SPAIN AND THE WESTERN TRADITION

The Castilian Mind in Literature from *El Cid* to Calderón

SPAIN AND THE WESTERN TRADITION

The Castilian Mind in Literature
from *El Cid* to Calderón

Volume II

Otis H. Green

Madison and Milwaukee, 1964
The University of Wisconsin Press

Published by the University of Wisconsin Press
P.O. Box 1379, Madison, Wisconsin 53701

Printed in the United States of America
by North Central Publishing Company

Library of Congress Catalog Number 63–13745

Preface

This is the second volume of a series, but its content and structure
are independent of Volume I, published by the University of Wisconsin Press in 1963. There will be four volumes in all, and each
volume of the series is designed to be a complete book in its own
right.

These later volumes are more diverse in their content than was
Volume I. Each chapter is a monograph on an important aspect of
the thought pattern that determined the content of works of literature composed in Spain during the centuries studied. This content
is clearly Western. In Volume I, I did not treat aspects of Spanish
thought and feeling where the Oriental influence — as a complicated set of overtones, not as a determinant of what was written —
is most clearly perceptible, or is most reasonably assumed. In the
final chapter of Volume II, I do investigate one of those aspects —
the Spanish conception of Fortune and Fate. The result is negative.
The Oriental influence simply is not apparent, nor is it necessarily
to be posited. Spanish beliefs regarding Fortune and Fate are close
to St. Augustine and to the whole body of Patristic literature. I
may say the same for the tenth chapter of Volume III, which treats
of Philosophy: the Spaniards are certainly less receptive to the
doctrines of Avicenna and Averroës than are, for example, the Ita-
lians or the French.*

My method is to avoid polemics, to refrain from writing a "no-
tional" book, to let the Spanish texts speak for themselves. Of
course, these texts are interpreted by one who is convinced that
Spanish culture is fundamentally Western, and this conviction
causes me to write a study essentially different from the efforts of
other interpreters who seek to find a "secret" — or *the* secret —

---

* See the interesting review by Steven Runciman of R. W. Southern, *Western
Views of Islam in the Middle Ages* (Cambridge, Massachusetts, 1962), *Speculum*,
XXXVIII (1963), 505–506.

v

that can explain the peculiarities of the Spanish culture pattern, of Spain's value system. That that value system differs from the Italian or the French or the English is true, but it is not known *why* Spain chose to remain faithful to the Aristotelian-Thomistic world view, passing up opportunities to contribute to the Europe of Newton and Darwin and Einstein, any more than it is clear *why* England chose to follow the lead of Hobbes and Locke and Bacon rather than that of Milton, Samuel Butler, and Richard Hooker; or *why* our American republic chose not to erect a statue to the Goddess of Reason and, on the contrary, adopted the motto: *In God We Trust*.

My texts will not settle these questions of collective preference, of what we might go so far as to call collective choice, or collective decision. But they do something that is important: they enable us to see why Cervantes and Calderón and their fellow Spaniards caused the characters in their plays and novels and poems to do and to say certain things — things inexplicable to one who reads these works without preparation. It will be much the same for some reader in the future who encounters a novel or a poem, or a play of our own day, full of Freud, of *e equals mc squared*, of other complex ideological concepts that will need to be interpreted if he is to understand fully our literature.

I would like to express my thanks to the Committee on the Advancement of Research of the University of Pennsylvania for various grants that have defrayed the cost of producing the typescript; to Dr. Nicholas Morcovescu for many critical suggestions that have improved the book; to my colleagues Arnold G. Reichenberger, Paul M. Lloyd, Peter G. Earle, and Ciriaco M. Arroyo for help in countless ways; and — very especially — to Mrs. Isobel Korbel, of the University of Wisconsin Press, for continued personal interest in my work and for help of the highest degree of competence in all matters pertaining to editing.

OTIS H. GREEN

Philadelphia, Pennsylvania
May, 1962

Contents

SPAIN AND THE WESTERN TRADITION

The Castilian Mind in Literature from *El Cid* to Calderón

I · The Creation and the Creatures

All things to which God gave existence
outside Himself were created by Him to
do honor to His power, His wisdom, and
His goodness.   *Raimundo Sabunde* [1]

In the year 1617 Alonso de Bonilla drew the following picture of
God and His universe:

> God is the original circumference
> Of every spherelike figure, every ring,
> Since every orbit of the encircling heavens
> Sweeps round the center of His holy Essence.
>   Forth from this center of His infinite
> Wisdom, extend the radii of the creatures,
> Sparks of the Light ineffable and pure
> Of the inaccessible Omnipotence.[2]

In his view the universe is a continual outpouring: the rays endlessly given off by the astral bodies are the radii of God's omnipotence overflowing into the world of things; and those things, in
their outermost overflow, are still God.

WHY THE UNIVERSE WAS CREATED

It was natural to wonder why an all-perfect and self-sufficing God
should have chosen to manifest Himself, His power, wisdom, and
goodness, by means of a descent from unity to multiplicity. Some

1. *Theologia Naturalis*, trans. Michel de Montaigne (*Oeuvres complètes de Michel
de Montaigne*, ed. A. Armaingaud [Paris, 1924–41]), vol. X, p. 102. Montaigne's French
translation of Sabunde is one of the famous books of the Renaissance. For all following citations of *Theologia Naturalis* from this translation, reference will be given as
op. cit. (or *ed. cit.*, as the need arises), I (vol. IX of the Armaingaud edition of Montaigne) or II (vol. X of Armaingaud). Translations into English are mine.
2. "Es Dios la original circunferencia / de todas las esféricas figuras, / pues cercos,
orbes, círculos y alturas / en el centro se incluyen de su esencia. / De este infinito centro
de la ciencia / salen inmensas líneas de criaturas, / centellas vivas de las luces puras /
de aquella inaccesible omnipotencia" (*BAE*, XXXV, 45b). Translations are always
mine; they are not always line-for-line.

writers attempted no answer — God works in a mysterious way. Lope de Vega (d. 1635) in his Biblical play, *La creación del mundo y primera culpa del hombre*, while declaring that the outpouring redounds to the glory of the Creator and the good of the creatures, is aware that in the last analysis he is dealing with things unknowable. In Adam's first lesson to the newly created Eve, the husband says:

> You must know that in His glory,
> Without beginning, middle, or end,
> God existed, when He willed
> To give being to the universe,
> Since for His mysterious ends
> (Known to Him in the beginning)
> This was needful, that His glory
> Might be manifest, and we
> Might be blest as He intended.[3]

Manifestation of glory

The same note of glory is stressed by Fray Luis de Granada (d. 1588): "the purpose for which God made and prepared this [the Empyrean] was the manifestation of His glory. For although all things that our Lord created exist for His glory . . . , this one was conceived and created in a very special way, since His greatness and magnificence are therein most resplendently revealed."[4]

How can He who is all-glorious receive glory from His creatures?[5] Pedro Malón de Chaide (d. 1596?), like Lope de Vega, faces the *misterios grandes* and declares that he does not understand:

3. "Sabed que en su misma gloria, / sin principio, fin ni medio, / estaba Dios, cuando quiso / dar principio al universo: / que para misterios grandes, / prevenidos abeterno, / convino así por mostrarnos / gloria suya y bienes nuestros" (ed. Real Academia Española, III [Madrid, 1893], 1972). S.A. Vosters, in his article, "Lope de Vega y Titelmans: Cómo el Fénix se representaba el universo" (*Revista de literatura*, XXI [1962], 5–35), does not mention the play here cited. His article is interesting and valuable, however. During a period of nearly twenty years, Lope relied, for cosmological information and interpretations, on the *Compendium Philosophiae Naturalis* of a Belgian Franciscan, Franz Titelmans, first published in 1530. Lope probably used an edition of 1582.

4. *Obras*, I (Madrid, 1768), 93–94.

5. Sabunde's effort at a solution seems altogether paradoxical: "God cannot grow inwardly because He is infinitely and supremely perfect, but He can do so exteriorly and outside Himself. . . . He grows outside himself when His honor, His praise and His glory increase, and they increase only in His rational creature. He therefore made His creature rational in order to increase in him, that is to say, in order that a new

Oh mighty Lord! How can you be interested in my redemption? How could you suffer loss, oh God, were I to perish, or what can you gain from my salvation? . . . Before you created the heavens, the angels, the earth, mankind, and every other creature, did you lack anything for your serenity of spirit and your glory? Were you not then as blest as now, as always? Was it not in your power to create whatever pleased you? Consequently, if all your creatures add not a jot or tittle to your glory, . . . tell me, great God of miracles, how can you show such passionate interest in me? . . . I hear you say, Lord, that unless a grain of wheat be buried in the earth and die, it remains alone unto itself. . . . I confess, great God, that I do not understand you. . . . I cannot grasp the secret of this saying. . . . You, oh Lord, are an only Son, hence the only heir; if you refrain from making us sons of God, you will still be the one and only Son in the house of your Father . . . and we will be excluded. Then what you say is true, Lord: *ipsum solum manet*, it remains alone; for you will be alone in your glory if by your death you do not also make me a son. You die in order that, sowing yourself like a seed in the earth, there shall come forth from you countless spikes of grain with innumerable kernels of faithful followers that bear your image.[6]

Malón de Chaide has answered his own questions. The divine outpouring, the descent from unity to multiplicity, is thought of as a condition necessary to the fullness of glory which God chose for Himself, as an enhancement of that which can know no increase, a perfecting of that which is supremely perfect. Well might Lope speak of "great mysteries" and Malón de Chaide confess his confusion and the difficulty of arriving at some sort of comprehension. For the mysteries remain: How can such an outpouring, such a burying in the earth of a seed already perfectly good, partake of the character of a necessity felt by the One who is indivisible, who knows, and can know, no need?

A veil of revelation

For Alejo Venegas del Busto (d. 1554), the created world is God's disguise: "Faith is a disguise, a veiling, of God. . . . Surely there could not be in all the world a king who could travel about his kingdom so incognito, so disguised as God is disguised in this visible world beneath the veil of the Catholic faith."[7] The world of the creatures is a disguise, a veiling, and at the same time a

knowledge and awareness of Himself should be engendered in His creature" (*op. cit.*, I, 338).

6. *La conversión de la Magdalena*, ed. P. Félix García (Madrid, 1947), II, 269–73.

7. *Agonía del tránsito de la muerte*, NBAE, XVI, 262b.

revelation, says Alonso de Orozco (d. 1591): "The Lord beheld all the things that He had created and saw that they were very good, because each created thing proclaims the power, the wisdom, and the goodness of God. His power is revealed, since He was able to create it; His wisdom,[8] for He brought it forth so excellent; His goodness, since without needing the world He chose to give it being." [9]

Goodness as liberality

This idea of an overflowing of goodness — a fundamental concept of Christian theology and of Platonic philosophy as we shall see — is interpreted by Baltasar Gracián (d. 1658) as generosity: "The wise Creator gave heed, not only to the needs of man, for whom all this universe was created, but also to his comfort and pleasure, showing thereby His infinite liberality, obliging man to serve and venerate Him with commensurate generosity." [10] Two centuries before Gracián, Raimundo Sabunde (d. 1436) had developed this idea in its fullness. God created the universe out of a need to share:

Inasmuch as giving is very characteristic of God, it remains for us to prove by the nature of liberality itself and by its special suitability to the nature of God, that there is in Him an eternal production. . . . That giving is natural to God we can realize by considering the creation of the world; for we see that He gave to each thing fullness of being in accordance with its capacity to receive, though He had taken nothing from it and was in no way obligated to it — a thing which He would not have done had giving not been natural to Him. We can confirm this by the method of His giving: for what He gave to each thing He gave in order that it might pass it on to another. We see that the creatures, in proportion as they are great and superior, take less for themselves and give more. The heavenly bodies ceaselessly send forth their in-

8. See Sir Thomas Browne (d. 1682) in his *Religio Medici*: "There are no *Grotesques* in nature; nor any thing framed to fill up empty . . . spaces; in the most imperfect creatures, and such as were not preserved in the Arke, but having their seeds and principles in the wombe of nature, are everywhere, where the power of the Sun is; in these is the wisdome of his hand discovered. . . . What wise hand teacheth them to doe what reason cannot teach us? ruder heads stand amazed at those prodigious pieces of nature, Whales, Elephants, Dromidaries and Camels; these I confess, are the Colossus and Majestick pieces of her hand; but in these narrow Engines there is more curious Mathematicks, and the civilitie of these little Citizens more nearly sets forth the wisedome of their Maker" (quoted in Joan Bennett, "A Note on *Religio Medici* and Some of its Critics," *Studies in the Renaissance*, III [New York, 1956], 176).

9. *Victoria de la muerte* (Madrid, 1921), pp. 240–41.

10. *El Criticón*, ed. M. Romera-Navarro (Philadelphia, 1938–40), I, 130.

fluences to those below, receiving nothing in return. . . . The elements teach us this more clearly, for they received their essence from God on the condition that they give themselves to each creature, so that the latter can build its being from their contribution. The things produced by the elements teach us the same lesson: the trees and the plants, for they give to men and animals for the conservation of their life not only what they produce, like leaves and fruits, but also they give themselves, their trunks, their branches, their roots. . . . Whereby is clearly revealed the nobility of giving, and that as a consequence this exists more fully in God than in any creature . . . , just as among men themselves the greatest and the most noble give most.[11]

Some writers, following the Neoplatonic tradition,[12] make a distinction between goodness and beauty, reserving the former for the Creator and applying the latter to the creatures. Malón de Chaide, in the following passage from *La conversión de la Magdalena*, seems to be echoing a text,[13] from the pseudo-Dionysius the Areopagite, which defines the Good as that which partakes of Goodness, and Goodness as participating in the Beneficient Cause of all things good:

But in order to express more briefly what we mean by Goodness or Good-in-God, and what we mean by Beauty, I say that Goodness is the superexcellent existence of God. Beauty is the act or ray which is born therefrom and spreads and penetrates through all things. This ray spreads first to the angels, and casts its light upon them; thence it passes to rational souls; and thence to all nature, and finally to the matter which is the substance of all things. It beautified the angels with the ideas or species of the things wherewith it endowed them when it framed them, for it produced them with knowledge thereof. It filled the soul with reason and the power of thought. It sustains nature with the seeds which it placed in each thing enabling it to reproduce itself. Finally, it adorns and bedecks matter with various forms, just as the potter who has before him a shapeless mass of clay beautifies it by making of it a platter, or a plate, or an urn; in the same manner God beautifies the matter of all things, clothing it with the form of plant or lion, horse or man. Hence it is that he who contemplates and loves the beauty of these four things [angel, soul, nature, matter] which constitute the whole of the creation,

11. *Op. cit.*, I, 72–73. This text anticipates ideas of "Order" and "Degree"; see below.
12. See Leo Spitzer, "Classical and Christian Ideas of World Harmony: Prolegomena to an Interpretation of the Word *Stimmung*," *Traditio*, II (1944), 409 ff., and III (1945), 307 ff.; Emmanuel Chapman, *Saint Augustine's Philosophy of Beauty* (New York–London, 1939).
13. "Bonum quidem esse docimus quod bonitati participat, bonitatem autem participationem benignefactricis omnium bonorum causae." This is from Hilduin's ninth-century translation; other translations are less close to the Spanish text. See Edgar de Bruyne, *Estudios de estética medieval*, trans. Fr. A. Suárez (Madrid, 1958–59), I, 375.

loving the splendor of God which he sees in them, may come to know and to love God Himself.[14]

Pedro Calderón de la Barca (d. 1681), being more of an Aristotelian than the writers so far cited, regarded the multiplicity of nature as having sprung from a single act of Power (the attribute of God the Father, as Wisdom is the attribute of the Son and Goodness, of the Holy Spirit).[15] In Calderón's *auto sacramental, La vida es sueño*,[16] the Divine Power, personified as one of the dramatis personae, addresses the Four Elements:

> You must exist bound together,
> So that, when Hate would divide you,
> Love will maintain you in union.
> Thus, as friendly enemies,
> In your harmony and discord
> You shall strive and rest forever.[17]

When this separation and binding has been accomplished by Power, Wisdom (the second of the Divine Attributes) takes command, saying:

> Now that Almighty Power
> Has divided you in four,
> In equal balance and authority,
> Let Wisdom come in and assign
> Unto each the post and task
> That shall be yours; so let the creatures
> See that, as creation was
> The attribute of Power Divine,
> The tasks of government belong
> To Supreme Wisdom.[18]

PROBLEMS: PHILOSOPHICAL, THEOLOGICAL, SCIENTIFIC

The universe, then, is conceived through the centuries by Spanish writers as having been created by a supremely good God in an

14. *Ed. cit.*, III, pp. 119–20.

15. See above, under "A veil of revelation," Alonso de Orozco's discussion of power, wisdom, goodness.

16. Not to be confused with the drama of the same title.

17. "Es fuerza que eslabonados, / cuando vaya a dividiros / el odio, os tenga el amor; / y que, amigos y enemigos, /duréis conformes y opuestos / lo que duraren los siglos" (*Obras completas*, ed. A. Valbuena Prat [Madrid, 1952–59], III, 1388).

18. "Ya que el sumo Poder /a los cuatro ha dividido, / mantenidos en igual /balanza, igual arbitrio, / entre la Sabiduría / a dar los puestos y oficios / que habéis de

initial act — "in the beginning" — of overflowing goodness and generosity, or as an act of adorning the universe. Fray Luis de Granada, in his *Introducción del Símbolo de la fe* (Book II, ch. iii) expounds the errors of pre-Christian philosophical interpretations of the creation. Nor could the Christian philosophers — the theologians — resolve the contradictions:[19] we remember that Lope de Vega caused Adam to bow before the *misterios grandes prevenidos abeterno*. We are now ready to consider the philosophical and theological background of thought and belief which caused the authors thus far quoted to write as they did.

This background of theory, from both the philosophical and the theological point of view, is optimistic.[20] The idea that a good God, out of the necessity of His own goodness, produced good things derives from Plato.[21] St. Augustine, taking over and adopting this Platonic idea, asked himself if Plato must not have known the Bible, so great was the conformity of his thought to that of the Scriptures.[22] Yet even for Augustine, the question of how an Unchangeable Being can have any relation to changing beings remained a mystery.[23] Accepting the mystery, he gave thanks for the

tener; vea el orbe / que si la creación ha sido /atribución del Poder, / lo es de la Ciencia el arbitrio" (*ibid.*, p. 1389).

19. "Yet plainly the conception of the creation as a ladder for man's ascent did not really reconcile the implications of the principle of plenitude as a theory of value with the otherworldly side of Platonic philosophy and Christian theology. For, in the first place, the parallel between the descending and the ascending process was little more than verbal. Conceived as steps in the stairway up to perfection, the lower grades had only to be spurned and transcended; and such a conception had little in common with the assumption that the existence of each of these grades is a thing so good on its own account that God himself had been, so to say, constrained by his very divinity and rationality to engender every one of them" (Arthur O. Lovejoy, *The Great Chain of Being* [Cambridge, Massachusetts, 1948], pp. 89–90).

20. Origen, however, is tinged with pessimism. He held that this world was created not for the production of good but for restraint of evil, so that souls might be assigned to stations in the universe and to diverse bodies as prison-houses, according to their respective merits. St. Augustine asks: How could a man "so learned and so well versed in the literature of the Church" have thought these things? See William A. Christian, "Augustine on the Creation of the World," *Harvard Theological Review*, XLVI (1953), 23.

21. Plato declared that "the most sufficient reason for the founding of the world" was "that by the good God, good works were made" (cited *ibid.*, p. 23).

22. J. M. Parent, *La doctrine de la création dans l'Ecole de Chartres* (Paris–Ottawa, 1938), p. 35.

23. See Christian, *op. cit.*, p. 9. I shall not discuss here the problem of what existed before the creation, of time-before-time, etc., since we are concerned with the universe as the theater of human action and the training place of Christian souls. Augustine held that the six active days of Genesis are to be understood "in some other way" than as literal days, marked by the circuit of the sun (cited *ibid.*, pp. 4–5).

creation of the creatures, himself among them, just as later Spanish writers in their own time did:

> Thanks to Thee, O Lord. We behold the heaven and earth. . . . We see . . . this space of air through which wander the fowls of heaven between those waters which are borne in vapors above them, and in clear nights distil down the dew, and those heavier waters which flow along the earth. . . . We behold the lights shining from above, the sun to suffice for the day, the moon and the stars to cheer the night; and that, by all these, times should be marked and signified. We behold on all sides a moist element, replenished with fishes, beasts, and birds. . . . We behold the face of the earth adorned with living things, and man, created after Thy image and likeness (that is the power of reason and understanding), set over all irrational creatures. . . . These things we behold, and they are severally good, and altogether are very good.[24]

The Platonic-Augustinian doctrine of "l'expansion créatrice du bien," [25] of an expanding Godhead and an expanding universe whose reason for being is the good, persists in the Middle Ages.[26] Guillame de Conches and Thierry de Chartres, leading thinkers of the twelfth-century School of Chartres, both make this affirmation: the divine goodness is the final cause of the world.[27] This assertion is offered as a solution of the dilemma of the philosophers of antiquity: i.e., if God needed the world He was not perfect; if He did not need the world, He committed a superfluous action in creating it. God acted, according to Guillaume, out of liberality, that is to say, in order to communicate His goodness to other beings. It was out of love of goodness that God sought to share it by making intelligent beings capable of knowing, of loving, and of participating in His beatitude. Hence man's privileged position in the Universe, to the discussion of which we shall return.[28]

24. Quoted in Christian, *op. cit.*, pp. 23–24.

25. These words constitute the heading of Parent's chapter III (*op. cit.*, pp. 59 ff.).

26. "The result was the conception of the plan and structure of the world which, through the Middle Ages and down to the late eighteenth century, many philosophers, and most men of science, and, indeed, most educated men, were to accept without question — the conception of the universe as a 'Great Chain of Being' . . . " (Lovejoy, *op. cit.*, p. 59). On the Great Chain of Being, see below.

27. Parent, *op. cit.*, pp. 59 ff.

28. See below, our discussion of the heading of "Degree." The nature of the preesnt work (which assumes that the Spaniards of our centuries necessarily lived beset with contradictions — see Vol. I, Ch. I) makes it unnecessary for us to investigate such problems as whether God in his goodness acted in freedom or was bound by the necessity of his nature; or whether He created the best of all possible worlds. Our writers answered (or if pressed surely would have answered) both of these questions in the affirmative. In answer to the first, the Catalan Sabunde says: "God delights and takes pleasure in

In the thirteenth century St. Thomas Aquinas addressed himself to the totality of problems arising from the shift of Christian thought from the Augustinian-Neoplatonic to the essentially Aristotelian world view. St. Thomas' solution of the problem amounts in the end to the same expansion of goodness that we have noted in Augustine and in the School of Chartres. Simply stated it is this: Supreme wisdom could not normally be concentrated in a single nature. The diffusion of the good through descending degrees from the Supreme Good must of necessity produce a multiplicity of goods, a variety of beings and of perfections whose combined effort would be to expand and distribute with greater richness the Highest Being. God multiplies beings just as man multiplies words in his discourse: one word is insufficient to tell all.[29]

The knowledge of the universe expanded so greatly between the thirteenth and the sixteenth centuries that the Scholastic philosophers and theologians of the Counter Reformation — Spanish and Portuguese for the most part, with Francisco Suárez (d. 1617)[30] at their head — felt the need of undertaking again the task assumed by St. Thomas Aquinas, namely, that of bringing factual knowledge and theological belief once more into harmony. The Jesuits were leaders in this activity, and it is a Jesuit, Father José de Acosta (d. 1600), who will concern us here. In 1590 he published his *Historia natural y moral de las Indias*, providing it with what amounts to an internal prologue[31] wherein he says: "He who wishes to understand the facts concerning this nature — so varied and so abundant — will have the pleasure provided by history, a history better

society; otherwise he would not have created the world" (*op. cit.*, I, 68). The goodness of the universe is everywhere taken for granted. "Hallo al eterno Padre en cualquier parte" — "I see God everywhere" — wrote Alonso de Acevedo in *La creación del mundo* (*BAE*, XXIX, 263a); and Fray Luis de Granada declared that, just as here on earth the creatures are a mirror wherein we perceive (though darkly) the beauty of God, so when we reach Heaven, we shall see in God the beauty of His creatures, and much more perfectly than if we beheld them in themselves, directly (*op. cit.*, I, 103). I find no appreciable concern with the problem of a plurality of worlds, although Democritus is mentioned as the originator of the idea by Cristóbal de Villalón in his *Ingeniosa comparación entre lo antiguo y lo presente* (ed. M. Serrano [Madrid, 1898], p. 183). See Grant McColley, "The Seventeenth-Century Doctrine of a Plurality of Worlds," *Annals of Science*, I (1936), 385–430.

29. A. D. Sertillanges, O.P., *Les grandes thèses de la philosophie thomiste* (Paris, 1928), p. 108.

30. See his treatise *De Opere Sex Dierum*.

31. Ed Madrid, 1792, I, 106. See José Rodríguez Carracido, *El padre José de Acosta y su importancia en la literatura científica española* (Madrid, 1899).

than others inasmuch as the deeds recorded are not the work of men but of the Creator. He who passes beyond and comes to understand the natural causes of the effects observed will have an exercise in good philosophy. And he who lifts his thoughts still higher, and, contemplating the supreme Artificer of all these marvels, takes delight in His wisdom and greatness, may be said to be dealing in excellent theology."

Father Acosta is keenly aware of the contradictions, not only between Aristotle and St. Thomas and the new data provided by the discovery of the western Indies, but also between these and the Bible. Early in his first volume (p. 60) he observes: "The Scripture also tells us that all the beasts and animals of the earth perished excepting those that were preserved for the propagation of their kind in Noah's Ark. We must therefore reduce the propagation of the said animals to the ones that emerged from the Ark on Mount Ararat. . . . Consequently, both for human beings and for beasts we must find some means whereby they could have passed from the Old World to the New." St. Augustine, he says, faced the problem on a much smaller scale when he wondered about the existence of animals on islands after the Deluge and suggested that man, after the flood, had conveyed useful animals to the islands. Others might have been conveyed by men, not because of their usefulness in man's economy but because men loved hunting as a sport; or perhaps God repeated the act of the original creation and produced insular fauna by a supernatural fiat. But alas! not even St. Augustine can guide us in our search for a solution to the new problem, since it is not in accord with God's good government that "perfect" animals such as lions, tigers, wolves (as apposed to tadpoles and vermin) should spring from the earth without having been sired. How, then, shall we find a means of passage from Eden for the beasts of the Indies? He suggests the "great conjecture" that some hidden land passage may exist: "My personal opinion," he says, "is that the two land masses somewhere come together or at least are very close to each other" (p. 62). This conjecture is strengthened by the fact that on the Caribbean islands and others that are at a distance from the mainland there exist no lions, tigers, bears, wild boars, foxes, etc., though these beasts, or ones similar to them, are found on the mainland. The presence on remote islands of useful creatures he attributes to the Spanish navigators themselves. There are partridges in Peru but not on the islands, nor have any insular species of guanacos or vicuñas been found (pp. 65–66).

This double conjecture of connecting land passageways and transportation by men in ships is of course inadequate to answer the question of the origin of species without precedent in the Old World. Acosta assumes that their ancestors left the Ark but were led by instinct or by Providence to establish their range in certain restricted places, as the elephant did in India, being native to no other part of the world. (Was the African elephant not yet discovered?) Acosta states the quandry in the following words (p. 272–73): "If the sheep of Peru, called llamas, alpacas, and guanacos, are found nowhere else in the world, who took them to Peru? Or how did they arrive? For no trace of them is found in all the world. And if they did not migrate from another region, how were they formed and produced there? Did God peradventure produce a new creation of animals? What I say in regard to these guanacos and alpacas, I shall say of a thousand varieties of birds, fowls, and animals of the forests that have never been known either by name or by sight."

As for the human inhabitants, Father Acosta regards them as newcomers to the lands they occupy, savage hunters from the Old World who had become lost at sea or had been driven from their homes by famine or other causes and who, finding land, had proceeded to occupy it, living by no law and with no culture except for a little bit of natural light [32] (faint and darkened by isolation) and at most a few customs remembered from the place of departure. This is not incredible even if they had left civilized lands, since even in Spain and Italy there exist human groups — *manadas de hombres* — who, except for their human faces and forms, are otherwise scarcely men. This would explain the "infinite savagery" of the New World (p. 73).

Finally, there are geological phenomena to be taken into consideration and to be harmonized with the Scriptures. "My opinion is," says Father Acosta, "that the signs and marks of a former deluge which are found were not produced by the flood of Noah, but

32. On "natural light," see below, our chapter on The Nature and Destiny of Man.

rather by some other limited deluge like those reported by Plato, or by the one the poets tell of in the story of Deucalion" (p. 74).[33]

THE GREAT CHAIN OF BEING

The metaphor of the Great Chain of Being serves to describe the manner in which, during the Middle Ages and until modern times, most educated Europeans viewed the structure of the universe. It expresses "the unimaginable plenitude of God's creation, its unfaltering order, and its ultimate unity. The chain stretched from the foot of God's throne to the meanest of inanimate objects. Every speck of creation was a link in the chain, and every link except those at the two extremities was simultaneously bigger and smaller than another: there could be no gap. The precise magnitude of the chain raised metaphysical difficulties; but the safest opinion made it short of infinity though of a finitude quite outside man's imagination."[34]

Order

This ideal concatenation of creatures accounted for the inequalities in nature (and human nature). Some thinkers attributed these to special causes or to the exercise of free will, but St. Thomas argued against them: just as participation in the Supreme Being had of necessity to be multiple or else fail to attain the degree of goodness perceptible in the universe, so this participation had also to be hierarchized, and, consequently, unequal.[35]

The hierarchized structure of the universe is at the very heart of the argument of Sabunde's *Theologia Naturalis*, a book whose influence extends throughout the Renaissance and down to St. Francis de Sales (d. 1622) and Blaise Pascal (d. 1662).[36] The book en-

33. See Marcos A. Morínigo, *América en el teatro de Lope de Vega* (Buenos Aires, 1946), and the additional references in the review of this work by C. E. Anibal, *HR*, XVI (1948), 183–85. The subject deserves study in many other authors.

34. E. M. W. Tillyard, *The Elizabethan World Picture* (London, 1948), p. 23.

35. Sertillanges, *op. cit.*, p. 109.

36. I. S. Révah, *Une source de la spiritualité péninsulaire au XVIème siècle: La "Théologie naturelle" de Raymond Sebond* (Lisbon, 1953), p. 5. See Tillyard, *op. cit.*, p. 25: "For a more detailed but quite popular account [of the Great Chain of Being] I know none better than that in a shortened version of the *Natural Theology* of Raymond de Sebonde. . . . The account of the chain of being found here must have been the common property of western Europe in the sixteenth century." (It should be remembered that Sabunde was a Catalan who died in 1436).

deavors to prove that the human mind, by ranging upward from rung to rung of the ladder of ascents, may come to know and to enjoy God; that man inhabits a rationally ordered universe, created and sustained by the will of a rational God; and that it is man's privilege, through the use of his God-given reason and the gift of grace, to attain by an act of ratiocination to the understanding of the truth and the contemplation of the good and the eternal.[37] Among many possible pertinent quotations, I select one:

> Having considered the similitude and general correspondence between man and the creatures of the three lower degrees . . . , let us ponder now this correspondence in its special and particular aspects. First, with the things of the first level which possess nothing but existence, such as the elements and the heavenly bodies, man has his correspondence in that just as they are arranged and ordered among themselves, so man is arranged and ordered within himself. For, as among the stars more worthy and noble things are above, and those less worthy are below and inferior, the sun above and the earth beneath, and among the elements, earth, being of less esteem occupies the lowest place, with water next above as more worthy, air higher still, and fire highest of all because of its excellence; so in man there is an above and a below, with his head at the highest point of his body, since it is more noble and worthy than any other exterior member; and by the same token, the feet are at the bottom, charged with supporting the other members, as earth carries and supports the other elements. Furthermore, just as the higher bodies [the stars] rule and control the lower ones, so it is with the organization of man's body.[38]

These concepts are part of the intellectual furniture of every[39] educated Spanish writer and reader. Fray Luis de Léon (d. 1591), preparing to develop his meditation on Christ's title of Prince of Peace in his great classic *De los nombres de Cristo*, defines peace in the words of St. Augustine as a peaceful, calm, and firm good order. As an example of his meaning he chooses the heavens "wherein the army of the stars, as if in seried rank and ordered file, shines in all its radiance and each one maintains its post inviolably; where none usurps the position of its neighbor, nor disturbs it in

37. See my review of Révah's monograph in *HR*, XXIII (1955), 131–32.
38. *Ed. cit.*, I, 90.
39. I think the word "every" can properly be used for Spain. In Italy there are signs of a breakdown of the idea of hierarchy in Ficino, Pomponazzi, and Pico della Mirandola. Montaigne rejected the idea of hierarchy completely: "Differences between creature and creature, between nation and nation, differences in physique, in function, in mores — all these he readily granted; but as for superiority, that he was loath to admit" (Abraham C. Keller, "Montaigne on the Dignity of Man," *PMLA*, LXXII [1957], 50).

the performance of its duty, and much less would think of breaking the holy and eternal law imposed on it by Providence; but on the contrary, in brotherly co-operation and having regard each for the other, the greater ones sharing their light with those of lesser magnitude, they show love and a sort of reverence each to each, and all together they at times temper their rays and influences, joining in a pacific unity of virtue, composed of different parts and aspects, universal and powerful above all conception." [40]

Malón de Chaide takes up the theme in his *Conversión de la Magdalena*: "The first object of our love must be God, since He alone is superior to our faculty for loving (*voluntad*). This we are taught by the very order of nature, because inferior and less worthy things convert themselves into things superior and more worthy. Thus the elements are converted into plants; these, through their fruits, are converted into the nature of animals that feed upon them; animals are converted into man, as he eats them and lives on their flesh, and in him they are perfected and ennobled. From this we argue that, in order for man in his totality to become better, he must first of all love God. All nature cries out that the first requisite is to love God, and when this hierarchy is upset, love becomes evil and uncontrolled." [41]

Gracián, the last great prose writer of the Golden Age, in *El Criticón* sets forth the same doctrine of order, as Critilo explains to Andrenio (the man who, long imprisoned in a cave, first beholds the wonder of the world as an adult) the reasons behind the marvelous order of the universe:

This is the prodigious effect of the infinite wisdom of the Creator, whereby He organized all things in accordance with their weight, number, and measure; for, if one observes carefully [one sees that] every created thing has its center with respect to place, its duration in time, and its special end in action and existence. For this reason you will see that they are subordinated each to each in accordance with the degree of their perfection. The elements, which are lowest in the scale of nature, join to form mixed bodies; and among the latter, the lesser ones serve the greater. Those herbs and plants which are at the bottom of the scale of life (since their life is merely vegetative), moving and growing till they attain the point of their perfection with the passage of time beyond which point they cannot advance, nonetheless serve as nutriment for sentient beings, which are in the second rank of life, enjoying senti-

40. *Obras completas castellanas*, ed. P. Félix García (Madrid, 1944), p. 597.
41. *Ed. cit.*, I, 76.

tive life in addition to life which is merely vegetative; and these [sentient beings] are the animals of the earth, the fishes of the sea, and the fowls of the air: these crop grass, live in trees whose fruit they eat, in whose branches they nest, among whose trunks they hide to defend themselves, with whose leaves they cover themselves, and beneath whose shade they take shelter from the sun. But all of them, trees and animals, live in the service of another and third rank of living beings, much more perfect and greatly superior, which, over and above growth and sense, can reason, ponder, and understand; and this is man, who at the end of the creative process is ordained and given existence for and toward God, to recognize Him, love Him, and serve Him.[42]

Degree

An extension of the idea of cosmic order is the idea of degree. The hierarchization which exists between the orders is present also in the various orders themselves. "Another form of excellence, found in most accounts of the chain of being and certainly to be connected with it, is that within every class there is a primate. . . . Sebonde [Sabunde] speaks of the dolphin among fishes, the eagle among birds, the lion among beasts, the emperor among men. . . . Other primates were God among the angels, the sun among the stars, justice among the virtues, the head among the body's members." In a short space in *Richard II* (Act III, scene 3), "we have . . . fire among the elements, the sun among the planets, the king among men, the eagle among birds. Again, at the beginning of act five Richard is first a rose and then a lion." [43]

These primacies were familiar in Spain as elsewhere. In *Las cortes de la Muerte* (1557) by Micael de Carvajal and Luis Hurtado de Toledo, they are specified:

> Among the gems of the Orient,
> Scholars everywhere declare,
> The ruby is most excellent
> By reason of secret virtues.
> And so great is its perfection
> That this single stone contains
> The qualities of all the others;
> God gave it such great distinction. . . .[44]

42. *Ed. cit.*, I, 134–35. See also Granada's *Introducción del Símbolo de la fe*, I, iii, 1, where the treatment is very full.

43. Tillyard, *op. cit.*, pp. 27–28.

44. "Entre piedras orientales / ser una más señalada / y en virtudes más señales [sic], / afirman los naturales / que es el carbunclo llamada. / Y es tanta su perfición, / que aquesta sola contiene / las gracias que en todas son; / dióle Dios tan alto don" (*BAE*, XXXV, 19a).

Mateo Alemán's picaresque novel *Guzmán de Alfarache* (1599) even establishes a primacy among evils: "And as among birds imperial rank is given to the eagle, to the lion among beasts, to the whale among fishes and to the basilisk among serpents, so among evils the greatest and the most powerful is deceit." [45] And Calderón says of the rose:

> The rose for this reason is queen
> Among flowers, since it has
> Thorns which as archers defend
> Its beauty from competition.[46]

Primacy and inferiority of man

Man, created in God's image (Gen. 1:26) and made by Him a little lower than the angels (Heb. 2:7), occupies the highest place in the order of all things outside Heaven. His is the highest degree, the primacy of all non-heavenly creatures. Fray Juan de los Angeles (d. 1609) wrote: "Among all the creatures there is order, as you know; and each one of them to a greater or lesser degree represents God and imitates Him: in greater degree the ones that live than those that have no life; to a greater extent those that understand than those that are without understanding. For all are reduced to these three orders; and in this scale of imitation which exists in them, man occupies the last stage in the act of imitation and is consequently the perfect image of God; upon him, as a seal impresses its lines and figures upon wax, God impressed His living image." [47]

The totality of the creatures exists for the service and the ennoblement of man, as Sabunde testifies: "This sky, this earth, this air, this sea, and all that in them is, is forever busy in your service. This diverse movement of the sun, this constant variety of the seasons of the years is all directed to satisfying your needs and to the continual renewal of fruits for your use. Think, therefore; think: Who is the Creator of this fair order who with such firm and lasting bonds has willed that all nature be bound to your necessities?" [48]

45. Ed. Clásicos Castellanos (Madrid, 1926–36), III, 112.

46. "La rosa por eso es reina / de las flores, porque tiene / archeros en las espinas / que su hermosura defienden" (*Obras Completas*, ed. Angel Valbuena Briones [Madrid, 1956], II, 354a).

47. Quoted in José Gallegos Rocafull, *La experiencia de Dios en los místicos españoles* (Mexico City, 1945), p. 88.

48. *Op. cit.*, I, 157–58.

Before the Fall, this beautiful order existed in all its perfection: the lion and the lamb lay down together, as Acevedo reminds us in *La creación del mundo*:

> These cruel animals, and others like them,
> That deal out death with claw or poisonous fang,
> In the beginning were without their poison,
> Nor knew fierce anger or impetuous wrath.
> Therefore let no malicious tongue berate
> Kind Providence, nor blame the heavenly Act
> That turned the serpent's tooth into a weapon,
> Bathing with poison its swift-darting barbs.[49]

It was man's transgression in the Garden that set the creatures against him to avenge the evil thing that he had done. Fray Francisco Ortiz wrote in his *Epístolas familiares* (1552): "If the very stones were to rise up against man, they would be doing him no injury; but would be visiting upon him merited punishment for his offenses against God." [50] Fray Luis de Granada declares that on the Judgment Day the creatures will fight against men who, by reason of their ingratitude to God, shall have deserved eternal damnation.[51]

It is not often, however, that the creatures are thought of as avenging enemies. The benefits which man derives from them vastly outweigh their occasional hostility. Man, in his turn, is obligated to requite these benefits by serving as the mute creatures' mouthpiece: it is through him alone that they repay their debt of homage for the inestimable gift of their creation. Sabunde writes an apostrophe of the world to man: "I serve you that you may serve Him who made me . . . for you, and you for Him. Since you enjoy these blessings, pay for them and give thanks." The cry is taken up by the heavens, the air, the water, the earth, by all creatures: "Receive, but pay; take my service, but be grateful for it. Enjoy these benefits, but give thanks therefor." [52] There can be no greater deafness, says Fray Luis de Granada, than to fail to hear

---

49. "Estos y otros crueles animales / que saetean muerte venenosa, / no ejecutaban ímpetus mortales / al principio con ira ponzoñosa; / y así, contra las obras celestiales / no se vuelva la lengua maliciosa, / ni culpe al Creador, porque los dientes / tan dañosos volvió de las serpientes" (*ed. cit.*, p. 278a).

50. *BAE*, XIII, 264b.

51. See his *Obras, ed. cit.*, V, "*Indice Alphabético*," *s. vv. Criaturas* and *Juicio universal.*

52. *Op. cit.*, I, 158–59; see also p. 163.

these cries. Each creature calls upon man: "Behold how greatly my Lord and Maker loved you, who for your sake created me, and for His sake wills that I should serve you in order that you may serve and love Him who created me for you, and you for Himself. These, O Christian, are the voices of all the creatures. Be assured that there can be no greater deafness than to be deaf to such cries and ungrateful to such benefits." [53]

Finally the world of the creatures would vanish into the nothingness from which it emerged were it not for the ever-exerted sustaining power of the Divine Hand: "For God . . . having produced them out of nothing, His assistance is at every moment needed for the conservation of His creation, which without it could not subsist a single minute, and which would in no time return to the void from which it sprang, were it removed from the eye of its Maker. That is why it is necessary that the entire essence of God be infused in all the beings of the world, though not contained therein, since it extends beyond [to infinity]." [54]

Ethical applications

The drawing of practical or ethical lessons from the animal kingdom is common to all Western cultures: "Go to the ant, thou sluggard!" (Prov. 6:6). An extension of this type of didacticism on a loftier and more universal level of thinking is the use of the concept of a stratified and hierarchized universe for purposes of ethical exhortation. Fray Luis de Granada, discussing animals noted for their fierceness, likens to them violent and angry men who, by an abuse of their divine gift of free will, forget or disregard their commission to serve as a link upward between the non-rational animals of the earth and the angelic ministers who do God's pleasure in Heaven: "and these [beasts] are imitated by the violent and furious men who, though able to control their anger by means of human reason and discretion, yet choose to follow their beastlike impulses and their rage, being pleased to give free rein to that part of their nature which they share with the animals rather than to that higher and more divine part which is characteristic of the angels." [55] Fray

53. *Obras, ed. cit.,* I, pp. 27–28. Fray Luis appears to be writing with Sabunde's text in mind.
54. Sabunde, *op. cit.,* I, 33–34.
55. *Obras, ed. cit.,* I, 479.

Luis de León in his book *The Perfect Wife* calls upon the humbler partner in the marriage contract to recognize the degree which God has assigned to her in the order of the Great Chain of Being: "Just as the good and self-respecting woman was not designed by Nature [56] for difficult undertakings, but for a single simple and domestic function, so also she was limited by Nature in her powers of understanding. . . . Just as the beauty of faces consists in the perfect proportion of the various features, so the beauty of a human life resides in the obedience with which each individual performs his tasks in accordance with what his own nature and his calling require of him. The wife's state, when compared with that of her husband, is humble."[57]

Devotional applications

In the history of Christian thought the attitude toward the natural has fluctuated between acceptance and denial. One group of thinkers sees in the supernatural a perfection of things natural; an opposing group regards the natural as a negation of the interests and aspirations of the soul. We have already hinted at the inherent conflict of Christian beliefs regarding the creation: after the overflowing of divine unity into a multiplicity of things, after the "descent" of the Godhead itself into innumerable souls, there is a need for restoration, for the purified soul to return to God and again enter into His unity, bearing with it as it comes not only its own tribute of praise but also the tribute of the voiceless creatures:

There was no way in which the flight from the Many to the One, the quest of a perfection defined wholly in terms of contrast with the created world, could be effectually harmonized with the imitation of a Goodness that delights in diversity and manifests itself in the emanation of the Many out of the One. The one program demanded a withdrawal from all "attachment to creatures" and culminated in the ecstatic contemplation of the indivisible Divine Essence; the other, if it had been formulated, would have summoned men to participate, in some finite measure, in the creative passion of God, to collaborate consciously in the processes by which the diversity of things, the fullness of the universe, is achieved. It would have found the beatific vision

56. Nature is here considered as the handmaiden of the Creator (*Natura naturans*), the agent charged with the endlessly repeated acts of creation which have followed and continue to follow the work of the Six Days. See below, Chapter III, Three Aspects of Nature.

57. *La perfecta casada*, ed. A. Bonilla (Madrid, 1917), p. 183.

in the distinterested joy of beholding the splendor of the creation or of curiously tracing out the detail of its infinite variety; it would have placed the active life above the contemplative; it would, perhaps, have conceived of the activity of the creative artist, who at once loves, imitates, and augments the "orderly variousness" of the sensible world, as the mode of life most like the divine.[58]

Here once again we are faced by the *Sic* and the *Non*, the yes and the no, the tensions and contradictions of the culture we are studying (see our Volume I, Chapter I). The Psalmist supports the creatures, for the heavens declare the glory of God (Ps. 19:1); yet God is a hidden God, as St. John of the Cross well knew, and the path to Him is negative, the *via negativa* of the mystics: "Verily thou art a God that hidest thyself" (Isa. 45:15); "I will give thee treasures of darkness" (Isa. 45:3). The mystic finds in the creatures merely a trace, a vestige, of the ineffable glory that exists in the Maker's essence: "When that which is perfect is come, that which is in part will be done away" (I Cor. 13:10).[59] Meditation upon the creatures, the mystics taught, "may take the soul a little way towards a knowledge of the Creator: it is, in fact, after the practice of self-knowledge, the first thing in order upon this spiritual road to the knowledge of God. But beyond a determinable point upon that road, the creatures begin to obscure God's image." [60] The doctrine of mystical theology is best expressed, I believe, by the fourteenth-century Catalan Raimundo (Ramón) Lull (d. 1315). There are three ways, Lull says, of worshipping God and adoring Him: first, in nature; second, in things nature cannot do, such as miracles; third, in what God is and does in, of, and by Himself. These three approaches represent three degrees of perfection, and the last is best. It is better to worship God in what He does in Himself than in what He does outside Himself, and the most perfect worshipper of all is the one who adores God in all of the three possible manners.[61] Ways one and two are the ways

58. Lovejoy, *op. cit.*, pp. 83–84. This is the doctrine of Plenitude; see our Volume I, Chapter III. The medieval Church rejected this doctrine, insisting that contemplation was "the better part" (Luke 10:42).

59. These texts are all cited by St. John of the Cross. See San Juan de la Cruz, *El Cántico espiritual*, ed. Clásicos Castellanos (Madrid, 1942), pp. 23 ff. and p. 111. The quotation from I Corinthians appears as "1 collocen. 13" — an obvious error as there is of course no "First Colossians."

60. E. Allison Peers, *Spirit of Flame: A Study of St. John of the Cross* (London, 1943), p. 138.

61. *Blanquerna*, ed. Colección Crisol (n.p., n.d.), pp. 478–79.

of ordinary piety; the third is the way of the mystic whose soul is "caught up to the third heaven" and hears "unspeakable words, which it is not lawful for a man to utter" (II Cor. 12:4). On the level of simple piety, the worshipper is merely one among many creatures. The mystic, in the ecstacy of union, knows no line of demarcation between himself and the One — precisely because he has risen above the creatures. Not that the creatures are in themselves an obstacle to contemplation: it is only by reason of our imperfection that we remain upon the steppingstones. Mystical theology is thus on an infinitely higher level than the natural theology of Sabunde.[62]

Fray Juan de Pineda (d. 1597) speaks of the lower levels of piety when he says: "All the world is a primer wherein is written the alphabet of the creatures, each creature being a living letter whereby the soul begins to learn to know God through the agency of his own outward senses. . . . Inasmuch as the creatures emerged from the hand of God marked with the image of the eternal Ideas which are in God, and inasmuch as like gives knowledge of like, when we understand the creatures we know that they have in God their ideal prototypes, and thus by means of the finite we derive a conception of the infinite Creator, in a confused and indistinct manner of knowing."[63]

As for the positive aid which the creatures provide in man's ascent back toward his Maker, if we "were to collect the passages which tell . . . of the natural immanence of God in the creatures . . . we should need to cite or mention a half of the great theologians and writers on spiritual subjects" of Spain.[64]

The transition from the second of Lull's levels to the third and highest level may seem negative and harsh. The ascent of the lad-

---

62. Mysticism was, however, potentially dangerous. Its insistence on the inwardness of worship and the unique and solitary character of the state of union contained the threat that the ministrations of the organized Church might become unnecessary. The unusual social activity of the Spanish mystics is noteworthy; they were reformers of orders and founders of convents and monasteries. For natural theology, see our chapter, below, on Reason.

63. *Primera Parte de los treynta y cinco Diálogos familiares de la Agricultura christiana* (Salamanca, 1589), fol. 298v.

64. R. Ricard, "Notes et matériaux pour l'étude du 'socratisme chrétien' chez Sainte Thérèse et les spirituels espagnols," Part II, *BHi*, L (1948), 5. In Calderón's *El gran teatro del mundo* (1649), created things are shown to exist "only for the purpose of awakening in men gratitude to, and praise of, God" (A. A. Parker, *The Allegorical Drama of Calderón* [Oxford–London, 1943], p. 128).

der of created things "is, after all, only another name for a progressive *contemptus mundi.*" [65] *Contemptus* is not, however, a word that a mystic would normally use. There is no contempt in these words of Fray Luis de Granada: "For just as now the creatures are a mirror that in some way reveals the beauty of God, so then [when we reach Heaven] God will be the mirror in which we shall see revealed the beauty of the creatures; and this we shall perceive with infinitely greater perfection than if we were contemplating the creatures themselves." [66] It is simply that the soul when in the state of union is "abysmally distant from that periphery wherein the creatures have their being and human words are formed." [67] Meister Eckhart says of the state of union: "All that a man has here . . . is intrinsically One. Here all blades of grass, wood, stone, all things are One. This is the deepest depth. . . . When the soul comes into the light of the supersensual it knows nothing of contrasts." [68] Here time and space are forgotten in an experience of the Infinite. To reach this state it is necessary to strive with all one's being toward the contemplation of God with no intermediary: to behold the Divine Majesty in all purity, in itself, with the mind bared and free of all images, memories or distractions of things created.[69]

This doctrine is stated in its harshest form by Diego Laínez, the second General of the Society of Jesus (d. 1565): "Surely the sinner falls from the heights to the depths when he centers the love of God — a thing so sublime — in the creatures, all of which, in comparison to God, are nothing." [70] Lull in his *Blanquerna* shows both stages, the lower and the higher, making clear the relative value of each in a language which is less passionate and consequently more accessible to persons having no direct knowledge of the mystical experience: "The monk again listened to Blanquerna's teaching, in which he showed him by the natural ratiocination of philosophy how the creatures show forth the Creator and his works." This is, of course, the stage of separateness, the lowly stage of the

65. Lovejoy, *op. cit.*, p. 92.
66. *Obras, ed. cit.*, I, 103.
67. Gallegos Rocafull, *op. cit.*, p. 93.
68. Quoted in W. T. Stace, *Religion and the Modern Mind* (Philadelphia, 1952), p. 231.
69. Fray Juan de la Cruz, the Dominican (not St. John of the Cross), quoted in M. Bataillon, *Erasmo y España* (Mexico City–Buenos Aires, 1950), II, 206.
70. Quoted in F. Cereceda, *Diego Laínez en la Europa religiosa de su tiempo,* (Madrid, 1945–46), I, 142.

ordinary worshiper. The highest stage is suggested in a single sentence: "The heart of the lover rose up to the Beloved in the heights, in order not to be distracted in his love of Him by the abyss of this world, and, finally in His presence, contemplated Him with sweetness and joy."[71]

The same spirit of ineffable fruition is expressed by Fray Luis de Granada: "This is taken from the supreme theologian St. Dionyius who, in his *Mystica Theologia*, seeks only to teach us the difference between the Divine Being and every created thing, teaching us (if we would know God) to turn our eyes away from the perfections of all the creatures in order that we may not be deceived in our effort to arrive at a conception of God from them; to leave them here below and rise up to contemplate a Being above all being, a Substance above all substance, a Light above all light, before which all light is darkness, and a Beauty above all beauty, compared to which all beauty is but ugliness. This is what is meant by that darkness into which Moses entered to speak with God, a darkness which hid from his sight everything that was not God, that he might thus more truly know Him." [72]

SUMMARY OF DOCTRINE

The mystery of the passage from "in the beginning" to "after the beginning," the mystery of why there should be a circular movement of descent from God and of return to Him, received in Spain, as in the rest of Europe, this answer: supreme Goodness must of necessity be manifested in a multiplicity of creatures, ranging from the humble elements to the sublime (the angels), each creature being placed, with the proper degree of dignity, in the order to which the heavenly Wisdom assigned it. The highest order of creatures below the Empyrean is composed of a single species — man — whose duty it is to effect the return from the material to the spiritual, to join God in an ultimate union (experienced for brief ecstatic moments by the mystics even in this life), placing at His

71. *Ed. cit.*, pp. 284–89, 568.
72. *Obras, ed. cit.*, I, 5. See also Sabunde, *op. cit.*, I, 33; Gallegos Rocafull, *op. cit.*, pp. 90–91; Julián Marías, *El tema del hombre* (Madrid, 1943), p. 144; Fidèle de Ros, *Le Frère Bernardin de Laredo* (Paris, 1948), pp. 258, 261; and Pedro Laín Entralgo, *La espera y la esperanza: Historia y teoría del esperar humano* (Madrid, 1957), p. 113.

feet the tribute of praise rendered by the entire ascending hierarchy of the beasts and birds and fishes, of the plants and stones, of
the four elements: fire, air, water, earth.

The theological and teleological explanation of the universe
was taken for granted. Why, it was asked, does part of the earth's
surface (though earth is the heaviest element) rise above the level
of the surrounding ocean? Not by natural inclination, for particles
of earth sink in water, but because of God's command in Genesis,
in order that man might have a dwelling place. "And the waters
that thus obey the Author and Creator of nature are more happy
in their obedience than if they bathed the whole of the earth as
is their natural inclination . . . , for in this obedience they serve
their Creator, converting into an ordinary occupation the reverence and obeisance which they owe to Him, since their obligation
is greater to Him than to their inherent tendency." [73] And the final
cause of the creation is none other than to effect the Eternal Return: "all things return to Him exactly as they came forth from
Him: that is the *causa final del mundo*." [74]

This created *uniuerso*, this rising scale of creatures, provided a
"Jacob's ladder" up which man's thought and love might mount
to a consideration of the beauty, the goodness, the wisdom, and the
power of Him who, as He made each rung, left thereon some im-
print of the shaping Hands, some fragrance of the Divine Breath.
The rungs themselves were adequate for the ordinary mortal not
gifted with the swift, strong powers of flight that enable the mystic
to mount up to the very Godhead and from there to view the creatures left behind exactly as God views them: as divine artifacts,
worthy of their Maker, but — in comparison with his Supreme Essence — humble witnesses, mere shadows of His Glory. The mystic,
in his awareness of their humility, often preached a negative consideration of (and a positive rising above) the creatures, and this
via negativa often went so far as to advise not stressing the
Humanity — the wounded hands and feet, the thorns, the bleeding
side, the cold sweat — of the Redeemer, since hands, feet, side, and
thorny crown, though sacred, partook of the creatural and the
human. This is not really a *contemptus mundi*; it was a *contem-*

---

73. Alejo Venegas del Busto, *De las differencias de libros que ay en al uniuerso*
(Salamanca, 1572), fol. 81 v.

74. Alfonso de la Torre (d. 1460?), *Visión delectable, BAE*, XXXVI, 367a.

platio Dei on a higher plane than that of simple piety and ordinary worship.

DOCTRINE TRANSMUTED INTO POETRY

This return from the material to the spiritual — from the creatures to the mind of the Creator — is a transformation that takes place in the human soul. In the realm of art a similar transformation takes place: pigments become "a light that never was," and words — poor dead things until the spirit is breathed into them — rise up from the brooding darkness of the poet's subconscious and by an act of creation are converted into poetry. The concepts we have been studying, when utilized by St. John of the Cross, become the stuff of mystical and poetic expression on the highest level.

In his *Cántico espiritual* or *Spiritual Canticle* the poet utilized the allegory of the *Song of Songs* to express, in forty short stanzas of incomparable beauty and simplicity, the seeking and finding of the soul's fulfillment in the state of mystical union. "The Song of Songs has always exercised a subtle charm upon those who have 'fallen in love with God.' Using the simple metaphor of Spouse and Bride, the Biblical writer sketches a series of rapid dialogues between God and the soul, made brilliant with the most suggestive colors of nature. The fragrant vineyard, the fig-tree laden with fruit, the voice of the trutle-dove and the springing of the flowers, the spikenard and saffron . . . , the fruitful valleys and green hills, . . . streams of Lebanon, beds of spices and gardens of lilies — all these and more speak to the mystic of the object of his love. So they spoke to St. John of the Cross, and one may be tempted to assert that never in their long and crowded history have the Songs inspired a greater masterpiece." [75]

The soul is portrayed as seeking her Beloved, first of all by exercise of self-knowledge, as St. Augustine instructed (so the author explains in his prose commentary). In stanza 4 she is ready to start upon her search along the road that leads, through consideration and knowledge of the creatures, to the knowledge of their Creator,

75. E. Allison Peers (trans.), *The Complete Works of St. John of the Cross*, II (London, 1934), pp. 1–2.

who is her Beloved. Thus this stanza initiates a meditation on the elements, on the lower and the higher creatures, on the heavens and the celestial spirits:

O bosques y espesuras	Oh, leafy groves and bowers,
plantadas por la mano del Amado,	Planted in love by my Beloved's hand,
O prado de uerduras	Oh, bright and shining flowers
de flores esmaltado,	That deck this verdant land,
dezid si por uosotros ha pasado.[76]	Tell me, has my Beloved trod this strand?

The creatures join in reply to the questioning soul (stanza 5):

Mil gracias derramando	Speeding in haste and trailing loveliness
passó por estos sotos con presura,	He passed these copses through,
y yéndolos mirando	Letting his gaze impress
con sola su figura	Its beauty ever new
vestidos los dexó de su hermosura.	On whatsoever felt his eyes' caress.

The soul, unable to content herself with mere traces and vestiges of the Beloved's passing, calls to Him for a direct and immediate vision. No messenger's report can satisfy (stanza 7):

Y todos cuantos vagan	All these created things
de ti me uan mil gracias refiriendo,	Reveal the loveliness you left behind
y todos más me llagan,	Dimly; their message brings
y déxame muriendo	New suffering, for my mind
un no sé qué que quedan balbuciendo.	Inteprets not mere murmuring of the wind.

At last the search is rewarded. The meeting is effected and the soul tells how, when the deep draught was drunk, the darkly-revealing glass was laid aside and forgotten, and she saw face to face (stanza 26):

En la interior bodega	Where the strong wine is kept
de mi Amado beuí, y quando salía	I drank of my Beloved, and at length
por todo aquesta bega	From the place where I slept
ya cosa no sabía	I stepped forth with new strength,
y el ganado perdí que antes tenía.	Forgetting all for which I once had wept.

76. This and the succeeding verse quotations are from the previously cited Clásicos Castellanos edition, pp. 9–18.

The experience is ineffable, but it must be told. She tells it (stanzas 36, 37):

Gozémonos, Amado;	Beloved, oh, be mine!
y vámonos a uer en tu hemosura	Let me behold myself in your fair face.
al monte y al collado,	Take me to yonder pine
do mana el agua pura;	Where flows the fount of grace;
entremos más adentro en la espesura	Hide me more deeply in the secret place;
Y luego a las subidas	And in the caverns there
cauernas de la piedra nos yremos	Where all is hidden and the stones arch high,
que están bien escondidas	Let us go in, away from noonday's glare;
y allí nos entraremos	There I'll beside you lie,
y el mosto de granadas gustaremos.	And with you drink love's cup, and never die.

There at last the Beloved will reveal to the soul the fullness of knowledge that existed in Eden before the Fall. She will receive the direct inspiration of the Holy Spirit and will experience the immediate enjoyment of God. She will perceive the creatures as God himself sees and knows them, from above, in the great light of His glory. Totally transformed into the love of God, she will have pure and complete contemplation of His Essence (stanzas 38, 39):

Allí me mostrarías	There you will show me all
aquello que mi alma pretendía;	That was the object of my heart's desire;
y luego me darías	There as before the Fall
allí tú, vida mía,	I'll see the Empyrean's fire,
aquello que me diste el otro día:	And hear the voices of the angelic choir;
El aspirar del ayre,	I'll breathe the heavenly air
el canto de la dulce Filomena,	And hear the song of Heaven's nightingale;
el soto y su donayre	And in Heaven's forest fair,
en la noche serena	In heavenly glade and dale,
con llama que consume y no da pena.	I'll burn with fire of love that cannot fail.

I offer apologies at these efforts at translating the soaring music of a poet of genuis. But somehow the indispensable form must be conveyed; somehow the alternating measures of heptasyllable and hendecasyllable and the haunting repetitions of the rhymes must be perceived and the connotation of the words at least suggested, though the echo be far from faithful; the visions of beauty must be seen as shapes, though the mirror distort and its darkness dim the image.

II · Three Cosmological Problems[1]

The spheres of the heavens are like
the layers of onions.
                    Alejo Venegas [2]

I stood dumbfounded. Who would not
be smitten by amazement beholding
so strange a harmony, produced by a
conflict of opposites?
                    Baltasar Gracián [3]

The principal cause why the ancients
made blue the color of jealousy was this:
just as in the heavens there is no real
color (for such color as we perceive is
merely false and apparent, being caused by
the immense distance between the heavens and
our eyes), so jealousy is a product of
imagination and suspicion which, on a basis
of convincing deceit, conjures up offenses
and guilt.
                    Manuel Fernández Villareal [4]

THE STRUCTURE OF THE UNIVERSE

Calderón's *comedia, La selva confusa,* begins with a eulogy of the
chase, in which one of the speakers praises hawking in language
intelligible only to those members of the audience who had at least

1. See W. F. Warren, *The Universe as Pictured in Milton's Paradise Lost* (New York, 1915); Marjorie Nicolson, "The 'New Astronomy' and English Literary Imagination," *SP,* XXXII (1935), 428–62; A. M. Schmidt, *La poésie scientifique en France au seizième siècle* (Paris, 1939); Arnold Williams, "Renaissance Commentaries on 'Genesis' and Some Elements of the Theology of 'Paradise Lost,'" *PMLA,* LXVI (1941), 151–64; John C. Lapp (ed.), *The Universe of Pontus de Tyard* (Ithaca, New York, 1950); P. H. Kocher, *Science and Religion in Elizabethan England* (San Marino, California, 1953); Thomas S. Kuhn, *The Copernican Revolution: Planetary Astronomy in the Development of Western Thought* (Cambridge, Massachusetts, 1957).
2. *Agonía del tránsito de la muerte, NBAE,* XVI, 308a.
3. *El Criticón,* ed. M. Romera-Navarro (Philadelphia, 1938–40), I, 137.
4. From a work entitled *Color verde: A la divina Celia* (Madrid, 1637). See B. J. Gallardo, *Ensayo de una biblioteca española de libros raros y curiosos* (Madrid, 1863–89), III, col. 1053 (hereafter to be abbreviated *Ensayo*).

a hearsay acquaintance with the Ptolemaic-Scholastic theory of the four "regions" of the elements — earth, air, fire, water — and of the eleven "spheres" [5] of the heavens:

> How wonderful to see the flying crane
> Mount up so high toward heaven
> That in her upward flight
> Her pinions brush one region, then another!
> For between fire and air,
> Speeding away in swift trajectory,
> Her wings, that brighten the thin realm of air,
> Are singed when upward bent toward the pure fire.[6]

Calderón, who died in 1681, stands at the very end of our period. Turning back to Fernando de Rojas, whose *Celestina* (1499?) was published nearly two centuries earlier, we find the same conception of *la gran fábrica del mundo*, of the structure of the world as a complex sphere composed of a series of concentric rings, wherein "everything is ruled and restrained by an unyielding bridle and all things move impelled by the same spur — heavens, earth, sea, fire, heat, cold; and where the author, like everyone else, felt geared to the secret movements of the high celestial firmament of the planets and the pull of the waxing and waning of the month-counting moon".[7]

The world above us, as pictured or suggested by the poets, had

5. The sphericity of the earth had been believed by Clement of Alexandria, Origen, Ambrose, and Basil. The Venerable Bede sought to prove it on scientific grounds. Albertus Magnus gave an elaborate demonstration of it, and it has been pointed out that his views on this subject led eventually to the discovery of America. The sphericity of the earth was denied by Lactantius and Augustine. The lowest of the "regions" was occupied by the two elements that make up our terraqueous globe: earth and water. Above these, on all hands, was the encircling envelope of air; and above that, the circle of elemental fire, clearly distinguished from fire as known on earth. Outside all of this were the concentric "spheres" of the planets and of the fixed stars. Still farther out were the *primum mobile* or prime mover, and the glowing Empyrean.

6. "¿Qué se iguala al ber la garça que altanera / al cielo se lebanta, / siendo en conquista tanta / término de una y otra esfera? / que entre el fuego y el viento / corre sin alterar el movimiento, / quando del ayre en la región suprema / bate las alas que en el fuego quema, / haciendo de su pluma al ayre esmalte?" (ed. G. T. Northup, *RHi*, XXI [1909], 186). The metaphor was popular, appearing in almost identical form in Tirso de Molina's *Luis Pérez el gallego* (ed. J. E. Hartzenbusch, II, 445c; cited by Northup).

7. This and what follows is taken from an article by Joseph E. Gillet, "*So la luna*: Notes on the Life and Death of a Spanish Idiom," in *Estudios Hispánicos: Homenaje a Archer M. Huntington* (Wellesley, Massachusetts, 1952), pp. 194–95.

an almost concrete reality which today it preserves only in the imagination of childhood. The pictures of the Ptolemaic cosmos: the Moon and Mercury, Venus, the Sun, Mars, Jupiter, and Saturn, the crystalline sky of the fixed stars, the *Primum Mobile*, where all motion originated, and, beyond Nature, the Empyrean, drenched in eternal light, the fiery dwelling of God, while all the spheres girated around the Earth, all this was a fairly familiar picture, and because it did not have to be realized first by an effort of the imagination, it could be transformed at a touch into a scene of awesome wonder:

> Dwelling of majesty,
> Temple of brilliance and eternal beauty.[8]

Because of this centuries-old concept of the universe, Acevedo in his *Creación del Mundo* (1615) could depend on the easy understanding of his readers when he wrote:

> God the Creator hung the earth in space,
> Fixed, ever motionless, by air surrounded,
> Center and fulcrum of revolving spheres.[9]

This is the geocentric universe of Ptolemy. While the Mohammedans and Jews recognized seven heavens, Aristotle eight, and Ptolemy nine, Alfonso el Sabio, following most Scholastic theologians,[10] counted ten plus the Empyrean.[11] Eleven was the usual number of spheres pictured by the Renaissance mind, a picture constantly renewed by the unceasing editions of John of Holywood's (Sacrobosco's) *Tractatus de Sphaera*. These ideas pervade Spanish literature during the Golden Age. For example, we find in *El príncipe perfecto of* Lope de Vega the following:

> — Eleven, you say, the heavens are?
> — Yes, sir;

8. "Morada de grandeza / templo de claridad y fermosura" (from Fray Luis de León's *Noche serena*, composed *ca.* 1576). Whenever Calderón speaks of the movements of our planetary system, he supposes that the sun revolves about the earth, in accordance with the system of Ptolemy.

9. "Y a la tierra, que un punto no declina, / el sumo Hacedor dejó suspensa / en el aire sutil sin movimiento, / y en la mitad del mundo hizo asiento" (*BAE*, XXIX, 247b).

10. Sometimes the crystalline heaven and the *Primum Mobile* were considered as one.

11. Gillet, *op. cit.*, n. 5.

and in Cervantes' *Persiles y Segismunda*: "By the eleven heavens that are said to exist, I swear to you. . . ." [12]

The earth

At the center of the *máquina del mundo* was the earth, a core composed of the two heaviest elements [13] — earth and water — which exist together in a single "region," part of the earth extending upward above the ocean's surface to provide man a dwelling place. Father Acosta, pondering the scientific knowledge gained from the circumnavigation of the globe (1522), wrote that "without doubt the sky has a round and perfect figure; and the earth, in its embrace with the element of water, has the form of a perfect globe or ball, made up of these two elements; and it has its limits, its roundness and its greatness." [14]

Some fifty years before Columbus and nearly seventy-five before the earth was circumnavigated, Juan de Mena (d. 1456) gave a similar picture of the world in his *Laberinto de Fortuna*. With Providence as his guide he is caught up and placed on a vantage point:

> And from there I beheld the spherical center,
> And the five zones: the austral, the brumal,
> The zone of the northwind, the zone equinoxial,
> And then last of all, the zone of the solstice;
> Next pacing toward me I saw a procession
> Of wild beasts and men of the strangest appearance,
> Monsters and forms both seen and imagined,
> As I too moved forward in that strangest of places. [15]

Air and fire

The regions of air and fire constitute the two first "onion rings"

12. "¿Once son, en fin, los cielos? / — Sí señor"; "Por los once cielos que dicen que ay, te juro. . . . " Other examples are cited by Gillet in note 5 (see n. 11 above).

13. On the combination of the elements to form species and varieties, see Alfonso de la Torre (d. 1460?), *Visión delectable*, BAE, XXXVI, 370.

14. *Historia natural y moral de las Indias* (Madrid, 1792), I, p. 5.

15. "De allí se veía el espérico çentro, / e las çinco zonas con todo el austral, / brumal, aquilón, e la equinoçial, / con los que solstiçia contiene de dentro; / e vi contra mí venir al encuentro / bestias e gentes de estrañas maneras, / monstruos, e formas fengidas e veras, / quando delante la casa más entro" (*copla* 34). J. M. Blecua, in his notes to the Clásicos Castellanos edition of Mena (Madrid, 1943), on page 19 refers this *copla* to its source in the *De Imagine mundi* attributed to St. Anselm.

that envelop the earth. The ring of air is palpably experienced by us all: we receive it in our lungs; and our persons, our buildings, and our ships bear the force of its tempestuous currents. The region, or ring, of fire, on the other hand, is imaginary, having been deduced by a sort of argument-from-design: "Nature made an element which is dry and cold, which we call earth; and another which is moist and cold, which we call water; and a third which it hot and moist, which we call air; the conjugation of opposites would seem to be imperfect if Nature had not created also a fourth element which should be hot and dry, which we call fire, in order that there might be an adequate combination of the four first qualities in order to guarantee the generation of mixed and composite things." Since the three elements — earth, water, air — have each its region, logic requires that the fourth element — fire — should have its region also, and that this should be the highest of all, since a flame rises upward through the air toward its source, which is the sun.[16]

The first heaven: the Moon

Above the elemental, earth-bound regions revolves the first heaven, that of the Moon. All things below the moon are subject to generation and decomposition: water can be boiled away or polluted, air exhausted or corrupted, fire extinguished, earth dissolved.[17] In the sphere of the moon, and above it, all things are changeless, and this is the reason for the existence of the Spanish idiom *so la luna* — beneath the moon — which corresponds to our own *under the sun*.

Each of the planetary spheres, moreover, was associated with the astrological ideas of the influence of the horoscope, and four of them — the Moon, Mercury, Venus, and Saturn — were assigned to the quadrants of the zodiac that corresponded to the four elements, to the four seasons, to the four ages of man, to the four humors of the human body — phlegm, black bile or melancholy, yellow bile or choler, blood — and to the four temperaments or "complexions"

16. Pedro Simón Abril in his *Filosofía natural,* a manuscript work (*ca.* 1589) studied by Margherita Morreale de Castro in her dissertation, *Pedro Simón Abril* (Madrid, 1949), pp. 151–52.

17. "The alterations which this planet [the moon] produces in the human body, with her periods of full moon and new moon and in her eclipses, when her light is . . . impeded by the shadow of the earth, are a matter of ordinary experience to us all" (Fray Luis de Granada, *Obras* [Madrid, 1768], I, 74–75).

of persons born under the influences of the respective quadrants.

The Moon, *Luna*, was the planet assigned to the zodiacal quadrant of *Taurus-Virgo-Capricornus* (Virgo undoubtedly suggesting the virgin Diana). Her element was water; her wind, Eurus, or the southeast wind; her season of the year, autumn; her season in man's life, the age of vigor; her bodily humor, phlegm; her bodily complexion, phlegmatic.[18] Persons born under her influence were considered to be cold and moist; neither good nor bad but indifferent, lazy, and negligent; sleepyheads [19] who seldom laugh or cry; taciturn, slow to learn, puffy of face.[20] This bill of particulars, drawn up by the fifteenth-century Alfonso Martínez de Toledo in a moralizing but remarkably realistic book to which was given the subtitle *Condemnation of Worldly Love*, seems not a little damaging; but over against this *Non* there is also a *Sic*. The Moon is Luna, Diana the Chaste, Diana the Huntress. Francisco Sánchez, known as El Brocense, in a note in his 1582 edition of Mena's fifteenth-century *Laberinto*, offers a happier picture of the person born under the influence of Luna: "The first planet which is the Moon causes men to be fond of the fields and of the exercise of the chase, lovers of chastity and bodily purity, and so among heroes of the past Hippolytus, son of Theseus, has first place. . . ." [21] In Mena's poem, Providence explains to her neophyte the Diana-like character of the exemplars:

> If you beheld chaste men with the hunters,
> It's because this is set forth by grave authors
> Who assign to this planet the virtue aforesaid.[22]

The second heaven: Mercury

Sebastián de Covarrubias in his *Tesoro de la lengua castellana* (1611) defines the adjective *mercurial* as applying to anyone born under predominance of the planet Mercury. Such a person will be "active and dangerous to deal with, because of his sharpness and

18. Lawrence Babb, *The Elizabethan Malady: A Study of Melancholia in English Literature from 1580 to 1642* (East Lansing, Michigan, 1951), p. 11.

19. The fiery Don Quijote on more than one occasion says to his phlegmatic squire Sancho Panza: "Sleep thou, who wert made for sleep."

20. Alfonso Martínez de Toledo, *El Arçipreste de Talavera*, ed. L. B. Simpson (Berkeley, 1939), pp. 208–9.

21. Cited in ed. Blecua, p. 37, n. 63a.

22. "Si viste los castos con los caçadores, / es porque assinan aquí los auctores / desta planeta tal grado bien quisto" (*copla* 69).

astuteness." El Brocense, commenting on Mena's *copla* 85 ("Here Begins the Second Order, of Mercury"), notes that: "In the second order, or circle of Mercury, the poet places prudent counselors and ambassadors, and the intermediaries in peace negotiations . . . , and those given over to just and honorable traffic in merchandise, and men who were liberators of their country. . . ." These are the qualities which classical mythology ascribed to the god Mercury. Mena's neophyte describes them:

> Those I beheld who in council were wise,
> And those who in wartime brought armies to terms,
> And no less those men who in different endeavors
> Acquired worthy gains in the traffic of merchants;
> Others who gained for their countrymen freedom,
> Exposers of plots whereby many were saved
> From dire evils of tyrants' oppression,
> From national dangers and great public perils.[23]

The third heaven: Venus

In Chapter IV of Volume I we saw how, in his moment of greatest emotional and artistic self-realization, Garcilaso de la Vega (d. 1536), the Prince of Castilian poets, fused the multiple elements of his Christian, classical, and Renaissance-Italian culture in fourteen lines of verse that are a joy forever — his *Egloga Primera* to Elisa *in morte*. Just as the loving spirits in Dante's *Paradiso* descend from the Empyrean singing *Hosana* to greet the poet on his upward flight, so Garcilaso imagines Elisa descending from the motionless Empyrean to meet him in the circle of the Celestial Venus,[24] the last stage in which the mounting souls preserve their earthly lineaments. We saw also how Fray Luis de León cast a play-

23. "Vi los que sano consejo tovieron, / e los que conponen en guerra las pazes, / e vimos a muchos fuera destas fazes, / que justas gananças mercando quisieron; / e otros que libres sus tierras fizieron, / e los que por causa de evitar más daños / han revelado los grandes engaños, / a muchos librando que non se perdieron" (*copla* 85; see *ed. cit.*, p. 49).

24. In the Renaissance, Venus was an ambivalent symbol. The humanists were familiar with her conventional role no less than with the more esoteric meaning attached to her in the dialogues of Plato, who speaks of two Venuses. The question as to what Venus represented to the Renaissance is too vague for the historian to obtain a well-defined answer, but it is certain that Botticelli painted her as representing Platonic beauty, and that to the Protestant Spenser it was from Venus' house that "all the world derives the glorious features of beautie" (see E. H. Gembich, "Botticelli's Mythologies: A Study of the Neoplatonic Symbolism of his Circle," *Journal of the Warburg and Courtauld Institutes*, VII [1945], 13-17).

ful horoscope for the newly born daughter of the Marqués de Alcañices in a poem which delicately suggests that the newly born
child will be endowed with riches and fame by Jupiter and with
beauty by Venus, the goddess identified with the planet of the
third heaven:

> Upon you were bestowed,
> With generous hand and overflowing heart,
> Blessings unnumbered by the god who rules
> The sixth planet of the heavens,
> And by the powerful goddess of the third.[25]

The fourth heaven: the Sun

Among all creatures having bodies, wrote Fray Luis de Granada,
"the one which best represents the beauty and omnipotence of the
Creator . . . is the sun. And the first way in which it does this is
that, though it is but a single star, it produces within itself such
great light that it illumines everything that God created from the
heavens down to earth, in such fashion that even when the sun is
in the other hemisphere below us, it gives light to all the stars of
the sky."[26]

Mena places in the Sun's circle doctors of the Church, mystics
of great learning, philosophers and orators, astronomers and poets:
Jerome, Gregory, Augustine, Thomas Aquinas, Aristotle, Socrates,
Plato, along with Tubal (the inventor of music), Orpheus, and
many others who are dear to Apollo the Sun God, who, because of
his omniscience, was also the god of divination, poetry, and music,
and president of the choir of the Muses.[27]

While it was natural to associate any king with the Sun, inasmuch
as the Sun held the primacy among the planets, the words *el Sol*
were especially applicable to Philip IV (d. 1665) because of his number — fourth in the series of the Philips as the sphere of the Sun
was the fourth among the heavens. In Calderón's *zarzuela*, *El lau-*

25. "Diéronte bien sin cuento / con voluntad concorde y amorosa / quien rige el
movimiento / sexto, con la alta diosa / de la tercera rueda poderosa" (see O. H.
Green, "The Abode of the Blest in Garcilaso's *Egloga Primera*," *RPh*, VI [1953],
276).
26. *Obras, ed. cit.*, I, 72. I do not have information to show when or how this
erroneous idea concerning the light of the stars was corrected. We shall meet it
again when we discuss the color of the sky (see below).
27. *Coplas* 116 ff. See Alfonso el Sabio, *Setenario*, ed. K. H. Vanderford (Buenos
Aires, 1945), pp. 60–61.

rel de Apolo, Philip IV is shown grieving for Queen Mariana who, it was believed, was on the brink of death in childbirth:

> Although the fecund Lucina
> Presided over his horoscope,
> A sudden turn for the worse
> Put an end to joy and hope,
> So that the Sun became shrouded
> With clouds, and we all assumed
> That the clouds were dropping rain;
> But the raindrops were tears of the Sun.[28]

The fifth heaven: Mars

Mars was assigned to the quadrant of the zodiac corresponding to the appropriately aggressive *Aries-Leo-Sagittarius*. His element was fire; his wind, Favonius, the west wind that ushered in the spring; his season of the year, summer; his season of life, youth; his bodily humor, hot-dry choler; his bodily complexion, choleric.[29] Martínez de Toledo, in the fifteenth-century work already cited (pp. 207–8), says the following of men of choleric temper: "These men are hot and dry, since their element is fire. They are of swift and violent anger, very proud, strong, dangerous in their emotional outbursts, though these are brief. They are gifted with natural eloquence, bold to take a stand in any public place, spirited, swift of movement, very wise, subtle, and *given to dreams and visions*.[30] They are competent. They love justice, though they are

28. "Y aunque fecunda Lucina / a su horóscopo asistió, / grosero accidente puso / el alborozo en temor; / tanto, que el Sol entre nubes, / como es de las nubes Dios, / presumimos que llovía, / y era que lloraba el Sol" (see E. W. Hesse, "Court References in Calderon's *Zarzuelas*," *HR*, XV [1947], 370). Calderón wrote of the newly-born Prince Felipe Próspero: "Let the Fourth Planet give him his name, / So that as Fourth and Fifth / He may excell in arms and letters" (cited *ibid.*, p. 372). In this text fourth refers to the Fourth Sphere, that of Apollo, god of poets, thinkers, musicians; fifth, to the Sphere of Mars, the god of war (arms). See Alfonso el Sabio, *op. cit.*, pp. 60–61.

29. Babb, *op. cit.*, p. 11.

30. For a justification of this translation of the word *ingeniosos* see my article, "El *ingenioso* hidalgo," *HR*, XXV (1957), 175 ff. In this article I relate not only this word but also all of Don Quijote's traits — his activity, his life, sickness, recovery, and death — to the typology of the elements and humors as conceived by contemporary physiology and psychology. Cervantes got his idea from Juan Huarte de San Juan's *Examen de ingenios para las ciencias* (Baeza, 1575), the first work of differential psychology directed toward vocational guidance ever written. For this book's influence in England see Hardin Craig, *The Enchanted Glass: The Elizabethan Mind in Literature* (New York, 1950), pp. 55, 117, 119 ff.

more suited to execute it than to make judicial decisions. They are vindictive when their choler is stirred up, ardent as fire. They are born under the planet Mars."

All of these traits are traits of Don Quijote, and the interplay of choler (yellow bile) and melancholy (black bile), of hot-dry and cold-dry, determine his original madness, his sorties, his returns, his mounting disillusionments, discouragements and depressions, his final return to his village, the recovery of his mental health as that of his body declines, his renunciation of knight-errantry and his death.[31] The parallels are striking. *Under the planet Mars*: "I was born," says Don Quijote, "if one may judge by my inclination to the career of arms, under the influence of the planet Mars" (Part II, ch. 6). *Violent in anger*: "Great Saints preserve us, and how great was the anger of Don Quijote as he heard the unbecoming words of his squire!" (II, 46 — the number of such outbursts of fury is legion). *Proud*: Don Quijote's sin is *hubris*, overweening pride, and it is only in the final chapters of the book (starting in II, 58) that he achieves Christian humility. *Gifted with natural eloquence*: We recall the flights of brilliant rhetoric displayed at the goat-herds' campfire (I, 11) and in the discourse on arms and letters (I, 38). *Bold to take a stand in any public place*: We recall the over-whelming boldness of his reply to the meddling ecclesiastic in the palace of the Duke and Duchess (II, 32). *Lover of justice, more suited to impose and execute it than to decide it*: We think of the galley slaves, freed out of love of justice, but unwisely freed. Finally we come to the key words: *mucho sabyos, sobtiles e engeniosos* — wise, subtle, and given to dreams and visions. Don Quijote is an *ingenioso*, as described by Martínez de Toledo and by other writers on the problems of psychology and psychiatry who came after him in sixteenth-century Spain. It is his visionary character, his power (made pathological by his lack of sleep) to dream up adventures and conceive great projects, that starts him off on his immortal journeys and sustains him in the tests of the *camino de perfección*, the way to perfection, that constitutes the story of his final years.

31. In addition to my article just cited, see two others also by me: "Realidad, voluntad y gracia en Cervantes," *Ibérida: Revista de filología*, III (1961), 113–28, and "El Licenciado Vidriera: Its Relation to the *Viaje del Parnaso* and the *Examen de Ingenios* of Huarte," *Linguistic and Literary Studies in Honor of Helmut A. Hatzfeld* (Washington, D.C., 1964), pp. 213–20.

There could be no more striking proof that the intellectual background, the philosophical and scientific or pseudoscientific ideas of a culture, are the ground from which its great art forms spring.

The sixth heaven: Jupiter

Jupiter, like the Moon and Mars, had his quadrant in the zodiac — that of the appropriately benign *Gemini-Libra-Aquarius*. His element was air; his wind Auster, the south wind; his season of the year, spring; his season in the life of man, youth; his bodily humor, hot-moist blood; his bodily complexion, sanguine.[32] We read in the *Arçipreste de Talavera* that persons born under Jupiter's influence are joyous, given to laughter, to games and dancing; that they are swift of movement, generous, friendly, ruddy in color, beautiful, upright in their dealings; controlled, just and merciful, even to the extent of grieving over the suffering of irrational animals; in short, that the sanguine person is *byenaventurado*, blest.[33] It will be remembered that Fray Luis de León imagined Jupiter, who governs the movement of the sixth sphere, as bestowing upon the newborn daughter of a Spanish nobleman the blessings — *bien sin cuento* — of riches and fame.[34]

Jupiter was also, in classical mythology, the father of gods and of men. It is therefore natural that the planet and the heaven assigned to him should be conceived of in terms of traits associated with the idea of fatherhood. Alfonso el Sabio's thirteenth-century *Setenario* says that the name Jupiter "signifies uprightness and worthiness, because all things accomplished under its influence are good and right . . . , its property is the love of justice, nobility and all goodness. . . . And for that reason they assigned to this planet the element of the air, which is bright and clear."[35] Mena, in *copla* 214 of his *Laberinto*, describes the neophyte's vision as he and Providence moved toward "la sexta orden, de Júpiter":

> Those I beheld who in glorious peace
> Hold gentle sway over all their subjects,

32. Babb, *op. cit.*, p. 11.
33. *Ed. cit.*, pp. 206–7.
34. See above, our treatment of Venus.
35. *Ed cit.*, p. 62.

And those who on earth, with no thought for themselves,
Bend every effort toward the public good.[36]

The seventh heaven: Saturn

Saturn's place in the zodiac corresponds to the quadrant of
Cancer-Scorpio-Pisces — cold-blooded creatures. His element is
cold-dry earth; his wind, Aquilo or the north wind; his season of
the year, winter; his season in man's life, old age; his humor, melancholy or black bile; his bodily complexion, melancholy.[37]

The planet Saturn brings to mind mythological associations
which are dark and bloody: castration, devouring of offspring.
Melancholy or Saturnine men, we read in the *Arçipreste de Talavera* (*ed. cit.*, pp. 209–10), are given to anger and lacking in moderation; they are excessively stingy; unendurable, quarrelsome,
inclined to strike their heads against the wall; gloomy, venomous
of tongue, pensive, given to sighing, hating all joy and merriment;
deceitful, cruel, and characterized by innumerable other defects.
Yet, if these tendencies are offset by the benign action of another
humor, the result may be highly favorable. Hence it is that men of
great mental power were regarded as saturnine: Empedocles, Socrates, Plato. Melancholy, being dry and cold, was regarded as aiding the intellect just as its opposite, dry-hot choler, fostered the
imagination.[38]

For our example of melancholy in literature we turn again to
Don Quijote. The knight's life-trajectory is composed of both
centrifugal and centripetal movement. Under the centrifugal impulse of his choleric nature, as determined by the complexion that
he received at birth, plus the exacerbating influence of a mania
for reading that deprived his heated brain of the restorative virtue
of sleep-produced humidity and coolness, plus an additional hot-
dry factor that resulted from hot and dry emotions of anticipated
knightly glory — under the impulse of these three disposing forces,
Don Quijote makes his successive sorties. As disposing forces of
the opposite character — defeat, the conviction that he is enchanted,
disillusionment, depression — operate upon him, he makes his suc-

---

36. "E vi los que reinan en paz gloriosa, / e los muy umanos a sus naturales, / e
muchos de aquellos, seyendo mortales, / que biven çelando la pública cosa."
37. Babb, *op. cit.*, p. 11.
38. Babb, *op. cit.*, pp. 59–60.

cessive returns to his village. In the Second Part, the number of humiliating and depressing experiences heaped on him by Cervantes (as he slowly and skillfully plans the knight's ultimate return, renunciation, and death) are almost unbelievably numerous. They are subtle, violent, or poignant, as the case may be. Their goal is ever the same: to curb Don Quijote's *hubris* and vainglory, to restore him to Christian humility, to cure him of his hot-dry mental disease so that he can see his error for what it is and, in his last moments, have a glimpse of the pure glory that lies beyond the Shining River. The phases of the metamorphosis are exquisitely planned and brought to their conclusion. They are three times repeated, each time with greater force: an exciting cause, a resolving crisis, a diminution of cerebral heat — all finally joined in a greater unity as the initial dry-hot choler yields to its opposite, the cold-dry emotion of melancholy, and to the ultimate cold of death.[39]

The eighth heaven: the firmament of the fixed stars

Venegas, in his *Primera parte de las Differencias de libros que ay en el vniuerso,*[40] explains that "above Saturn is the eighth heaven, which is called the starry heaven or the firmament, because all the stars, excepting the seven planets, are set and established firmly in it, like knots in a board." To Fray Luis de Granada [41] this firmament is a source of awe and wonder: "Nor should we be less moved to admiration by the creation of stars so numerous that only He who created them can count them. And if each one of the stars is greater in size than this world of ours . . . how can we imagine the creation of innumerable worlds, vastly more beautiful and precious than ours, inasmuch as the matter of which they are composed is more excellent than our four elements? And all of them, together with the sun and the moon, were created by the uttering of a single word."

Again, as we have often done before, we appeal to the other Luis, Fray Luis de León, who in his *Night of Stars* [42] has given poetic

39. See my three studies on the psychopathic aspects of *Don Quijote* listed in notes 30 and 31 above.

40. Ed. Toledo, 1540, fols. xcii (read xcix) ff.

41. *Obras, ed. cit.,* I, 387–88.

42. Aubrey F. G. Bell (trans.), in *Ten Centuries of Spanish Poetry,* ed. Eleanor L. Turnbull (Baltimore, 1955), pp. 186–87.

form to the wonder inspired in a sixteenth-century Spaniard by the contemplation of the firmament of the eight heaven:

Rodéase en la cumbre	And yonder in the height
Saturno, padre de los siglos de oro;	Whirls Saturn, father of the Age of Gold,
tras él la muchedumbre	And after him the bright
del reluciente coro	Stars in fair choir enrolled
su luz va repartiendo y su tesoro;	Their light and all their treasures still unfold;
. . . .	. . . .
Inmensa hermosura	Here beauty infinite
aquí se muestra toda; y resplandece	Unveils itself, and light, quintessence pure,
clarísma luz pura,	Transparent gleams; no night
que jamás anochece;	Its radiance may obscure;
eterna primavera aquí florece;	Spring's flowered splendour here is ever sure.
¡Oh campos verdaderos!	O fields of truth most fair!
¡Oh prados con verdad frescos y amenos,	Oh meadows verily ever fresh and bright,
riquísimos mineros!	Mines full of riches rare!
¡Oh deleitosos senos,	Oh fountains of delight!
repuestos valles de mil bienes llenos!	Deep valleys with a thousand blessings dight!

The ninth or crystalline heaven [43]

Above the firmament of the fixed stars, says Venegas,[44] is the crystalline heaven,[45] which in the Scriptures (Ps. 148) is called the "waters that be above the heavens." Acevedo, in *La creación del mundo*, relating the activity of the Second Day, says that a portion of the waters was retained in heaven, while other waters were assigned their place on earth:

> Much of the water that was thus poured forth
> God in His wisdom placed above the stars,

43. See Harry F. Robins, "The Crystalline Sphere and the 'Waters Above' in *Paradise Lost*," *PMLA*, LXIX (1954), 903.

44. *Differencias de libros* . . . , *ed. cit*, fol. xcii [read xcix].

45. "Alphonso X, the astronomer-king of Spain (1252–1284), added the crystalline sphere to the geocentric sphere so that the motion of trepidation might be accounted for mechanically." Prior to this addition there had been no more than nine major spheres in any cosmological heaven (those of the seven planets, that of the fixed stars, and the Prime Mover). See Robins, *op. cit.*, p. 905 and n. 9.

That by their chilling flood the burning fire
Of all those flaming bodies might be cooled,
Lest they consume themselves and thus might fail
To exert the influence that to each He gave.[46]

It seems strange that a single verse of the Psalter should have so influenced cosmological thinking,[47] and stranger still, perhaps, that the resulting concept should have formed part of the mental furniture of the ordinary Spaniard. Agustín de Tejada, one of the poets included in Pedro Espinosa's famous anthology, *Flores de poetas ilustres de España* (1605), gives expression to it in a lyrical poem on the Assumption of the Virgin:

The starry Heaven to you makes its obeisance,
The Heaven of waters, and the swift Prime Mover,
As you move up to where all motion ceases.[48]

The tenth heaven: the Prime Mover[49]

Above the crystalline heaven, says Venegas,[50] "is the *Primum Mobile*, which moves so fast that it almost has the speed of thought, for in the space of twenty-four hours it makes a full revolution." This is the sphere which communicates its motion to all the others. "What lightning flash can be so swift," asks Fray Luis de Granada,[51] "that its speed will not seem that of a tortoise in comparison? What human mind can there be that will not falter as it considers the greatness of the Power that could cause such speed? And there is a still greater marvel, which is this: a single angel, applying his vir-

46. "Gran suma de las aguas derramadas / puso el eterno Padre sobre el cielo, / para que de las llamas levantadas, / templando el fuego ardiente con su hielo, / los varios astros hagan la influencia / que ordenó la divina Providencia" (*ed. cit.*, p. 251a).

47. "The famous astronomical dialogue in Book VIII [of *Paradise Lost*] reveals Milton's scepticism about the capacity of science to solve cosmic secrets; . . . while he borrowed eclectically from the astronomical lore of two thousand years, he did not hesitate to discard any theory which conflicted with his ultimate authority, the Bible" (Robins, *op. cit.*, p. 914).

48. "Y el firmamento octavo se te humilla, / el áqueo cielo, con el primer moble, / hasta que llegas al empíreo inmoble" (ed. J. Quirós de los Ríos and F. Rodríguez Marín [Seville, 1896], p. 253).

49. The concept of the *Primum Mobile* was a very late development in European astronomy, added in the thirteenth century to account for the precession of the equinoxes as described by Ptolemy. See Robins, *op. cit.*, p. 905, n. 9.

50. *Differencias de libros* . . . , *ed. cit.*, fol. xcii [read xcix].

51. *Obras, ed. cit.*, I, 385.

tue to this great mass which is the tenth heaven,[52] has been moving it without ceasing since the beginning of the world . . . without ever losing a beat in the tempo, or the slightest portion of the glory which he enjoys as he beholds the face of the Creator. It is because of this regularity that astronomers proclaim eclipses. . . . Who will not humble and prostrate himself . . . in the presence of such Majesty?"

The eleventh heaven: the Empyrean

The concept of the motionless Empyrean, a limitless, waveless ocean glowing with the spiritual fire of love, is familiar to readers of our first volume: in the resplendent light of this unmoving dwelling of God and His saints, treading and measuring the heaven with her immortal feet, moves the deceased Elisa visualized by Garcilaso de Vega.[53] To Fray Luis de Granada the Empyrean is "the royal palace and abode of God and his elect." [54] Mena, in his *Laberinto*, designates it as the dwelling place of the Most High:

> Oh God of our love, in whom we believe!
> Alas! How can human tongue hope to explain
> Or tell how your Will conveys ceaseless motion
> To all your creation, though you, God, be still? [55]

In the seventeenth century Diego de Hojeda repeats the theme:

> The circle of the Empyrean, drenched in light,
> God's radiant palace, meets the gazer's eye,
> Stable and fixed, brilliant in glowing splendor.[56]

52. Fray Luis' text reads "noveno cielo" but he is referring unquestionably to the *Primum Mobile*; cf. his vol. VI, *Obras*, ed. cit., p. 770: "y porque en este mundo . . . huviese un príncipe y governador . . . crió [Dios] el primero de los cielos (comenzando dende lo alto) que llaman el primer movile, y junto con él un Angel nobilísimo que lo mueve con increíble ligereza . . . y este cuerpo así movido es causa de quantos otros movimientos . . . hay en la tierra." The discrepancy in the numbering of the heavens (ninth, tenth) arises from the fact that Fray Luis, like Dante, identifies the Prime Mover and the crystalline heaven, reducing them to one. Fray Luis may have been following Alfonso de Madrigal, known as El Tostado, who, according to Fray Juan de Pineda, *Primera Parte da los treynta y cinco Diálogos familiares de la Agricultura christiana* (Salamanca, 1589), fol. 55v, "places above the crystalline heaven only the Empyrean, and identifies the Prime Mover with the crystalline heaven, against the majority opinion of astronomers."

53. See Chapter IV of our Volume I.

54. *Obras*, ed. Fray Justo Cuervo (Madrid, 1906–8), V, 309.

55. "¡O dios admirable, según nuestro credo! / Cierto, no bastan las lenguas agudas / decir el modo en que vuelves y mudas / todas las cosas estándote quedo" (*copla* 16 of the *Adiciones*).

56. "El cielo empíreo, trono rutilante / y palacio de Dios allí se vía, / estable,

"The Empyrean, which does not move, gives permanence and constancy to the universe, offsetting the instability of the other heavens," says Venegas.[57] The concept of the Empyrean is an entirely Christian one, unknown to the philosophers of antiquity,[58] and its name arises from the fact that it surpasses all the other heavens, not in heat, but in splendor.[59]

In another place [60] I have shown how the fifteenth-century *Bías contra Fortuna* of the Marqués de Santillana yields its full meaning only to one acquainted with this concept of the Empyrean. *Bías contra Fortuna* is a poem of consolation which upholds the Graeco-Roman ideal of the *vir fortis* and also the idea of the fifteenth-century Spanish knightly warrior. Its ethic, according to Professor Rafael Lapesa in his luminous study of Santillana,[61] is Stoic. But there remains a mystery which it is necessary for us to explain. The Christian poet, says Lapesa, at the end of his poem felt unable to admit that "supreme happiness consisted merely in the enjoyment of flowery meadows, hunting, and the exercise of noble arts," and therefore "he imagined another superior dwelling, free from change, where the souls of the redeemed enjoy a purer blessedness, singing we know not what." Lapesa points to the parallel between this "superior dwelling" and Dante's *Paradiso*; but he also states that the poet does not indicate that he is thinking of the Christian heaven, "probably in order not to break the line of thought of a poem which he had tried to keep within the framework of Classical thought." Lapesa's reader is thus induced to make an inference which Santillana's own words do not permit one to make, namely, that Santillana, in this poem, gives no direct consideration to the Christianized idea of Fortune (to which he was no stranger). Such an inference would be incorrect. The "superior dwelling" to which Bías, an ancient Greek, makes an anachronistic reference is none other than the Christian Empyrean. Santillana did not need to proclaim it as such, since he counted on his readers to recognize the

fixo, espléndido, radiante" (*La Christíada*, ed. Sister Mary Helen Patricia Corcoran [Washington, D.C., 1935], p. 62).

57. *Differencias de libros* . . . , ed. 1572, fol. 151.

58. "The Empyrean, which is known only through theology" (Fray Juan de Pineda, *op. cit.*, fol. 55).

59. Calepinus, *Dictionarium* (Antwerp, 1572), art. *caelum*. For fuller details, see my previously cited article, "The Abode of the Blest . . . ," pp. 272 ff.

60. See below, note 63.

61. *La obra literaria del Marqués de Santillana* (Madrid, 1957).

allusion. Bías is presented as knowing — again anachronistically — that Christ will come to open the gates of Heaven to the just who lived before the Redemption. Bías says to Fortuna:

Este camino será	This path I shall tread,
Aquel, que faré yo Bías	At the end of my days,
en mis postrimeros días,	O Fortune,
si te plaçe o pesará,	Strive against me as you may.
a las bienventuranzas;	To the home of the blest it will lead me,
do cantando	Where in song
viviré, siempre goçando	And in endless joy I'll dwell
do çessan todas mudanças.	Forever untouched by change.

Do çessan todas mudanças — "where there is no variableness, neither change nor shadow of turning" (Jas. I:17). For the men of the fifteenth century no further identification was necessary: only in the Empyrean is there no change.[62] Nor should we entertain any doubt as to what, in that Abode of the Blest, Bías might be singing: in the Empyrean his song could have only one theme — *Holy, holy, holy, Lord God of Hosts.*[63]

Here again we become convinced that in order to understand the art forms of a past culture we must enter fully into the ethos of the artist who created them. The reward which we obtain from the effort is the expansion of the self as it perceives new resonances in its own enhanced experience.

The impact of Renaissance science

Sir Francis Bacon (d. 1626) never did become a convert to the Copernican hypothesis which was set forth in 1543, confirmed early in the seventeenth century by Galileo's invention of the telescope, and refined and corrected as the new century progressed.[64]

---

62. "O life . . . without variableness or change . . . where love is perfect and fear is non-existent. . . . Sweet is the shade after the glowing heat of noonday, sweet is the fountain to the weary traveler and rest to the laboring slave; much sweeter still to the saints is peace after war, security after danger, and permanent rest after the weariness of their past labors" (Fray Luis de Granada, *Guía de pecadores*, Bk. I, ch. iv: "De la gloria de los bienaventurados").

63. I have treated this subject at length in my article, "Sobre las dos Fortunas: de tejas arriba y de tejas abajo" in *Studia Philologica: Homenaje ofrecido a Dámaso Alonso* . . . (Madrid, 1960–63), II, 143–54.

64. Don Cameron Allen, *The Legend of Noah: Renaissance Rationalism in Art, Science, and Letters* (Urbana, Illinois, 1949), p. 15. See also *idem, Doubt's Boundless Sea: Skepticism and Faith in the Renaissance* (Baltimore, 1964), pp. 113–14.

It is not surprising, therefore, to find, in 1590, Father José de Acosta making a forcefully unambiguous statement of the Ptolemaic conception of an earth-centered universe. Basing his conclusions on the evidence provided by the circumnavigation of the globe in 1522, he says: "From this we infer, without any possibility of doubt, that the heavens envelop all parts of the earth, moving ceaselessly around it, so that one should no longer make question of this problem." [65] But neither should we be surprised to find that the Copernican theory was expounded at the University of Salamanca in the second half of the sixteenth century and was clearly set forth in Diego de Estúñiga's commentary on the Book of Job (1584) [66] and in Andrés García de Céspedes' volume *Theoria de los planetas según la doctrina de Copérnico (ca.* 1606).[67] The fact is that advocating the Copernican theory was first prohibited only in 1616, and then only *donec corrigatur,* the corrections prescribed being such as were necessary to exhibit the Copernican system as an hypothesis, not as an established natural law.[68]

The interest in the theory manifested by the University of Salamanca, by García de Céspedes, and by others was, however, insufficient to change Spanish habits of thought during our period. About the year 1589 Pedro Simón Abril marshaled arguments against the hypothesis of a moving earth; [69] he chose to follow the traditional Ptolemaic system as simply the more convenient and reliable, but he was not scandalized by the new theory. He says: "All astronomers place the earth in the center of the world, and the sun in the fourth heaven, and the other heavens in their order, and they make predictions of conjunctions, oppositions, eclipses and similar matters, and make a good case [*salvan las apariençias*], and their predictions prove to be accurate. Then comes Nicholas Copernicus, and turns things upside down, and makes the sun the center of the world, and raises the earth up to the fourth heaven, and he makes a good case, and on the basis of these assumptions

---

65. *Op. cit.,* p. 8. The last phrase of the quotation is explained by the fact that St. Augustine had rejected the idea that the world was round.
66. M. Menéndez y Pelayo, *La ciencia española* (Madrid, 1915–18), I, 98.
67. *Ibid.,* I, 97, n. 5, and III, 387.
68. *Catholic Encyclopedia, s. v.* Galileo. The name of Copernicus does not appear in the Index of Henry Charles Lea's *A History of the Inquisition of Spain* (New York, 1906–7).
69. Morreale, *op. cit.,* pp. 152 ff.

he makes the same predictions, and they too prove to be accurate." [70] Here we have palpable proof that "the theories of Copernicus, at least so far as they were concerned with the relative positions of the earth and the sun, interested much more than they troubled thoughtful minds." [71] Certain it is that in the practical realm of navigation, where maintaining a course successfully was more important than philosophical or theological implications, a pragmatic compromise was readily made: the Copernican tables were followed by Spanish navigators for the three highest planets, whereas the traditional ones of Alfonso the Learned (i.e., of Ptolemy) were used for the four lower planets. [72]

It is also a matter of record that on October 23, 1616, Galileo, who had tried on various occasions to sell to the Spanish Crown his *Pianeti Medicei* for determining longitude at sea, wrote from Rome to Curzio Picchera, secretary to the Grand Duke of Tuscany: "The Rector of Villahermosa, secretary to his Excellency the Count of Lemos, by whose order he came to see me, is here; and among other things we talked about my invention. . . . Within six days he will return to Naples, and from there he will pass quickly to Spain, where I think we shall have to tie the threads up again. . . . " [73] The Rector of Villahermosa was the Aragonese poet and historian Bartolomé Leonardo de Argensola, and the Count of Lemos was Don Pedro Fernández de Castro, Spanish Viceroy of the Kingdom of Naples. On May 16 of the following year Galileo wrote to Argensola at Naples a letter in which he thanked him for his kindness and promised to report their conversations to the Grand Duke of Tuscany, whose ambassador at Madrid, it was hoped, would arrange for Galileo to visit Spain. [74] On May 31 Ar-

---

70. *Ibid.*, p. 146, especially n. 1. In the year 1600 a copy of Copernicus' *De revolutionibus orbium caelestium* was sent from Seville to Vera Cruz in Mexico along with some seven hundred other books for sale to the trade, "for cash or on credit," as the recipient might prefer; see O. H. Green and I. A. Leonard, "On the Mexican Book Trade in 1600: A Chapter in Cultural History," *HR*, IX (1941), 7 and 31.

71. Nicolson, *op. cit.*, p. 428.

72. Morreale, *op. cit.*, p. 146, n. 1. See also F. Picatoste, *Apuntes para una biblioteca científica española del siglo XVI* (Madrid, 1891), p. 56.

73. For the material on Galileo, see Eugenio Mele, "Tra vicerè, scienzati e poeti," *BHi*, XXXI (1929), 256–67; and O. H. Green, "Bartolomé Leonardo de Argensola, secretario del Conde de Lemos," *BHi*, LIII (1951), 382–83.

74. Galileo had sought to go to Spain earlier, in 1612, but the Grand Duke of Tuscany did not permit it (Picatoste, *op. cit.*, p. 57).

gensola wrote Galileo a letter in connection with the great astronomer's intended journey, and on June 20 a report was sent to the
Secretary of State of Tuscany, together with a cordial greeting to
the Rector of Villahermosa — written, we may be sure, by Galileo
himself. In spite of these efforts the negotiations were not carried
through.

Galileo's research, based as it was on sense perception aided by
newly devised instruments, disturbed thoughtful minds in England from 1610 onwards.[75] I find no such disquietude in Spain. In
literature — in Lope de Vega, Calderón, and countless others — a
firm and motionless earth and a revolving sun continue to be taken
for granted; and I have found one text which shows that in 1641 a
Spaniard could be as lighthearted about Galileo's telescope (the
revealer of "new stars") as Simón Abril had been two generations
earlier in his discussion of the prognostications of Copernicus.
(Nor should this lightheartedness surprise us greatly; Galileo's
name appears nowhere in the Indices of the Spanish Inquisition,
which was at all times independent of the Inquisition of Rome.)[76]

The text in question is a dialogue between the devil and Don
Cleofás in Luis Vélez de Guevara's *The Limping Devil* (1641), as
the visitor from the nether regions excuses himself in the following terms for declining to discuss matters of astronomy: "Don
Cleofás, our fall [with Lucifer from Heaven] was so swift that we
had no chance to observe anything; and I swear that if Lucifer
had not brought with him a good third of the stars, as we constantly
hear in the allegorical plays at Corpus Christi time, astrology
would have even greater means than it now has to play tricks on
you. I say this with all due respect for Galileo's telescope and the
other one used by Don Juan de Espina, whose famous house and
remarkable chair are the offspring of his own imagination; [77] for
I speak with reference to things below the telescope and things
below the rooftops, and with no less respect for the optics (and
the whims) of those whimsical gentlemen who have discovered that

75. Marjorie Nicolson, "The Telescope and Imagination," *MPh*, XXXII (1934–35),
233 ff.

76. Lea, *op. cit.*, III, 537.

77. See Emilio Cotarelo y Mori, *Don Juan de Espina: Noticias de este célebre y
enigmático personaje* (Madrid, 1908), p. 24.

the sun has a sunspot on its left side, have traced mountains and valleys on the moon, and have seen horns on Venus." [78]

These jesting remarks are very accurate and show unexpected familiarity with the significance of Galileo's telescopic discoveries. Galileo found, just as Vélez de Guevara's devil says he did, hills and valleys on the moon; he found a spot on the sun, thus bringing into question the idea of the sun's incorruptibility; and he showed that Venus had phases like those of the moon — hence the reference to that planet as having "horns" (*cornuta*).

So, in the Spain of 1641, Vélez de Guevara felt no need to take sides in these grave matters. In the England of 1604, however, George Abbot, who later became Archbishop of Canterbury, showed himself much less receptive. He put down in writing and published in a book his recollection of a lecture at Oxford University in the year 1583, in which Giordano Bruno (d. 1600) endeavored to establish the truth of the Copernican hypothesis: "Not long after returning againe, when he had more boldly then [sic] wisely put vp into the highest place of our best & most renowned schoole, stripping vp his sleeues like some Iugler, and telling vs much of *chentrum & chirculus & circumferenchia* (after the pronunciation of his Country [sic] language) he vndertooke among very many other matters to set on foote the opinion of Copernicus, that the earth did goe around, and the heavens did stand still; whereas in truth it was his owne head which rather did run round & his braines did not stand still." [79]

CONCORD IN DISCORD [80]

The second Prologue to *La Celestina*, which first appeared in the expanded version of this masterpiece (twenty-one acts), begins with a discussion of the significance of the philosopher Heraclitus' *Fragment 26*:[81] "It should be understood that war is the common

78. *El diablo cojuelo*, ed. Clásicos Castellanos (Madrid, 1941), pp. 126–27.

79. Quoted in Robert McNulty, "Bruno at Oxford," *Renaissance News*, XIII (1960), 303.

80. On Calderón's treatment of the discord and harmony of the elements, see A. A. Parker, *The Allegorical Drama of Calderón* (Oxford–London, 1943), pp. 205–24.

81. Wheelwright's numeration (see next note). According to H. Diels, *Die Fragmente der Vorsokratiker* (4th ed.; Berlin, 1922), I, 94, it is no. 80; according to I. Bywater, *Heracliti Ephesi Reliquiae* (Oxford, 1877), it is no. 62.

condition, that strife is justice, and that all things come to pass through the compulsion of strife." [82] Because of this circumstance, critics have seen in *La Celestina* a foreshadowing, in the year 1502, of modern existentialist *Angst* over the lot of man cast by an indifferent Fate into an essentially hostile universe.[83] I shall show that such a philosophy of *Angst* is not properly attributable to Heraclitus, much less to Fernando de Rojas or, in general, to Spanish writers of our period. The fact is that the author of the Prologue presents only the strife (not the harmony) of the elements and of the creatures [84] because he is making a very special use of the quotation, a use so obvious that the passage should never have served as a springboard for a philosophical interpretation of *La Celestina*. The author of the Prologue, after nearly three pages of discussion, comes to his point: "Well, since this long misery has been known through all the ages, I will not be astonished if this present work may not also have served as a cause for dissention and battle for its readers, for everyone will judge it the way he likes." [85]

It is necessary to quote more fully, beginning with Rojas' first sentence (*ibid.*, p. 8):

> The great and wise Heraclitus tells us that all things are produced as if in contest or battle: *Omnia secundum litem fiunt.* This maxim is in my opinion ever worthy of being borne in mind. And although it is true that every word of a man of learning is pregnant with meaning, it may be said of the statement just quoted that it is really bursting with significance. It is like

82. Philip Wheelwright, *Heraclitus* (Princeton, 1959), p. 29. The Spanish author's immediate source was Petrarch's *De remediis utriusque Fortunae*; see A. D. Deyermond, *The Petrarchan Sources of 'La Celestina'* (Oxford, 1961), Index, *s. v.* Heraclitus. Julio Cejador, in his edition of the *Celestina* (Madrid, 1913), in a note on the passage involved, states that the idea also occurs in Origen. Heraclitus' system is discussed by at least two other Church Fathers: Clement of Alexandria (see *Clement of Alexandria with an English Translation* by G. W. Butterworth [London–New York, 1919], Index, *s. v.* Heraclitus) and Hippolytus (see *The Ante-Nicene Fathers*, eds. Alexander Roberts and James Donaldson [Grand Rapids, Michigan, 1951–53], V, 126–27).

83. "Rojas' choice of prologue thus reveals his thematic 'postura ante la vida,' yet at the same time fails to make it explicit" (Stephen Gilman, *The Art of La Celestina* [Madison, Wisconsin, 1956], p. 150). See also *idem*, "Fortune and Space in the *Celestina*," *RF*, LXVI (1955), 342 ff.

84. See Gilman, *The Art of La Celestina*, p. 166: "the whole vision of the universe which we know from Rojas' *Prólogo* is substantially that of Petrarch. Thus, although Rojas consistently eliminates from his adaptation Petrarch's philosophical commitment to harmony, in doing so he continues a transition that was already apparent in the *De remediis*."

85. *Celestina: A Play in Twenty-One Acts Attributable to Fernando de Rojas,* trans. Mack H. Singleton (Madison, Wisconsin, 1958), p. 11.

a tree so richly dressed in boughs and leaves that its tiniest bud may provide some intellectual fruit for the discerning.

Rojas knows that "the discerning" are as familiar as he is with the *topos* "Concord in Discord," and he refrains from showing Heraclitus' thought in its fullness because his Prologue is not concerned with philosophy:[86] he simply has hit upon a graceful means of saying that the *genus irritabile vatum*, the ill-tempered citizens of the republic of letters, are sure to contrive to lambaste him and his work. In accordance with this purpose, he presents an impressive picture of the battle of the elements.

Although most of the other writers who discuss this war of Nature balance their picture of war and contention with a corresponding picture of harmony, love, and Providence so as to form a diptych, it will be convenient (for purposes of exposition) to isolate and present in chronological order, first of all, the statements that would seem to establish the cruelty of the universe, after which I shall present the opposing statements of harmony and concord, frequently made by the same authors and occurring in the same places as the statements of hostility.

Cosmic strife

Juan Luis Vives (before 1540): "Man's life on earth is a continual war"; [87] *Pedro Mexía* (1540); "We see between many things a natural enmity"; [88] *Cervantes* (1585): "It is well known that our life on earth is war"; [89] *Simón Abril (ca.* 1589): The antipathies of the elements cause "perpetual war"; [90] *Alonso López Pinciano* (1596): "Man, a combination of body and soul, is a field of battle";[91] *Mateo Alemán* (1599): "Night follows day, light follows darkness, the shadow follows the body. Air is ever at war with fire, earth with water, and all the elements with each other"; "Everything is topsyturvy, a tangled mass in endless movement. No man is at peace

86. Cejador, in note 18 of his edition, expresses the same opinion, although he blames the author for using the theme of "universal conflict" in a humble prologue.
87. *Introducción a la sabiduría* (Madrid, 1944), p. 106.
88. *Silva de varia lección*, ed. La Sociedad de Bibliófilos Españoles (Madrid, 1933–34), II, 19–20.
89. *La Galatea* (in *Obras completas*, ed. Angel Valbuena Prat [Madrid, 1956]), p. 692.
90. Cited in Morreale, *op. cit.*, p. 160.
91. *Philosophía antigua poética*, ed. Alfredo Carballo Picazo (Madrid, 1953), I, 86.

with his neighbor; we lie in wait for each other as the cat does for the mouse, the spider for the snake . . .";[92] *Acevedo* (1615): "Everything below the Prime Mover is in continual war of restlessness and struggle, all is in flux: whirling heavens, winds, lightning, earthquakes, seasons, animals, birds, men, lovers, toilers, young men and old; our life is a vast field of battle";[93] *Francisco de Quevedo* (before 1645): "Nothing holds sway in this world as discord does. Discord reigns perpetually in the elements; there is no truce in their war. Our bodily humors know not a minute of peace. If you believe the astronomers, the firmament is a resplendent discord: there is no star that is not opposed to some other, and all strive with each other by means of their contrary aspects. By war we live, of it we are composed, to it we are subjected by Nature."[94]

Cosmic harmony

I now present the second half of our diptych. *Joanot Martorell* (1490): "Your Highness should be aware of the value, power, and force of love, which moves the heavens and the intelligences that never weary of taking delight in that movement, merely because of the love they have for the First Cause. The elements repose in their spheres because of the love they feel for the places assigned them; thus all the elements love with true affection the things that partake of their nature, and cannot be found in any places except those that are conformable to their condition and state."[95] *Vives'* words quoted above are Christianized, being introduced by the words, "How right Job[96] was when he said. . . ."[97] In like manner, *Mexía* recognizes that in discord there is harmony: "Heracli-

92. *Guzmán de Alfarache* (Madrid, 1926–36), II, 54, and V, 108.
93. *La creación del mundo*, ed. cit., pp. 283a–87b.
94. *Epistolario completo de D. Francisco de Quevedo Villegas*, ed. Luis Astrana Marín (Madrid, 1946), p. 423. Picatoste says of Calderón: "All the great upheavals, the most terrible cataclisms, the most amazing phenomena of nature were attributed to the violent confusion of these elements as they mutually penetrated one another. Calderón frequently indicates this, referring to [all violent manifestations in nature] as riots, rebellions, and confusions" (*Memoria premiada por la Real Academia de Ciencias Exactas, Físicas y Naturales para conmemorar el Segundo Centenario de D. Pedro Calderón de la Barca* [Madrid, 1881], p. 69).
95. *Tirante el Blanco* (in *Libros de caballerías españoles*, ed. Felicidad Buendía [Madrid, 1954], p. 1256).
96. Job said (VII, 1, of the Vulgate): *Militia est vita hominis super terram* — "Man's life on earth is warfare."
97. See n. 87.

tus . . . held that all things are caused and produced by harmony and discord . . . and that their amity and enmity produce all generation and corruption. I do not care to discuss this philosophy here . . . , but let us establish that in all truth . . . we do see natural enmity between many things, and natural friendship between others." [98] *Cervantes'* quotation, like the one from Vives, is a Christian echo of the Book of Job. The speaker adds (1585): "but in the pastoral life there is less strife [99] than among dwellers in cities, since here there are fewer things to upset and disturb the spirit." [100] *Fray Luis de Granada* speaks of universal government (1588): "The agents that create all things [from the four elements] are the heavens with their planets and stars. For although God is the first cause of all other causes, yet these bodies with the intelligences [angels] that move them are the principal instrument He makes use of for the government of this world below. . . . If this movement [of the heavens] were to cease, all movement would cease so that fire would not even ignite a bit of tow [flax] lying beside it." [101] *Simón Abril* speaks of the affinities as well as of the antipathies of the elements and of bodies, describing graphically and in a primitive way the nature of the factors which in a chemical reaction normally produce equilibrium.[102] *López Pinciano*, after saying that man, as a composite of body and soul, is a battlefield, adds that this battle is a struggle between reason and appetite, productive both of vices and of virtues.[103] *Acevedo* presents not cosmic war, but a beautiful cosmic dance. Recognizing, with Job, that our life on earth is an endless strife, and that we live in disquietude from birth till death, he asserts that all will be set right on the Eighth Day of the creation, the day of the Second Coming,

98. See n. 88.

99. The pastoral life is a Platonic utopia: "One must go back to Nature, the pastoral novel teaches us. But this nature is half symbolic and altogether transposed; it is a dream of love: 'Look about you, Silvio. All beautiful and pleasant things in the world are the work of Love; the heavens love, the earth loves, and that fair star that you behold announcing the dawn loves likewise . . . ; the beasts love . . . and that bird that sings so sweetly . . . all things love.' The pastoral proclaims without ceasing that, in Nature, happiness exists for pure hearts" (Jean Rousset, *La littérature de l'âge baroque en France: Circé et le Paon* [Paris, 1953], pp. 32–33).

100. See n. 89.

101. *Obras* (Madrid, 1768–71), V, 56 (see also p. 70).

102. See n. 90.

103. See n. 91.

when time and change shall cease and our hearts shall rest in God in peace and glory.[104] *Quevedo* ends his eloquent description of universal strife by adding: "Providence has a great part in this dissention, which orders, sustains, and vivifies."[105] *Tirso de Molina* declares (before 1648) that "love binds the elements together in gentleness and love." [106] *Gracián*, in *El Criticón* (before 1658), speaks of the divine Providence which enclosed water within the limits of the ocean's sands and fire within the boundaries of a piece of flint, without which restriction the earth and all its inhabitants would long since have come to a disastrous end. And he defines the universe in terms that are glowingly optimistic: "My book, the unlettered wise man [Job] called it, wherein he studies the divine perfection. . . . It is a banquet, said Philo Judaeus . . . where the spirit finds food. A well-tuned lyre, Pythagoras called it, which with the melody of its great concert delights and amazes us. Tertullian called it the pomp of uncreated majesty, and Hermes Trismegistus, the pleasant harmony of divine attributes." [107] Finally *Calderón* declares that the elements, however great their rebellions and confusions, obey a law of universal order:

> Nothing departs
> Without resistance from its center:
> The waters, wherever they flow,
> Seek inevitably the ocean;
> No matter whose hand has thrown it,
> The stone returns to the earth;
> The wind embraces the wind,
> Whatever the course of its current;
> And no matter what feeds its flame,
> Fire mounts upward to heaven.[108]

Sources and analogues

The doctrine that the equilibrium of the elements alone differentiated the established world from chaos was expressed by many

104. See n. 93.
105. See n. 94.
106. *Siempre ayuda la verdad*, in *NBAE*, IV, 209.
107. *Ed. cit.*, I, 143.
108. "No se aparta / fácilmente de su centro / cosa ninguna: las aguas / van siempre buscando el mar / por donde quiera que vagan; / la piedra corre a la tierra / de cualquier mano que salga; / el viento al viento se añade / de cualquier parte que vaya; / y el fuego a su esfera sube / de cualquier materia que arda" (*Las tres justicias en una*, cited by Picatoste, *Memoria* . . . , p. 70; see also pp. 45–46).

thinkers of the ancient world and was incorporated into the Scholastic system.[109] First of all, it should be stated that Heraclitus, although he is said to have asserted that war and Zeus are the same thing, held that the major occurences of the universe "run along by themselves, as a result of many forces, which are most characteristically in conflict, but which sometimes enter into temporary and limited alliances, and which somehow manage in their fluctuations to reveal glimpses of a subtle and hidden harmony."[110] The Heraclitean harmony was very different from the Christian which was to adapt and transform it. Heraclitus rejected any teleological interpretation and described the guiding force of the universe, not as a wise and kindly God, but rather as an irresponsible child idly moving counters in a game (*ibid.*, p. 35). Seneca sounds very close to Job: "To live, Lucilius, is to engage in war; life is not a delicate thing."[111] Ovid's description of chaos-harmony was perhaps the best known. He "begins his cosmogony with a description of chaos [*Met.*, I, 5 ff.]. Cold battles with hot, wet with dry, soft with hard, heavy with light. The conflict was composed by a god or milder Nature: *Hanc deus et melior litem natura diremit.* Ovid does not decide between Nature and the god: 'whichever of the gods it was. . . .' Four centuries later Claudian takes up the theme again. The concept of the universe has changed. Not a god but Natura parted the ancient strife of the elements. For Claudian she is a powerful goddess."[112] Substantially the same thing was held as a belief by other ancient authors. It could be, and was, adapted to the account of the creation in Genesis, and was accepted as Christian natural science[113] (as our quotations from Granada and from Acevedo clearly show). In Boethius' (d. 524) *Consolation of Philosophy*, procreative love is identified with God's providence, and "Lady Philosophy relates it to the universal force which holds all things in concord. . . . The harmonious action of the elements, the sun, the moon, and the sea is governed by love. If love should

109. E. M. Wilson, "The Four Elements in the Imagery of Calderón," *MLR*, XXXI (1936), 43.

110. Wheelwright, *op. cit.*, p. 36; see also José Ferrater Mora, *Diccionario de filosofía, s. v. Heráclito.*

111. *Letters to Lucilius*, XCVI, 3.

112. E. R. Curtius, *European Literature and the Latin Middle Ages*, trans. Willard R. Trask (New York, 1953), p. 106.

113. Wilson, *op. cit.*, p. 34.

slacken its restraining force, all things would be at strife to destroy the order of the world" — a doctrine taken over by Geoffrey Chaucer (d. 1400?).[114] Joannes Scotus Erigena (d. 877?) said that "those things which in parts of the universe appear opposed to each other and contrary and dissonant, when considered in the general universal harmony, are seen to be harmonious and consonant."[115]

At the Renaissance, Nicholas of Cusa (d. 1464) based his philosophy on the coincidence of opposites, defining God as the One in whom all contradictions are comprehended. Pico della Mirandola, in his *Oration on the Dignity of Man* (1486?), said that, according to Heraclitus, nature was begotten of war and that it is not, therefore, in the power of natural philosophy to give us in nature a quiet and unshaken peace but that this function is the privilege of holiest theology, who will show us the way and, seeing us coming from afar, will exclaim: "come unto me and I will give you peace."[116] Pico in his definition of beauty declared: "Nor do contrariety and discord between various elements suffice to constitute a creature, but by due temperation the contrariety must become united and the discord [be] made concordant; and this may be offered as the true definition of Beauty, namely, that it is nothing else than an amicable enmity and a concordant discord. For this reason did Heraclitus say that war and contention are the father and master of all things."[117] Louis Le Roy (or Regius), in his *Of the Interchangeable Course, or Variety of Things in the World* (1572), declared that the basis of all form, order, decorum, and beauty in a world composed of contrary and conflicting elements is to be found in the unity of God's nature, and that the principle of unity must exceed the principle of contrariety, or chaos will come again.[118]

In the Baroque period the dualism continues. Said John Donne (d. 1631): "Woe be to that man that is so at peace, as that the spirit

---

114. E. E. Slaughter, *Virtue According to Love — in Chaucer* (New York, 1957), pp. 108–9.

115. E. de Bruyne, *Estudios de estética medieval*, trans. Fr. A. Suárez (Madrid, 1958–59), III, 379.

116. Ernst Cassirer *et al.* (eds.), *The Renaissance Philosophy of Man* (Chicago, 1948), p. 231.

117. Quoted by Edgar Wind, *Pagan Mysteries in the Renaissance* (New Haven, 1958), p. 83.

118. Craig, *op. cit.*, p. 54; see also Herschel Baker, *The Wars of Truth: Studies in the Decay of Christian Humanism in the Earlier Seventeenth Century* (Cambridge, Massachusetts, 1952), p. 71.

fights not against the flesh in him; and woe to them, too, who would make them friends, or reconcile them, between whom, God hath perpetuated an everlasting war." [119] And Sir Thomas Browne (d. 1682) states: "I find there are many pieces in this one fabrick of man; this frame is raised upon a mass of Antipathies. I am one methinks, but as the World; wherein notwithstanding there are a swarm of distinct essences, and in them another World of Contrarieties; we carry private and domestic enemies within, publick and more hostile adversaries without. . . . Let me be nothing, if within the compass of myself I do not find the battail of Lepanto, Passion against Reason, Reason against Faith, Faith against the Devil, and my Conscience against all" (*ibid.*, p. 151). This is no doctrine of despair; it is the acceptance of our world as a place, and one's own life as a time, wherein the Christian is tested.

Discord and harmony in Spanish literature

Leo Spitzer, in the second part of his study of "Classical and Christian Ideas of World Harmony," [120] has reviewed the occurrences of the idea of universal harmony in Castilian letters from Berceo onward. Since very often his quotations stress harmony only, without the tensions evoked by the opposite idea of chaos or discord, they are, on the whole, somewhat removed from the purpose of our survey of the idea of conflict and resolution, of harmony in discord. The one idea, however, can scarcely exist without evoking the other, as in the seventeenth-century *Epístola moral a Fabio*:

> Without tempering and tuning, did you ever
> Behold a perfect thing . . . ? For harmony shows me
> Truth in its essence, and thereby my will,
> Stilled in its agitation, is composed.[121]

Spitzer summarizes: "In this detour of the historical development of the idea of the 'concert of the stars' it has surely become evident that this idea was but a consequence of the *topos* of World Harmony. And underlying this cosmic 'concert' are the associations of

119. Quoted in Margaret L. Wiley, *The Subtle Knot: Creative Scepticism in Seventeenth-century England* (Cambridge, Massachusetts, 1952), p. 128.

120. *Traditio*, III, (1945), 307 ff.

121. "Sin la templanza ¿viste tú perfecta / alguna cosa . . . ? / Así, Fabio, me muestra descubierta / su essencia la verdad, y mi albedrío / con ella se compone y se concierta" (cited by Spitzer, *op. cit.*, p. 347). This poem is anonymous.

order, *consensus*, harmony, peace, 'numbers,' the reflection of World Harmony, of its Institutor and Ruler, and of love inspiring his praise: 'Brudersphären-Weltgesang' in the words of Goethe" (*ibid.*, p. 350).

Rojas' picture of cosmic strife

It is time for us to draw our own conclusions. There is no need to see in Fernando de Rojas, as Américo Castro does, "a despairing genius"; [122] he is merely a man capable of creating a tragic tale of passionate love in which the wages of sin are ruin and death. The evidence does not support the contention, inspired by Rojas' use of Heraclitus' "universal struggle," that the *Celestina* is founded on the idea of baleful cosmic strife; that its author "attempted to objectify what was to him the insoluble conflict of life"; or that the *Celestina* "indicates the departure characteristic of the seventeenth century (man's worst crime is having been born)" (*loc. cit.*). Nor can we allow to go unchallenged statements which have had too ready acceptance, namely: that the Prologue in question presents "a whole vision of the universe"; [123] that the whole of the *Celestina* is a dramatization of "the theme of the vulnerability of life in an indifferent universe" — of "human insignificance in a world not just 'objective', as the Stoics would have it, but agonizingly indifferent in its enormity." [124]

The linguistic level on which Rojas presents his picture of cosmic strife is anything but "tragic." To enforce this point, let us consider also the Prologue in verse which preceded the 1501 edition of *La Celestina*. In its heading "the author excuses himself for his error in writing this work," and to this end compares his own recklessness to that of the proverbial winged ant which, not content with her condition as one of the creeping things of the earth, made bold to fly through the air (decidedly not her element: *no sabe dónde yr*), supported by her newly-born and transparent wings, only to be swallowed in full flight by an insect-catching bird. Rojas makes this application: "Just as this creature dreamed

---

122. "Incarnation in Don Quixote" in *Cervantes Across the Centuries*, ed. A. Flores and M. J. Benardete (New York, 1947), p. 173, n. 14.

123. Gilman, *The Art of La Celestina*, p. 166.

124. Gilman, "Fortune and Space . . . ," pp. 355, 360. See also M. Bataillon, *"La Célestine" selon Fernando de Rojas* (Paris, 1961).

of the exultation of flight, and I of obtaining honor with my pen, so the two of us came to grief: she devoured, and I as the object of reproaches of all sorts" (*ed*. Cejador, I, pp. 9–10). Surely we must see in this comparison an intent to place the whole discussion on the level which the author considers most fitting his purposes as prologue writer. He is saying, in effect: "I know I am in for some whacks!"

Reverting to the Prologue in prose which we have been analyzing, we find the same low stylistic level. Not only are the great beasts of prey offered as examples of cosmic war, but also ("if one may be excused for introducing an old wives' tale"—*si no pareciesse consejas de tras el fuego*) the elephant: a huge beast that "is scared by, and flees from an insignificant and contemptible [*suziuelo*] mouse, and even is greatly frightened if he hears one squeak." In our barnyards (does a writer seek tragedy in a barnyard?) the marauding kites [*milanos*] "insult" our domestic fowls, invading our very domiciles to snatch chicks from beneath their mothers' wings! And besides—in the realm of folklore, now—there is the fabulous bird known in Arabic tales as the *roc*, a creature "born in the Indian Ocean, so great that in its beak it can carry not only one man or ten men but also an entire ship with its rigging and its crew, so that the wretched sailors, suspended thus in mid-air, are by the fluttering of the flight shaken from their portholes and fall to a cruel death in the sea beneath" (*ibid.*, pp. 19–22).

This language, with its humble and even contemptible expressions of terror (elephant-mouse) and of death (seized chicks, dropping sailors) is not the language of tragedy. Its "naive" display of learning is not altogether naive. Some of the detractors may be *suziuelos*, no more to be feared than a mouse; others will be utterly cruel at the expense of the author—like marauding kites—, but they will be kites, not eagles.

We shall address ourselves to the problem of despair in Volume III of the present work. The point on which it is now necessary to be clear is that the theme of cosmic discord in Rojas' Prologue is but one half of a concept of discord-concord that had been familiar for something like two milleniums; that the concept is optimistic, not pessimistic; and that Rojas simply utilized the negative half of the concept because that was the part that suited his immediate purpose as *prologuista*: if there is strife among the elements and strife among the creatures, surely there will be contention both between the author and his critics and among the critics themselves.

But let us return to the point from which this discussion of cosmic harmony-discord took its inception, and to the author — Baltasar Gracián — who provided the keynote for the present excursus. Gracián died near the mid-point of the seventeenth century, a century whose characteristic outlook in Spain is not, as has been argued, that man's worst crime is to have been born,[125] or that man's "circumstance" is "utterly incapable of being integrated into the process of his own existence."[126] In Crisi III of the First Part of *El Criticón*, in a section entitled "Composition of Opposites,"[127] Critilo is made to ask: "And how can that surprise you, if within man himself . . . this discord is even more violent?" Andrenio is taken aback and asks: "What's that? Man at war with himself?" And Critilo replies:

Yes; being a microcosm, he has all the opposition of opposites of the macrocosm. The fight begins with his bodily humors: in accordance with the predominance of special humors, the radical humor resists his native heat. . . . His lower part is always at variance with his superior part; appetite attacks reason and at times overcomes it. Even his immortal soul it not free from this general discord, since within it the passions struggle: fear against valor, sadness against joy . . . ; now the vices triumph, now the virtues, and all is war. So that man's life on the face of this earth is nothing but warfare. But oh, how marvellous, how infinitely wise the providence of the great Moderator of all creation, by whom this continuous and varied strife among all the creatures is tempered, and who sustains and preserves the vast composite structure of the world![128]

125. This phrase is spoken by a character in a play (Calderón's *La vida es sueño*) who outgrows the concept as the play progresses.
126. Castro, *loc. cit.*
127. On the theory of opposites, see *Torres Naharro and the Drama of the Renaissance*, edited, transcribed, and completed by O. H. Green (Philadelphia, 1961), pp. 60–64. (This is volume IV of *Propalladia and Other Works of Bartolomé de Torres Naharro*, ed. J. E. Gillet, and it will be cited as "Gillet-Green, *op. cit.*" throughout this volume.)
128. *Ed. cit.*, I, 138–39.

THE COLOR OF THE SKY

"To judge between one ethos and another," writes C. S. Lewis, "it is necessary to have got inside both, and if literary history does not help us to do so it is a great waste of labour." [129] Failure to have done so has caused critics and historians to see in such expressions as the third epigraph at the beginning of this chapter (and in others, appearing in purely scientific or didactic works, to the effect that the sky we see above us "is neither sky nor blue") evidences of the collapse of the Renaissance world view, as the Baroque found "all coherence gone" — Nature "deceives us." An example is ready to hand in Ramón Menéndez Pidal's essay on the Spanish language of the sixteenth century, "El lenguaje del siglo XVI," in which he writes:

> The dominant ideas have changed radically. In this generation of Cervantes, . . . Argensola writes the famous sonnet on the charm of the white and rose complexion of Doña Elvira, a deceitful beauty unequaled by that of any genuine face. How many commentaries have been written on this poem! . . . But its true meaning is revealed to us only when we recall the insistence with which the two preceding periods [in the history of the language] condemned women's use of cosmetics, since art should not deceive the human spirit which rests confidently in its idea of the goodness and the beauty of everything that is natural. Now this poet, at the end of the sixteenth century, finds that truth and beauty are no longer one and the same thing; Nature has lost her divine privilege: she deceives us; [130] the sky "is neither sky nor blue," a disturbing apothegm which Calderón will repeat in his *Saber del mal y del bien*. Confidence in the natural is gone; so also is confidence in the simple veracity of language. . . .[131]

What I propose to show in the following pages is that this concept has nothing to do with the "new science"; that it is, in fact, "old science"; and that it was no more disturbing in the Spanish Golden Age than it is today to remark that an oar entering the water at an angle is not really bent or that the sun does not really

129. *English Literature in the Sixteenth Century, Excluding Drama* (Oxford, 1954), p. 331.
130. For bibliography see my article, *"Ni es cielo ni es azul:* A Note on the 'Barrosquismo' of Bartolomé Leonardo de Argensola," *RFE*, XXXIV (1950), 137–50.
131. The Spanish text is available in my article (n. 111 above); the entire essay, in Ramón Menéndez Pidal, *Mis páginas preferidas: Estudios lingüísticos e históricos* (Madrid, 1957), in *idem, España y su historia* (Madrid, 1957), II, and in other reprintings.

"rise." In this connection it will be helpful to make use of another observation of C. S. Lewis (*op. cit.*, pp. 4–5):

Historians of science or philosophy, and especially if they hold some theory of progress, are naturally interested in seizing those elements of sixteenth-century thought which were later to alter Man's whole picture of reality. Those other elements which were destined to disappear they tend to treat as mere "survivals" from some earlier and darker age. The literary historian, on the other hand, is concerned not with those ideas in his period which have since proved fruitful, but with those which seemed important at the time. He must even try to forget his knowledge of what comes after, and see the egg as if he did not know it was going to become a bird.

Let us examine the "egg." James Fitzmaurice-Kelly, writing before the "Barock Mensch" had been discovered,[132] was content to see Argensola's "famous sonnet" as both an example of classic correctness (as against Luis de Góngora's disconcerting innovations), and as "a polite, humourous fancy" which he reproduces in the translation of James Young Gibson:

> I must confess, Don Juan, on due inspection,
> That dame Elvira's charming red and white,
> Though fair they seem, are only hers by right,
> In that her money purchased their perfection;
>   But thou must grant as well, on calm reflection,
> That her sweet lie hath such a lustre bright,
> As fairly puts to shame the paler light,
> And honest beauty of a true complexion!
>   And yet no wonder I distracted go
> With such deceit, when 'tis within our ken
> That nature blinds us with the self-same spell;
>   For that blue heaven above that charms us so,
> Is neither heaven nor blue! Sad pity then
> That so much beauty is not truth as well.[133]

132. "Many present-day art critics and literary historians . . . have pushed the 'Renaissance Mensch' into the background to make room for the 'Barock Mensch,' who will doubtless remain on the stage until research in this newly exploited period shows that this type is also unstable" (Robert Herndon Fife, "The Renaissance in a Changing World," *Germanic Review*, IX [1934], 81).

133. *A History of Spanish Literature* (New York, 1900), p. 278. The original bears the title "To a Woman Applying her Make-Up and Artificially Beautiful" — *A una Mujer que se Afeitaba y Estaba Hermosa*. I quote it in Foulché-Delbosc's critical edition (*RHi*, XLIII [1920], 417): "Yo os quiero confesar, don Juan, primero / que aquel blanco y color de doña Elvira / no tiene de ella más, si bien se mira, / que el aberle costado su dinero. / Pero tras eso confesaros quiero / que es tanta la beldad de su mentira, / que en vano a competir con ella aspira / belleça ygual de rostro

I shall first show that the idea that the heaven which we all see "is neither sky nor blue" has nothing to do with the science of Copernicus or Galileo. Fray Juan de Pineda regarded the concept as Aristotelian. According to this view, the first heaven properly so called, the heaven of the Moon, was too remote for the human eye to perceive and was by nature colorless:

> The fourth condition necessary for a thing to be visible is that it not be of such transparency as to offer no resistance to the eye, or nothing for the eye to feed on; otherwise no vision is formed. This happens to us with the air, which although it has body, is so thin and transparent that the eye does not perceive it, as it does not perceive the sky because of its remoteness; and indeed the sky, if it is a quintessence [fifth element] as Aristotle would have it, has no color at all, since it cannot receive outward impressions; and without these the secondary qualities (one of which is color) cannot be engendered. All the more so, since before we come to the heavens we find the sphere of fire, which would have to be perceived first, and is not seen because it does not have sufficient substance to produce a glowing effect . . . It is a matter of ordinary speech to say that this substance is lacking also to the sky, which is so diaphanous and transparent that rays of the heavenly luminaries pass through it, as through very clear glass; and our vision fails us there in the region of the air, without seeing anything; because from a combination of the brightness reflected from below and the darkness from above [134] there is produced the appearance of that blue which seems to us to be the sky and is really nothing at all.[135]

Search in Aristotle's works for the idea so clearly set forth by Pineda is disappointing, and it is rather from the Aristotelian commentators, as we shall see, that sixteenth-century Spaniards derived

verdadero. / mas ¿qué mucho que yo perdido ande / por un engaño tal, pues que sabemos / que nos engaña así Naturaleza? / porque ese cielo azul que todos vemos / ni es cielo ni es açul. ¡Lástima grande / que no sea verdad tanta belleça!"

134. The "darkness from above" is the blackness of the stratosphere.

135. "La quarta condición necessaria para que la cosa se vea, es que no sea de tanta transparencia que no halle la vista resistencia en que se ceue, so pena de no formar visión: como nos acontece con el aire, que aunque tiene cuerpo, es tan sutil y transparente que no le percibe la vista, ni al cielo por su mucha distancia: y aun por ventura el cielo, si es quinta essentia (como quiere Aristóteles), no tiene color alguna, como no es capaz de impressiones peregrinas, y sin éstas no se pueden engendrar las segundas qualidades, vna de las quales es el color. Quanto más, que antes del cielo está el fuego, que ouiera de ser visto primero, y si no se vee por le faltar materia en que se ceuar para resplandecer . . . también es común lenguaje que le falta al cielo, y es tan diáfano y transparente que passan los rayos de las luminarias celestiales por él, como por vidrio muy claro: y nuestra vista se desuanece por la región del ayre sin ver nada, porque con lo claro de abaxo y lo escuro de arriba, se haze la muestra de aquel azul que nos parece cielo, y no es nada" (*Agricultura christiana*, I, fol. 142).

the idea of "neither sky nor blue." For the time being I quote from the work of two of these commentators: "And it is Aristotle's opinion that the heavenly bodies are colorless because they belong to the fifth essence. Every color comes from the four elements."[136]

Pineda's explanation, which is at least partially Aristotelian as has been seen and as I shall continue to show, becomes clearer when we examine a similar statement made by Venegas in his *Differencias de libros* . . . :

> The heavens, if we were to weigh them, would not weigh an ounce or the weight of a pin: they are so solid and dense that neither steel nor diamond could scratch them. They have no color, for the blue which we see here below is not more than ten leagues from the earth's surface: [137] because it is the result of the coming together of the blackness of the stratosphere with the reflected rays of the sun which rise from below [i.e., are bounced off the earth]: because blue is nothing other than a mixture of white and black, as if we mixed a dish of powdered lime with a dish of powdered charcoal: we would produce a very perfect blue.[138]

Pineda and Venegas thus tell us, in 1589 and 1540 respectively, that the blue which the eye perceives in the sky is an illusion, produced relatively near the earth's surface by the mingling of white light reflected back from the earth's surface against the black of what today we call the stratosphere. This implies a belief that there is but one light in the heavens — the sun — , since otherwise the idea of a stratosphere all black except for light reflected from the *partes de abajo* would have been impossible.[139] If Aristotle has anywhere

136. "Excerpta ex Commentariis Alexandri et Olympiodori in Librum III," in *Aristotelis Meteorologicorum libri IV* (Leipzig, 1836), pp. 130–31.

137. According to Pineda, it is over 16,000 leagues to the heaven of the moon, or first heaven. See Green, "Ni es cielo . . . , p. 142, n. 3.

138. "Los cielos si los pesássemos, no pesarían vna onça ni vn alfilel: son tan sólidos y maciços que ni azero ni diamante les podría hazer mella. No tienen color, que el azul que vemos acá no dista diez leguas de la tierra: porque es la juntura de la tiniebla de partes de arriba con la reuerberación de los rayos del sol que sube [sic] de partes de abaxo: porque no es otra cosa color azul sino blanco y negro mezclado, como si mezclássemos vna salsera de cal molida y otra de poluos de carbón: haríamos vn azul muy perfecto" (*ed. cit.*, fol. 151). On fol. 105v. Venegas has the following to say of the color of the sea: "The sea . . . takes its blue color from the so-called color of the sky, not because the sky has color, but because the coming together of darkness and brightness produces that color . . ." ("Tornando al color de la mar, digo que aunque el agua de sí tira a lo blanco, toma el color azul que dizen del cielo; no porque el cielo tenga color, sino porque la juntura de la tiniebla y claridad hazen aquel color . . .").

139. "Placé au centre des planètes, le soleil est cause de toute illumination. Albert le Grand consacre un chapitre de son *De Coelo et Mundo* à cette question: 'Et est

stated the theory in the clear and definite terms used by Pineda and Venegas, I am not aware of it.[140] We are faced with two problems: the nature of the color blue, and the nature of the optical illusion which produces the appearance of blueness in the sky. We shall consider first the nature of the color blue.

"The primary colors are two, namely white and black; the others are called colors only by participation," we read in Calepinus' *Dictionarium, s.v. color.* This is good Aristotelian doctrine.[141] "All the intermediate colors are produced from black and white," is repeated from Aristotle in Vicente de Burgos' translation of Bartholomaeus Anglicus' *Liber de proprietatibus rerum,* (XIX, 8), published at Toledo in 1529. And Juan de Padilla, known as El Cartujano (d. 1502?), wrote in his rhymed life of Christ:

> Between black and white
> Green is a sort of intermediate.[142]

One of the various "intermediate" colors was blue. Concerning it we have the following statement from Leonardo da Vinci (d. 1519): "Let him who wishes the final proof take a board painted with diverse colors, among which there should be a fine black, and over all these colors let there be applied a thin and transparent white; then one will see that over no color will the brightness of that white manifest itself as a beautiful blue so successfully as over the black. . . ."[143] Quevedo applies the same prin-

digressio declarans qualiter stellae omnes illuminantur a sole' " (G. Paré, *Le 'Roman de la Rose' et la scolastique courtoise* [Paris–Ottawa, 1941], p. 68). See also Fray Luis de Granada, *Introducción del Símbolo de la fe,* in *Obras,* ed. Fray Justo Cuervo, V, 67; Tirso de Molina, *Cigarrales de Toledo,* ed. V. Said Armesto (Madrid, 1913), p. 110; and Alessandro Piccolomini, *Parte seconda della Filosofia naturale* (Venice, 1576), fol. 90v.

140. No such clear statement was found by Dr. Samuel G. Barton, of the Department of Astronomy of the University of Pennsylvania, to whom I am grateful for assistance in this connection.

141. *De Sensu et sensibili Liber unus* in *Aristotelis Opera,* ed. P. Sylvester Maurus, IV (Rome, 1668), pp. 341–42.

142. "entre la negra color y blancura / casi lo verde es el medio formado" (*Cancionero castellano del siglo XV,* ed. R. Foulché-Delbosc, *NBAE,* XIX, p. 430).

143. "Ma chi vuol vedere le vltime prove tinga vna asse di diuersi colori fra li quali sia messo bellissimo nero e sopra tutti sia datta sottile e transparente biacca [bianca], allora si uedra la chiarezza di tal biacca non si mostrare soppra nessun colore di piv bello azzurro che sopra il nero. . . ." (*The Literary Works of Leonardo da Vinci,* compiled and edited from the original manuscripts by Jean Paul Richter [London–New York–Toronto, 1939], I, 238). See also his *Trattato della Pittura,* ch. CLI: "Da che nasce l'azzurro nell'aria."

ciple to the blue color of mountains. Mountains, he says, are naturally green or earth-colored, yet when seen from a distance they appear blue. This is the result of the mixture of the brightness (white light) of the sun reflected by the mountains and the darkness (blackness) resulting from the eye's failing vision, as its power to see is overcome by distance.[144]

So much for the black-white character of the composite color blue, as explained by Aristotle, whose authority could deceive Leonardo da Vinci, a practical painter and a scientific genius. Our second problem — the nature of the meteorological phenomenon which causes the eye to see the sky as blue — offers more difficulties. There is apparently nothing in the Aristotelian texts which could give Pineda and Venegas their clear-cut explanation, although the principal elements of that explanation are indeed found in Aristotle. The main point, as already seen, is Aristotelian. The sky is colorless because: (a) its substance is the fifth essence, absolutely different from the four elements of earth, water, air, fire; and (b) colors cannot exist separated from the four elements of the sublunar world. The second point, that the blue of the sky is a mixture of light and darkness in space, is merely suggested in the third chapter of Aristotle's *On Colours*. The passage is too long to be quoted in full. Speaking of transparent substances such as water, glass, and air, Aristotle says:

as the rays from all directions fail owing to the density, we cannot see accurately into their inner parts. But the air when examined from near by seems to have no colour . . . but when examined in depth, the air appears from very near by to be blue in colour because of its rarity. For where the light fails, there, being penetrated by darkness at this point, it appears blue. But when dense, just as with water, it is the whitest of all things.[145]

It will be instructive to document this concept as it appears in non-Spanish writers in the sixteenth and seventeenth centuries and, finally, to suggest a hypothetical source for its more elaborated form. We shall first examine Otto von Guericke's report of his experiments at Magdeburg[146] in 1672: "The blue color in the

144. *Providencia de Dios, BAE*, XLVIII, 171b.

145. *Minor Works*, trans. W. S. Hett, I (London, 1936, Loeb Classical Library, vol. 307), p. 19.

146. *Experimenta nova ut vocantur Magdaburgica de vacuo Spatio* (Amsterdam, 1672), p. 142.

upper part of the air is born of black and white; since at the place
where the air begins to be free of vapor and watery humors or becomes altogether free of them, in that place the white ceases and
the black begins (for since the pure air . . . freely transmits the
light it appears black, that is, without any color). In between the
black and the white, however, the cerulean color exists, just as a
drop of milk and a drop of ink, when placed together, at the point
of contact produce a blue color." J. C. Scaliger's *Exotericarum
exercitationum libri XV de Subtilitate* (Frankfurt, 1607) contains
a similar passage: "Nor is the sky itself visible, though it transmits
rays from above. Nor does the blue color which we see exist at all
in the sky; but because of the distance and density the translucent
parts offer the appearance of a condensed body." [147]

Of like character is a passage in Erasmus' *Colloquia*: "Is the sky
then colored? — Not really, but it appears to us to be so because of
the air and moisture in between, just as the sun appears to us now
red, now yellow, now white, though the sun itself suffers no such
transformations. Similarly the rainbow is not really in the sky, but
in the humid air." [148] And in Leonardo da Vinci's *Trattato della
Pittura* (ch. CLI) we read: "The blue in the air is born of the density of the body of the illuminated air interposed between the upper
darkness and the earth: the air itself does not have the qualities of
odors or tastes or colors, but takes unto itself the likeness of things
that are placed beyond it; or rather it will be the more beautifully
blue in proportion as behind it there exists greater darkness, provided the distance is not too great nor the humidity too dense." [149]

Following a suggestion made by a learned colleague that Leo-

147. "Neque caelum videtur ipsum: transmittit enim radios superiores. Neque
enim caeruleus, qui videtur color, vllus in caelo est: sed propter distantiam translu-
cidae partes propter densitatem in recta linea, praebent speciem corporis condensati"
(Exercitatio LXI, Distinctio 3). Scaliger was read and admired by Argensola, who
regarded him as "el Aristarco de nuestros tiempos." See *Obras sueltas de Lupercio y
Bartolomé Leonardo de Argensola*, ed. el Conde de la Viñaza (Madrid, 1889), II, 301.

148. "*Cv.* Est igitur coelum coloratum? *Al.* Non vere, sed tale nobis videtur propter
aërem, et liquorem medium, quemadmodum sol nobis nunc rubet, nunc fulvet,
nunc candidat, cum is nihil talium mutationum recipiat. Itidem et iridis pictura
non in coelo est, sed in aëre humido" (Leiden, 1729, p. 729).

149 "L'azzurro nell'aria nasce dalla grossezza del corpo dell'aria alluminata, inter-
posta fra le tenebre superiori e la terra: l'aria per se non ha qualità d'odori, o di
sapori, o di colori, ma in se piglia le similitudini delle cose che dopo lei sono
collocate, o tanto sarà di più bell'azzurro quanto dietro ad essa saran maggior tenebre, non essendo lei di troppo spazio, ne di troppa grossezza d'umidità."

nardo might have been following an Arabic source, and knowing that Leonardo was familiar with the works of al-Kindi, I was able to locate (with the assistance of an Arabist) the following passage in Wiedemann's translation (p. 123) of that commentator on Aristotle: "The air that surrounds the earth assumes a faint lightness because of the dust particles that become fiery through the heat which they have absorbed from the rays reflected from the earth. The dark above the earth becomes visible through a mixture of earthly light and the light of the sun; it is seen as a light halfway between darkness and light. That is the lazuli-blue tint. We have shown that this color is not the color of the sky, but rather something which affects our vision because our eyes have been struck by light and darkness." [150]

It is time to return to Argensola and his sonnet. His phrase, "neither sky nor blue," was a scientific commonplace stemming from Greek philosophy and was certainly recognized as such by his contemporaries. But he associated the idea with the unrealiability of the senses, the *engaño a los ojos*. Is the latter concept revolutionary? The speech in Calderón's play, *Saber del mal y del bien*, in which Argensola's phrase occurs, begins as follows:

> There are times when our poor vision
> Is deceived, and objects seem
> So different from what they are
> That they leave the soul perplexed.[151]

This subject has been studied for Cervantes by Américo Castro and for Calderón by Arturo Farinelli.[152] Gracián causes a character in *El Criticón* to remark "that there [are] no true colors in objects,

150. "Die die Erde umgebende Luft wird rein passiv zum schwachen Leuchten gebracht durch die in ihr verteilten erdigen Teile, die in feurige verwandelt sind durch die Hitze, die sie durch die Reflexion der Strahlen von der Erde aufgenommen haben. Was über dieser an dunkler Luft sich befindet, sieht man durch das, was an irdischem Licht beigemengt ist und dem Lichte der Sonne als ein Licht, das in der Mitte steht zwischen Dunkelheit und Licht. Das ist die lasur-blaue Farbe. Wir haben nun nachgewiesen, dass diese Farbe nicht die Farbe des Himmels ist, sondern etwas, was sich an unseren Blicken dadurch ereignet, dass sie von Licht und Finsternis getroffen werden." See E. Wiedemann in *Festschrift für Elster und Geitel* (Braunschweig, 1915), pp. 118 ff.

151. "Que tal vez los ojos nuestros / se engañan, y representan / tan diferentes objetos / de los que miran, que dejan / burlada el alma . . ." (*Comedias*, ed. J. Keil [Leipzig, 1827–30], I, 160).

152. Castro, *El pensamiento de Cervantes* (Madrid, 1925), pp. 79–88; Arturo Farinelli, *La vita è un sogno* (Turin, 1916), II, 130, 135, 137.

that green is not green, nor red red, but that all consists in a different disposition of the surfaces and in the light that bathes them" (ed. cit., III, 172).

This unreliability of the human powers of vision is clearly suggested by the third chapter of Aristotle's On Colours: "We do not see any of the colours pure as they really are, but all are mixed with others; or if not mixed with any other colour they are mixed with rays of light and with shadows, and so they appear different from what they are. Consequently things appear different according to whether they are seen in shadow or in sunlight, in a hard or soft light, and according to the angle at which they are seen." [153]

The history of skepticism need not be reviewed here. It was in no sense new.[154] Though the condemnation of Nicholas of Autrecourt (fl. 1340) in the year 1347 put a damper on the skeptical movement of the fourteenth century, the Renaissance was no stranger to its uncertainties, and many years before Francisco Sánchez published his Quod nihil scitur (ca. 1576), the Christian humanist Vives had declared: "This knowledge of yours is but a sad illusion. . . . To eliminate the urge for investigation would be folly; but it is no less folly to fail to recognize the extreme fragility of our faculty for examining the truth." [155] "The things of this life,"

153. Minor Works, ed. cit., I, 17.
154. See C. Michalski, Les sources du criticisme et du scepticisme dans la philosophie du XIVe siècle (Krakow, 1924). St. Augustine "avait compris de bonne heure . . . que le sensualisme pur engendre inévitablement une doute universel. Si le réel se réduit en effet à l'apparence sensible, comme elle est en perpétuelle contradiction avec elle-même, aucune certitude de quelque ordre que ce soit ne demeure possible. De là ces conclusions, d'une sévérité que rien n'atténue, et sur lesquelles tous les grands philosophes du XIIIe siècle seront appelés à réfléchir: 'Tout ce qu'atteignent les sens du corps: ce que l'homme nomme le sensible ne cesse pas un instant de changer. . . . Or, ce qui ne demeure pas ne peut être perçu . . . et l'on ne peut comprendre ce qui n'arrête pas de changer. Il n'y a donc pas à espérer que les sens corporels nous livrent la vérité dans sa pureté.' Le non est igitur expectanda sinceritas veritatis a sensibus corporis va rester comme un avertissement solennel à méditer, et l'on s'y est d'autant plus volontiers arrêté, qu'en fait de nombreux philosophes du moyen âge pouvaient aisément s'en accommoder" (E. Gilson, L'esprit de la philosophie médiévale [Paris, 1944], pp. 234–35).
155. Quoted in Farinelli, op. cit., I, 114–15. See also J. de Iriarte, Kartesischer oder Sanchezischer Zweifel? Ein kritischer und philosophischer Vergleich zwischen dem Kartesischen Discours de la méthode und dem Sanchezischen Quod nihil scitur (Bottrop in Westphalen, 1935); Robert G. Hoopes, "Fideism and Skepticism during the Renaissance: Three Major Witnesses," Huntington Library Quarterly, XIV (1951), 319 ff.

wrote Fray Luis de Granada, "have little substance, for St. Paul [I Cor. 7] chose to call them, not real things, but only images or figures that have not being but merely semblance — which makes them all the more likely to deceive us." [156] And Quevedo said: "Human eyes are forever looking at enigmas. They see the black powder, in which are hidden the flames and the angry explosion of fire, as it lies quiet and motionless; they apply a spark to it and it thunders, flies in a rocket, glows and gives forth light. We pass from one enigma to another. The eyes deem it to be a star; it falls, a skeleton of paper and string; the eyes learn the truth of two deceits as they contemplate the sad remains to which the contrary figments have now been reduced. Warned by these examples and considerations, let us kindle a light to illumine this darkness, wherewith we may see dimly by the light of Christ Jesus who is the Sun of Justice. . . . Let the blind see with His doctrine and His example." [157]

The "skepticism" of Argensola's sonnet is therefore as normal as Quevedo's awareness that gunpowder, seemingly dead and cold, can spring into motion and give forth heat and light; it is as normal as our awareness of the effect of refraction, seen when we observe an oar dipped into the denser element of water. Every Christian knows that in this life we see "through a glass darkly."

There is one final question to be asked: what importance shall we concede to this sonnet as an expression of approval of artificiality, of cosmetics in contrast to "a true complexion?" Menéndez Pidal in his commentary said that the true significance of our sonnet could be grasped only when one remembers how, in the preceding periods of the history of the Spanish language, women's artificial enhancement of their charms was condemned. But the fact is that cosmetics are condemned at all times and in all periods by poets who write as moralists. It is quite a different matter when they write as poets, for the sheer delight of creating a literary artifact. Indeed, our poet himself, in a poetic epistle to Don Nuño de Mendoza, declares that all cosmetics are

156. Quoted in Pedro Laín Entralgo, *La antropología en la obra de Fray Luis de Granada* (Madrid, 1946), p. 315.
157. *Providencia de Dios*, in *Obras en prosa*, ed. Luis Astrana Marín (Madrid, 1932), p. 1031b.

To the eyes a laughing stock, and to the nose
A stench to heaven, and no less a stench
To heaven's fallen angels down in hell.[158]

From all that has gone before we may conclude that Argensola's sonnet is a literary toy, a manifestation of Spanish *agudeza y arte de ingenio*, of wit. The author was known to his contemporaries as a stern moralist: *Leonardo recto juez, Catón severo* — "censorious Cato and unswerving judge"[159] — but not always. *Tetrica sunt amoenanda jocularibus* — "things serious should be enlivened by the interspersing of things jocular," wrote the fifth-century bishop Sidonius Apollinaris.[160] What we studied as medieval laughter in our first volume does not disappear when the Middle Ages are over. Aristotelian meteorology as interpreted by Arabic science, together with memories of Horace, of Juvenal, and perhaps of the *Greek Anthology*, is converted by Argensola in a moment of poetic relaxation into what Gracián called a *concepto*, a conceit, which had, for the feelings, the same effect as dissonance,[161] and which is, for us, an example of art as release from tension, as play.[162]

158. "Risa a la vista, hedor a las narizes, / mentira aborrezible a todo el Cielo, / i a los que dél cayeron infelizes" (*Rimas de Lupercio i del Dotor Bartolomé Leonardo de Argensola* [Zaragoza, 1634], p. 244).

159. *Rimas de Lupercio y Bartolomé L. de Argensola*, ed. José Manuel Blecua (Zaragoza, 1950–51), II, 617.

160. See our Volume I, Chapter II.

161. T.E. May, "An Interpretation of Gracián's *Agudeza y arte de ingenio*," *HR*, XVI (1948), 298.

162. See Konrad Lang, "Art as Play," and Karl Groos, "Art and Play," in Melvin M. Rader (ed.), *A Modern Book of Aesthetics* (New York, 1935), pp. 1–52.

III · Three Aspects of Nature[1]

Everywhere, in medieval philosophy, the natural order
rests on a supernatural order, on which it depends,
as its origin and its end. Man is created in the image
of God, the beatitude which he desires is a divine
beatitude, the adequate object of his intellect and of
his will is a being that transcends him, before whom
his moral life unrolls and by whom it is judged. . . . The
physical world itself, created by God for his own glory,
is worked upon from within by a sort of blind
love which impels it towards its Maker, and each creature,
each operation of each creature, depends at every
moment, for its efficacy and its existence, on an
all-powerful Will which sustains it. If this is so, can
one speak of nature in a Christian philosophy, or
would it not be better to say . . . that nature is par
excellence an anti-Christian idea, a vestige of pagan
philosophy utilized by unwise philosophers? The
thinkers of the Middle Ages did not believe so.

Etienne Gilson [2]

St. Thomas Aquinas understood Nature as the inner principle of
a universal power of generation or of activity — the intrinsic principle of movement; his concept also included the word in the sense
of the "nature" of a given thing, as well as the thing itself and the
totality of all things, especially of those that lack the power of
reason. The "absolute nature" of a thing is its pure essence. Furthermore, St. Thomas speaks of *Natura condita, creata, increata,
corporalis, spiritualis*; and of *Natura naturans*, which is God, "the
Universal God . . . , the cause of all things which are brought
into being naturally, for which reason some call Him *Naturantem*:

1. See Gerhart B. Ladner, "Bibliographical Survey: The History of Ideas in the
Christian Middle Ages from the Fathers to Dante in American and Canadian Publications of the Years 1940–1952," *Traditio*, IX (1953), Section II, 447 ff.; H. S. Wilson, "Some Meanings of 'Nature' in Renaissance Literary Theory," *JHI*, II (1941),
430 ff.; Gillet-Green, *op. cit.*, Part II, ch. VI (Man and Nature), and index, *s. v.
Nature*.

2. *L'esprit de la philosophie médiévale* (Paris, 1944), p. 345.

Nature in her operation imitates the operation of God." [3] Our concern in the present chapter will be to isolate and to document for Spain the philosophical and literary distinctions of three of these forms of Nature: Creating Nature (*Natura naturans*); Created Nature (*Natura naturata*); and Nature as the universal law, inherent in things, whereby they are moved toward a determined end (*Divinus omnium rerum ordo*). This done, we shall possess — at least in part — the key that is necessary for the interpretation of countless references to, and many expanded treatments of, *Natura* and *Naturaleza* in the pre-classical and classical literature of Spain.

NATURA NATURANS

Unfamiliarity with theological concepts can be the cause of fundamental misconceptions in the interpretation of Spanish literature and of the spirit of the age that produced Spain's literary masterpieces. The *Celestina* is an important example. The first scene of this *tragicomedia* begins with a statement, a question, and an answer. Calisto, encountering Melibea in her garden, says to her: "In this I see, Melibea, a manifestation of the greatness of God." — "In what, Calisto?" — "In His having given to Nature the power to endow you with such perfect beauty."

In these words Américo Castro saw what was to him an early manifestation of a current of essentially un-Christian nature-philosophy extending from the *Celestina* through *Don Quijote*.[4] "Why," asks Professor Castro, "does the author set before us with such vehemence a theological problem as grave as the relation of God to the world? The Middle Ages lived in the firm conviction that the world has in God, not only its reason for existence but also the logical and scientific explanation of its meaning. The universe revealed the glory of God. . . . And now, with no regard for things so sacred, Calisto 'deduces' the Divine Magnificence from his contemplation of the lovely Melibea, created by Nature, the vicegerent of the Great Artificer. . . . *La Celestina* is a book

3. See Rudolf Eisler, *Wörterbuch der philosophischen Begriffe und Ausdrücke* (Berlin, 1904), I, 708, s. v. *Natur*; L. Schütz, *Thomas-Lexikon* (Paderborn, 1895), s. v. *Natura*, pp. 513, 515.
4. "El problema histórico de *La Celestina*," in *Santa Teresa y otros ensayos* (Santander, 1929), pp. 193–215, especially pp. 203 ff.; idem, *El pensamiento de Cervantes* (Madrid, 1925), pp. 156–77.

filled with a human and autonomous conception of life . . . ; its moral philosophy rests on the ideas which, with respect to the world, to Nature, and to the divine, were then current in the humanistic circles of Renaissance Italy." [5]

The necessary correction of the misconceptions we have been discussing was provided by Leo Spitzer in 1930: The beginning of the *Celestina*, he wrote, at least as far as its thought content is concerned, "is to be interpreted not as an expression of Renaissance (*idem est natura quod Deus*) but rather of medieval ideology. A glance at Gelzer's beautiful essay on Nature . . . provides Old French examples of the idea of Nature as the Vicaress of God, as the creator of beautiful creatures. Gelzer traces these expressions back to the Averroist-Scholastic concept of God as *Natura naturans*." [6]

The concept of *Natura naturans*, of Nature as creator and establisher of all other natures, is present in St. Augustine (d. 430): *Ea Natura quae creavit omnes caeteras instituitque naturas.*[7] Joannes Scotus Erigena (d. 877?) in his work *On the Divisions of Nature* gives to Nature a hierarchic structure: "the nature which creates and is not created; the nature which is created and which creates; the nature which is created and does not create. Here is God as uncreated first cause . . . and as uncreated end . . . ; the second division, the created and creating nature, is the Ideas in God, which, since they have proceeded from a principle, are subordinate to God, and can in a sense be called created; the third division is the universe of things modelled on the Ideas." [8]

5. "El problema histórico . . . ," pp. 203–4. J. E. Gillet has documented many early Spanish occurrences of *natura* and *naturaleza* in his edition of Torres Naharro, *Propalladia and Other Works of Bartolomé de Torres Naharro* (Bryn Mawr, Pennsylvania, 1943–51), III (Notes), pp. 10–11.

6. "Zur *Celestina*," *ZRPh*, L (1930), 238–39. Gelzer's essay is in *Stilistische Forschungen*, Heft I (Halle, 1917): "Natur: Zum Einfluss der Scholastik auf den altfranzösischen Roman," pp. 1–95. When, in 1640 — almost a century and a half after the book's first appearance — the Inquisition finally decided to expurgate *La Celestina*, eliminating certain passages regarded as having dangerous doctrinal implications, Rojas' concept of Nature the Creator was not disapproved. See O. H. Green, "The *Celestina* and the Inquisition," *HR*, XV (1947), 212.

7. *De Trinitate*, 14, 9. See Edmond Goblot, *Le vocabulaire philosophique* (Paris, 1901), p. 358.

8. Richard J. Thompson, "Early Christian Scholasticism," in Virgilius Ferm (ed.), *A History of Philosophical Systems* (New York, 1950), pp. 189–90. We shall return to the idea of subordination to God when we discuss heretical or semiheretical deviations; see below.

St. Anselm (d. 1109) designated God as "summa Natura."[9]
Alanus de Insulis (Alain de Lille, d. 1202) grants to Nature only the
power to shape matter — not to create a soul, this being uniquely
the power of God. "Nature, after receiving the soul from God,
produces the substances by mixing the essences from the four
elements." Nature is thus "mediator between God and things,
and is ministrant to man."[10] She is "the shaper of matter according
to spiritual forms derived from God."[11] After Alanus, the distinction between *Natura naturans* and *Natura naturata* finds wide acceptance. It occurs in the writings of Vincent de Beauvais (d. 1264),
St. Bonaventure (d. 1274), Averroës (d. 1198), Pierre d'Abano
(d. 1316), Meister Johannes Eckhart (d. 1327); William of Ockham
(d. 1350).[12]

It is thus obvious that the idea was embraced by thinkers of the
most diverse tendencies, from a Franciscan saint to an Arabic
commentator on Aristotle. Indeed, it is to the latter, to Averroës,
that Rudolf Eisler (*loc. cit.*) attributes the spread of the doctrine
into Scholastic philosophy. *Natura dicitur duplex,* wrote Albertus
Magnus.

In Spain the concept finds ready acceptance in the *Setenario* of
King Alfonso the Learned (d. 1284), where we read:

Nature is the second part of this *Setenario*, which shows whence things are
born and how and in what manner they operate by themselves or in reciprocal
relationships; and likewise how they are decomposed. And this matter philosophers divided into seven parts: NATURA NATURADOR, NATURA NATURADA, NA-
TURA SSINPLE, NATURA CONPUESTA, NATURA ORDENADOR, NATURA OBRADOR,
NATURA ASCONDIDA. And the first is *Natura naturador* [*Natura naturans*]; this
is God, who was and shall be, and from Him come all things and within Him
they are enclosed. . . . The second is called *Natura naturada* [*Natura naturata*], which means that it is the creature of *Natura naturador*. And these are
the creatures that are called angels, who possess in themselves power and
virtue to work on the things that God wishes each one to produce according
to the task which has been assigned him. The third is *Natura ssinple*, which
exists of itself according to the simple matter of which the thing is made.
The fourth is *Natura conpuesta*, which composes certain things with others
without producing form. The fifth is *Natura ordenador*, which orders every

9. Eisler, *Wörterbuch, s. v. Natur.*
10. See his *Anticlaudianus* in *Patrologia Latina*, vol. 210 (Paris, 1855), pp. 549–50,
and Slaughter, *Virtue According to Love* . . . (New York, 1957), pp. 114–15.
11. Slaughter, *op. cit.*, p. 119.
12. Elie Blanc, *Dictionnaire de philosophie* (Paris, 1906), *s. v. Nature.* Blanc refers to studies by Denifle and J. E. Erdmann.

thing in its proper time and place. The sixth is *Natura obrador*, which gives form to the nature which has been prepared. The seventh is *Natura maravillosa* which is hidden from the understanding of men. . . . These are the miracles produced by God's own nature and the power that emerges therefrom. . . .[13]

The Catalan Raimundo Lull (Raymond Lully) wrote in his *Liber de efficiente et effectu* that *Natura naturata est facta sub Natura naturante* [14] — "Created Nature is produced by command of the Nature that Creates." Sabunde, also a Catalan, said of Nature (in Montaigne's translation: "[Elle] n'engendre rien sans effet," [15] which is an echo of St. Thomas: *Deus et Natura nihil frustra faciunt* — "God and Nature never act in vain."

Early Spanish poets — no less than Jean de Meun (d. 1305?) in France and Geoffrey Chaucer (d. 1400) in England [16] — present Nature as "vicaire of the Almighty Lord" and as the creator of beautiful and wonderful things, including — very often — the human body. In the *Cancionero de Baena* (*ca.* 1445) we read in a poem by Alfonso Alvarez de Villasandino, composed for Juan II of Castile while he still was Prince, that

Obró rrycamente la naturalesa en este señor bienaventurado, que l'fiso commo ángel fermoso, apurado, onesto, loçano, león en bravesa.[17]	Nature worked splendidly to produce this fortunate Prince, making him beautiful as an angel, exacting, pure in his conduct, crowned with graces, a lion in valor.

13. Ed. Kenneth H. Vanderford (Buenos Aires, 1945), pp. 26–27. These doctrines cast a shadow across the centuries. The men of the seventeenth-century Cambridge School (Henry More *et al.*) conceived the "plastic natures," which they looked upon as indispensable to all organic processes, principally as subordinate forces which they placed under the guidance and rule of the divine will. "God stands over all the world as its 'telos' and transcendent principle, while the plastic natures act within the world, being, as it were, entrusted by the First Cause, which is merely concerned with general aims, with the task of executing the details of creation" (Ernst Cassirer, *The Philosophy of the Enlightenment* [Princeton, 1951], p. 85).

14. Cited in Eisler, *loc. cit.*

15. *Theologia naturalis*, in *Oeuvres complètes de Michel de Montaigne*, ed. A. Armaingaud (Paris, 1924–41), IX, 134. Montaigne's translation of the two volumes of Sabunde falls in vols. IX and X of this edition, but hereafter *Theologia naturalis* will be cited as *op. cit.*, vol. I or II.

16. A. F. M. Gunn, *The Mirror of Love: A Reinterpretation of "The Romance of the Rose"* (Lubbock, Texas, 1952), pp. 226, 244, *et alibi*; P. Miroczkowski, "Medieval Art and Aesthetics in *The Canterbury Tales*," *Speculum*, XXXIII (1958), 204–21, especially pp. 212–13.

17. Ed. F. Michel (Leipzig, 1860), I, 16.

Juan de Mena, in his commentary on his own *Coronación*, speaks of "creatures of strange shapes such as Nature never created," and in a lyric poem uses the same verb, *crió*, to praise the lady of his thoughts:

Desde niñez en la cuna,	From the time you lay in
cobrastes fama, beldad,	your cradle you possessed fame,
con tanta graciosidad	beauty, and all the charm that
que vos dotó la fortuna,	Fortune bestowed upon you,
que assí vos organizó	shaping and forming your hu-
y formó	man frame so that you are the
la composición humana,	most exquisite and queenly crea-
que vos soys la más loçana	ture that Nature ever created.
soberana	
que la natura crió.[18]	

Although we shall devote a chapter of the present volume to a consideration of Fortune and Fate, it is necessary to digress here in order to provide an explanation of the disconcerting appearance of Fortune as cocreator, with Nature, of this beautiful lady. Mena, in the poem just quoted, seems actually to confuse — or identify with each other — Nature and Fortune, the two givers of gifts.[19] This confusion (or identification) was the subject of polemics in the fifteenth century, especially as certain writers sought to identify Fortune with Divine Providence. In the *Cancionero de Baena*, Fray Alfonso de la Monja declared that "Fortune is God," that is to say, that God "holds the balances and gives to each person what he deserves": "Dios es Fortuna, e El tiene el pesso,/ El da a cada uno lo que le meresçe." Santillana in his *Comedieta de Ponça* says that Fortune is the delegate of God; and Mena (though in his *Laberinto* he is unable to keep separate arbitrary Fortune and Fortune-subject-to-God's-plans) in the text cited

18. *Cancionero General*, ed. La Sociedad de Bibliófilos Españoles (Madrid, 1882), I, 114; see also *HR*, XX (1952), 276: "animals [such as the chimera] . . . not created by Nature" (J. Homer Herriott, "The Ten Senses in the *Siete Partidas*" [of Alfonso the Learned]).

19. It was normal to regard the "goods of Fortune" as consisting of lineage, wealth, dignities, and other things that fall to one's lot; the "gifts of Nature" as consisting of beauty, fine proportion, charm of personality, proper balance of the bodily humors, health, and strength. See Fray Martín de Córdoba (15 c.), *Compendio de la Fortuna*, ed. P. Fernando Rubio Alvarez (El Escorial–Madrid, 1958), p. 11, and Luis Alfonso de Carvallo (or Carballo), *Cisne de Apolo*, ed. A. Porqueras Mayo (Madrid, 1958), II, 59.

above is clearly in agreement with Fray Alonso: *Dios es Fortuna,*
i.e., Fortune is God.[20] Both Fortune and Nature are God, and God
gave the lady her beauty.

Reverting to our proper subject of Nature, we find that the
Marqués de Santillana (d. 1458) actually used the formula *Natura*
naturante:

Mas natura naturante,	But Nature the Creator, without noise
sin rumor e sin rebate,	or opposition, put an end to the debate
desvolvió tan gran debate	and commanded as one who exercises
e mandó, como imperante,	authority that the heavens should dis-
que los çielos sus lumbreras	play their lights, and that the other
demostrassen,	lesser spheres should assume their or-
e por cursos se ordenassen	dered courses.
las otras baxas espheras.[21]	

Francisco Vaca wrote before 1511:

Yo passando vn espessura	As I passed through a grove adorned
de flores muy hermosas,	with lovely flowers, I would have you
sabrés, señor, que ventura	know, sir, that — as Fortune would
m'encontró con la natura,	have it — I came face to face with Na-
criadora de las cosas.[22]	ture, the creator of all things.

In the year 1493 Gonzalo García de Santa María argues against
the belief that Nature (as St. Cyprian had contended) is declining
through old age: [23] "Nor have the forces of Nature suffered decline,
so that she would today be unable to produce a man as excellent
as [any ancient]." [24] Somewhat earlier Alfonso de la Torre, in his
Visión delectable, had declared that Nature *hizo los montes* —
"made the mountains" — and in another passage had spoken of Nature as acting in accordance with the Divine Will: "And then
Nature, aware of the will of God, began her operations, producing movement and bestowing upon the elements the first qualities,

20. See Rafael Lapesa, "El elemento moral en el *Laberinto* de Mena," *HR*,
XXVII (1959), 258–60; and my article "Sobre las dos Fortunas: de tejas abajo y de
tejas arriba," in *Studia Philologica: Homenaje ofrecido a Dámaso Alonso*, II (Madrid, 1961), 143–54.
21. *Cancionero castellano del siglo XV*, ed. R. Fouché-Delbosc (Madrid, 1912–15),
I, 488.
22. *Cancionero General, ed. cit.*, I, 314.
23. There was, of course, ample precedent for such a view. See Ernest Tuveson,
Millenium and Utopia (Berkeley–Los Angeles, 1949), p. 13. See also our chapter
on Optimism-Pessimism in Volume III of the present work.
24. Quoted by Gallardo, *Ensayo*, III, col. 31. See Chapter XI of our Volume III

that is to say: heat, dryness, cold, and wetness, and producing the generation and decomposition of things." [25]

As we pass into the sixteenth and seventeenth centuries, we find that the concept of *Natura naturans* has not lost its vitality, either in Catholic Spain or in Protestant England. Order is everything, according to Sir Thomas Elyot (d. 1546); over this order, this unity, rules Nature. Or, to quote Richard Hooker (d. 1600): "Obedience of the creatures unto the law of Nature is the stay of the whole world"; and, "Nature is God's deputy, just as, according to Spenser, order is Nature's sergeant. . . . Nature rules over three domains, each of which is a reflection of the others, since they are all parts of the same ordered unity. She rules over the cosmos — the universal world; she rules over the world of created objects on earth; and she rules over the world of human government, of man in society." [26] God being the author of Nature, according to Hooker, her voice is but His instrument.[27] In his *Of the Laws of Ecclesiastical Polity*, Hooker regards the law of Nature and the law of Scripture as promulgated by the same authority.[28] Nature's law, he says, can be discovered in both of the "books" — the book of the Scriptures, and the book of the world — which God has given to man.[29] To these two "books" the Spaniard Venegas added two others. In his *De las differencias de libros que ay en el vniuerso* he enumerates them all: the first is *El Primero Original*, the Book of God's Mysteries; the second is the Book of the Visible World; the third, the Book of Man's Reason; and the fourth, the Scriptures. It is with the greatest naturalness, therefore, that Venegas writes: "Nor could Nature produce so humble a creature as the ant, if God were not cooperating with her." [30]

It will be well to trace the concept in works of a didactic or doctrinal character, and — as an initial proof that the concept was

25. *BAE*, XXXVI, 360b; cf. p. 372a.
26. Cited in Theodore Spencer, *Shakespeare and the Nature of Man* (New York-Cambridge, Massachusetts, 1945), pp. 6–7.
27. Cited in Herschel Baker, *The Dignity of Man: Studies in the Persistence of an Idea* (Cambridge, Massachusetts, 1947), p. 235.
28. Cited in Hardin Craig, *The Enchanted Glass: The Elizabethan Mind in Literature* (New York, 1950), p. 23.
29. Cited in Spencer, *loc. cit.* See also Sabunde, *op. cit.*, I, pp. ix–x.
30. Ed. Salamanca, 1572, fol. 204.

acceptable to the directors of the national conscience — we shall begin with Fray Luis de León's manual of advice to the perfect wife, *La perfecta casada* (1583): "Nature did not produce the good and self-respecting woman for the study of the sciences." [31] This done, we shall follow the chronological order:

1534. Juan Boscán's translation of Castiglione's *Courtier* had great influence in the sixteenth century as a "mirror" for gentlemen and ladies. Its faithfulness to accepted ecclesiastical doctrine is noteworthy. God cooperates with Nature: "All this structure of the visible world with its bright sky adorned with shining stars . . . , we may say that it is nothing else than a great painting composed by the hands of Nature and of God." [32] Nature is strictly subordinate to the Creator and acts at one remove as His agent: "True it is that by favorable influence of the stars or by the goodness of Nature some persons are born with so many graces that one would think that they were not born, but were made by God's own hands, purely and with no intermediary. On the other hand, others are seen to be so stupid and ill-organized that one can only think that Nature cast them into the world in anger or as a jest" (*ibid.*, p. 52). Surely Castiglione would seem to be falling from grace in this last sentence, but such is not really the case; rather, he takes into account the misshapen creatures that are always with us and allows himself to think of nature (not Nature) as having human attributes, just as Mena and Santillana think now of one fortune, now of another (the heavenly and the earthly), or as the poets play with the idea of the celestial and the noncelestial Venus. Nature in Castiglione's last sentence is *naturaleza de tejas abajo,* nature from the roof downward, earthly nature that can make mistakes. Toward the end of his book Castiglione identifies Nature with the Author of the Golden Rule: "And this was also contrary to the law of Nature, which decrees that we may not do unto another what we would not wish to have done to us" (p. 446).

1553. In Antonio de Torquemada's *Coloquios satíricos,* Albanio says: "Surely it is a delightful thing, my dear Jerome, to see the

31. Ed. Madrid, 1917, p. 183.
32. *El Cortesano,* ed. A. M. Fabié (Madrid, 1873), p. 122.

freshness of this garden . . . with the varied colors of the flowers and roses that Nature produces, intermingled with the verdure, in accordance with the will of Him who produces all things. . . ." [33]

1556. Fray Luis de Granada, in his *Guía de pecadores,* or *Sinners' Guide:* "So, wretched man, you cannot excuse yourself by saying that you owe this debt of gratitude to Nature, and not to God; for there is no Nature without God." [34] "What else is Nature but God, who is the source and origin of all nature?" [35] "The works of Nature are the works of an Intelligence that does not err." [36]

1589. Fray Juan de Pineda, in his *Agricultura christiana:* "You must realize that Nature, being a most wise disciple of her Creator . . . , is the mistress of all her children, men, beasts, and plants; and so great is her prudence (in which she resembles her Master, God) that with one lesson she teaches any of her children all he needs to know; for, just as God, when He engendered His Son, infused into Him all His infinite wisdom . . . , so Nature, as she engenders any of her children, gives to it the natural instinct whereby it may know how to (and wish to) obtain what it needs for its preservation." [37]

1591. The Jesuit José de Acosta, in his *Natural and Moral History of the Indies,* speaking of the Peruvian vicuñas and guanacos: "all this was given them by Nature without price, thereby manifesting her desire to favor the poor Indians." [38]

1598. Jerónimo de Mondragón in his *Censure of Human Folly:* "Nature wished to outdo herself, showing herself partial in having endowed you with such singular gifts and benefits." [39]

1615. Acevedo, in his *Creación del Mundo,* says that Nature

33. Quoted in Menéndez y Pelayo, *Orígenes de la novela* (Madrid, 1905–15), II, 531b. Cf. p. 512b: "Nature makes and produces all things. . . ."

34. *Obras,* I (Madrid, 1768), 21.

35. *Ibid.* See also Pedro Laín Entralgo, *La antropología en la obra de Fray Luis de Granada* (Madrid, 1946), p. 68.

36. *Ed. cit.,* V (Madrid, 1769), p. 52. Cf. St. Thomas: *Opus Naturae est opus intelligentiae* (Schütz, *loc. cit.*). One might challenge the testimony of Granada in view of the fact that he was required by the Inquisition to alter the second edition of the *Guía de pecadores.* The fact is, however, that he was at all times orthodox. What the authorities regarded as dangerous (in a work intended for the general reader) was his emphasis on inner, as against outward and institutionalized, religion. See Marcel Bataillon, *Erasmo y España* (Mexico City–Buenos Aires, 1950), index, *s. v.* Granada, *Guía de pecadores.*

37. Salamanca, 1589, II, fol. 152 (the first of the folios so marked).

38. Madrid, 1792, p. 66.

39. *Censura de la locura humana,* ed. Antonio Vilanova (Barcelona, 1953), p. 42.

gave to certain marine creatures arts and tricks for their security to make up for not having provided them with a hard exoskeleton, and that with these special gifts the soft-shelled creatures can avoid death, and deal death to creatures much more powerful.[40]

Before 1645. Quevedo explains that "Nature is the possession of all. She is magnificent in her largess; . . . there is no worm, fish, animal, bird nor plant that can complain of having received from her an inadequate patrimony. Only man, for whose benefit she produced all things (in accordance with the will of God) defames her, and says that she is stingy. . . ."[41]

1663. In an *Academic Discourse* by the Portuguese Dr. Silón Cardoso Pereira, we read: "Of what avail would it be that Nature created the diamond, if Art did not cut it and polish it. . . . Nature gave it its being; Art, its lustre."[42]

In Spanish *belles-lettres,* as distinct from doctrinal works or didactic statements, the conception of Nature as Creator continues to have vitality throughout the Renaissance and the Post Renaissance.

1508. In chapter lxxiii of Book III of the *Amadís de Gaula* the author says of the daughter of Bandaguido that when she grew up to be a maiden, "Nature so adorned her and increased her beauty that in much of the world . . . her equal could not be found."

1528. In the scandalous *Lozana andaluza* of Francisco Delicado a woman sees in her lover such Apollo-like beauty "that it seemed to her that Nature had held nothing back and that there was nothing that she had not bestowed upon [him]."[43]

Before 1536. In his *Egloga Segunda* (lines 781 ff.), Garcilaso de la Vega, echoing Ariosto, wrote:

> One single work like this one Nature made,
> And then in haste destroyed the lovely mold
> That shaped the figure of a form so fair.[44]

1548. Juan de Segura, in his epistolary novel, *Processo de cartas*

40. *BAE,* XXIX, 271a.
41. *Obras en prosa,* ed. Luis Astrana Marín (Madrid, 1932), p. 741a.
42. Quoted in Gallardo, *Ensayo,* I, col. 902.
43. Ed. Javier Farías (Buenos Aires, 1942), p. 20.
44. "Una sola obra quiso la Natura / hacer como ésta, y rompió luego apriesa / la estampa do fué hecha tal figura." Cf. *Orlando furioso,* X, 84.

de amores, letter III, speaks of "the most excellent lady that Nature could form," and in letter XXIII conceives of her as showing "in everything . . . how perfect Nature formed [her]."

Before 1550. Cristóbal de Castillejo, in a *Diálogo* between Adulation and Truth, causes Truth to sound the warning that in life

> Nature produces nothing
> To be held in safe possession.[45]

Before 1558. Jorge de Montemayor, author of the pastoral novel *La Diana,* in his *Cancionero* addresses the Marchioness of Alcañices and the Countess of Lerma:

> In you did Nature form such lovely figures,
> Hoping to see herself as in a mirror,
> That she surpassed the limits of her art
> And what she painted did herself excel.[46]

1559. Early in *La Diana,* the heroine is described by Montemayor as "the one in whom Nature concentrated all the perfections which in many other persons she had distributed and divided," [47] and in the Libro Segundo of the novel the author characterizes three nymphs as being "so beautiful that Nature seemed to have provided, by creating them, a clear demonstration of her power" (*ibid.,* p. 71).

Ca. 1587. In the *Auto de Sant Christóval,* the anonymous author exclaims:

¡O supremo criador!	O God, Creator of all, oh joyous
¡O saber alto y jocundo,	and awe-inspiring wisdom, since
pues nos diste en este mundo	in this world you gave us such
muestras de tu gran valor!	evidence of your power! This
este honbre y su grandeça	man of amazing stature is worthy
cosa es digna de alabar:	of all praise; Nature endowed
dotóle Naturaleza	him with a great body. . . .
de gran cuerpo. . . .[48]	

45. "No produce la Natura / cosa quieta y segura / sin questión y sin querella" (*Obras,* ed. J. Domínguez Bordona [Madrid, 1926–28], IV, 122.)

46. "Formó Naturaleza una figura / por tener un espejo en que mirarse, / do quiso en tanto estremo sublimarse, / que a la pintora excede la pintura" (ed. Bibliófilos Españoles ([Madrid, 1932], p. 50).

47. Ed. F. López Estrada (Madrid, 1946), p. 10.

48. *Colección de autos, farsas y coloquios del siglo XVI,* ed. Leo Rouanet (Barcelona–Madrid, 1901), I, 455.

1590–91. The concept had lost none of its force when the members of the Academia de los Nocturnos were holding their nightly sessions in Valencia. On one of those evenings Guillem Bellvís addressed this quatrain to a lady who had lost her eyesight:

Formóte Naturaleza con toda su perfección porque con justa razón se estimase tu belleza. . . .[49]	Nature formed you with all the perfection she could bestow, in order that your beauty might be justly esteemed.

1599. In the gloomy and moralizing picaresque novel *Guzmán de Alfarache* of Alemán, the rogue, reviewing his life of willful deviations from the good, refuses to hold Nature responsible for his misdeeds: "I would not be right in trying to blame Nature, since I possessed no less ability to follow the good than to pursue what was evil. Mine was the fault, since none of Nature's works was ever beyond the pale of reason. . . ."[50]

1585–1616. From the early *Galatea* (1585) to the posthumous *Persiles* (1617) Cervantes adhered to standard doctrine regarding Nature. It would be easy to multiply significant passages. Here is one, taken at random, from the play *Pedro de Urdemalas*, in which Clemente complains of the indifference of

Esa, a quien Naturaleza dió el extremo de belleza que has visto . . .[51]	Her to whom Nature gave sur- passing beauty . . .

"In one respect," writes Aubrey F. G. Bell, "Cervantes did not probe the tragic depths. In representing Nature as the steward or handmaid of God, he includes in it that perfection which he attributes potentially to human nature also. He does not contemplate, much less attempt to explain, the mysterious contradiction that Nature, with its serene swans . . . and flowered loveliness, is red in tooth and claw."[52] Without accepting Américo Castro's declaration that Cervantes' doctrine of Nature is a *doctrina naturalista*, we can take as accurate his statement of Cervantes' position

49. *Cancionero de los Nocturnos*, ed. F. Martí Grajales (Valencia, 1905–12), IV, 132.

50. Ed. Clásicos Castellanos (Madrid, 1926–36), II, 288–89. Cf. St. Thomas: "Opus Naturae est opus intelligentiae" (Schütz, *op. cit.*, p. 515).

51. *Obras completas*, ed. Angel Valbuena Prat (Madrid, 1956), p. 499.

52. *Cervantes* (Norman, Oklahoma, 1947), p. 49.

in *El pensamiento de Cervantes* (p. 171): "Nature, the major-domo of God, has formed each being, placing in it virtues or defects which impress on every individual ineradicable imprints that determine its character, the realization of which is the theme of the life of each one."

1618. In his semiautobiographical work of fiction entitled *Vida del escudero Marcos de Obregón*, Vicente Espinel appears to give to the doctrine of Nature-the-Creator a sort of deistic turn. Nature creates but does not watch over; once the creature has left her hands, it can complain but cannot change itself. This is, however, not deism or determinism but rather a recognition that Nature is not "the same as God." The "everlasting arms" that sustain the creation are not hers; nor can she, as her Maker can, intervene miraculously to alter, in a given instance, the natural sequence of cause and effect. "When once Nature forms her works with the qualities that she gives them, she no longer has control over the work of her hands, unless God, as her superior, chooses to change it. If it has been made large, large it remains; if small, it must be small forever. . . . What comfort can one have in trying to contravene the works of Nature herself, the representative of the will of the First Mover and Author of all things? If Nature should have happened to produce you with ill-matched members, you might voice complaint, but you could not correct your defect." [53]

1623. Pedro Soto de Rojas, in his *Desengaño de amor en Rimas*, calls his lady to account for breaking the laws of Nature, her maker:

> If Nature bestowed upon you
> With lavish hand the wealth of all her beauty,
> Why do you contravene her laws, dear enemy? [54]

Before 1641. In Juan de Jáuregui's curious *Diálogo* between Nature and the two arts, Painting and Sculpture, Sculpture claims superiority over Painting because it is three-dimensional and therefore possesses being, whereas Painting is a mere illusion (*un falso parecer*). Painting, more reasonable, rejects Sculpture's contention, insisting that neither art has to do with being, but only with representation, for

---

53. Ed. S. Gili Gaya (Madrid, 1922–23), I, 317–19.
54. "Si en vos Naturaleza / puso la perfección de su belleza, / ¿por qué quebráys sus leyes, enemiga?" (*Obras*, ed. A. Gallego Morell [Madrid, 1950], p. 72).

> Art has no power to form
> The essence of any thing.

Nature intervenes in the dispute with three words — *fuera querer-me igualar*:

> To think otherwise would be
> To assume a power that's given to me.

The contention between the two arts, she continues, is silly. They are equal in that each one copies the essence that Nature forms.[55] *Before 1648*. Tirso de Molina speaks of a lady endowed with

> the greatest beauty
> That on this Spanish soil of ours
> (To serve as mirror to the sun)
> Was formed by Nature.[56]

Before 1658. The sixth Crisi of Graciáns *Criticón* is entitled "On Knowing How to Reign." Pointing out correspondences between physical features and moral traits, el Cuerdo (the Wise Man) remarks that the human nose is the feature of prudence, the inn-sign of the soul, the indicator of sagacity and foresight. Thereupon Critilo observes: "I have noticed many times that Nature handles with easy success the other features: she produces a good pair of eyes (though these are such complex organs), a broad and serene brow, a well-formed mouth, but when she comes to the nose, she gets lost and often fails."[57]

Nature as *Natura naturans*, as Nature-that-creates, is thus the producer, the former, the shaper, of things. As such she is the Vicaress of God, one of "those ministers of His that do His pleasure" (Ps. 103:21). It is, of course, hard for men of letters to think of her with philosophic or theological rigor. She is generally thought of as producing fine and beautiful things; yet the world also contains its loathsome creatures, and occasionally an author speaks of nature's inability or failure — as Gracián does in our last

55. "Mal puede el arte formar / el ser mismo de la cosa." — "Fuera quererme igualar. . . . Digo pues que no dudéis / ser vuestra nobleza igual / en una parte esencial / que es el fin a que atendéis, / copiando mi natural" (*BAE*, XLII, 116a–7b).
56. "Como la mayor belleza / que en nuestro suelo español, / sirviendo de espejo al sol, / formó la naturaleza" (*NBAE*, XI, 418).
57. Ed. M. Romera-Navarro (Philadelphia, 1938–40), III, 200.

text — and sometimes of her acting in anger or in jest — as Casti
glione does in *The Courtier*. The subject is beset with difficultie
and, since it involves the question of the existence and the natur
of God and of his distinctness from the world — not to speak of th
possibility of miracles — its discussion can border on, or even in
volve, heresy. Is Nature as a whole self-sufficient, or does it requir
a transcendent ground as its cause and principle? Is *Natura natur
ans* one and the same with *Natura naturata*? By some these ques
tions were answered in a pantheistic sense — and long befor
Giordano Bruno (d. 1600).[58] "If nature alone exists, and if all it
changes are absolutely necessary, everything takes place accordin
to a strict determinism. If, on the contrary, God exists as a tran
scendent, intelligent, and free cause of nature and its laws, no
only nature in all its details depends ultimately on God's will, bu
its ordinary course may be suspended by a miraculous interven
tion of the First Cause."[59]

Pliny had written in his *Historia Naturalis*: "One may believ
that the world is an eternal deity, immense, not engendered, incor
ruptible for all time."[60] Lorenzo Valla (d. 1457) declared in hi
De voluptate: Idem est natura quod Deus, aut fere idem — "Natur
and God are the same, or almost the same."[61] Between the Roman
Pliny and the Italian Valla there had been a centuries-old contro
versy. "That the goddess Physis or Natura had power over men'
souls is proved by the Christian polemics against her."[62] "Th
pagan Natura never entirely vanishes from consciousness."[63] Nor
indeed, does she vanish altogether from Christian and Catholic
Spain. I present three examples, the only ones I know.

The historian Lucas de Tuy (d. 1249) reported that toward th
end of the twelfth century there spread in western Spain a heres
similar to that of the Albigensians, based on the ideas of Amalric
de Chartres and David of Dinant:

Under the appearance of philosophy they seek to pervert the Holy Scriptures
They prefer to be called naturalists or philosophers. . . . They attribute to

58. Cassirer, *op. cit.*, pp. 41; cf. pp. 44–45.
59. C. E. Dubray in *Catholic Encyclopedia, s. v.* Nature.
60. Trans. J. de Huerta, cited by Castro, *El pensamiento* . . . , p. 159.
61. Cited *ibid.*
62. E. R. Curtius, *European Literature and the Latin Middle Ages*, trans. Wil
lard R. Trask (New York, 1953), p. 107 and note.
63. *Ibid.*, p. 108.

Jature everything that God achieves daily by means of his marvellous or-
er. . . . They say that God conferred upon Nature the power to do everything. . . . Their purpose is to introduce the sect of the Manichees, and to
how that there are two gods, one of whom, the evil one, created all visible
things.[64]

In chapter VII of Alfonso de la Torre's *Visión delectable*, Na-
ure, called upon by Wisdom (*Sabiduría*) to help convince Under-
tanding (*Entendimiento*) with her palpable proofs — as against
Wisdom's imponderables —, makes this excuse (*ed. cit.*, p. 350):

should be very pleased to bear the message you suggest; but you know full
well that I am the one whom he [*Entendimiento*] most hates, imputing to me
ll manner of false testimonies, saying that I assert the eternity of the [visible]
world, a thing which he declares to be contrary to the truth; and the error
which he commits in not knowing how to distinguish between priority of
ause and effect produced, between nature and time — that error he imputes
o me, saying that I deprive God of His omnipotence. . . . *Entendimiento*
lso thinks it improper that God should have entrusted to me things capable
f being engendered and decomposed. And I say that God in His blessed
lory, my master and governor, could indeed take it upon Himself directly
o cause existing things to be decomposed, should He wish to do so; but I
now that that will never be His wish, because it would detract from His
reatness were He to be changeable in His will. . . .

The reasoning in this passage is abstruse and refers to debates
f which the uninitiated can have only the slightest inkling, but
which were taken very seriously — and not only in the fifteenth
entury. Marcel Bataillon in *Erasmo y España* reports a third case,
hat of the physician Dr. López de Illescas, a Christian of Jewish
lescent who had doubts concerning the existence of God, perhaps
ecause of "a vague professional naturalism." He was accused of
aving said that *Naturaleza obrava todas las cosas y no Dios* — "that
Nature and not God was the author of all things." When de-
ounced in 1537, he claimed not to have made such a declaration.
Whatever his exact words were is a matter of no importance, says
Bataillon; what is important for us is that what he said could be
nterpreted as if he were opposing Nature to God, and that the
words in question came from the lips of a man for whom the exist-
nce of God was problematical. He was, apparently, a man touched
y the philosophical naturalism of the Italian Renaissance. He was
lso, as we know (for he said so himself), a man who had been

64. Cited by Castro, *España en su historia* (Buenos Aires, 1948), pp. 298–99.

saved from despair by reading the *Enchiridion of the Christian Soldier* and other works of Erasmus (II, pp. 70–71).

Dr. López de Illescas was given a light sentence: he must abjure his error, offer a candle, and pay thirty ducats to cover the costs of his trial. The twelfth-century heretics reported by Lucas de Tuy were undoubtedly dealt with severely. Alfonso the Learned's *Setenario* could identify with a single copula, the verb *es*, Nature-that-creates and God; but when language became rigorous it was necessary to insert some such expression as "in accordance with God's will," as we have seen in more than one of our quoted examples. So long as Nature-the-Creator was regarded as distinct from God, so long as God was held to exist as a transcendent, intelligent, and free cause of Nature, the concept *Natura naturans* offered no difficulty, and theologians like Luis de León and Luis de Granada employed it as readily as did the novelists and poets. What was necessary was to avoid fusing *Natura naturans* with *Natura naturata* — that one not identify the two in a naturalistic pantheism. *Natura* as a whole is not self-sufficient; its transcendent ground, its principle, is God. Fernando de Rojas is quite clear on this point in Calisto's first speech in *La Celestina*. It is to God, not Nature, that glory is due: "In this I see, Melibea, a manifestation of the greatness of God. . . ."

NATURA NATURATA

It is time now to turn our attention to that other Nature — nature in all its details, nature that is created but does not create — *Natura naturata*.

Nature is, first and foremost, the child and the creature of the Almighty. We read in the anonymous thirteenth-century *Libro de Alexandre* (ms. pp. 2339–40):

Pesó al Criador que cría la Natura,	God, the creator of Nature, was
ovo de Alixandre saña e grant rencura.	offended, and felt his wrath stir against Alexander.

In Alfonso the Learned's *Setenario*, also of the thirteenth century, the term *Natura naturada* is defined as meaning *que ffué ffecha del Naturador* — "that it was created by *Natura naturans*" (*ed. cit.*, p. 27).

St. Augustine and many others down through the centuries were convinced that nature was a work of God and an emblem of moral ideas; that every detail and every event in nature represented some divine truth — the new grass, the Resurrection; the sunrise, the light of Christ dispelling the night of sin.[65] An example is the ninth-century Rhabanus Maurus' *Allegoriae in universam Sacram Scripturam*, in which an elaborate allegorical reading of the "book of nature" is worked out, with the realities of nature serving as a system of divine symbols.[66]

In the thirteenth century there came about a change. Nature did not remain merely a symbol, an emblem of truth; she suddenly became a source of knowledge parallel to Revelation. Alongside the Book of Scripture was placed the Book of Nature — a book that now possessed epistemological validity and independence. "The Aristotelian revival rekindled a desire for a genuine science of nature, of nature considered in itself as an independent reality, and not merely as an obscure and confessedly inadequate clue to the character of its Creator." [67] St. Thomas Aquinas, in answer to the challenge of this thirteenth-century "discovery of the world and man," affirmed, like all Aristotelians, "the absolute primacy of perception in our thought, and the impossibility, in this life, of any direct apprehension of God." The beatific vision he postponed to the next world; in this world, truth must come, for the Christian as for all men, through reason and the senses (*ibid.*, p. 75). The source of intellectual knowledge is *Natura naturata*, created nature, the world of stars and stones and trees.

At the end of the fifteenth and the beginning of the sixteenth century, again something new was added. The task which the Christian humanists then set themselves was the sanctification of nature. "At this time . . . one no longer places the accent on original sin, but on the Grace which revives nature in its pristine purity. To Grace, nothing human can be foreign. That is why, in this world where the arts bring forth a fruit so new, where the

65. Wilhelm Ganzenmüller, *Das Naturgefühl im Mittelalter* (Leipzig, 1914), pp. 36–37; see also Alfred Biese, *The Development of the Feeling for Nature in the Middle Ages and Modern Times* (London, 1905), pp. 42–43.

66. Joseph A. Mazzeo, *Structure and Thought in the "Paradiso"* (Ithaca, 1958), p. 178.

67. J. V. Langmead Casserley, *The Christian in Philosophy* (New York, 1951), p. 87.

sciences are awakening, the Christian humanists concern themselves with ethnography and geography, with history and with
literature, with everything that is human." [68]

For Spain we shall choose, among countless texts that might
serve our purpose, the testimony of four men, two of the sixteenth
and two of the seventeenth century. The first is the layman Alejo
Venegas (d. 1554), who gave up theology for marriage, and whose
Differencias de libros has been so often cited in the course of the
present work:

Of the books which we must read (because they were written for us), the first
is the book of nature, which is the totality of the creatures. This book is so
open that any man unable to read therein must lack the power of reason,
for it is so clear and legible that if it is read with attention, it can be read
without a human master to teach one. In this book St. Anthony read the
marvels and virtues of the Creator. . . . This saint, when asked how it was
that he could live in the desert without human contacts and without books,
replied that the book of nature was his entire library, wherein were contained
as many volumes as there were things for him to contemplate, and all of
them the more trustworthy in proportion as a book written by the hand of
God exceeds books written by the hands of men. In this book St. Anthony
read of the great power of God in the creation; of the wisdom of God in its
government; of the goodness of God in His great act of sharing — an example
which, by reading in this book, we may be induced to follow. He learned to
fear God, by reason of His immense power; to believe in Him, by reason of
His infinite wisdom; to love Him, because of His infinite goodness. And let
us not be like children, or demented persons, who, seeing the book's letters all
beautifully illuminated, take delight in the work of the illuminator without
giving inward thought to what the writing says.[69]

Mere delight in nature is not enough; it can not be an end in
itself. The book of nature exists for the purpose of leading us to
its Author.

Our second witness is the Dominican Fray Luis de Granada
(d. 1588), who marveled that philosophers like Pliny could be
content only to study nature, with no other aim "than merely to
feed the natural appetite of curiosity, the desire which men have to
know extraordinary and admirable things, an appetite which might
better be checked and mortified than fed; whereas with a single
mounting up of the imagination we can come to a knowledge of

68. Francis Hermans, *Histoire doctrinale de l'humanisme chrétien*, (Tournai-
Paris, 1948), I, 42–43.
69. Ed. Salamanca, 1572, fol. 49rv.

that infinite goodness and wisdom of the Creator of so many marvels; in which exercise men would find, not only great fruit, but
also great delight, which is what men commonly seek in life." [70]
Fray Luis' remarkable interest in such small creatures as the mos-
quito, and his dwelling upon them in his works, corresponds to
his belief that he can persuade the Christian that the contemplation of nature necessarily leads one to discover and worship God. [71]

Vincente Espinel (d. 1624) was a restless person, who in his youth
enjoyed the income of a chaplaincy founded by his family and
late in life, after extensive travels and many escapades, took final
orders as a secular priest. At the beginning of *Descanso* XVII of
his *Vida del escudero Marcos de Obregón* he describes, with a
musician's ear for the thrill of birdsong, his arrival on muleback
at a point from which the city of Málaga lay spread out beneath
him (*ed. cit.*, I, 254):

So great was the comfort that I received from the sight of the city, and
from the fragrance with which the wind burdened itself as it played through
the marvelous orchards, crowded with all species of orange and lemon trees,
full of blossoms at all seasons of the year, that I seemed to be beholding a
portion of Paradise, because there does not exist in all the circuit of that
horizon a single thing that does not delight some one of the five senses.
The eyes are delighted with the vision of the sea and the land, the latter covered with as great a diversity of beautiful trees as can be found in all the
multitudinous places where such plants grow, [and] with the view of the city's
site and buildings, both private dwellings and excellent churches, especially
the Cathedral, for in all the known world no more pleasing temple is known
to exist. The ears are stirred to admiration by the abundance of the birds
which, imitating each other, do not cease night or day to give forth with artful
artlessness their sweet song; for as they produce neither harmony nor dissonance, their singing is a sweet confusion which lifts one's thoughts to the Maker
of All Things. The abundant and substantial fruits appeal to the taste and
maintain the health. . . . All this is sufficient to make one wish to write a
great book on the excellencies of Málaga. . . .

Is Espinel's remembering of the Creator inserted here merely
pro forma? We can not know; even if such were the case, the
passage would have significance as giving evidence of how a seventeenth-century Spaniard was supposed to view God's wonders. I
suspect, however, that the pious thought was inserted spontane-

70. *Obras, ed. cit.*, V, 29–30; see also the index of this volume, *s. v. Naturaleza*.
71. Laín Entralgo, *op. cit.*, p. 25.

ously, with a true sense of cosmic wonder. This is no ordinary set piece of rhetoric; it is the sweet notes of music — Espinel's great love — that lift him out of himself, out of his *circunstancia*, into a Higher World.

Last of all, we come to our Jesuit historian of the Spanish Indies, in whose account of the natural history of the New World Aristotle comes in for more than one correction, made necessary by a truly Aristotelian observation of the world of visible and tangible things. This text shows a keener awareness of nature as the Romantics were to feel it than any other of our period that is known to me. In his *Historia natural y moral de las Indias*, Father José de Acosta prefers to temples and palaces, to paintings, carvings, or precious stones, the sight of the ocean, of a lofty crag, of a furious torrent (*ed. cit.*, pp. 12–13):

> Whether they be pleasant gardens or palaces and proud temples, whether they be buildings of imposing architecture, or paintings, or carvings, or gems of great value marvelously cut, and even if these things have all the exquisiteness imaginable, it is a matter of common experience that, when we have looked at them two or three times, our eyes scarcely focus on them any more, but immediately wander to look at something else, as if tired of what they have seen. But the sea, if you gaze upon it, or focus your eyes on some high cliff rising boldly in the distance, or on a field clothed with its natural verdure and bright flowers, or on the current of a furiously dashing river that ceaselessly beats against its stony walls and seems to roar as it fights against them; and in short any of the works of nature, no matter how often it is seen, always causes new delight and never wearies the vision, so that it really seems a copious and magnificent banquet set before us by the Divine Wisdom which silently, without ever causing satiety, feeds and delights our mind and lifts it up.

The last words of this passage, *apacienta y deleyta nuestra consideración*, carry all the meaning I have given them in my expanded translation. *Consideración*, in the devotional literature of this century, meant a grateful taking into account of the inestimable wealth of blessings showered upon man by a God — all goodness — who created the universe for him. Here again, in this paragraph from a book of natural history, there is a note of enthusiasm that seems as individual and as spontaneous as Espinel's prose hymn to Málaga. And here, as in the other three texts, Nature — however much she may delight us directly — leads us beyond ourselves to the Creator of the tiny, feathered ball of song, of the dashing foam and crashing roar of the river as it struggles through the canyon.

DIVINUS OMNIUM RERUM ORDO

Covarrubias, in his *Tesoro de la lengua castellana* (1611), defined *Natura* as "the divine order of things, whereby all things are moved, have their origin, and cease to be. This indeed has been said to be God, by whom all things are created." [72] Although, as Covarrubias' definition shows, the distinctions between this meaning of Nature and the two we have so far studied are not really clear-cut, it will be profitable to consider in some detail this third use of the word as signifying "the divine order of things." [73]

The twelfth-century Alanus de Insulis, in his *De planctu Naturae*, "chose to work as a philosopher and poet within a well-defined tradition of philosophical poetry, and he made it clear that he was quite aware of the limits imposed by his choice. . . . Nature (who is significantly in full control of the dialogue) insists that the dreamer be aware of her limitations as a creative power, and of her total incompetence to restore the moral order once it has broken down. She is the figure of the natural universe and of its inherent governing and reproductive forces; she is herself a creature who acts in the name and power of the Creator. The limits of her own power are shown most clearly in the defection of man, her most perfect work, a defection which she can condemn but not remedy." [74]

In the thirteenth century, Thomas Aquinas defined Nature as

72. "divinu[s] omnium rerum ordo, quo omnia mouentur, oriuntur, et occidunt. Hanc quidem Deum esse dixerunt, a quo omnia sunt creata."

73. "The word 'nature' had long since come to designate, along with its many other meanings, the whole world of sensible objects and its ordinary processes and empirically known laws — the sense which is perhaps the most current one in contemporary usage. There is in this sense no obvious or necessary normative implication; the term is simply a summary name for things as they are, not as they ought to be. Nevertheless, even this widest and primarily descriptive signification of 'nature' and 'natural' early took on a eulogistic coloring (which for many it still has) and became the source of value judgements" (A. O. Lovejoy, "Nature as a Norm in Tertullian," in *Essays in the History of Ideas* [Baltimore, 1948], p. 324).

74. Richard H. Green, "Alan of Lille's *De Planctu Naturae*," *Speculum*, XXXI (1956), 653.

ratio cuiusdam artis, scilicet divinae, indita rebus, qua ipsae res moventur ad finem determinatum — "the law of a certain activity, namely of the divine activity, inherent in things, whereby things are moved toward a determined end." For St. Thomas, "every fact of nature is organically related to the total pattern of the great design. Thus the body . . . is viewed . . . as merely an instrument of the soul. Even the sexual organs have their proper 'end,' and 'that which is the end of any natural thing cannot be evil in itself: since that which is according to nature, is directed to an end by divine providence.' God is rational, and rationally orders the universe with regard 'not only to the species, but also to the individual' — which delicate and double obligation He codifies into natural law." [75]

In the generation following St. Thomas, in the *Romance of the Rose* of Jean de Meun, "Nature — in spite of the dialectic that fills her discourse — and Genius, her deputy, do not argue; they promulgate their doctrine as the all-encompassing and all-binding truth. They speak with authority concerning the things of the natural order, as Reason speaks with authority concerning the things above Nature." [76]

In the sixteenth century, Hooker wrote in *Of the Laws of Ecclesiastical Polity*: "The general and perpetual voice of men is as the sentence of God himself. For that which all men have at all times learned, Nature herself must needs have taught; and God being the author of Nature, her voice is but his instrument." [77] Most men of the sixteenth century, except outright skeptics and atheists,[78] "could have given reasonably sincere lip service to the ethics of More's *Utopia*. There would inevitably have been some quibbling of the definition of terms . . . but the basic principles would have

75. Baker, *op. cit.*, p. 198.
76. Gunn, *op. cit.*, p. 403.
77. Quoted in Herschel Baker, *The Wars of Truth: Studies in the Decay of Christian Humanism in the Earlier Seventeenth Century* (Cambridge, Massachusetts, 1952), p. 95.
78. Serious skepticism "is scarcely discoverable prior to the very end of the sixteenth century, in Bruno, Campanella, and Vanini, and they expiated their temerity at the stake [or in the torture chamber] after the manner of the High Middle Ages" (Roland H. Bainton, "Man, God, and the Church in the Age of the Renaissance," in *The Renaissance: A Symposium*, Metropolitan Museum of Art [New York, 1952], p. 59). See also my review of Paul Oskar Kristeller, *The Classics and Renaissance Thought* (Cambridge, Massachusetts, 1955), in *RPh*, X (1957), 282–83.

been as sweetly reasonable to Sir Thomas Elyot as to Rabelais. Man's felicity, said More, is the result of a virtuous life, and a virtuous life consists of living according to nature, that is, rationally, after the pattern of God." [79]

In Spain, in the fourteenth-century *Libro de buen amor*, Juan Ruiz declares that men and beasts desire *segunt natura* — "in accordance with Nature's laws" — a companion of the opposite sex, and that man, unlike the animals, sins knowingly but inevitably, *ca natura lo enriza* — "because Nature eggs him on" (*coplas 73c* and *75d*). In the same sense Fernán Pérez de Guzmán (d. 1440?) writes in the fifteenth century:

Muy difícil, digo yo,	It is most difficult, I claim — let
diga imposible quien osa,	him who dares say it is impos-
vencer la muy poderosa	sible — to overcome the power-
natura que Dios crió;	ful inclination of Nature, the
e qualquiere que alcançó	child of God. And any man hav-
vigor a tal resistencia,	ing strength to make such resist-
regracie la grant clemencia	ance should thank God for the
del Senyor que lo esforçó.[80]	great mercy whereby he was en-
	abled to do so.

In the same century Juan de Lucena wrote in his *De vida beata* (1463): *sólo era pecado lo que natura . . . les prohibió* — "the only sin was what Nature forbade them." [81]

It is recognized that the laws of Nature often appear to produce conflict. When a writer speaks responsibly, as a thinker, the conflict is resolved in a superior harmony: "In spite of the great variety and the continual conflict of so many laws of Nature, everything remains subject to order and is governed by an imperturbable rule; everything reveals the most marvelous cunning, the most judicious and best-directed harmony," wrote Sabunde.[82] When, on the other hand, one was thinking in terms of Nature *de tejas abajo* — earthly and earthy Nature, sister of the "earthly" Fortune and unidentified with any thought of Providence — in such circumstances one could speak of Nature as a stepmother: *con nusco mostrarse madrastra natura*, as did Hernán López de Yanguas in

79. Baker, *The Dignity of Man*, p. 293.
80. *Cancionero castellano . . . , ed. cit.*, I, 579–80.
81. See Gillet (ed.), *Propalladia . . .* , III, 10.
82. *El hombre y sus deberes* (Madrid, n.d.), p. 22. (This is an anonymous partial translation into Spanish of the *Theologia naturalis*.)

the sixteenth century and Gracián in the seventeenth.[83] In similar
vein, Gil Vicente (d. 1536?) speaks of being saddled by Nature
(cited *ibid.*):

Que natura nos ensilla,   For nature so saddles us that we
que no podemos torcer   are ever subject to her.
de sujetos suyos ser.

Among the responsible, or seriously didactic statements, the
following may be taken as typical:

Before 1458.

Oyo los secretos de philosophía   I hear the secrets of Philosophy
e los fuertes passos de naturaleza.[84]   and the sound of Nature's firmly
                                      planted feet.

1526. "A single hope remains to me and it is this: each day destroys false opinions and confirms true judgments founded on
Nature."[85]

1534. "The best knowledge for living wisely is the natural law
which God implanted in things."[86]

Before 1540. "The order of Nature is this: that wisdom govern
and rule the entire universe; that everything we see obey man;
that within man the body serve the spirit, for that is the name we
now give to the inferior part of man [subject to the passions]; that
this inferior part be subject to the understanding [free from the
passions]; and the understanding be subject to God. He who departs from this order is guilty of sin."[87]

Ca. 1550. "What philosophy, what astronomy, what science, no
matter how lofty and sublime, has heretofore been able to master,
oblige, or compel Nature so as to make it possible (withdrawing
the stigma which she, overcome by the illness suffered and making
herself a party thereto, had imposed on men by withdrawing from
them the power of speech) . . . for our human spirit and human

83. Gillet (ed.), *loc. cit.*
84. Santillana, cited *ibid.*
85. Vives writing to Cranevelt. See M. Bataillon, "Du nouveau sur J. L. Vives,"
BHi, XXXII, (1930), 111.
86. Feliciano de Silva, *Segunda comedia de Celestina*, ed. J. A. de Balenchana
(Madrid, 1874), p. 396.
87. Vives, *Introducción a la sabiduría* (Madrid, 1944), p. 41.

wisdom to enable the deaf to talk — by no other means than industry and a spirit of research?" [88]

1556. "Grace is more powerful than Nature, and God more powerful than the devil, and the good angels than those that were evil and rebellious; and finally, spiritual delights are beyond any comparison greater and more efficacious than the joys of sense." [89]

1575. "When Aristotle said: *Deus et natura nihil faciunt frustra* [God and Nature do nothing in vain], he did not mean that Nature is some universal cause having jurisdiction apart from God, but rather that it is the name of the order and harmony which God gave to the composition of the world to the end that the effects necessary for its sustenance shall take place. In exactly the same way, we commonly say that the king and the civil law do injury to no man, without anyone thinking that this same law indicates some prince having jurisdiction apart from the jurisdiction of the king, but rather that it is a term which embraces in its meaning all the laws and royal ordinances which the king has made for the preservation of the peace in his kingdom." [90]

Ca. 1581. "Consequently one must disagree with Scaliger when (in spite of his immense learning) he calls Vives absurd for having said that the investigation of Nature by the human mind is full of darkness. If the opinion of Vives is absurd, I would wish to be absurder still. For I not only regard such investigation as full of obscurity, but as tenebrous, full of pitfalls, abstruse, inaccessible, undertaken by many and by none achieved or achievable." [91]

Before 1645. "If kings are careless in maintaining their authority, they are likely to be overcome by Fortune. For I believe that just as the soul has a guardian angel and a public prosecutor (who is the devil) in spiritual matters; so Nature (like a mother) has care for our conservation in temporal matters and is analogous to the

---

88. Licenciado Lasso, *Tratado nuevamente compuesto . . . en que por nuevo estilo y manera de decir se examina y funda de derecho como el mudo 'a natura,' excluso en la institución de algunos mayorazgos . . . , es capaz el tal mudo, si hablare, para suceder en el dicho mayorazgo,* cited in Gallardo, *Ensayo,* III, cols. 299 ff., especially 307.

89. Granada, *Guía de pecadores,* in *Obras,* ed. cit., I, 431.

90. Juan Huarte de San Juan, *Examen de ingenios,* ed. R. Sanz (Madrid, 1930), p. 74.

91. Francisco Sánchez, *Que nada se sabe* (Madrid, n. d.), p. 109.

guardian angel; while Fortune (like a stepmother and a scourge) would encompass our destruction and is analogous to the devil." [92]

Before 1658. "With perfect justification all learned men confess that even if all the minds that were ever created should come together and should make a distillate of all their reasoning, they could not emend a single circumstance or a single atom of Nature." [93]

Let us review these seriously didactic, these "responsible" statements concerning Nature as the divine order of things. They range from Santillana's "secrets of philosophy" and "resounding footsteps of Nature," to Vives' last and best hope for the victory of judgments founded on Nature and for the subjugation of man's passions to his reason, in accordance with Nature's command. They include (in a lawyer's allegation on behalf of deaf mutes) an amazing paean to the power of man, who with thought and skill and determination can actually repair a natural defect caused by an accident of birth. They include Luis de Granada's placing of Grace above Nature, and Huarte de San Juan's refusal to see in Nature a universal cause with jurisdiction apart from God, seeing her, on the contrary, as a useful vicegerent of the Creator, just as the civil law is a useful tool (or servant) of the king. [94] Included also is Francisco Sánchez's insistence on Nature's inscrutability, an idea which he carries to an extreme but which had had earlier expression in Vives and in others. [95] The gloomy Quevedo sees in Nature a secular counterpart of man's guardian angel—a motherlike power concerned with his preservation and an enemy of downcasting "material" Fortune. Finally, in Gracián there is a bowing of man's reasoning and his philosophizing before the perfection of Nature governed by Providence.

92. Quevedo, *Obras en prosa, ed. cit.,* p. 810b.

93. Gracián, *El Criticón, ed. cit.,* I, 141. On page 280 Gracián appeals to "the supreme Providence that governs Nature."

94. Huarte, indeed, regarded this order of Nature as competent to guarantee the concert and evolution of the world with a minimum of direct intervention (i.e., through miracles) of the Creator. See Mauricio de Iriarte, S. J., *El doctor Huarte de San Juan y su Examen de Ingenios* (Madrid, 1948), p. 206; J. Dantín Gallego, "La filosofía natural en Huarte de San Juan," *Estudios de historia social de España,* II (1952), 205.

95. This stands in sharp contrast to the exultant confidence of the Licenciate Lasso as he contemplates man's power to correct a defect of Nature.

As we look back over the ground traversed in this chapter, we find, amid shifting points of view, a general consistency of attitude. There is general agreement that Nature in her operations imitates the operation of God, that she serves Him as the agent He has appointed for the producing of His creatures. In that capacity she is *Natura naturans*, God's Vicaress or Major-domo, ever separate from the Godhead and subordinate to it. She creates bodily forms, not souls; nor may she perform miracles — i.e., she may not reverse an action she has completed. Only God may interfere with her "determinism."

There is general agreement, also, in applying the word Nature to the totality of things created: the *res extensa* as opposed to the *res cogitans* of Descartes. In this sense Nature is *Natura naturata*, created in accordance with God's will and for the use and the edification of man. Learning the lessons of *Natura naturata*, man may come to know God. *Natura naturata* is the basis of the *Theologia naturalis* of Sabunde, and of the appeal for *consideración* — for awareness of God's inestimable love — in the works of Fray Luis de Granada.

Finally, Nature is a set of laws, a *divinus ordo*, a "civil code" for governing the kingdom which is the world, a machinery or an agency set up for the preservation, without miraculous intervention,[96] of the universe. In this sense Nature is the *ratio indita rebus, qua ipsae res moventur ad finem determinatum* of St. Thomas — an inherent active principle whereby things move to their divinely appointed end.

There is also a *Naturaleza de tejas abajo*, an "earthly" and "material" nature, physical not spiritual; a nature that can be called stepmother — a stepmother whom one could blame for his inordinately large nose or the hump on his back; a nature that could be overcome by, and could yield to, disease, producing persons deaf or blind from birth and producing other "errors" of nature, some

96. It was not only thinkers like Pompanazzi who sought to explain so-called miracles as the effect of natural causes (E. Cassirer *et al.* [eds.], *The Renaissance Philosophy of Man* [Chicago, 1948], p. 277). The Inquisitor Martín Castañega, e. g., in his *Tratado de las supersticiones* (Logroño, 1527), sought physical and psychological causes for many phenomena regarded as extraordinary. He wrote: "Things should not be considered miraculous as long as they can be produced naturally" (Castro, *Santa Teresa y otros ensayos*, pp. 159–60). Cf. Huarte de San Juan, *op. cit.*, I, 73.

of them (like the speechlessness of deaf mutes) correctable by man. This does not mean, of course, that man has had the temerity to think he can correct God; it means simply that in certain matters God's majesty is not committed. In similar fashion, when one speaks, in connection with the meteorology and the physics of the sky, of Nature's deceiving us (and here I have again capitalized Nature), the deception suffered by the eye is no real deception at all, nor is there any "mistake" of Nature. When once the physical factors involved are understood (even on the basis of the false Ptolemaic premises), the "deceit" vanishes. The blue color of the sky is merely an optical illusion, and the real sky (as against the optical illusion) is moved up hundreds of leagues to the invisible heaven of the Moon.

Even nature's "mistakes" cannot really be mistakes. Under the broad dome of the Almighty's will, evil itself is somehow good, as in the tempting and the suffering of Job. The universe was created for the benefit of the human soul, and the human soul has free will, a fact which necessitates the existence of evil, else there could be no choice.[97] Even the physician of Jewish descent, who had difficulty organizing his religious beliefs and appears to have been troubled by the idea that nothing exists but Nature, found comfort and avoided despair by reading an eminently devotional book: The *Handbook of the Christian Soldier* by Desiderius Erasmus of Rotterdam. The *Sic* and the *Non* are gathered up and subsumed (sometimes by a resort to fideism, sometimes by the efforts of rational theology) into a greater, an all-embracing *Sic*.

97. We shall treat of free will in a subsequent chapter. It is the foundation of Spanish thought.

IV · The Nature and Destiny of Man

O God, by whom the dignity of
human nature was wondrously
established . . .
    From the Mass.

En la Soberana Idea
de Dios miré la pintura
del alma hermosa del hombre,
cuya gran belleza, cuya
perfección había de ser,
al cuerpo mortal conjunta,
Humana Naturaleza,
reina del mundo absoluta.
        Calderón [1]

"When Francis Bacon analyzes human reality, he is, perhaps, most typically himself, appearing as a man of the Renaissance. First of all, the effort to understand man from the point of view of revelation, while not absent in Bacon's work, is reduced to a secondary plane, or even given third place; furthermore, there is a triumphant optimism in his words when he speaks of man's 'prerogatives,' or of the 'marvels of human nature': Bacon does not forget the testimony of antiquity, since he is a good humanist; but what is most interesting of all is that he interprets everything from the point of view of technology, of the mastery of nature by man. This

---

1. "In the sovereign Idea in the mind of God I beheld the image of the beautiful soul of man, whose great beauty and perfection, when joined to a mortal body, were to become Human Nature, absolute queen of the world" (from the *auto sacramental*, *El pintor de su deshonra*, cited by Eugenio Frutos, "Origen, naturaleza y destino del hombre en los autos sacramentales de Calderón," *Revista de filosofía*, X [1945], 539). In *El Divino Jasón*, Calderón speaks of the Cross as an arch, a passageway, whereby the human heart, *una vez casi Dios y otra gusano* — "at times little lower than God, at times a worm" — is lifted up till its forehead reaches the Empyrean (Frutos, *op. cit.*, p. 535). As Frutos points out (p. 554), "Baroque" melancholy and lamentation have to do with the vanity and emptiness of human affairs here below, not with the supernatural destiny of man. In *El año santo de Roma* Calderón says that Caesar is not born to be Caesar, nor the mighty lord to be lord, nor is the beggar born to his grief: *todos nacen a otro fin / que es, si lo examinan cuerdos, / servir a Dios y gozarle* — "all are born to another end, which, if they would only see it, is to serve God and enjoy Him forever" (cited *ibid.*, p. 555).

is, indeed, a recapitulation of the themes of the Renaissance as they expand and open out in anticipation of an age already mature in its achievement: the modern age." [2]

Spain produced no Francis Bacon, nor did Spanish thinkers care greatly about technology. To ask why this was so, and to seek to provide the answer, would launch us upon the limitless ocean of speculation concerning what constitutes a culture pattern and determines the attitudes and choices of peoples — their "style of life." Avoiding speculation as much as possible, I shall endeavor to establish the fact that, whatever the determining cause or causes — and these are indeed multiple — in Spain the interpretation of man's nature in the light of revelation is of prime importance, although certain authors will stress — within that framework, and in that light — the physiological and the psychological, that is to say the astral, climatological, even dietary basis of man's achievements and failures. Notes of triumphant optimism will be based primarily on the Biblical assurance that man bears God's image and possesses the God-given power of reason and free will. When material or technical achievements such as the circumnavigation of the earth in 1522 give to man a sense of conquest and dominion, the status of lord of the universe is not thought of as something new that man has accomplished after emerging from a "Gothic night," but rather as something ordained from the beginning by the Creator, as recorded in Genesis. This sense of optimism will be offset (as indeed it was in England) by an awareness of the immensity of the calamity represented by the Fall in Eden. As for the testimony of ancient writers, in Spain both humanists and antihumanists will utilize the authority of the Greek and Roman philosophers exactly as the "founders of the Middle Ages" [3] and the Church Fathers had done.

CHRISTIAN ANTHROPOLOGY: THE FOUR MAIN POSITIONS

From the Catholic point of view, the problems of "theological anthropology" are of two classes: those having to do with the component parts of the human composite (body-soul) and their mutual

2. Julián Marías, *El tema del hombre* (Madrid, 1943), p. 184.
3. E. K. Rand, *Founders of the Middle Ages* (New York, 1957).

relations; and those concerned with the end, powers, and tendencies of man (natural and supernatural). The problems of the first classification have not caused great dogmatic controversies; those of the second, on the other hand, have been the theme of keen argument and the root of dogmatic divergences. Inevitably, the different personal experience of each theologian influenced decisively his interpretations. On the one hand, a theologian with a pessimistic view of himself and of other men necessarily will interpret pessimistically the effect of the Fall (Augustine; exaggerated by Luther); or he will make his interpretation on the basis of a pessimistic view of human nature itself (Origen, who represented the soul as imprisoned in the body as a punishment). On the other hand, an optimistic temperament and a favorable view of human life will cause a theologian to interpret optimistically the effects of the Fall (Pelagianism); or to stress optimistically the saving effects of Grace (the Christian humanists; exaggerated by all groups of *illuminati*).[4]

Christian anthropology in Spain

The diversity of Spanish ideas on man and his nature is indeed striking; but when our necessarily limited survey has been completed, I am sure that we shall find it reasonable to conclude, in words used over a decade ago by Hardin Craig with reference to the England of Queen Elizabeth, that the road to truth, as conceived by our Spanish thinkers, "was not the free use of reason, but reason restricted to the discovery or rediscovery of a universe whose laws were the legacies of a wiser past, or fiats of an unimpeachable God."[5]

God was unimpeachable, and the past was — for the most part —

4. Miguel Benzo Mestre, "La pura naturaleza humana en la teología de Suárez," *Anthologica annúa*, III (1955), 406–7. As an early example of the optimistic view, we may take Godefroy de Saint-Victor's (*fl. ca.* 1184) *Microcosmus*. "The personal contribution of this stubborn humanist is his steady refusal to denigrate nature for the sake of grace, the body for the glory of the soul, or, as he puts it himself, the water of human science for the wine of theology. He is persuaded . . . that the best way to guarantee the value of the human is to honor the work of God in nature, to insist that the human persists even in an era of grace" (E. A. Synan, reviewing Philippe Delhaye's edition and critical study of *Le Microcosmus* [Lille–Gembloux, 1951], in *Speculum*, XXIX [1954], 805).

5. *The Enchanted Glass: The Elizabethan Mind in Literature* (New York, 1950), p. 3.

wiser. Sometimes the past was impeached; in the past, obviously, there had been no inkling of the Spanish and Portuguese discoveries. In 1540 Venegas declared that only the poles of the earth remained to be discovered, since the Equatorial regions "in our own time have been very adequately traversed by the feet of men." [6] Father José de Acosta exclaimed in 1591: "Who can fail to believe that the ship Victoria, by circumnavigating the globe, has shown that the earth, no matter how vast, is subject to man, since with his feet he has measured it?" [7]

Yet there is no Promethean arrogance, nor any Pascalian awareness of the dwarfing of man by infinity. Man was dwarfed and exalted, but only by the exercise of his free will—dwarfed by the wretchedness of sin, exalted by the glory of its conquest. The one dark note is a certain localized determinism (accidental, not substantial—arising from the influences, exerted on man's body and mind by horoscope, food, water, and air), a determinism about which the Spaniards, a nation of conquerors in strange lands and under foreign constellations, found it most difficult to make up their minds, as we shall see.

The dramatist-musician Juan del Encina, one of whose plays was performed in Rome in the year 1513, called man a worm of a thousand malices, subject to two thousand appetites, a sound carried off by the wind, a building without foundations, yet a creature who held in his hand the reins of his governed or ungoverned passions. [8] Bernardino de Laredo, a physician turned mystic (d. 1540?), declared man to be a vessel composed of lead (the body) and of brass (the soul infected by original sin); yet a vessel which the Divine Goldsmith has chosen to adorn with gold and silver, enamel and precious stones. [9] St. Thomas of Villanueva, the last Father of the Spanish Church (d. 1555), apostrophizes man: "Oh man, recognize who you are; be aware of your great dignity, in

6. See my article, "The Concept of Man in the Spanish Renaissance," *The Rice Institute Pamphlet*, XLVI (1960), 41

7. *Historia natural y moral de las Indias* (Madrid, 1792), p. 5.

8. See his poem on the theme *Memento, homo, quia cinis es et in cinerem reuerteris*: "Gusano gusarapiento / gusano de mil malicias / hombre de dos mil codicias / que contino estás hambriento: / sonido que lleva el viento / viento de poco provecho / hedificio sin cimiento / hazes tuerto del derecho. / Abre, ciego, bien los ojos, / no mires como mundano / pues que tienes en tu mano / la rienda de tus antojos" (*Cancionero*, ed. facsimile [Madrid, 1928], fol. xxv).

9. See Fidèle de Ros, *Le Frère Bernardin de Laredo* (Paris, 1948), p. 108.

order that your life may match your nature. You are a man; live a human life." [10] Alonso de Orozco (d. 1591) addresses the sinner: "Oh, sinner: consider the rational nobility that the Creator bestowed upon you. Be not a bastard son; renounce not the glorious nature given you when you were made like unto the angels." [11] Hernando de Zárate (d. 1596?) says that, as a result of the Fall, man, tormented by his passions, may be considered the most miserable animal on earth. [12]

What must man do to rise above this misery? He must live like a man, as St. Thomas of Villanueva urged. Already in 1521 Alonso de Madrid has the formula: "Then is man fully in the image of God when he busies himself with knowing and loving the manifestations of His greatness." [13] Nearly three generations later, in 1596, Alonso López Pinciano, author of one of the best commentaries on Aristotle's *Poetics* produced anywhere during the Renaissance, declared that human happiness consists in the contemplation of the truth. [14] Juan Eusebio Nieremberg (d. 1658) said in his *Epistolario* that "so glorious is the end of man, that not only the human means of attaining it are glorious, but the divine sacrifice that made this possible — God's having become flesh to dwell among us — is the greatest conceivable honor of man, which even the angels could envy." [15] For Gracián, who died in the year that Nieremberg wrote the above-quoted words, man was an enigma. The best book in the world, says Gracián, is the world itself. The heavens are an extended parchment, and the stars are letters whose message is easily understood. The difficulty consists in understanding sublunar things, where all is written in cipher and human hearts are inscrutable. There, the best of readers is at a loss. [16]

Whether these writers regard man as worm or angel, as triumphant traverser of the antipodes or as a sealed enigma, they agree on one thing: man's soul is infinitely precious, and can be saved. His salvation depends on his own free will. Pedro Malón de Chaide

10. Cited by R. Ricard, "Notes et matériaux pour l'étude du 'socratisme chrétien' chez Sainte Thérèse et les spirituels espagnols," Part II, *BHi*, XLIX (1947), 183.
11. *Victoria de la muerte* (Madrid, 1921), p. 3.
12. *Discursos de la paciencia cristiana*, *BAE*, XXVII, 421b.
13. *Arte para servir a Dios*, *NBAE*, XVI, 590ab.
14. *Philosophia antigua poética*, ed. Alfredo Carballo Picazo (Madrid, 1953), I, 212.
15. Ed. Narciso Alonso Cortés (Madrid, 1915), pp. 238–39.
16. *El Criticón*, ed. M. Romera-Navarro (Philadelphia, 1938–40), III, 118–9.

in the rather late year of 1588 uses figures of speech employed in Italy a century earlier by Pico della Mirandola in his *Oration on the Dignity of Man*. At the time of the Creation, says Malón de Chaide, God took man, still without individual face or image, and, placing him in the midst of the other animals, said to him: "I give you neither fixed abode, nor a face of your own, nor any particular gift. You shall have a seat of your own choice. The face and the gifts you may prefer, shall be yours. You are bound by no law, by no limit. By your own will — in whose charge I place you — you shall make your law. I have made you neither celestial nor eternal, neither mortal nor immortal; you shall be the determiner and the sculptor of yourself. You can degenerate to lower things or transform yourself into superior things, as it may seem best to you." [17]

SOUL AND BODY

With this brief summary as an introduction, we may now profitably examine some of the anthropological problems that Spanish Christian thinkers sought to solve. The first of these concerns the nature of the human being — a composite of two not easily reconciled parts, an immortal soul and a mortal body.[18]

17. *La conversión de la Magdalena*, ed. P. Félix Garcia (Madrid, 1947), I, p. 103.

18. "For others . . . the ultimate explanation of our contradictions lies in the essential composite character of our being: body and soul. . . . This can be understood in two very different ways which correspond to two conceptions of the composite soul-body, that is to say, to two conceptions of man. For some, indeed, the human composite must be understood as a prison of the soul [Origen (d. 254)], which is impeded by the body in its effort to satisfy its own tendencies, producing thus in man an internal struggle on the part of his spiritual aspirations against the barriers of the flesh, until death frees the soul from its slavery, permitting it to live its own life, happy, harmonious, and without internal contradictions: such an opinion Suárez attributes to Scotus and indeed it is latent in many ascetic writers. For others . . . , the composite soul-body is to be understood as the union of two elements which, although of different nature, are essentially destined to form such a union, so that when death separates them, one of them (the body) ceases to exist as such, and the other (the soul) subsists in a state of incompleteness, retaining a natural appetite for reunion with the other part. And even within this last conception one may distinguish between those who believe that the union with the body gives the soul more benefits than disadvantages, and those who hold the opposite view" (Benzo Mestre, *op. cit.*, p. 514). All of these solutions to the problem of man are *católicas* ("Catholic"), according to Mestre. On whether or not Origen and Origenism were condemned as heretical, see below. Important writers have held that they were.

Vives, in his *De anima et vita* (1538), declared: "To know what the soul is, is of no importance to us, though it is important, immensely so, to know . . . what its operations are." [19] Foster Watson has said of Vives that he "is the first, in modern times, to lay stress on what the soul does, or on what its manifestations are, instead of confining inquiries into what the essence of the soul is." [20] That may be true; but Vives' insistence on studying the soul's operations is based on centuries of uncertainty as to how the soul should be conceived, i.e., of vacillation between the two great poles of medieval thought: the Platonic-Augustinian and the Aristotelian-Thomistic. It implies the acceptance of the concept of the soul as activity or operation, as this was worked out by the philosophers and theologians of Scholasticism. The difficulty of the matter lay in the apparent irreconcilability of the conflicting ideas of man as an indivisible composite of body-and-spirit. How could the personality survive the breaking of this union; i.e., how could the union be immortal? How could an eternal soul escape the consequences of the break-up? How could it continue, after death, to be what it had been — a composite? The answer, as we shall see more clearly, was found by considering the soul as an operative force.

"God is spirit, and they that worship Him must worship Him in spirit and in truth" (John 4:24). Almost everyone, says Etienne Gilson,[21] holds the mistaken belief that Christianity is a clear-cut spiritualism. There are many passages in the Bible which tend to re-enforce such a belief. What shall it profit a man to gain the whole universe, if he lose his soul? To cultivate his soul, to free it by purifying it and to save it by freeing it — such would appear to be the proper end of the Christian. And yet Christian philosophers do not direct all their effort or concentrate all their thought on the spiritual part of man to the neglect of the mortal part (the body). St. Bonaventure, St. Thomas, Duns Scotus, even St. Francis of Assisi respected their bodies, extolled the dignity of their human frame, and never consented to separate the destiny of the body from that of the soul. How can this be explained, and what

---

19. *Tratado del alma*, trans. J. Ontañón (Madrid, 1923), p. 61.
20. *Luis Vives, el Gran Valenciano (1492–1540)* (Oxford, 1922), p. 98.
21. In the chapter on Christian anthropology in *L'Esprit de la philosophie médiévale* (Paris, 1944), p. 175. The following discussion is from this chapter.

does its explanation tell us of the true nature of Christian man both in and outside of Spain?

How does it happen that Christian thought, which for so many years after St. Augustine followed the doctrine of Plato as set forth in the *Phaedo*, should have yielded progressively (and so greatly) to the influence of Aristotle? [22] Gilson, in answering this question, points out first of all that the "Good News" of the Gospel announced not merely the salvation of souls but the salvation of men, that is to say, the salvation of each of those individual beings, with his flesh, his members, all the structure of corporal organs without which each one of them would feel himself to be nothing but the shade of himself. The resurrection of Christ was the promise and the proof of the resurrection of all Christians: the dead shall rise up incorruptible, and we shall be transformed; the corruption of the body shall put on incorruption (I Cor. 53). In their effort to give to this "Good News" a philosophic basis, the Christians of the first twelve centuries leaned now toward Plato, now toward Aristotle. It was only with St. Thomas in the thirteenth century that, passing beyond both Plato and Aristotle, Christian philosophy revealed its creative originality.

In the doctrine of Plato, the body is perishable; the soul, by means of philosophy, rids itself progressively of matter until death enables it to give itself over to the contemplation of the Ideas. Man is thus "a soul that makes use of its body." St. Augustine gives the definition: "man is a rational soul which possesses a body," adding, however, that this soul-and-body form a single man. As against Plato, Augustine would preserve the unity and the permanence of the human composite. The Christian can not believe, as Plato did, that the soul's presence in the body was the result of a fall; it was in the Garden and before the Fall that God formed man of the dust of the ground and breathed into Adam's nostrils "and he became a living soul." For the Christian, there-

22. "Parmi les problèmes qui, pendant la seconde moitié du XIII⁰ siècle, séparent ce que l'on est convenu d'appeler l'augustinisme et l'aristotélisme, figurent trois questions de psychologie: l'âme est-elle simple ou est-elle composée de matière et de forme; l'âme est-elle unique ou multiple en l'homme; l'âme est-elle identique à ses facultés ou en est-elle distincte?" (D. Odon Lottin, *Psychologie et morale aux XII⁰ et XIII⁰ siècles* [Louvain–Gembloux, 1942–60], I, 427). See also W. Ellis, *The Idea of the Soul in Western Philosophy and Science* (London, 1940).

fore, man is a substantial composite, not an accidental juxtaposition, as he was for Plato. Augustine, firm in his affirmation of this compositeness, was unable to justify it philosophically (Gilson, *op cit.*, p. 181). It is for this reason that the Aristotelian definition of the soul, apparently so ill-adapted to Christian thought, was at an early date taken into account by certain philosophers and theologians, in the face of strong opposition (e.g., by Nemesius of Emesa). By the thirteenth century, Aristotle's definition normally appeared as one among various ones considered as acceptable.

The soul, according to Aristotle, is the act or the form of the organized body. The relation of body to soul is thus a particular case of the relation of form and matter. With this definition, the substantial unity of man presents no difficulty, but certain consequences of the unity so conceived are disturbing: to follow Aristotle is to run into difficulty in the matter of the soul's immortality, as the anti-Averroist controveries of the thirteenth century attest.

Yet there existed a partially satisfactory solution (which would be replaced by a better one when philosophical progress made possible an acceptable solution). Strange to say, it was the Arabic philosopher Avicenna (d. 1037), whose works became known in Latin early in the thirteenth century, who provided Christian philosophers with a formula capable of saving both Plato's immortality and Aristotle's unity of the human composite. It is Avicenna's solution that is found in the *Summa* of Alexander of Hales (d. 1245), in the *Commentarium* of his pupil, St. Bonaventure (d. 1274), and in other lesser theologians. St. Bonaventure strengthens the doctrine of Avicenna with that of ibn Gabirol (13 c.). Albertus Magnus (d. 1280) holds to the definition of Avicenna.

But all of this was too easy an eclecticism and was first upset and later superseded by St. Thomas Aquinas. Asserting that union with the body is not included in the essence of the soul *as soul*, Aquinas uses the Aristotelian terms: the soul is a form which possesses and bestows subantiality. Wherever there are acts of thought, there are thinking substances: it is a man, not a sensibility, that feels; it is a man, not an intellect, that thinks. Man is a substantial being, and it is to the substantiality of his soul that he owes his own substantiality. The human soul is therefore essentially an act. The body has no subsistence except as it receives subsistence from its form, which is the soul. Hence, if at death the principle which gives to the body its being is withdrawn, the body is dissolved without affecting the soul. The soul is an immortal substance which can develop its activity only with the aid of sense organs; to obtain this aid, it actualizes a bit of matter; this bit of matter becomes a body only through the soul's operation. Man, therefore, is neither his body nor his soul, because the body subsists only because of the soul. Man is the unity of a soul which substantializes his body, and of a body in which this soul subsists as a substantializing force.

We can now return to Vives who, after all, does venture to give a definition of the soul in a chapter of his *De anima (ed. cit.,* pp. 159–60):

We can therefore say that the human soul is a spirit which makes possible the life of the body to which it is united, possessing the power to know and to love God, and to join itself to Him to achieve everlasting blessedness. Indeed, just as our soul [at the time of its incarnation] descends from the highest to the lowest (which is our body) by virtue of the love which God, as its author, bears it . . . , so also the [incarnated] soul rises and returns to its origin by means of divine knowledge and love. So it is that it descends from the heights to the depths; it rises later from this to that, a process which is manifest in our entire life, since man lives at first as a plant [vegetative life], later as an animal [conscious life], and finally with truly human [or rational] life. When purified, he mounts above terrestrial things, is converted into an angel, and finally, joined to God, he himself is also deified in a certain way. Such is our ascending progression from inert matter to the senses, from the senses to the imagination and the fancy, from the imagination to reason and reflection, and finally to love. The descent [of the sinning soul] is just the opposite; for the soul becomes perverted when it yields its judgment to the passions, or when reason submits to the fancy, as if the body were to try to walk with its feet extended aloft and its head upon the ground.

The soul, says Calderón,

vive en la tierra obligada	lives here below under obliga-
a subirse a ser estrella	tion to mount to Heaven and
o a reducirse a ser ascua.[23]	become a star, or sink to Hell as
	a coal of fire.

Body and soul carry within them their destiny: the body returns to the dust from which God fashioned it; the soul rises to Heaven

23. From *Los alimentos del hombre,* cited by Frutos, *op. cit.,* p. 552.

or descends to Hell. Since man is a dual creature, the elements of the composite do not have a univocal destiny; but the true destiny of man is, as phrased by Tennyson (*In Memoriam, CXVIII*), to

> Move upward, working out the beast,
> And let the ape and tiger die.

In *La nave del mercader*, Calderón again addresses himself to the problem (cited by Frutos, pp. 552–53):

Hombre de tierra terreno,	Earthy man of the earth, know
sabe que también ha habido	that the Son of Man in Heaven
Hombre de cielo celeste,	existed and exists, and if you by
y si tú con albedrío,	exercise of free will (though you
siendo terreno, te unes	be earthy) rise to join Him on
al Celeste, ten creído	high, you too will become heav-
que a celeste de terreno	enly like Him, and He in grati-
subas, y él agradecido,	tude will come down to meet
a terreno de celeste	your soul, so that at one and the
baje; con que a un tiempo mismo	same time a bond of brotherhood
serán, en un lazo de hermandad unidos,	will join the Divine to the hu-
Divino el humano, y humano el Divino.	man and the human to the Divine.

The three souls of man

As St. Augustine taught, man occupies an intermediate position between the angels and the beasts: the brute is irrational and mortal; the angel, rational and immortal; man, inferior to the angels, is superior to the brutes, sharing the mortality of the latter and the rationality of the former. He may be defined, therefore, as a rational, mortal animal.[24] This is echoed in the *Visión delectable* of Alfonso de la Torre, who says: "it is fitting, therefore, that just as man has his place between the angels and the animals, his life should be an intermediate life"; and that "On the second level, man is considered as an animal; and according to this, it is fitting that his make-up should be like that of the beasts, and that he obey the dictates of the concupiscent appetite and of anger; consequently, certain men are envious, others are gluttonous and winebibbers and proud; or timorous or miserly, and so on with respect to the other passions."[25] And he concludes: "The third

24. Marías, *op. cit.*, p. 112.
25. *BAE*, XXXVI, 383b and 367b.

aspect is, that man, considered in his human quality should be just, liberal, prudent, temperate, strong and orderly in his behavior. The first life is called angelic, the second bestial, the third human life" (*ibid.*). The details of man's angelic life are specified somewhat farther on in the *Visión* (p. 372 ab):

And in this manner man is gifted with the virtue of understanding, because of which he is honored and compared to the angels . . . and is similar to God (for he resembles Him in no other way); on the contrary, in other things he resembles the dumb beasts. And so great is the excellence of him who understands when compared with those who do not understand, that it would be like comparing a man with the mule he rides; for this one virtue is incorruptible . . . nor can the body prevail against it; rather it prevails against the body, and he who lives in accordance with this virtue is an angel, and when he dies he becomes an intelligence [i.e., a spiritual being]. . . . And there is no doubt that there is nothing so excellent on the earth as man's intelligence, which is not composed of earthly matter, but of the light and the largesse of intelligence. . . .

Man, we are told by Hernán Pérez de Oliva in his *Diálogo de la dignidad del hombre* (before 1531), has a soul which is similar to God and a body similar to the world,[26] so that he lives like a plant, feels like a brute, and understands like an angel.[27]

Two generations later the same ideas appear in the *Diálogos de la conquista del Reino de Dios* (1608) of Fray Juan de los Angeles: "In man we behold three different kinds of men: animal, rational, godlike or divine. Each one of these men has an inner force or faculty whereby he recognizes and understands, and another which inclines him to flee from — or to desire — that which the former faculty has already appraised as being dangerous or desirable." These "three men" are considered by Fray Juan as being really three parts of the soul: inferior, intermediate, and superior. Of the superior part of the soul he tells us little: it is the "apex of the soul," the *synteresis* of the mystics: "here there is supreme calm and supreme silence, for this center is never approached by any representation of a created thing, and because of it we are divine or resemble God, or are so similar to God that the supreme wisdom calls us gods. This intimate and naked place, empty and without

26. See below our treatment of *macrocosmos-microcosmos.*
27. *BAE*, LXV, 390b.

figures, is raised above all other created things, and above all the senses and the powers of the soul, beyond time and place . . . in perpetual union with God. . . ."[28]

Matter

We have already seen that, once St. Thomas had arrived at his conception of the soul as a form which possesses substantiality and bestows it on the material body, the nature of the human composite of body-and-soul did not cause great difficulty to Catholic thinkers. We have seen also, in the quotations reproduced in the preceding section, that the triple nature of man — animal, rational, godlike or divine — was regarded as a natural consequence of the place which God had assigned to man in the Great Chain of Being, midway between angel and beast. It is therefore not surprising to find that few of our thinkers show distress or concern over the fact that man is not pure spirit, that he has a body, and that this body is composed of matter.

Living spirit and intelligible reality, St. Thomas taught, have a lower limit below which their existence takes place attended by a strange and unspeakable weakening. The light of understanding has its penumbra in the senses and its darkness in matter. Matter is a residue of spirit, a degenerating of the spirit. And when we seek to decipher nature . . . we become aware everywhere, and in ourselves as well, of this obscure power which circulates through phenomena, ever identical to itself and free from phenomenal transformations, ungraspable, unthinkable, and yet forming a substratum both of thought and of being. . . .

Spirit and matter are, in the last analysis, only degrees of more and less — of more and less perfection, of more and less being. Matter is only weakened spirit . . . a precipitate of spirit, and indirectly it tends back toward spirit, under the auspices of being. . . . The universal ocean ever floods us with its substance and its forces. By means of knowledge it seeks to flood us also with its forms and its secret reasons. Maternal in her relation to spirits as well as to bodies, Nature prepares for the nourishment of mankind songs as well as milk. But what songs can be fully understood by the dulled hearing of a soul that is earth-bound? Earth-bound it may be, but our soul is spirit. Its thinking faculty . . . does not exclude matter. . . . Its object is universal, and object and subject must of necessity correspond, each to the other.[29]

28. Cited by A. González Palencia, *Del Lazarillo a Quevedo* (Madrid, 1946), pp. 189 and 193–94.
29. A. D. Sertillanges, *Les grandes thèses de la philosophie thomiste* (Paris, 1928), pp. 30, 33, 35.

The Hermetic writings (*ca.* 150 A.D.) offer a different statement of the duality of man, much more optimistic, under the picture of the intimate, loving embrace of heaven and earth. Material nature, far from being evil, is "a beautiful image of God." From

the Stoic, Hermetic, and Cabalistic writings these convictions were taken over by Cusanus [d. 1464], Pico [d. 1494], Reuchlin [d. 1522], and others, and poured into the main stream of Renaissance thought. . . . This approval of the world of phenomena and matter was a welcome philosophical confirmation of what was already a firm, vital conviction and a mainspring of action. Most of Renaissance art, even of religious art, was an apotheosis of the material, a glorification of the human body, of fabrics, jewels, and all the accessories of living, of human environment in man-made architecture and God-made landscape. The expansionism of the era . . . represents altogether a positive turning of man toward the material world for the purpose of suffusing it with man's own mediatorial spirit, forming and ennobling it, humanizing it, raising it toward the divine.[30]

New as this fifteenth-century development may at first glance appear, it is after all not out of keeping with St. Thomas, who taught, as we have seen, that it is the human spirit that gives substantiality to matter in the composite of body-and-soul; who declared that spirit does not exclude matter and asserted that, in the last analysis, spirit and matter are only degrees of greater or less perfection.

Yet the old Neoplatonic flight from matter is not altogether forgotten. The Spanish writer in whom I have found it as a main preoccupation belongs precisely to the period that extends from Cusanus to Reuchlin. He is Alfonso de la Torre, author of our frequently cited *Visión delectable,* a work whose first six chapters furnished to Lope de Vega the material on the Seven Liberal Arts that he incorporated into his *Arcadia* (1598).[31]

La Torre's position, essentially, is this: "It is impossible to make anything from material that is not in the proper state, in the same way that a mirror does not receive images unless it has been cleaned and polished" (*ed. cit.,* p. 365b).

Since before anything can be made there must first exist material from which to make it, the Creator "saw that the world could not

30. Harold Jantz, *Goethe's Faust as a Renaissance Man: Parallels and Prototypes* (Princeton, 1951), pp. 103–4.

31. J. P. Wickersham Crawford, "The Seven Liberal Arts in Lope de Vega's *Arcadia,*" *MLN*, XXX (1915), 13 ff.

be caused without having material, efficient, and final causes; and therefore he produced matter, which came into being from non-existence, and from it He made all things, except the angels; and He made the heavens of the fifth essence, and all inanimate things He made of matter" (*ibid.*, p. 363a). This matter, however, proved refractory. God could have created an Adam who would never have sinned, but neither the world nor man could have received this divine action *por la inobediencia de la materia* — "because of the resistance of matter." And the author gives as illustration the carpenter whose workmen failed to hew a straight beam from a crooked log, though their skill and the measurements given them were perfect (*ibid.*, p. 362a).

The questions raised become deep. Understanding asks of Wisdom if the angels are capable of sin, and Wisdom replies: "I must insist that all evil arises from matter . . . and as they are immaterial, they can in no way sin." When pushed in connection with the problem of evil and its first appearance in the universe, Wisdom says that the angels sinned by willing what was evil. "And what gave them that will?" asks Understanding. Wisdom replies: "This is one of the questions which can be apprehended not by knowledge but by faith . . . ." (p. 364ab).

The question of evil and its source in matter will not down. Farther on the author insists that things receive the goodness of God in proportion to their receptiveness, and that if the *material* from which an ant or a fly has been created were able to receive human form, God in his generosity would give human form to those creatures. Consequently, man *fué el mejor que pudiera ser* — "emerged from the hands of God with as great perfection as he could receive" — and God did not make him better because He saw that, being formed of corruptible matter, he could receive no further perfection. Understanding then asks: "And why could not God make man like an angel, free from sin?" Wisdom replies: "If He were to have made him more perfect, it would have had to be without admixture of matter, and in that case he would not have been a man" (p. 386b).

There is a further complication which arises from the differences between individual men. Not all matter is the same, since the heavenly bodies have the power to dispose matter so that it is favorable or unfavorable: "the imperfections of man have their source in matter, which, if it is well disposed, causes men to be better, or worse [if ill disposed]. Some men long to eat sour things, others sweet, or dry; others lust after women, or are given to thieving. But these inclinations—and here the problem shifts from that of evil to that of free will—cannot compel the human spirit, which retains its liberty of choice, and will choose wisely if it possesses the virtue of Prudence" (p. 387b).

La Torre fails to reconcile evil and goodness: if man were to have been better, he would have had to be free from matter, but God chose to make him "from the dust of the ground." Genesis relates this act of creation with no repugnance, simply and beautifully. Fray Luis de León in *De los nombres de Cristo* (1583) regards the substance of the body and of the soul as good:

between these two things I have mentioned, of which one is the substance of the body and of the soul, and the other is this poison and evil spirit [of original sin], there is this difference . . . : that the substance of the body and of the soul in itself is good, and is the work of God, and if we trace things to their source, we have it only from Him. Because the soul is created by Him alone; and He alone is the maker of the body, having made it originally from a bit of earth; and it is no less true that He is also the author of all bodies produced from that first body in the succession of time, as each human being is born. But the other poisonous and haughty spirit is in no way the work of God, nor is it produced in us by His desire and will, but rather it is the work of the devil and of the first man: of the devil, inspiring and persuading; of man, voluntarily and culpably receiving it within himself. And thus, this and this only is what the Scripture calls the old man in us, or the old Adam, because it is the work of Adam: that is, because it is, not what Adam received from God, but what Adam produced in himself by his own sin and with the power of the devil.[32]

This defense of the goodness of the body, with its interpretation of the old Adam that every just man is required to overcome in himself, is perfectly consistent with the traditional attitude of the great theologians mentioned earlier: St. Bonaventure, St. Thomas, Duns Scotus, St. Francis of Assisi.[33] The defense would not have been written, however, had Fray Luis not been aware that for some persons the old Adam represented—no matter how confusedly—an original taint; that for such people our material

32. Ed. Clásicos Castellanos (Madrid, 1914–22), I, 205–6.
33. Gilson, *op. cit.*, chapter on Christian Anthropology.

bodies are in some way the enemy of God and His righteousness. The theologian Alfonso de Castro in his *Adversus Haereses* (Antwerp, 1591) felt it necessary to combat what he regarded as the heresy of Origen, who taught that the souls of men were guilty before their incarnation in the body, and that it was as a punishment that the souls were incarcerated in the flesh.[34] If Origen's contention were true, wrote Castro, Christ (who never sinned) would not have been incarnated in a material body. Yet had not St. Paul said that "the flesh lusteth against the Spirit, and the Spirit against the flesh?" (Gal. 5:17) — *Sic et Non*: human dignity and human misery.

SELF-KNOWLEDGE

"Christian self-knowledge centers about an awareness of the dignity of the creature and a simultaneous recognition of his misery, without risking the dangers of pride and despair of self; it is a more ontological self-knowledge than the Greek in the sense that it is involved both with intellect and emotion."[35] "Provided it is subordinated to the doctrine of salvation, self-knowledge becomes an absolute necessity, one may even say that it is at one and the same time the beginning of all knowledge, the only object of knowledge, the ultimate object of knowledge. Not that the rest is useless — far from it — but it is so unless it is founded on the knowledge of man. . . . In order to know oneself, it is . . . necessary to set oneself in one's place, below the things to which one is inferior, above all things to which one is superior."[36] Such assessments bring one to a contemplation of what Pascal called the *grandeur et misère de l'homme*. By his intelligence, man is above the beasts; by reason of his ignorance, below the angels. Man's dignity arises from the fact that he bears God's image. By his liberty, he commands Nature and uses her; by his intelligence, he comes to know

34. F. G. Sánchez-Marín and V. Gutiérrez-Durán, *Doctrina de Trento: Imagen del hombre según nuestros teólogos* (Madrid, 1946), p. 170.
35. Marion Monaco, "Racine and the Problem of Suicide," *PMLA*, LXX (1955), 445.
36. "La connaissance de soi-même et le socratisme chrétien," ch. XI of Gilson, *op. cit.*, pp. 219 ff. See also Ricard, *op. cit.*, I, 5 ff. and 170 ff, and II, 5 ff. (Gilson neglects Spain).

her and to dominate her; but at the same time, he knows that his dignity does not come from himself, and this is the first step in the recognition of his misery. Created in the honor of his resemblance to God, man loses that honor if he forgets its source. The analogical argument leads man from knowledge of self to knowledge of God.

"Since the awareness of our nature leads us to the nature of God, he who knows not himself simply as a man fails to know his Maker," wrote Sabunde in his *Theologia naturalis*.[37] He proceeds to explain: "Inasmuch as no work of God is so close to man as man himself, the knowledge which man will construct by coming to know himself (who is one of God's works) will be greater than any other knowledge. He who knows himself, and who knows himself as a creature and artifact of God, will learn incomparably more about the nature and grandeur of his Creator than he will acquire by studying any other creature whatsoever."[38]

This doctrine is repeated by Spaniards throughout our period. Vives in his *Introduction to Wisdom* says: "This is life eternal, says our Lord Christ Jesus, that we know the Father and Jesus Christ, the only begotten Son whom He sent. This is the path to perfect wisdom, whereon the first step is for man to know himself, and the last step, to know God."[39]

Fray Luis de Granada, after copying St. Augustine's Soliloquy in Book X of the *Confessions* ("Thanks to Thee, o my Light; because with thy light I found Thee, and found also myself"), quotes St. Bernard, who imagines God as addressing His creature: "O man, if you but knew yourself well, you would be discontented with yourself, and would be grateful to me; but since you do not know yourself, you are full of self-pride, and are displeasing to me. There will come a time when you will satisfy neither yourself nor me. You will not satisfy me, because you sinned; nor yourself, because you will be burning in eternal fire."[40] The human body, center and sum of the perfections of the visible world, is the material reality which most ostensibly reveals the character

37. Trans. Michel de Montaigne (*Oeuvres Complètes de Michel de Montaigne*, ed. A. Armaingaud [Paris, 1924–41]), II, 249.
38. *Ibid.*, I, 354.
39. *Introducción a la sabiduría* (Madrid, 1944), p. 108.
40. *Obras*, I (Madrid, 1768), 18 and 444.

and condition of the world of phenomena. The study, therefore, of human anatomy is the noblest testimony to the greatness of the Creator. It is with this thought in mind that Fray Luis includes, in his magnificent exposition of the Creed, *Introducción del Símbolo de la Fe,* a brief treatise on the structure of the human body, in which the researches of the school of Vesalius are utilized.[41]

The other Luis, Fray Luis de León, declares that the beginning and foundation of all blessings is that each person know himself; and, inversely, that not to know oneself, and to consider oneself to be what one is not, is the source of human error in this life.[42] The same theme is developed in his *Ode* to the musician Salinas. When Salinas plays, says Fray Luis in his first stanzas, the air becomes serene and clothes itself with unaccustomed light and beauty; at the sound the poet's soul rises from its forgetfulness and recovers its lost recollection of its heavenly source:

> For this new knowledge then
> Its nobler thoughts and destiny restores:
> Of gold, vain lure of men,
> Which the blind crowd adores,
> The perishable beauty it ignores.
>
> Up through the fields of air
> It wings, till in the highest sphere it dwells,
> And a new music there
> It hears, music that wells
> Undying and all other kinds excels.
>
> The great Master it sees,
> His hand upon the mighty lyre, with train
> Of skillful cadences,
> Create the holy strain
> That this eternal temple doth sustain.[43]

41. Laín Entralgo, *La antropología en la obra de Fray Luis de Granada,* p. 216. See also my review in *HR,* XVII (1949), 180.

42. Alain Guy, *La pensée de Fray Luis de León* (Limoges, 1943), p. 428.

43. Trans. Aubrey F. G. Bell, in Eleanor I. Turnbull (ed.), *Ten Centuries of Spanish Poetry* (Baltimore, 1955), pp. 175 f. Here is the original text: "Y como se conoce / en suerte y pensamientos se mejora, / el oro desconoce / que el vulgo ciego adora, / la belleza caduca, engañadora. / Traspasa el aire todo / hasta llegar a la más alta esfera, / y oye allí otro modo / de no perecedera / música, que es de todas la primera. / Ve cómo el gran maestro, / a aquesta inmensa cítara aplicado, / con movimiento diestro / produce el son sagrado, / con que este eterno templo es sustentado."

In the ninth Crisi of *El Criticón*, Gracián, following the same line of thought as did Granada in his treatise on anatomy in *Introducción del Símbolo de la fe*, causes Andrenio (whose first years were spent in a cleft in the mountains, with no view of the world or of himself) to tell of his joyous amazement when he first beheld himself (after his release) reflected in the waters of a fountain. He thus became, to himself, "the greatest prodigy," and he evokes again the thoughts then suggested to him by the various parts of his human form; after which his mentor Critilo (who adds the commentary of experience to the amazement and admiration of youth) formulates the traditional argument by design: "Here I have noted . . . that, although the parts of this great republic of the human body are so numerous that the mere number of the bones equals that of the days of the year, and this greatness of number [is controlled by] a harmony such that there is no number (among the various digits) that does not correspond to some of the various parts (the senses being five, the bodily humors four, the faculties of the soul three, the eyes two), all these parts are pyramided upward toward the single head, which is thus an image and *figura* of the Divine Prime Mover. . . ." [44]

Calderón, ever conscious of theological problems, in the *auto* entitled *El pintor de su deshonra* points out that the supreme information concerning man's being must come, in the last analysis, not from man himself but from his Creator. This is the doctrine of Grace. Without enlightenment from God, self-study cannot give self-knowledge:

¿Quién eres,	Who are you, powerful Painter,
Pintor, de tanto poder,	who, lifting non-being into be-
que dando ser al no ser,	ing, proclaim by that very act
diciendo a voces estás	that you are more and are greater
que eres más y vales más,	than all, since your Being comes
pues muestra el Ser que mantienes	to you from no other, while you
que Tú de nadie le tienes	are a bestower of being upon
pues para todos le das? [45]	others?

44. The text (*Obras, ed. cit.*, I, 267–68) is difficult and therefore I give the original: "Y aquí he notado yo con especial atención — dixo Critilo — que aunque las partes desta gran república del cuerpo son tantas, que solos los huessos llenan los días del año, y esta numerosidad, con tal armonía que no ay número que no se emplee en ellas, como, digamos, cinco son los sentidos, quatro los humores, tres las potencias, dos los ojos: todos vienen a reducirse a la unidad de una cabeça, retrato de aquel primer móbil divino a quien viene a reducirse por sus gradas toda esta universal dependencia."
45. Cited by Frutos, *op. cit.*, pp. 532–33.

Without this gift of Divine Grace, even the self-searcher is at a loss: in order to know who he is, man must know who he has been, and this is hidden from mere human intelligence (*ibid.*, p. 531):

pues si quien a mí sin mí me hizo, no me informa aquí a mí de mí, será llano, de ansias mis discursos llenos, torne mi discurso atrás; pues cuando sé de mí más es cuando de mí sé menos.	For if He who created me without my participation in the act of creation does not inform me concerning myself, it is obvious that my searching will be mere wandering in a circle; since when I know most about myself is when I find myself most deprived of self-knowledge.

To Alexander Pope man was

The glory, jest, and riddle of the world.[46]

Calderón could have accepted the definition, but with this reservation: jest and riddle man might be, but with God's gift of Grace there could be no question of his glory; and the gift of Grace would not be lacking. In *La siembra del Señor*, God the Father says to his fallen children in Eden: *De la tierra alzad, amigos* — "Rise up from the earth, my friends." And Adam replies: [47]

Sí haremos, pues tú lo mandas, porque se vea en aqueste rasgo de piedad tan vana, que los que a servirte llegan de la tierra se levantan.	That we will, since you command us, and in order that this act of filial piety — though in itself it have no merit — may proclaim that those who come to serve you are lifted from the ground.

This "rising from the ground," says Frutos (*ibid.*) is effected by the call of Grace, and He who places man under the Law of Grace is Jesus Christ. This is the call to the heavenly Jerusalem:

que verás dibujada del Celestial Pincel en bosquejos, si acaso la Apocalipsi lees.	which you will see portrayed, or rather suggested as in a sketch, by the Divine Brush if you should chance to read the Book of Revelation.

Dignitas hominis

Study of his own nature inevitably leads man to a consideration of the fact that he partakes both of the God-like and the non-

46. Cited by Tillyard, *The Elizabethan World Picture* (London, 1948), p. 61.
47. Frutos, *op. cit.*, p. 541.

God-like. *Terram diligis?* asked St. Augustine, and gave the answer: *Terra eris*—"Dost thou love the earth? Thou shalt become earth." And he then presents, in a similar question and a similar answer, the opposite pole of man's destiny. *Deum diligis?* . . . *Deus eris*—"Dost thou love God? Thou shalt be deified."[48] Man is a proud yet a wretched thing. "Let us consider diligently the comparison of these two diverse conditions," wrote Sabunde; "let us see what man was like in his original innocence, what he is like now; where he was then, where he is at present; the infinity of the blessings he has lost and the incomparable greatness of the evils he has acquired, in order that we may instruct ourselves in the full knowledge of our nature, which consists in an awareness of man's perfection and of his fall."[49]

Leaving man's misery for a later section, we shall here provide the historical background necessary to understand what have been regarded as "Renaissance" eulogies of the human condition in Spanish literature of the Golden Age.

The Christian philosopher Boethius (d. 524) in his *De musica* established a Platonic-Pythagorean psychology of harmony. The harmony manifest in man is an essential condition of the ontological accord between the I and the Other. Since man is a microcosm, a world *in parvo*, it is evident that human music is but a concretion of world harmony. The rhythm of our bodies corresponds to the rhythm of things. Man is thus an instrument whose strings respond in sympathetic vibration with the Infinite.[50] Over a thousand years later, Alfonso Salmerón, in his *Commentarii in omnes Epistolas B. Pauli* (1602) declares man to be, among all the works of the Almighty, the most noble creature: *Inter omnia autem opera Dei, homo nobilissima creatura opus eius dicitur;* and Domingo de Soto, in his *De justitia et jure* (1569), after asserting man's dominion over the cosmos, adds: "And in order that the gift of the Divine Mercy might be complete, God gave us even the angels themselves, though their nature be much more worthy than our own."[51]

48. *Tractatus in Epistolam Johannis*, II, cap. 2.
49. *Op. cit.*, II, 115.
50. Edgar de Bruyne, *Estudios de estética medieval*, trans. Fr. A. Suárez (Madrid, 1958–59), I, 36.
51. Sánchez-Marín and Gutiérrez-Durán, *op. cit.*, pp. 142, 146, 163–64.

Between these extremes (from the sixth century A.D. to the period after Trent) there are, in Spain, many declarations of human dignity to be recorded — many more than can possibly enter into our discussion. Before recording the ones that I have chosen, it will be well to see what happened, for example, in England.

E. M. W. Tillyard begins his presentation of *The Elizabethan World Picture* with an introductory short chapter in which he quotes Hamlet's famous words on man: "What a piece of work is man: how noble in reason; how infinite in faculty; in form and moving how express and admirable; in action how like an angel; in apprehension how like a god; the beauty of the world, the paragon of animals."

"This has been taken," says Mr. Tillyard, "as one of the great English versions of Renaissance humanism, an assertion of the dignity of man against the misconceptions of medieval misanthropy. Actually it is in the purest medieval tradition: Shakespeare's version of the orthodox encomia of what man, created in God's image, was like in his prelapsarian state and of what ideally he is still capable of being. It also shows Shakespeare placing man in the traditional cosmic setting between the angels and the beasts. It was what the theologians had been saying for centuries. . . . What is true of Hamlet on man is in the main true of Elizabethan thought in general." [52] Herschel Baker, in his Preface to *The Dignity of Man: Studies in the Persistence of an Idea*,[53] defends the same position: "in its estimate of human nature the Renaissance marked no radical departure from the late Middle Ages."

Indeed, we find no radical departure in Spain. Don Juan Manuel (d. 1349?), grandson of King Ferdinand III *el Santo*, wrote in *El libro infinido*: "Certain it is that the reason why man is the noblest of the creatures, is that man is composed of soul and body, and has understanding and the power of reason, and has free will to do

52. Pp. 1–2. Tillyard quotes as typical the following text from Nemesius, a Syrian bishop of the fourth century: "no eloquence may worthily publish forth the manifold pre-eminences and advantages which are bestowed on this creature. He passeth over the vast seas; he rangeth about the wide heavens by his contemplation and conceives the motions and magnitudes of the stars. . . . He is learned in every science and skilful in artificial workings. . . . He talketh with angels, yea with God himself. He hath all the creatures within his dominion."

53. Cambridge, Massachusetts, 1947.

good or evil. And these things are possessed by no other creature, in heaven or on earth, except man." [54]

The doctrine of Sabunde's *Natural Theology* circulates in the *Pensées* of Pascal, and is one of the main influences on St. Francis de Sales (d. 1622). Its influence in Spain extends through all the sixteenth century.[55] This book, so often quoted in the present work, is an affirmation of the belief that God is a rational Creator whose existence is demonstrable from his creation; that man inhabits a rational universe; that it is man's privilege, through use of his free will and the divine gift of grace, to attain to the understanding and the contemplation of the good and the eternal. So excessive is this confidence that the book was, temporarily, placed on the Index. According to Sabunde, man is raised above all earthly things by the freedom of his will. His frame is perfect. God has lifted him from degree to degree, to the dignity of God's very image — which is none other than the freedom of his will. Because he bears this image, all the creatures serve him. All of this is a tremendous hymn of optimism. Some fifty years before Pico della Mirandola, Sabunde finds that among livings things, only man is capable of perfecting himself; only he, in his task of self-perfection, cooperates continuously in the stupendous task of creation. Sabunde shows how, in the Great Chain of Being, fibrous rocks are a link upward with the vegetable kingdom; how sensitive plants are a link with the animal kingdom; and how intelligent animals are a link upward with mankind. In like manner, stupid men with degraded souls are a link downward with intelligent animals like the beaver. Man, according to Sabunde, was created to praise God on behalf of the whole universe. By doing so he saves his soul.

That Sabunde regarded the will as the dominant faculty is patent. Yet his whole system is based on man's ability to reason his way to a knowledge of God. This is likewise the doctrine of St. Thomas, who argues by analogy and design to prove God's existence, but who declares that knowledge through faith surpasses knowledge through demonstration, and goes on to state that in this most excellent knowledge through faith, the Will has the

54. Ed. J. M. Blecua (Granada, 1952), p. 10.
55. I. S. Révah, *Une source de la spiritualité péninsulaire au XVIeme siècle: la "Théologie naturelle" de Raymond Sebond* (Lisbon, 1953), pp. 5–6.

leading place.[56] From Sabunde's hymn of praise to man, I shall quote just one sentence: "Man is distinguished from other beings, not by any defect of his qualities and gifts, but by a superiority of prerogatives which give him distinction and a place of privilege. His reason and his perfectibility, the elevation of his desires and his free will, lift him to a great height, and make of him the sovereign of the earth."[57]

Yet all is not pure optimism in Sabunde. In accordance with his belief in the supremacy of the will (the appetitive and loving faculty), he composes this prayer: "Uncreated Father, Supreme Being, . . . awaken in us, in so far as our hearts are capable of receiving it, an intense flame of love. Turn toward men, these creatures of yours that succumb and falter, who would wish to love and cannot; who knowing how greatly they should love you, love you not."[58]

I shall quote but one other text from the fifteenth century, a stanza from the *Bias contra Fortuna* of the Marqués de Santillana:

Capaz e sancto animal, sobre todos convenía que toviese mayoría e poder universal; pues que éste fué el hombre racional, a los celestes igual al qual fizo e puso nombre.[59]	It was fitting that a holy animal, supremely capable, should have primacy and universal power over all the others; this was rational man, equal to the creatures of Heaven, whom God created and to whom He gave a name.

The line *a los celestes igual* may seem to offer difficulty, when applied to a creature "a little lower than the angels." I shall not attempt to solve the theological problem involved. It will be remembered that Don Juan Manuel in the preceding century pointed up the fact that understanding, reason, and free will were given to no other creature but man, either in Heaven or on earth.[60]

The humanist Pérez de Oliva was one of the important men of his day in Spain. He was one of the first to translate into a modern

56. See my article, "The Concept of Man . . . ," pp. 44 ff.
57. *El hombre y sus deberes* (Madrid, n.d.), p. 25.
58. *Ibid.*, p. 86.
59. From *El Cancionero de Roma*, ed. M. Canal Gómez (Florence, 1935), II, p. 133.
60. See above. It seems to me unnecessary to take Santillana and Don Juan Manuel to task for not taking into account the rebellion of Lucifer and his followers.

European tongue classical dramatic works. Many years before the French Pléiade, he sought to ennoble and elevate his native language by showing how it could be made to express the concepts of, and serve as the vehicle for, certain genres of Greek and Roman literature. His *Diálogo de la dignidad del hombre* is a debate between pessimism about, and confidence in, the goodness of the universe. One of the interlocutors, Aurelio, is the voice of pessimism: all human activity is vanity, and could man but know the ills of life, he would prefer to seek death. Antonio answers him: man is created in God's image. He is master of his fate; all he has to do is to will it, and he can be an angel, made to behold the face of the Father. The human body, reviled by Aurelio, is defended by Antonio in an eloquent passage. Our hands are more precious than all the weapons with which Nature has equipped the brutes, and "great are the miracles of the tongue, which in itself is sufficient to honor the entire body." Man's will, protected by the understanding, is the temple in which we honor God. The artist's ability to create brings him near to his Maker, and contemplation puts the scholar in touch with God. Even death is not terrible: to be forever present with our Creator is "the last . . . for which the first was made."

This dialogue was translated into Italian by Alfonso de Ulloa and was printed in French at Paris in 1583. I shall give but one direct quotation: "For if man emerges from the womb crying, it is not because he is the outcast child of nature, or because the world is not fit for his service, but rather . . . because he finds himself an exile from his true home. He who is a native of Heaven, how can he be happy in any other place, though he be treated well enough? Man is a native of Heaven; therefore do not marvel if you see him weep when he is removed therefrom." [61]

For Vives, all Christian doctrine consists in eliminating the passions and achieving a serenity of spirit which shall expand and rejoice the human heart and make it like unto God and the angels. Man is thus capable of a sort of deification. Indeed, Vives' *Fabula de homine* is an adaptation of Pico della Mirandola's *Oration on*

61. *Ed. cit.*, p. 392a. See W. C. Atkinson, "Hernán Pérez de Oliva: A Biographical and Critical Study," *RHi*, LXXI (1927), 309–484.

the Dignity of Man.[62] Man has three natures: he lives, as an embryo, like a plant; later, like an animal; finally, as a man. By purification of passion he may be joined to God and become, in a sense, a god himself. Thus our life is a long progression from matter to sensitive life; therefrom to imagination, creative fancy, reason; and, finally, to love. Or, it is a degradation, by surrender to the passions, with loss of human qualities. The fact that we can conceive of God proves our immortality; that which understands immortality must itself be immortal. When we achieve such understanding, God recognizes in us a likeness to his Divine Nature and delights therein, more than in the richest temple hands could erect.

Vives is thus a Christian humanist. But he too has his dark side. Our intellect, he insists, is weak. We can comprehend but little in this life, and what we understand is uncertain and obscure. Our minds, imprisoned in the flesh, live in darkness and ignorance; the edge of the intellect is so dull that it cannot cut even through the surface of things. Yet Christ chose to redeem all men: let no man scorn his soul, or risk it, since God, for its redemption, suffered crucifixion. Julián Marías has written of Vives: "When he touches on the immortality of the soul, his pages are enlivened by a strange fire. He expresses, with masterly success, the emotion of the humanist who has investigated all reality, and finds it admirable and worthy of perduration. If Vives did not greatly advance the ontology of the human entity, it is true that in his writings we see human reality portrayed with great vividness by a man who, knowing he must die, would not die completely." This, says Marías, is an essential dimension of all anthropology.[63]

Here again I shall give but one brief quotation from the author under consideration: "The more you rise above bodily things and mount toward things spiritual, the life you live will be more divine. So it will come to pass that God will perceive in you, as it were, a relationship or resemblance to his Divine Nature and

62. See Cassirer *et al.* (eds.), *op. cit.*, pp. 19, 385 ff. See also José Corts Grau, "La dignidad humana en Juan Luis Vives," in his *Estudios filosóficos y literarios* (Madrid, 1954).

63. *Op. cit.*, pp. 166, 170–73.

will take delight therein and dwell therein as in a true temple all his own, much more acceptable than temples of stone or metal." [64]

In the year of Vives' death — 1540 — Venegas published a work entitled *On the Different Kinds of Books in the Universe*, of which we already know something. This is a setting forth of what man can derive from his three sources of knowledge: the Book of Nature, which provides the natural philosophy of the visible world; the Book of Reason, by which we construct our rational philosophies; and the Book of Revelation, the Scriptures, the ultimate source of assurance and authority. These books proliferate into multiplicity, and into them, alas! the devil inserts his own false transcripts.

Venegas is a continuator of Sabunde. One of his chapter headings reads: "Wherein it is shown that man should love God, not only in his own name, but also in the name of all other creatures, whose debt of love is charged to man." Venegas marvels at man's negligence: the elements obey the laws of their own perfection, yet man neglects to seek some guide who will declare to him the way he should follow and its dangers. Venegas finds man an essential duality: the interior man, all reason; and the exterior man, all sensuality. These engage in open battle, and when the strife is over, one is triumphant, the other in subjection. Philosophy enables wisdom to temper the appetites; the reason dominates madness and folly.

Venegas is aware of the pagan concept of Nature as stepmother, not mother — a concept repeated in our own time by José Ortega y Gasset, who called man an unfortunate offshoot of the animal kingdom, unable to realize his humanity as the horse realizes his equinity. Nature, says Venegas, has given the brutes all they need for their perfection. Man only has weaknesses, ignorance, discontent, insatiability. But the pagans did not know that man's true home is Heaven. This stepmother treatment Venegas relates to Divine Providence. Our hearts must be ever restless till they rest in God. This is a rational argument for the immortality of the soul, which Venegas places alongside the dictates of faith. Man's striving cannot be senseless; it must have a goal; otherwise there would be disorder in the universe.

64. *Introducción a la sabiduría, ed. cit.*, p. 65.

Venegas' doctrine has also a social aspect. There is a law of compensation operating among the elements. No element exceeds another in mass, but only in density. This may well be pondered by man, in whose society similar compensations are at work. Let not the rich swallow up the poor, who partake in the Redemption no less than the rich. The same may be said of the wise and the ignorant, the slave and the master, the peasant and the king, the sexton and the Pope — even of man and angel, since all are capable of the supreme blessedness.[65]

In any full treatment of human dignity in Spain, the mystics and ascetics of the sixteenth century must have their place. St. Teresa insists that self-knowledge makes us aware of our dignity — a thing most necessary, first because it prevents us from falling into despair, and second because such self-knowledge reveals to us clearly our duty to our own soul. She therefore advises persons who have known the blessedness of the mystical experience "to recognize themselves and esteem themselves greatly, with a holy and humble pride." That which constitutes the dignity of the human soul is not merely its resemblance to God but — even more — that is both the image and the dwelling place of the Creator.[66]

Fray Diego de Estella, in his *Meditaciones devotíssimas del amor de Dios* (1578), warns that he who loves things that are unworthy of him does injury to himself. "Let each man consider himself, and when once he has come to recognize his dignity, let him not love things which are of less value than he is. . . . Behold your own beauty, and you will understand what sort of beauty you ought to love." Yet self-knowledge also produces humility: "Oh Lord, you love us so greatly that in even our punishments you seek our good. . . . You wish us to recognize ourselves, to humble ourselves and make amends." Yet along with humility there must be a sense of worth: "Consider, oh my soul, your great value, since, though you were lost through sin, God gave his only begotten Son to seek you in this world. . . . Lift up your eyes, open the eyes of your understanding, and consider how you have fallen and the wretched state of your folly-seeking will. Recognize your dignity and the honor in which you have been placed by Him who made you out

65. See my article, "The Concept of Man . . . ," pp. 47 ff., and references, p. 56.
66. *Las Moradas* (1557) and *Vida* (1562). See Ricard, *op. cit.*, Part I, pp. 12–13.

of nothing. Let there be born in you a holy pride; esteem your self as your nobility deserves, and consider it an act of ignominy to employ your love on anything other than God." [67]

The works of Grace, as against those of nature, says Fray Luis de Granada, have as their end the deification of man. Fierce and angry men, by the choice of their free will, decide to use the vile part of their natures — which, in accordance with the idea of the Great Chain of Being, they have in common with the beasts — instead of using the heavenly part, which could join them to the angels. All of man's dignity consists in two things: reason and free will. It is the passions which dethrone man from his seat of dignity, obscure his reason, and pervert his will.[68]

As we pass into the seventeenth century, the waning of Spain's political star brings with it an intensification of the tendency to dwell on life's precariousness, its brevity, its essential inability to satisfy man's longings (a tendency strongly present also in the preceding centuries, as we shall see in the next section). Many have spoken, for example, of Quevedo's anthropological pessimism. "What sort of man is this?" asks Dámaso Alonso. "What did he believe?" [69] I have shown in various places [70] that, whatever the depths of Quevedo's pessimism *quoad vitam,* he is clearly no pessimist *quoad ens.* No true pessimist could regard man's emergence from nothingness into life as a "reward given in advance," a prize already received, a foretaste of divine glory, as does Quevedo. Quevedo says, echoing the words of St. Augustine, that we should give thanks to God for our punishments as well as for our blessings; that we should sing the *Te Deum* for our losses and defeats, no less than for our victories. But what does he say of human dignity? In his *Política de Dios,* arguing for the immortality of the soul, he asks his imaginary opponent to consider his personal life from its source: the female womb, the seedbed of the body. Starting

---

67. Quoted *ibid.,* Part II, pp. 177–78.

68. See my article, "The Concept of Man . . . ," pp. 48–49.

69. *Poesía española: Ensayo de métodos y límites estilísticos* (Madrid, 1950), p. 558. See my review, *HR,* XX (1952), 70; also my review of Amédée Mas, *La caricature de la femme, du mariage et de l'amour dans l'oeuvre de Quevedo* (Paris, 1957), in *HR,* XXVIII (1960), 72 ff., especially pp. 75–76. See also Pedro Laín Entralgo, "La vida del hombre en la poesía de Quevedo," *Cuadernos hispanoamericanos* (1948), no. 1, 63–101.

70. See the two reviews just referred to; also see my monograph, *Courtly Love in Quevedo* (Boulder, Colorado, 1952); and the review by Rafael Lapesa, *HR,* XXI (1953), 237–43.

with a quotation from Tertullian to show that Nature is venerable — *Natura veneranda est, non erubescenda* — he proceeds to "write the secrets of your formation." Man starts as a mass of horror, filth and poison — a confused, untidy and ugly chaos, into which, however, God infuses a soul, and which, by the acquisition of the power of reason, becomes fully human. The crying at birth is in recognition of the temporary suspension of the reason which will, in time, distinguish the babe from the brutes. In this suspension, in this delay in the use of reason and of speech, says Quevedo, we can recognize the dignity which sets off the rational creature from the vegetative and the sensitive creature (plant, animal), since the prolonged infancy of man is evidence of greater care on Nature's part. Then, in the child's life, comes the age of seven: the light of reason flashes like lightning, *y poco a poco se va dilatando como en llama espléndida* — "and little by little is expands as in a splendid flame." And later: [71]

> Behold him, as a man, and consider the harmony of that living edifice, seeing in what a brief space there appears an epitome of the higher and of the lower world — the macrocosm and the microcosm — reduced without offense to their dignity. Listen to him, and you will hear that his discourse, in spite of height and depth, has investigated the cloisters of the heavens, observing the silent steps of the stars and determining their aspects, as well as the depths of the earth, seeking precious stones though mountains cover them. And man has achieved other conquests: the sea, the mariner's compass. Even the fowls of the air must take into account man's mastery, along with all beasts and serpents: all creatures recognize the dominion of the power of reason, and serve that power in the capacity of slaves. Even the majesty of the elements renders tribute to man. Then comes the final question: Tell me, how can a soul that ennobles the base materials of man's frame be mere dust? And how can the human mind be compared to that of beasts, since it alone offsets the advantages which the animals have over man in their physical equipment?

The nakedness of man's body is but another proof of man's dignity: *Tú, para que conocieses la dignidad de tu alma, naciste con un cuerpo más desabrigado que las ovejas* — "As proof of the dignity of your soul, you were born more naked than the sheep." It is only when the rational soul is debased to the rank of the body

---

71. I use Quevedo's words as much as possible in the following but condense and summarize his text (from *Obras en Prosa*, ed. Luis Astrana Marín [Madrid, 1932], pp. 1032–33).

that the body, in insolence, rises up to assume the functions of the soul: the only evil is sin.

Contemporary with Quevedo was another great figure of the Spanish Baroque, Baltasar Gracián. For all his cult of the art of worldy wisdom, Gracián's essential Christianity is unquestionable: "Very natural . . . in man is the inclination toward his God." "Among all the marvels created for man, man himself was the greatest . . . he is the most noble creature . . . , monarch in this great palace of the world, in possession of the earth and with the expectation of Heaven; created of God, by God and for God." We have this on the authority of the Creator himself: "Look, take heed, and know that I formed man with my hands to be my servant and your lord and king," says the Supreme Master to the other animals. Man knows no limits: God made him "without bounds or *termini*"; he is "that famous microcosm, the smaller replica of the universes." He is God's masterpiece: "an animated palace, a sonorous, harmonious instrument," "the greatest work of art." His glories are two: reason and free will: "Man is the best of the visible universe, and the best of man is his understanding." His free will is both his glory and his greatest danger: "No other thing misses its end in life except man; he alone goes astray, the victim of the very nobility of his free will." In Gracián, as in Quevedo, the only evil is sin.[72]

Calderón is keenly aware both of the *dignitas hominis* and the *miseria hominis*. Leaving discussion of the latter for the next section, I would point out here that for him, as for Quevedo and Gracián, man's sin makes him bestial; his redemption is through Grace; and his dignity derives from his filial relation to the Almighty. As we have seen in Quevedo, so in Calderón "it is evident that God bestowed on man greater care than on all else."[73] And God called on him to work out his own salvation, in struggle. In *La cura y la enfermedad*, the allegorical figure Human Nature speaks:

> Sweet peace, sweet war, sweet never-ending struggle,
> That in beneficient and friendly strife

---

72. These and numerous other texts are brought together under the rubric *Dignitas hominis* by Hellmut Jansen, *Die Grundbegriffe des Baltasar Gracián* (Geneva–Paris, 1958), pp. 173–74.
73. Cited by Frutos, *op. cit.*, p. 540.

Preserves and holds together all this vast
Structure in one eternal harmony!
　How happy I, to whom dawn brings the day,
The zephyr comfort from the noonday heat,
The riverbank a bed beneath the trees
That guard my sleep from night's too chilling dews!
　Happy, I say again and yet again,
He who such union and such beauty knows,
Feasting his eyes in glorious possession!
　But, oh my thoughts, refrain from vanity!
Alas, I cannot, though I Nature be,
Forget that I am human, not divine! [74]

The human soul is born "for heaven and lives on the earth under the obligation of mounting to heaven to become a star, else it will descend to be a firebrand in Hell" (cited *ibid.*, p. 552):

> pues naciendo para el cielo
> vive en la tierra obligada
> a subirse a ser estrella
> o reducirse a ser ascua.

　In Calderón, life is spoken of as a dream. Man's days are as grass. He plows in the sea and writes in the wind. Yet all the doctrine of the Christian Epic — the Fall, the Redemption, the deification — is clearly set forth in his dramas and *autos sacramentales*. The chief end of man, he says (cited *ibid.*, p. 556), is

servirle, dije primero,　　　　　To serve him, I said, first of all;
porque para amar gozando　　　For to have the joy of love,
se ha de merecer sirviendo.　　The first requisite is service.

Miseria hominis

　The medieval Church extended its function and achieved its importance on the premise that St. Augustine's view of man was accurate.[75] Augustine, like Calvin who was to follow him a thousand years later, stressed the power of an offended God and the

---

74. "Dulce paz, dulce guerra, que a porfía, / en lid amiga, en amistad opuesta, / conserváis esta fábrica compuesta / en número de métrica armonía. / Feliz yo, a quien tu albor ofrece el día, / tu céfiro el halago de la siesta, / tu orilla el de la tarde y tu floresta / el blanco lecho de la noche fría. / Feliz, digo otra vez y otras mil veces, / quien tal por tal unión y tal belleza / posee fiel, mira alegre y goza ufana. / ¡Mas, ay discurso, que me desvaneces, / si no puedo, aunque soy Naturaleza, / dejar de ser Naturaleza Humana!" (cited *ibid.*).

75. Baker, *op. cit.*, p. 182.

impotence of offending man, except as saved by Grace. A heading in Augustine's *City of God*, XIX, 15, reads (in the English translation of 1620): "Nature's freedom and bondage, caused by sinne; in which man is a slaue to his own affects, though he be not bondman to any one besides." Augustine's concept was a product, of course, of his nature and nurture. Plato, his principal guide in matters philosophical, had said that if man had no immortality, he would be the most unfortunate of terrestrial beasts, for, unlike the animals, he possesses an awareness which multiplies and makes permanent his daily griefs. Fortunately, however, above his corporeal mass (agitated by the infinite stirrings of the passions) he has a rational soul which humanizes him.[76] And even Aristotle, the prince of rationalists, suggested that it were better never to have been born.[77]

It is not necessary here to review the history of the concept *miseria hominis* in classical and Christian thought.[78] It constitutes one of the great poles of Christian theology. While Luis de Molina (d. 1600) and the Jesuits proclaimed human liberty and its active part in the application of Grace to salvation, the Dominican Domingo Báñez (d. 1604) attributed the efficaciousness of Grace to God alone, reducing man's part almost to nothingness.[79] In Báñez's view, man inevitably is as dependent on God for the preservation of his being as is the poorest and vilest of the creatures, and his action is always that of an instrument in the hand of God, who dominates him as naturally as the hand of a human writer dominates a pen.[80] Here again we have our *Sic et Non*. Not even Catholic theologians agree.

Pope Innocent III's *De contemptu mundi* (12–13 c.) was translated into Spanish in the fourteenth century with the title *Libro de miseria de omne*.[81] The Prince Don Juan Manual (d. 1349?), in

76. Francis Hermans, *Histoire doctrinale de l'humanisme chrétien* (Tournai–Paris, 1948), I, 81.

77. A. H. Butler, "The Melancholy Greeks," in *Some Aspects of the Greek Genius* (1893), cited by Baker, *op. cit.*, p. 109.

78. See Alfonso Reyes, "Un tema de *La vida es sueño*," in his *Capítulos de literatura española* (Mexico City, 1945); and Michele Federico Sciacca, "Verdad y sueño en *La vida es sueño*, de Calderón de la Barca," *Clavileño*, núm. 2 (1950), 1–9.

79. Guy, *op. cit.*, p. 58.

80. J. M. Gallegos Rocafull, *El hombre y el mundo de los teólogos españoles de los siglos de oro* (Mexico City, 1946), p. 70.

81. See José Simón Díaz, *Bibliografía de la literatura hispánica* (Madrid, 1950–58), III, nos. 1481–83.

his *Libro de los estados*, I, xxiv, compares man unfavorably with the animals, in that the latter never make war on their own kind, nor will a starving lion kill another lion for food; ungulates and pacific creatures never overeat or overdrink, and all creatures, including the birds, indulge in sex only at times appropriate for generation. In all of this, they obey the Law of Nature, which mankind so shamelessly flaunts.

In the *Cancionero de Baena* (c. 1445), Ferrán Sánchez Calavera calls man a *podrido gusano* — a decaying worm — and Gonzalo Martínez de Medina uses, along with the same metaphor (worm) the words "dream, wind, thing corrupted, evanescent as the dew." Sleeping like a beast, man sees not what is before his eyes; he dreams of worldly glory and forgets God.[82] At about the same time Don Pedro de Portugal (d. 1466) produces his *Coplas del contempto del mundo*, in which a dejected *Ubi sunt* is answered by a doleful *Memento mori*.[83]

In 1525 the young Juan de Valdés published a boldly Erasmian catechism, the *Diálogo de doctrina christiana* — so boldly Erasmian, indeed, that Valdés left Spain permanently to avoid difficulties with the Inquisition. Marcel Bataillon finds that this catechism is mysteriously linked to a doctrine of the nothingness of man when left to his own forces, with Grace supplying the solution of the antinomy.[84] There is, of course, nothing un-Christian in this Augustinian position, but the Inquisition saw in it an element of danger. In a way which is more explicit than in any work of Erasmus, in the *Diálogo de doctrina christiana* the soul is invited to confess its nothingness and to place all its faith in a supernatural intervention which will convert the nothingness into plenitude. The soul will not be able to satisfy the commandments of God unless it is conscious of its own radical impotence.

In 1528 there was published at Logroño a translation of Erasmus' *Sermon on the Mercy of God*, one of the books which contributed to the spread in Spain of the pessimistic vision of man's earthly life as he moves unarmed and naked among the other creatures. In this anonymous translation, Divine Mercy is exalted as the remedy for two enemies that threaten the soul: excessive self-confi-

82. Ed. F. Michel (Leipzig, 1860), II, pp. 232 and 48.
83. Gillet-Green, *op. cit.*, p. 70
84. *Erasmo y España* (Mexico City, 1950), 1, 408–11.

dence on the one hand, despair on the other. The wretched weakness of the human animal is painted with the dark colors used by Pliny in his *Historia Naturalis* — offset by all the lyricism of the Psalms and all the persuasive force of the Gospels. The Inquisition, which forbade the circulation of this work in the vernacular, found nothing that required expurgation in its Latin text (*ibid.*, pp. 329–30).

Pérez de Oliva's *Diálogo de la dignidad del hombre* begins with an exposition of the point of view which the work as a whole will combat. The interlocutor Aurelio finds that death is merciful when it snatches away the young; that man would be better off without his understanding (with it he is in a worse situation than animals controlled by natural instinct); that man is the only creature not provided by the Creator with a natural defense against the things that threaten him in life (*ed. cit.*, pp. 387a, 388a, 389a).

The year 1552 is probably the date of composition of the anonymous *Crotalón*, for years wrongly attributed to Cristóbal de Villalón, in which the pessimistic view of man, when compared to the animals, is dependent on an important proviso: "Herein the author wishes to convey the thought that when men are sunk in vice, and principally the vices of the flesh, they are much worse than brutes. And there are even many wild beasts that beyond comparison exceed men in the exercise of virtue."[85] When Micilo commiserates the spirit of the talking cock on the misfortune of his early death, the cock replies: "Oh, Micilo, how mistaken you are. The opposite opinion was held by the Greeks, who were considered the wisest men of those times and who said that it was better, much better, either never to be born, or to die right after birth" (*ibid.*, p. 185b).

I have not been able to consult Baltasar Pérez del Castillo's *El Theatro del mundo de las miserias y de la dignidad del hombre* (Alcalá, 1574), but its title announces it as an exposition of both sides of the debate: *miseria et dignitas hominis.*

In 1588 there was published a book of poems entitled *Cancionero y vergel de flores divinas*, by Juan López de Ubeda. It contains this sonnet:

85. *Orígenes de la novela* (Madrid, 1905–15), II, p. 120a; cf. p. 126a.

Ashes moved by a soul, most horrid mixture,
Man, compounded of worthless dust and tears,
Bound and condemned to misery itself,
Whence comes, disgusting creature, all this pride?
Contract your peacock's tail, forget your folly,
Expel the air that puffs your poor hide up;
Dust born of dust you are, dust that tomorrow
Will be entombed, trodden by other men.
That pampered body that you now regale,
When you most care for it most eggs you on;
And those two eyes of yours that so deceive you,
Those thoughts of vanity and ostentation,
They and you and all you have are ashes,
Vile rotting trash, hot tears, and cold despair.[86]

Between this sonnet and the apostrophes to the *podrido gusano* —
"vile worm" — of the fifteenth-century *Cancionero de Baena* there
appears to be little difference, other than a greater maturity of
expression in the poem of 1588.

The unfavorable comparison of man with the animals — a commonplace in our debate — is summed up by the historian Juan de
Mariana (d. 1624). It is nonsense, he says, to accuse Nature, as
some persons do, calling her stepmother of the human race for
having created man so bereft of resources and defences. That apparent weakness is amply offset by the greatness of the destiny
which God has assigned to man, which is to love, living together
in mutual charity and friendship, since, by means of the strength
and industry of all, men can satisfy their needs and defend themselves from the evils and dangers to which they are exposed.[87]

In the summary at the beginning of the present chapter, I
quoted Gracián's view that man is an enigma. This pronouncement occurs in a passage that provides the key to both the understanding and the misunderstanding[88] of Gracián. When it is real-

86. Ceniza espiritada, vil mistura, / hombre de polvo y lágrimas formado, / a la
miseria misma sujetado, / ¿de qué te ensoberbeces, vil criatura? / Deshaz la rueda,
abaja tu locura, / vomita el aire de que estás hinchado, / que un polvo de polvo eres,
que hollado / serás mañana en la sepultura. / Y el cuerpo delicado que regalas, /
cuanto le curas más, mas él te atiza, / y esos tus ojos que te engañan tanto, / tus vanos
pensamientos y tus galas, / tú y ello y cuanto tienes sois ceniza, / basura y podrición,
lloro y quebranto (*BAE, XXXV*, 54a).

87. Gallegos Rocafull, *op. cit.*, pp. 120–21.

88. See B. B. Ashcom, reviewing Miguel Romera-Navarro's edition of Gracián's
Oráculo manual y arte de prudencia (Madrid, 1954) in *HR*, XXIV (1956), p. 163:

ized that in his writings he is considering, almost exclusively, things under the moon, things of this world and of this life, his "intellectual pessimism" is seen in proper perspective and his "worldly wisdom" appears not unlike that of the Biblical book of Proverbs. Jansen (op. cit.) has brought together and classified all of Gracián's dicta on the nature of man. What distinguishes them is their concentration on the unworthiness of man's behavior in the world of men; yet in their totality they present a picture which is essentially the picture found in the whole of Christian literature. The command *Know thyself* is a hard saying: *Enigma es, y dificultoso, esto de conocerse un hombre* — "It is an enigma, difficult of solution, for a man to come to know himself" *(ibid.,* p. 177). As for man, his days are as grass: *Ayer nada, hoy poco más, y mañana menos* — "Yesterday nothing, today little more, tomorrow less" *(ibid.).* After reviewing definitions of man from Plato to St. Bernard, Gracián gives his own: "But I, with the authority of God himself, say that he is earth, dust, and grandson of the void: *Memento, homo, quia pulvis es, et in pulverem reverteris*" *(ibid.).* Man is characterized by both *dignitas* and *miseria:* "Democritus and Heraclitus: the former laughed at all things; the latter wept over them, whereby both expressed most adequately the misery of human kind" *(ibid.,* p. 175). "When well tempered and attuned, [man] produces a marvellous harmony; when not so tempered, he is confusion and dissonance" *(ibid.).* To be in tune with the Infinite, one thing is lacking: Divine Grace willingly and reverently received: *cuan poco valen los humanos medios sin los divinos* — "how unavailing are the human means unaided by the Divine" *(ibid.).*[89]

"Gracián, says Romera-Navarro, was uninterested in *simpatía humana.* He is lacking in *candidez,* he is *eminentemente intelectual,* and he is *escaso de emociones* [lacking in emotion]. It is doubtful, therefore, that Gracián (or anyone so constituted) *llega a las raíces de lo humano universal* [reaches the depths of universal human feeling]. One who believes that *casi todo el mundo es una etcétera* [almost all the world is an *et cetera*] does not penetrate to universal truths about humanity. Gracián's view of life was a partial one. . . . He was an erudite and intellectual pessimist, with an equivocal ethic that at times is prudent (and I do not use the word in a favorable sense), at times cynical, and at times heartless. If Gracián believed in the perfectibility of man he gave no sign of it."

89. It is interesting to compare Gracián's gloomy view with that of the theologian Francisco Suárez (d. 1617): "There is no doubt that, within the limits of Catholic dogma which does not permit extreme optimism or pessimism . . . , Suárez is on the whole pessimistic in his judgment of mankind since the Fall, in harmony with the

With Calderón concepts become deeper and more complex. He imagines the human body as having consciousness, *before its creation*, of the uncertain fate that awaits it, and he gives it speech. The Body wavers between Hamlet's alternatives: to be or not to be, but finally it decides:

Mas ser quiero, que es error	But I wish to be, for, if I have
no ser, si en mi mano está,	the choice, it would be a mistake
pues peor no ser será	to choose non-being, since non-
que, siendo, ser lo peor;	existence is worse than even un-
y tengo ya tanto amor	worthy existence; and I am so
al ser que espero tener,	anxious to receive the being that
que por ser, tengo de hacer,	I expect, that I shall make efforts
juzgando a más pena yo,	to become, judging it more dis-
dejar de ser, que no	tressful to be denied being than
ser para dejar de ser.[90]	to enter into life only to cease
	to exist.

Somewhat later, the Body, eager for its being, asks: "Where am I going?" and Death replies: "To be mine!" Similarly the Soul, faced with imprisonment in the body, asks: "Am I to become a slave, when I come to rule as mistress?" And Death answers: "Yes; for thus I give you fair warning of the miseries of your estate." And Sin adds: "Yes; it is an inherited penalty." Both speakers warn Man (*ibid.*, pp. 530–31): "Your first step is toward death; your origin is sin." Man accepts (p. 534):

Ya lo veo, y pues es fuerza	Yes, I see; and since it must
que el hombre a que muera nazca,	needs be that man be born unto
nazca ya para que muera.	death, let me now be born, that
	I may die.

This same spirit of acceptance is beautifully expressed in the *auto, El gran teatro del mundo.* Before the breathing of God's

Augustinian tradition. . . . Thus we have seen that in the questions discussed, such as the possibility that man love God with all his powers, or resist a single strong temptation (or lesser temptations for a long time), or perform a perfect task of penitence, Suárez inclines toward the pessimistic position. We have seen likewise the great limitations which he assigns to the natural possibilities of man in regard to really knowing natural truths and, above all, those that refer to God. We have seen . . . his insistence on stressing the internal contradiction of body and soul, the miseries and pains of human life, and the fundamental role therein of concupiscence. To that can be added his assertion that the majority of mankind is eternally condemned" (Benzo Mestre, *op. cit.*, pp. 514–15).

90. Cited by Frutos, *op. cit.,* p 529.

spirit into the "dust of the ground," the King — one of the characters in the play soon to be performed on the stage of *The Great Theater of the World* — addresses his Maker (cited *ibid.*, p. 527):

Ya estamos a tu obediencia, Autor Nuestro, que no ha sido necesario haber nacido para estar en tu presencia. Alma, sentido, potencia, vida, ni razón, tenemos; todos informes nos vemos; polvo somos de tus pies. Sopla aqueste polvo, pues, para que representemos.	We stand ready to do your bidding, oh our Maker, for it is not necessary for us to have been born in order to be in your presence. We have neither soul, senses, faculties, life, nor reason; we lie as shapeless dust at your feet. Blow, then, upon this dust, that we may assume and perform our parts in your play.

At times the burden, after having been accepted, seems too great, and the Human Race cries out (p. 541):

Perezca, Señor, el día en que a este mundo nací; perezca la noche fría en que concebido fuí para tanta pena mía.	Perish, oh Lord, the day when I was born into this world; perish the cold night when I was conceived to suffer thus.

But protesting Humanity realizes the senselessness of its protest and corrects itself (pp. 541–42):

Mas, ay Señor, no enojado os deje la queja mía, que no de desesperado os maldigo vuestro día, sino en él a mi pecado.	But, oh Lord, be not angered by my complaint; for it is not out of despair that I curse your day, but because of the sin I committed therein.

In another place (p. 536) it is made clear that if man is almost an angel because of his precious soul,

por la culpa es bruto el hombre.	because of sin man is a beast.

It is Grace that comes to man's aid. I can do no better than to repeat a text already quoted. God the Father bids Adam and Eve to rise up from the ground (p. 541), and Adam, with deep symbolism, replies that they obey, in order that it may be seen how

. . . los que a servirte llegan de la tierra se levantan.	those who come to do your service from the ground are lifted up.

Dignitas et miseria, but the greatest of these is *dignitas.* Segismundo's pessimistic soliloquy in the play (not the *auto*), *Life Is a Dream,* is uttered before the unfortunate prisoner is enlightened. That enlightenment — through a glass, darkly — comes after he has learned that he is a composite of body and soul (Act II, sc. vii):

Fué porque ignoré quién era;	It was because I did not know
pero ya informado estoy	myself; but now I know my iden-
de quién soy, y sé que soy	tity, and can affirm that I am a
un compuesto de hombre y fiera.	composite of man and beast.

By this pale light he makes the necessary choice: *Acudamos a lo eterno* — "let us cleave to things eternal."

THE LITTLE WORLD OF MAN [91]

The concept of man as microcosm — as an epitome of the universe he inhabits — is another one of the commonplaces of Christian anthropology. The twelfth-century Godefroy de Saint-Victor (*fl. ca.* 1184) and the sixteenth-century Maurice Scève (dates unknown) wrote long poems on the subject. In Spain, the theme appears prominently in Don Juan Manuel's *Libro de los estados,* chapter XXXVIII, wherein the aged knight replies to the *caballero novel*'s question concerning the nature of man:

The way in which man resembles the world, and is all things, is as follows: man is a stone in that he is a body. . . . Likewise, just as the tree and the other plants are born, grow, have their estate, and become old and decay, so man also does these things. . . . Similarly, as the beasts, the birds, and creeping and crawling things do all this, and over and above this they feel, reproduce, and live composed of the four elements, air, fire, water, earth, so man has in his body four humors, which are blood, yellow bile, phlegm, and black bile. And as the angel is a spiritual being and immortal, so any man who by God's grace shall have earned the glory of Paradise, shall have that glory and shall have no end. . . . And thus, my son, you can understand

91. See G. Paré, *Le Roman de la Rose et la scholastique courtoise* (Paris–Ottawa, 1941), pp. 111 ff.; John B. Bamborough, *The Little World of Man* (London, 1952); Cassirer *et al.* (eds.), *op cit.,* p. 149; George P. Conger, *Theories of Macrocosmos and Microcosmos in the History of Philosophy* (New York, 1952); Robert Pring-Mill, *El microcosmos Lul·lià* (Oxford–Palma, Majorca, n.d.); Craig, *op. cit.,* p. 13; Curtius, *European Literature and the Latin Middle Ages,* trans. Willard R. Trask (New York, 1953), p. 109; Jantz, *op. cit.,* pp. 92, 132 ff., and Index; Tillyard, *op. cit.,* pp. 84–85.

that man resembles the world greatly, since he has within himself all things, and since God created the things of the world for man's service. . . .[92]

The *Visión delectable* of La Torre contains a similarly extended comparison, followed by this conclusion: "and for these reasons man is called a lesser world; for he carries within his person the image and the fulfillment of the greater world; and we say this not of every man, but only of the intellectual; for any other is not really a man, but is only slightly higher than the ape or other brute" (*ed. cit.*, p. 372b).

Vives, in his commentary on Cicero's *Dream of Scipio*, draws the same parallels, adding an apotheosis of the mind and soul of man: "Your immortal soul, derived from the divine Nature of Heaven, is like the sky and very closely related to it. But your mind, which without a doubt is a god, tempers and governs the mortal body and the spirit itself, exactly as the Optimus and Maximus Creator of Nature[93] rules both the fragile and perishable parts of the world and the parts that are stable and eternal. And as the Divine Architect of the world, whose divinity rules the universe, is not born in Time, but is immortal, so your spirit has no beginning nor will it have an end or termination. . . ."[94]

A special application of the comparison is made by Francisco Terrones del Caño in a book on homiletics, *Instrucción de predicadores*, published in 1617: "The most marvelous thing in the world is man, and in him the entire world appears in abbreviated form; and among men, the most marvelous is Christ, in whom God abbreviated, enclosed and epitomized all the human race and all the world."[95]

Calderón draws again the same picture, adding that man shares the power of thought with the angels, and immortality with God himself.[96] This sharing of attributes with God and the angels, with the spheres and the earth, and with the world of living things, is the expression of man's special nature as a link in the Great Chain of Being, reaching upward toward the Highest, and downward to the lowliest of creatures.

92. *BAE*, LI, 246ab.
93. The Roman Scipio is speaking, hence *Optimus* and *Maximus* applied to God.
94. *Obras completas*, trans. Lorenzo Riber (Madrid, 1947–48), I, 674a; cf. 676b.
95. Ed. Félix G. Olmedo (Madrid, 1946) pp. 121–22.
96. In *Los alimentos del hombre*, cited by Benzo Mestre, *op. cit.*, p. 544.

EQUALITY OF HUMAN SOULS

Montaigne tells of seeing, in the French civil wars, amazing exhibitions of courage by peasants under torture and notes that in people of low social rank "it is not so new to see some trait of rare goodness." Pondering this, he concludes that "the souls of emperors and cobblers are cast in the same mold . . . they are led to and fro in their movements by the same springs as we are in ours." [97] In 1637 William Austin applied the idea of soul equality to the perennial "woman question": "In the sexe is all the difference; which is but onely in the body. For, she hath the same reasonable soule; and, in that, there is neither hees, nor shees; neither excellencie, nor superiority: she hath the same soule; the same mind; the same understanding; and tends to the same end of eternall salvation that he Doth." [98]

This same universalist note is struck by Fray Bernardino de Laredo (*fl.* 1535) in his appeal to all human beings to seek the gifts of the spirit. No one, he says, is excluded from the school of divine love. Every person, whoever he may be, even the ignorant and the lowliest of women, is capable of acquiring the science of mystic theology, if he takes God as teacher.[99]

The doctrine of the equality of souls was the keystone of the teaching of Juan Huarte de San Juan in his *Examen de ingenios para las ciencias* (1575).[100] That doctrine may be summarized as follows: individual differences which exist in aptitude and in learning are a matter of common observation; these differences are independent of the will of the persons in question and have causes which are organic; the organic cause is not in the soul of the person (as distinct from the body), since souls are equal; the cause must be sought in the temperation of the bodily humors.

Huarte assumes that his key argument may be taken as an axiom: "All rational souls possess equal perfection, that of the savant and that of the fool" (cited *ibid.*, p. 205). Stated with greater

97. Donald M. Frame, *Montaigne's Discovery of Man* (New York, 1955), pp. 131–32.

98. *Haec Homo Wherein The Excellency of the Creation of Women is Described: By Way of an Essaie*, quoted in Carroll Camden, *The Elizabethan Woman* (New York–London, 1952), p. 30.

99. Fidèle de Ros, *op. cit.*, pp. 294–95.

100. Mauricio de Iriarte, S.J., *El Doctor Huarte de San Juan y su Examen de Ingenios* (Madrid, 1948), p. 153.

clarity: "rational souls possess an equal and supreme wisdom, capacity, and perfection; although they possess this equality to a much greater degree when separated from the body, since the body fails to afford them the perfect admixture of humors which they need. For if this were not the case, all men would be equally learned and prudent; and the failure in this is not to be attributed to the soul, but to the bad or good temperation of the individual" (pp. 283–84).

In so arguing, Huarte was taking rather much for granted. Ancient writers did indeed favor equality, if their conception of the soul was in any way comparable to Huarte's. The Scholastics were divided: in 1277 the Bishop of Paris condemned the supposition of equality, on the ground that, thus considered, the soul of Christ would not have been superior to that of Judas Iscariot. Cajetan (Tommaso de Vio) argued that St. Thomas was against equality. Domingo de Soto claimed the opposite, as did the Coimbra commentators on Aristotle (pp. 153–54).

We can only conclude that, in spite of some arguments against it, the doctrine found general favor. We have seen it taken for granted by Montaigne and by William Austin. In 1589 Fray Juan de Pineda wrote as follows in his *Agricultura christiana*: "On the subject of woman and her relation to man, [St. Thomas] says that, as the image of God resides in the soul, and as all souls are of equal specific perfection whether they be the souls of women or of men, in this respect men and women are equal; but since man is, as it were, the woman's 'head,' and masculine, he is more representative of God than she is and has an ill-defined excellence of being more perfectly God's image than she. And for this reason St. Thomas says that the image of God is more perfect in the superior angels than in the angels of lesser rank." [101]

In a *Sermón de San José*, Fray Diego de la Vega affirmed: "So God made Adam like unto himself, and made women like unto Adam and consequently like unto God, in order that the two might be equal in everything, and the woman in nothing inferior to the man, except by reason of the fact that she is his wife." [102]

---

101. Ed. Salamanca, 1589, I, fol. 294.

102 "De manera que a Adán le hizo [Dios] semejante a sí, y a la muger semejante a Adán, y por el consiguiente semejante a Dios, para que sean en todo iguales, y en nada la muger inferior al varón, sino sólo en ser su muger" (*Sermonario clásico*, ed. M. Herrero García [Madrid, 1942], p. 22).

Cervantes places these lines on the lips of his character, La Gitanilla:

Si las almas son iguales,
podrá la de un labrador
igualarse por valor
con las que son imperiales.103

If souls are equal, the soul of a peasant may equal in value the soul of an emperor.

The thought recurs in Cervantes' last work, *Persiles y Segismunda*, published posthumously in 1617: "all souls are equal, created and formed from a single mass at the beginning by their Creator" (*ibid.*, p. 1564).

In Lope de Vega's *Dorotea*, the heroine says: *las almas ni son mujeres ni hombres* — "souls are neither female nor male." 104

Quevedo repeats the *topos*: "all the faculties which compose the soul are common to all individuals of this species Man, since God differentiated them only in the body and in the endowments and operations thereof." 105

And Calderón, in *Afectos y odios de amor* declares — as did William Austin in 1637 — that among souls there are neither *he's* nor *she's*:

Y no es
hombre ni mujer el alma.106

And the soul
Is neither male nor female.

Individual differences

Having cited the testimony of Huarte de San Juan on the subject of the equality of all souls, we must now study his *Examen de ingenios* in its own right.107 It was first published in 1575, and is based on the false but widely accepted psychology of the bodily humors, which in turn correspond to the four elements — earth, water, air, fire — whose mixture in the human body is ever in precarious balance, or in outright imbalance. Huarte sets out to explain individual differences on the basis of physical differentiations. Man's habitat, his food, his drink, the air he breathes, the

---

103. *Obras Completas*, ed. Angel Valbuena Prat (Madrid, 1956), p. 799a.
104. Ed. E. S. Morby (Berkeley–Los Angeles, 1958), p. 417.
105. "todas las potencias que se sujetan en el alma, son comunes a todos los individuos de esta especie *hombre*, que Dios sólo en los cuerpos, dotes y oficios dél los diferenció" (*Obras en verso*, ed. *cit.*, p. 680b; See *HR*, XX [1952], 257).
106. Arturo Farinelli, *La vita è un sogno* (Turin, 1916), II, p. 96.
107. The book was widely read and widely translated. Its influence in England is studied by Hardin Craig, *op. cit.*, pp. 119 ff.

influences of latitude and of the stars at his birth (e.g., different constellations in the southern hemisphere), cause alterations in his organism. All men are therefore more or less ill — or distempered, as Huarte would say — but never in exactly the same way. All this had its origin in the sin in Eden, which drove man from Paradise, depriving him of the fruit of the tree of life. In such sad circumstances, Cain was engendered. Through Adam's descendants this ill health and disorder were transmitted to modern man. At this point there enters an element of paradox. All is not lost. Plato had said that geniuses are half mad. Perfectly adjusted individuals, says Huarte, lacking the beneficent element of illness, are inevitably mediocre. Indeed, from man's essential illness, Huarte derives consoling doctrine: no man, no matter how great his rudeness, is without some special aptitude. At the same time, there is determinism: food, air, water, environment, or the horoscope make the fool or the wise man — *Natura facit habilem*. There is also here a certain noble pride: fallen creature though he be, man has made progress and is capable of making much more. If Huarte could only enter the schools and conduct his tests, he would change students from one career to another, sending many back to the fields, rescuing many others from a life of toil and setting them to following their true bent — letters! Believing in the equality of souls, as we have seen, Huarte makes the brain the seat of the soul, since it is the organ of the psychic faculties. His book had tremendous influence. The very structure of Cervantes' *Don Quijote* is based upon it.[108]

Shortly after the publication of Huarte's book, Francisco Sánchez (d. 1632) issued his *Quod Nihil Scitur* (1576?), a work of skepticism which helped to prepare the way for the methodical doubt of Descartes. How can man know anything, Sánchez asks, when he cannot know himself? What an astounding variety in the single species of mankind! Some are pygmies, some giants, some totally naked, others hairy or clad in skins; some speechless, some

---

108. See O. H. Green, "Ed *ingenioso* hidalgo," *HR* XXV (1957), 175–93. See also my articles, "Realidad, voluntad y gracia en Cervantes," *Ibérida: Revista de filología,* III (1961), 113–28 (volume in homage to Marcel Bataillon), and *"El Licenciado Vidriera*: Its Relation to the *Viaje del Parnaso* and the *Examen de Ingenios* of Huarte," *Linguistic and Literary Studies in Honor of Helmut A. Hatzfeld* (Washington, D.C., 1964), pp. 213–20.

treedwellers. Some are cannibals; some hold wives and children in common; some have no homes. Others, for religion, will suffer martyrdom, and still others flee death at all costs. Some, after death, are buried or burned with live companions. Others receive no burial. You may refuse, Sánchez says, to grant that all of these are men.[109] Sánchez will not argue the case. He follows reputable accounts, he says, both ancient and modern. None of these things seems to him impossible. What is more: there may be corners of the world where even stranger things have been, are, or shall be. How, then, can man possibly know himself, let alone know the universe in which his lot is cast?

The Indians of the Americas

This insistence on diversity invites us to go back and examine the doctrine of natural inferiority and natural slavery which harassed the makers of Spain's colonial policy and sorely troubled the nation in her struggle for justice, and for justification, in her conquest of America. The controversy between the supporters of the doctrine of equality and those who held that inferior men were born to slavery or subjugation assumed the greatest importance in the sixteenth century when conquistadores and missionaries, theologians, royal counselors, and the King himself were struggling to arrive at a just (and practical) solution of the problem of the political and social relation of Spain to its subject peoples in the Indies.[110]

In the year 1433 Nicholas of Cusa proclaimed that "every constitution is founded on natural law (*jure naturali*)" and that "since all men are free, all government . . . arises solely from agreement and consent of the subjects. For if men are by nature powerful and

109. On the shadowy world of "semi-human" creatures and on the theologians' concern to determine whether their souls were human and could be saved, see my article, "Lo de tu abuelo con el ximio (*Celestina*, Auto I)," *HR*, XXIV (1956), 1–12, especially p. 8.

110. See Lewis Hanke, *The Spanish Struggle for Justice in the Conquest of America* (Philadelphia, 1949); idem, *El prejuicio racial en el Nuevo Mundo* (Santiago, Chile, 1958); Edmundo O'Gorman, "Sobre la naturaleza bestial del indio americano," *Filosofía y letras* (1941), núm. 1, pp. 141–48, and núm. 2, pp. 305–15. See also Silvio Zavala, *Servidumbre natural y libertad cristiana según los tratadistas españoles de los siglos XVI y XVII* (Buenos Aires, 1944); and Robert E. Quirk, "Some Notes on a Controversial Controversy: Juan Ginés de Sepúlveda and Natural Servitude," *HAHR*, XXXIV (1954), 357–64.

equally free, a valid and ordained authority of any one person, whose power by nature is like that of the rest, cannot be created save by election and consent of the others, just as law is established by consent." [111] This is the voice of *Sic*, but there were also those who said *Non*. At about the same time Sabunde, after showing in his *Theologia Naturalis* how fibrous rocks like asbestos are a link upward with the plants, and how living plants are a link upward with the animals, while intelligent animals are a link upward with man, proceeds to examine the descending scale: "Now, therefore, disregarding certain . . . privileges which are exclusively human, we can say that certain stupid men and certain degraded souls come to form this link of union, which elevates them only very little above the beaver, the horse, the dog, or the monkey." [112]

In 1449 Don Alonso de Cartagena, seeking to bring about the incorporation of the recently converted Jews into the body of Christian believers without impediment or discrimination, wrote in his *Defensorium unitatis Christianae* that there are three types of slavery: natural, civil, and theological. Natural slavery is suffered by stupid persons who need to be directed by their intellectual superiors. Civil slavery is one of status only: that of the enslaved prisoner of war, for example, who may be manumitted. Religious slavery is the "slavery" of him who has infringed the law of God: Jesus taught that whoever sins is the slave of his sin. [113] There were thus two types of inferiority or incapacity that might be attributed to the Indians.

There existed, as a consequence, two poles between which the Spanish colonial administration might fluctuate. The position of Nicholas of Cusa — government by the consent of the governed — seems to be reflected in the doctrine of Francisco de Vitoria (d. 1546), who "based his entire theory of political and international law on human conscience. . . . The action of the State is neither outside nor above the conscience of individuals: whether these be governors or subjects, it is in accordance with their conscience that they must decide what it is licit to command, or what it is

111. *The Portable Medieval Reader*, eds. J. B. Ross and Mary M. McLaughlin (New York, 1953), pp. 306–7.

112. *El hombre y sus deberes, ed. cit.*, p. 17.

113. Albert A. Sicroff, *Les controverses des statuts de "pureté de sang" en Espagne du XVᵉ au XVIIᵉ siècle* (Paris, 1960), pp. 41 and 50.

permissible for them to obey."[114] In accordance with this principle, Bartolomé de las Casas, the Apostle to the Indians, could argue that it was not lawful for Spaniards — not even the King of Spain — to rifle the treasures found in the tombs of the Incas.[115]

Over against this set of standards, closely related to the idea of the equality of souls and the general dignity of the whole of the human race, there were other considerations. In the first place, there was the doctrine of natural light.

Dante held that even a pagan could have knowledge of God, *per speculum,* that is, by observing the nature of the creation.[116] It was held that God is the cause of truth in the human soul because He has formed and illuminated it with the intelligible light of natural reason. Truth flows from the divine essence as a kind of formal and intelligible light which assures man's capacity for perceiving and receiving truth. The power of reason is such that, unaided, it can adequately reach its sapiential end, grasping its highest and particular good.[117] Descartes accepted the theory that a missionary could "draw from the lips of an unregenerate savage all the basic facts of the Christian faith."[118] How great was the guilt, therefore, of human beings who, had they listened to Nature, might have arrived by their own efforts at a knowledge of God, but who nonetheless would not receive that knowledge when missionaries preached and expounded it to them:

What an importance must have been attached to political utterance which might by its mere impact on the ears of the people shake the king upon his throne, or surround him with loving subjects; and what a weight of earnestness must have rested upon the preacher of the Word, who was veritably a dispenser of the bread of life! Those who heard would inherit eternal life, and those who did not hear would suffer eternal torment. Now, those into whose ears the truth had passed had no choice, if they were normal human beings, but to obey that truth. Those who heard the established truth and

114. Gallegos Rocafull, *op. cit.,* p. 29.
115. See *HR,* XXVIII (1960), 397.
116. J. A. Mazzeo, *Structure and Thought in the "Paradiso"* (Ithaca, New York, 1958), p. 97.
117. Eugene F. Rice, *The Renaissance Idea of Wisdom* (Cambridge, Massachusetts, 1958), pp. 82–84.
118. Don Cameron Allen, *The Legend of Noah: Renaissance Rationalism in Art, Science, and Letters* (Urbana, Illinois, 1949), p. 20. See also Pedro S. Achútegui, *La universalidad del conocimiento de Dios en los paganos, según los primeros teólogos de la Compañía de Jesús, 1534–1648* (Pamplona, 1951).

did not thereupon profess it, were condemned on the doctrine of persuasion as children of the devil. It was just and right that such persons should be led to the stake and burned.[119]

This leads us to the quarrel as to the responsibility of the American Indians for their sinful and subhuman condition. According to the doctrine of natural light, natural man is possessed of a power whereby, though he may not know the true God, he yet knows the necessity of God and seeks, or should seek, to remedy his weakness. Fray Luis de Granada repeats, as his predecessors had done, the injunction that man must assume responsibility for passing upward, along the ladder of Being, the expressions of praise from the lower creatures, whose voices otherwise would be silent. Fray Luis knows how badly man does this. And he knows that man is beset by endless miseries. These, he asserts, are inherent in Nature, because of the sin in Eden. Yet man always has the capacity to rise above Nature — *sobrenaturalizarse* — by the gift of heavenly grace.[120]

With knowledge of this body of thought as background, we can understand the need felt by the Spaniards for theological justification for their acts of colonial expansion and their efforts to arrive at a conviction that their action was just. Spain was a semitheocracy, with theology as the party line. The Aristotelian idea that there were natural-born hewers of wood and diggers of mines [121] appealed greatly to a nation of *conquistadores*. As early as 1519 a first application of Aristotle's doctrine of natural inferiority was made. And in those same early years the Indians were passionately defended by Father Las Casas, who was to have a long life, influencing Spanish thought over many years. The debate was fierce around 1550, as Juan Ginés de Sepúlveda, Spain's great Aristotelian, argued the case for a policy of subjugation and forceful conversion.[122]

119. Craig, *op. cit.*, p. 181.
120. See my article "The Concept of Man . . . ," p. 49.
121. We read in the *Visión delectable* of La Torre: "The second manner of servitude was that men dwelling in climates and regions of evil complexion, where human reason is weak, are very lacking in understanding, and these naturally are slaves of those who dwell in climates and countries of good complexion where reason abound . . . and the ones achieve salvation through the efforts of the others, and . . . this servitude is reasonable and natural" (*ed. cit.*, p. 396a). Notice particularly the date *ca.* 1440, of this work.
122. This was natural enough. Such a policy had been followed in Spain in dealing with the Jews and the Moors.

So successful was Sepúlveda's advocacy of this policy that the historian Francisco López de Gómara (d. 1572?) considered the matter
closed, merely referring his readers to Sepúlveda's Latin writings. Others called the idea pure tyranny. The Spanish crown inclined, officially, away from Aristotle and his disciple Sepúlveda
and decreed peaceful persuasion as a means of converting the Indians. The colonial government of Mexico City even suggested
that there be always six Indians on its Council. In 1573 a basic
law was promulgated, an eclectic sort of thing, based largely on
the ideas of Father Las Casas but taking into account the interests
of the Crown and the general usefulness of applying, in some measure, the Aristotelian concept of natural inferiority.

Law or no law, the debate went on. In practice there were great
difficulties. Some claimed that the Indians, inferior creatures,
could only be coerced; and in spite of all theories, there developed
an abyss between conquerors and conquered. Yet to Spain's honor
be it said that no other colonial power took so vehemently to
heart the problem of the ideal just treatment to be meted out to
its subject peoples.

I wish to quote yet another text of the sixteenth century, Fray
Juan de Pineda's *Agricultura christiana*, which shows the persistence of the religious and philosophical thinking that made it possible to regard the Indians as worse than benighted — as both
willfully and determininistically inferior and guilty.[123] Pineda
quotes St. Paul to the effect that the Gentiles — peoples who have
never received a law for living the good life — possess, nevertheless,
natural light, or natural law, which dictates what is sufficient for
salvation. Their synteresis — that is, their inborn inclination to
embrace the good — either excuses them or condemns them, according as they have chosen, or failed, to follow their inner light,
to respond to the higher law. He says in another place that there

123. The historian Gonzalo Fernández de Oviedo (d. 1557) regarded the religious
rites of the Indians as inspired by the devil. This error of the Indians (ultimately the
result of original sin) required a punishment and an opportunity for correction. The
punishment and the opportunity for correction were provided by the Spanish conquest, which would spread anew the religious truths which the Indians were supposed
to have apprehended long ago by natural light and to have forgotten because of their
sins. See *Trabajos y conferencias: Seminario de estudios americanistas* of the Faculty
of Philosophy and Letters of the University of Madrid, Vol. III, nos. 2/3 (Madrid,
1960), pp. 112–13.

are men of such powerful inner chemistry that, though nourished on cheese and garlic, they can purify this grossness and become men of lofty intelligence. On the other hand, there are sons of nobles who, though fed on delicate viands, live bestially, because of an evil admixture of the elements in their bodies. This baseness they pass on to their offspring. Hence, certain families and races normally produce persons of good endowment; others, with equal normality, are ill disposed, malicious, lustful, incapable of good. None of this, to be sure, has to do with essence. It is a question of exterior accidents. Like the stars, these other influences (diet, etc.) may incline to evil, but free will and the natural light are always there and should be heeded, or guilt ensues.[124]

THE CHIEF END OF MAN

Neither Gracián, the "erudite pessimist," nor his sixteenth- and seventeenth-century predecessors conceived of the chief end of man as essentially different from what it had been since the days of the founders of the Middle Ages: to know God and to enjoy Him forever. Gracián makes his statement in *El Criticón*: "man . . . is ordained for, and directed toward the knowledge of God, to serve Him and love Him."[125] As we survey in retrospect the evidence presented in this chapter, we find man declared to be a semigod *or* an enigma; his life, a triumphant mediation between the temporal and the eternal *or* a dream, an illusion, a tale that is told; a song of triumph *or* a dirge in a vale of tears. Whatever the extremes of any individual point of view, however, all[126] the writers whose testimony we have examined found one belief un-

124. *Ed. cit.*, fols. 22 and 118v.
125. Jansen, *op. cit.*, p. 173.
126. One naturally asks if Francisco Sánchez might be an exception. The answer is that he is not. He planned to follow his work of metaphysical demolition with another work which would be the basis for a new and reasonable science, based on observation and judgment. He did not carry his skepticism into the religious sphere: "Excusatio aliquam habet philosophorum opinio; sed nullam pertinacia in non credendo et contumacia in fide." He was a Christian: "Et hac ratione dicitur Christus Dominus miserias humanas subire voluisse ut expertus calamitates nostras magis misereretur." In his works there is no clear or covert attack on the faith; the divinity of Christ is expressly accepted. For a comparison of his doubt with that of Pascal, Bonald, Ráulica, and Donoso Cortés among Catholics, and of Algazel among Muslims, see Eloy Bullón y Fernández, *De los orígenes de la filosofía moderna: Los precursores españoles de Bacon y Descartes* (Salamanca, 1905), pp. 190–91.

questionable: human paths lead—if man does not betray himself through sin—to human happiness, and that happiness, as Aquinas had said, "consists not in externalities, or even such good of the soul as Aristotle's intellectual virtues; it consists in 'contemplation of truth.'" [127] As Vives taught, human rational life, brought into existence in order that it may know and love God, has as its end and destiny eternal happiness acquired by means of such knowledge and love.[128] And a century before Vives, Alfonso de la Torre also had said it: the final cause of man is the *vida angélica*, to know God and all His manifestations in the universe, to understand what God's power is like, to know His wisdom, His goodness, His light, to know the power of the prophecy and of the Grace which men receive from Him, and, together with all this, to be obedient to God and His commandments" (*ed. cit.*, p. 367ab). The following statement of Ignatius de Loyola was regarded as an axiom, one to which Spanish culture clung with the greatest tenaciousness during our entire period: "man is created to praise, revere, and serve God our Lord and by this means to save his soul; and all the other things on the face of the earth are created for man, to help him achieve the purpose for which he is created." [129]

At the end of our survey we are no nearer to modern philosophy or modern anthropology than we were at the beginning of this chapter on the nature and destiny of man. But we have seen into the heart and into the life of a nation—a nation that ardently believed in human [130] and in superhuman [131] values. We have found,

127. Baker, *op. cit.*, p. 195.
128. *De anima et vita*, I, ii, cited by Marías, *op. cit.*, p. 168.
129. Cited by Gallegos Rocafull, *op. cit.*, p. 18.
130. Altogether typical of Spain, with its general disinclination to study science (as against the social sciences), is Lupercio Leonardo's decision to say very little about geography and very much about saints, kings, and captains in the text which he prepared for printing on the margins of Juan Bautista Labaña's map of Argensola's native province of Aragon: "The most worthy of all I judged to be the saints, the kings, the captains, and, to say it all in a word, the men [of Aragon]" (O. H. Green, *The Life and Works of Lupercio Leonardo de Argensola* [Philadelphia, 1927], p. 155, n. 36).
131. The same Argensola, issuing in a private letter a prospectus of his proposed *Historia General de la España Tarraconense*, said that he did not intend to enter the uncertain field of the ancient history of the Aragonese region: "and thus leaving those centuries as a rude and shapeless mass, I begin with the fortunate times of Augustus Caesar, in which God sent his Son and the foundations of the Church were laid" (*ibid.*, p. 128).

with Professor Roland H. Bainton,[132] that the contrast of Renaissance thinkers with those of the Middle Ages — in the matter of
the concept of man — is not pronounced.[133] That man has the
power to fall to the level of the brute, or to mount the ladder and
to enjoy the vision of God, is an old and recurrent theme, ranging
from the early Greek Fathers of the Church to the Dominican and
Franciscan mystics in the age of the Renaissance. Although in
other countries of Renaissance Europe the Christian epic of Creation, Fall, and Redemption played a diminished role as the period
advanced, this was not so in Spain. In Spain there was no tendency
to pass from Christianity to universal religion. Calderón is the
end product of a Catholic culture, preserved in essential purity.
Perhaps for that reason it seems incredible that he was a contemporary of Thomas Hobbes and Baruch Spinoza, and a partial contemporary of John Locke and Gottfried Leibniz.

132. "The Thirst for God in the Renaissance," *Renaissance News*, V (1952), 10.
133. It hardly seems proper to speak (as Charles Edward Trinkhaus, Jr., does in
Cassirer *et al., op. cit.*, p. 149) of "the *Humanist* notions of man as a microcosm" (italics
mine), when we know that about the year 1184 Godefroy de Saint-Victor wrote a long
Latin poem entitled *Microcosmus*, and that Don Juan Manuel (d. 1349?) incorporated
the idea into *El libro de los estados* (see above). We read in the French dialogue
Placides et Timeo (written before 1303): "L'homme est un microcosme. Il est rond
comme le monde" (see Spitzer, "Classical and Christian Ideas of World Harmony,"
Part II, *Traditio*, III [1945], 311).

V · Reason

Though I know it's my undoing,
Winsome will sends reason packing.[1]
    Francisco de Castilla

May my reason have the power
To release the will from error.[2]
    Hernando de Ludueña

THE HUMAN SOUL: *E PLURIBUS UNA*

In his much quoted *De las differencias de libros que ay en el vniuerso* (1540), Alejo Venegas is admirably clear in his definition of the various faculties of the soul. "Although it is true," he writes, "that the rational soul is a single, indivisible substance, that fact does not prevent it from having — for various reasons and according to its various operations — different names, just as we see that a certain man is called a father because he has a son, and a son because he has a father or mother. In this fashion the rational soul, being one, is called *memory* insofar as its function is to retain; it is called *intellect,* insofar as its function is comprehending; it is called *will* insofar as its appointed task is to crave and to desire; it is called *intuition* insofar as its business is to investigate and trace the nature of things. It is called *free will* insofar as it chooses by an act of conscious election what it desires. It is called *reason* because it discerns the bad from the good, the just from the unjust, the false from the true, etc. But with all these functions the soul is ever one indivisible substance." [3]

1. "Y aunque veo que me daña / dulce voluntad destierra / a la razón" (*Cancionero General,* ed. Bibliófilos Españoles [Madrid, 1882], II, 390). Readers of this chapter will find it profitable to consult Don Cameron Allen's latest book, *Doubt's Boundless Sea: Skepticism and Faith in the Renaissance* (Baltimore, 1964), especially Chapter IV, "Rational Theology against Atheism."
2. "Pueda tanto la razón / que saque la voluntad / de la sujeción del yerro" (*Cancionero castellano del siglo XV,* ed. R. Foulché-Delbosc [Madrid, 1912–15], II, 727).
3. Ed. Salamanca, 1572, fols. 185v–186. Italics in this quotation are mine.

The soul's three faculties[4]

In our analysis, in Chapter II of Volume I of the present work, of the parodied sermon which serves as prologue to the *Book of Good Love* of Juan Ruiz, Archpriest of Hita, we found it necessary to anticipate somewhat this doctrine of the triune nature of the human soul. It is now time to penetrate more deeply into a matter which was then of but passing interest.

Dom Odon Lottin writes: "Everyone in the Middle Ages . . . was familiar with the trilogy: memory, intellect, will, wherein St. Augustine, in his *De Trinitate*, found traces (in the human soul) of the Trinity of the Divine Persons. . . . [Peter Lombard] had been struck by the text in which St. Augustine affirms that these three human faculties form a single essence — *haec tria una vita, una mens, una essentia* — and he objects: these three faculties differ among themselves, so how can they constitute a single essence?" Albertus Magnus likewise finds difficulties. He distinguishes the soul itself, *id quod est*, and its power of action, *id quo est*. Aquinas "takes up the solution of his master Albert, not, however, without detaching it still further from the Franciscan formulas: the faculties are properties which flow from the very essence of the soul considered as a potential whole."[5]

The functions of these three faculties or powers of the soul are indicated negatively (by stressing their failure to measure up to their possibilities) in St. Bonaventure's *Itinerarium*, IV, 4: "It seems strange that (since God is as close to our spirit as has been demonstrated) there are so few mortals who devote themselves to a consideration of His presence in themselves. The cause is that our soul, distracted by the tasks and cares of daily life, does not penetrate into its own secret place with the aid of the memory; that blinded by the vain images of worldly things, it does not reflect on its own essence with the aid of the intellect; and that, seduced by the attractions of concupiscence, it does not return to its true self with the desire [i.e. the will] to enjoy the inner peace and gladness of the spirit. Therefore, submerged in its entirety in

4. See Adolphe Garnier, *Traité des facultés de l'âme*, 3 vols. (Paris, 1852 and later eds.).

5. *Psychologie et morale au XIIe et XIIIe siècles* (Louvain–Gembloux, 1942–60), I, pp. 483–84; see also p. 501.

the world of phenomena, the soul is incapable of finding in itself the image of God."[6]

E DUOBUS UNA: INTELLECT AND REASON

In 1521 Fray Juan de Padilla el Cartujano, one of the last cultivators in Spain of Dantesque allegory, published a poem entitled *The Twelve Triumphs of the Twelve Apostles*. It is divided into chapters and in the heading of the first chapter the poet sets forth the plan of the entire work "and shows his intention . . . , introducing the Beast of Idolatry and taking St. Paul the Apostle as his guide and master, who is intended to symbolize Superior Reason which is Synteresis, while the author in his own person is a *figura* of the Lower Reason and of Sensuality."[7]

This is a statement of the Scholastic doctrine of synteresis. First used by St. Jerome as equivalent to the "spark of conscience," the term became very common in the thirteenth century. St. Thomas regarded it as a habitus of the intellect, enabling it to know first principles of practical reasoning. Franciscan thinkers tended to regard synteresis as a quality of the will, inclining it to embrace the good. We have the following from the fifteenth-century Augustinian Fray Martín de Córdoba: "And therefore the Philosopher [Aristotle] says that the principle of reason is not reason, but something better than reason, for just as God is the prime mover in all the universe, so He moves that tiny and divine part which is in us: this is the intellect."[8]

A quotation from St. Thomas will help to clarify the problem: "Hence the intellect and the will can be compared in three ways. First of all and without qualification, with regard to this or that object; and then the intellect is more eminent than the will, as possessing the worth of an object is more perfect than being related to that worth. Second, in regard to the natural objects of the

6. Cited by Julián Marías, *El tema del hombre* (Madrid, 1943), p. 145.

7. *Cancionero castellano* . . . , ed. cit., I, 290.

8. "E por esto dize el Philosopho que el prinçipio de la razón non es la razón, mas algo que es mejor que razón, que así como Dios es mouiente primero en todo el uniuersso e mueue toda cosa, así mueue aquella partezilla diuinal que es en nos: ésta es el entendimiento" (*Compendio de la Fortuna*, ed. P. Fernando Rubio Alvarez, O.S.A. [El Escorial-Madrid, 1958], p. 82). Cf. Aristotle's *Eudemian Ethics*, VII, 14.

senses; here again the intellect is as such nobler than the will, seeing that it is nobler to grasp a stone by knowledge than to want one; and the reason is, that the form of a stone exists in a nobler way in the intellect, when it knows it, than it does in the stone itself as desired by the will. Thirdly, in regard to divine things, which are higher than the soul; here the will is more eminent than intellect, as it is nobler to desire and love God than to know Him; seeing that the divine goodness exists more perfectly in God Himself, who is the object of desire, than it does as partaken of by us when it is possessed by the intellect." [9]

In his *Vniuersal vocabulario en latin y en romance* (1490), Alfonso Fernández de Palencia defines reason as "a movement of the spirit . . . which is divided into intellect and opinion. The reason is the eye of the spirit with which, by its own powers and not by means of bodily perception, it gazes upon truth." [10] In 1524 Vives brought out his *Introductio ad sapientiam*, in which intellect is the superior faculty and reason the handmaiden: "In our spirit there are two parts: one superior and the other inferior. The superior is called mind, which we may more conveniently designate as intellect, provided we remember that this part contains in itself the will; and in everything that it understands, or remembers, or knows, this faculty makes use of the reason, or of the judgment, and of the *ingenium*, or intuition. Because of this men are similar to God, and more excellent than all the other animals." [11] Venegas, in his *Agonía del tránsito de la muerte* (1537), declared that before the Fall Adam possessed "the original justice wherewith God created him, which was a spiritual order in which the lower faculties existed together with the superior ones without distress and without rebellion, being in perfect subjection to the superior portion which is the reason." [12]

In the second half of the century Fray Luis de Granada wrote: "For you must know that within our soul itself there exist these very different women, namely spirit and flesh, which the theolo-

---

9. *De Veritate*, Q. 22, art. xi, c, cited by M. C. D'Arcy, *The Mind and Heart of Love, Lion and Unicorn: A Study of Eros and Agape* (London, 1946), p. 307.

10. In *"Universal vocabulario" de Alfonso de Palencia: Registro de voces españolas internas* by John M. Hill (Madrid, 1957), p. 158a.

11. See the Spanish translation, *Introducción a la sabiduría* (Madrid, 1944), pp. 40–41.

12. *NBAE*, XVI, 120ab.

gians call the upper and the lower parts. The upper portion is that part of our soul in which are located the will and the reason, which is the natural light with which God created us. . . . And this is the noble woman whom God gave to man as his wife, that he should live with her, guiding all his affairs by her advice, which is to say, by this celestial light. But in the lower portion is located the sensitive appetite, about which we have spoken; which was given us in order that we might desire the things necessary to life and to the preservation of the human species, this to be done within the restrictions set by the reason. . . . For this appetite is the slave of which we spoke; who, since she lacks the light of reason, was created not to guide or command, but to be guided and to receive orders. And this being so, unfortunate man becomes so attached and given over to the joys and desires of this bad woman that, abandoning the advice of reason, by whom he ought to be guided, he comes to be ruled by her." [13]

From what has preceded it is apparent that there is some confusion in the use of the terms *entendimiento* and *razón*, or intellect and reason.[14] In the fifteenth-century *Visión delectable* (ca. 1440) of Alfonso de la Torre, reason and intellect are presented as distinct allegorical figures, with the particular circumstance that reason (often regarded as having an ethical function) instructs intellect (whose task is more usually epistemological, that is to say of a more abstract and higher order). In the seventh chapter of *Visión delectable,* Reason, addressing her companions Truth, Wisdom, and Nature, makes clear that Intellect is the lower portion

13. *Obras*, I (Madrid, 1768), pp. 222–23.
14. It may be helpful to examine the situation in Shakespeare's England: "Many sixteenth-century writers . . . were extremely hopeful. For man has more than reason to work with; in fact reason is merely the lowest of his three intellectual powers. It is reason's relatively humble job to work on the sense-data which sensation, memory and imagination place on the 'white paper,' the *tabula rasa*, of his mind, and to abstract from those sense-data the immaterial forms which they contain. These forms are then apprehended intuitively by the understanding or intellect, which is akin to the pure intellect of the angels, and which is therefore a higher power than the 'discourse of reason.' And finally there is will — 'which we use,' says Sir Walter Raleigh, 'to stir us up to seek God and . . . heavenly things. . . . This is the one point by which we are men, and do excell all other creatures living upon the earth.' Reason works downward on the material of sense; understanding or intellect works upward toward the immaterial world, and, as Cardinal Bembo says in Castiglione's *Courtier*, 'from understanding, by the which man may be partner with Angels, ariseth will' " (Theodore Spencer, *Shakespeare and the Nature of Man* [New York–Cambridge, Massachusetts, 1945], pp. 12–13).

of the mind, whereas she herself is synteresis: "I do not believe that I am any less hated than you three; but bearing in mind that Intellect has been in the house of Logic and Geometry and Rhetoric, where he has been taught the value of proofs and what their nature is, I shall now go . . . and explain to him what was said to him in each of those houses. And I am sure that although he at present holds us in abhorrence, when once he has got rid of his passions and false opinions, he will love us more than his life and will never wish to depart from us." [15] Thus, for La Torre, reason is that portion of the human spirit which seeks the highest truth; intellect, on a lower plane, seeks to interpret the world of phenomena.

In the allegorical *autos sacramentales,* or Eucharistic plays, which were introduced in the sixteenth century and have their own "golden age" in the seventeenth, Reason and Intellect appear as dramatis personae with considerable frequency, either in company with the other two faculties (Memory, Will), or in isolation. In Juan de Pedraza's early *Farsa llamada Danza de la Muerte* (1551),[16] Reason and Intellect appear in dialogue (as in La Torre). The two figures admit in conversation that Anger (*Ira*) can overcome and banish them, because of which weakness on their part the Shepherd (Humanity) must look to his defenses, scorning earthly things and earthly passions and devoting himself to the service of the *Verbum,* while Reason and Intellect must guard against temptation. It is Reason, not Intellect, who awakens the Shepherd from his figurative dreaming and directs his attention to the Bread and Wine. *Razón* is thus implicitly recognized as superior to Intellect (again as in La Torre a century before), though both are explicitly stated to be subject to defeat by the passions.

In the rest of the *autos* in González Pedroso's collection (*ibid.*) the splitting of reason into upper and lower parts does not occur. One play has a character named *El Entendimiento Niño,* or Intellect the Child; in another the same character is called *El Ciego Entendimiento,* or Blind Intellect. This is but to insist that without divine grace the intellect is powerless to arrive at ultimate truth. In the former play (beginning p. 46) Intellect the Child is

15. *BAE,* XXXVI, 350b.
16. In *BAE,* LVIII, ed. Eduardo González Pedroso, pp. 41–46.

accompanied by Will and Memory; Blind Intellect appears alone in the latter (p. 62). Will, Memory, and Intellect are characters in Lope de Vega's *Representación moral del Viaje del alma* (pp. 147 ff.) and in Calderón's *La nave del mercader* (pp. 440 ff.). Reason appears alone in Juan de Timoneda's (d. 1583) *Auto de la fe* (pp. 89 ff.); Will appears in isolation in Lope's *El pastor lobo* (pp. 191 ff); Reason is unaccompanied in José de Valdivielso's (d. 1638) *La Serrana de Plasencia* (pp. 244 ff.); Intellect is alone in Calderón's *El veneno y la triaca* (pp. 327 ff.) and *La divina Filotea* (pp. 531 ff.).

Reason defined

Venegas in his *Differencias de libros* says of reason that "it is none other (as St. Augustine affirms) than an activity of the soul sufficient to distinguish and to interrelate things under consideration. This activity (as Seneca says) is an imitation of Nature. Finally (as Josephus writes) reason is that faculty to which pertains everything that we do with rectitude. Compunction of spirit and detestation and abhorrence of vice are derived from her. Reason is like a good vinedresser who cuts off the useless shoots and tendrils and stifles the effect of every evil humor, allowing to grow only that which reason believes can in some way, at some time and place, be productive of good" (*ed. cit.*, fol. 187v.). This definition, derived—most interestingly—from Greek, Hebrew, and Christian authorities, suggests points that we shall need to discuss in this chapter: the definition of St. Augustine points to problems of epistemology, of knowing; that of Josephus, to problems of ethics, of conduct; and both together attribute to reason powers and activities whose end is salvation, the ultimate self-realization of the soul through union with God.

Fray Damián de Vegas, in his *Coloquio entre un alma y sus tres potencias (ca.* 1590), causes the Soul to say to Intellect (*Entendimiento*): "Be still, for you should be humbled by the realization that you are not my essence but merely a faculty, an accident, a part of me." [17]

As Venegas in his definition of reason made use of Seneca as well as of St. Augustine, so in the analysis of the structure of

17. "Calla, criatura vana; / pues humillarte debría / ver que tú no eres mi esencia, / sino sólo una potencia,/ accidente y parte mía" (*BAE,* XXXV, 530b).

the soul was Christian thinking reinforced by the thinking of the ancient world. In 1596 Alonso López Pinciano, in his *Philosophía antigua poética*, having considered man as an animal in the biological sense, proceeds to a consideration of his psychic nature:

> Let us now pass to the faculties which he possesses as a rational and intellectual being. They are three: intellect, memory, and will, and their benefits to man are of the highest order, according to the Philosopher [Aristotle] in his *Ethics*; by them the wise man is called happy and a friend of the gods. . . . Let us speak, therefore, of the first faculty, called intellect. This is a faculty which enables man to understand things without the intervention of any bodily instrument . . . , performing its operations by heeding the incorporeal percepts [i.e. the *species intelligibiles impressae*] received from the [Aristotelian] common sense. In this operation the common sense (when in good working order), the memory of the outward senses, and the inner or intellectual memory all work together effectively. . . . Then comes, in last place, the will, which is none other than appetite guided by reason; therefore it is called rational appetite — as against irrational appetite, . . . with which it is always at strife . . . ; from which strife are born good and bad moral habits: good, if the winner is the rational appetite; bad, if right reason is vanquished.[18]

REASON, WILL, AND HUMAN DIGNITY [19]

Don Juan Manuel, Infante of Castile (d. 1349?), wrote in his *Libro infinido* these words, which the reader will surely remember (see Chap. III, section *Dignitas hominis*): "the reason why man is a more noble creature is because man is made up of soul and body, and possesses intellect and reason, and has free will to do

18. "Vamos a las que como racional y intellectual tiene, que son tres: entendimiento, memoria y voluntad, cuyos bienes son proprissimamente tales, según el Philósopho en sus Ethicos, y por quienes es llamado feliz y amigo de los dioses el hombre sabio. . . . Digamos, pues, de la potencia primera dicha entendiminto. Esta es vna facultad para entender las cosas sin interuención de corporal instrumento . . . , sino que haze su operación conuirtiéndose a las especies incorpóreas e que el común sentido le da; para la qual el sentido común bueno es de mucha eficacia, assí como la memoria sentitiua para la intellectual . . . que conoce diferencias de tiempos. . . . Viene en el vltimo lugar la voluntad, la qual no es otra cosa que el apetito guiado por razón; por esto, dicho apetito racional, contrario al irracional . . . siempre anda con él en lid . . . , de cuya lid nacen los hábitos morales buenos y malos: buenos, si es vencedor el buen apetito racional, y malos, si es vencida la razón buena" (ed. Alfredo Carballo Picazo [Madrid, 1953], 1, 70–71). The idea is also Platonic: Plato taught that harmony is achieved when the desires and the aggressive will are under the control of the intellect.

19. See *Patrologia Latina*, vol. 219, p. 59: "Index de Ratione humana et eius excellentia, potentia et infirmitate"; Eugenio Garin, "La *Dignitas Hominis* e la letteratura patristica," *Rinascita*, I (1938), 102–146.

good or evil. This is possessed by no other creature in heaven or earth, except man." [20] Here intellect and reason are regarded as separate (see above, section *E duobus una*), and are mentioned in conjunction with the will. In 1535 Fray Bernardino de Laredo, whose teaching influenced the mysticism of Santa Teresa of Avila, gave preference, with all clarity, to reason: "All our nobility . . . consists in reason which makes us capable of knowing God and of esteeming every creature according to its true value. Let us therefore make use of reason: God himself requires it of us." [21] In 1538 Vives saw, in the ability of the reason to apprehend God and the angels, a proof of the soul's immortality and spoke of: "the reason, which (alone of all sublunar things) is the faculty that perceives, knows, and comprehends them and is, like them, a spirit. That which understands their immortality must itself be immortal; if this were not so, it could not in any way conceive of what exceeds itself in magnitude to an infinite degree." [22] In 1583 Alonso de Orozco exclaimed in his *Victoria de la muerte*: "O sinner! I beg you, consider the rational nobility with which the Creator so generously endowed you; be not a bastard son, departing from the illustrious state of being that God gave to you by making you similar to the angels." [23] And finally Sebastián de Covarrubias, in his *Tesoro de la lengua castellana* (1611) defines reason as: *Latine ratio. Nobilissima animae facultas, qua una a ceteris animantibus homo secernitur et a qua rationalis appellatur* — "In Latin, reason. The most noble faculty of the soul, whereby alone man is distinguished from other living creatures and because of which he is called rational."

The fountainhead of these conceptions, of course, lay in Greek philosophy. Both Platonism and Aristotelianism made knowledge central, and the Stoics proclaimed that "knowledge — of man's true Good, of its conditions in man's nature, and of its grounding in the Divine Reason in the cosmos — was a necessary condition

20. Ed. J. M. Blecua (Granada, 1952), p. 10.
21. See Fidèle de Ros, *Le Frère Bernardin de Laredo* (Paris, 1948), p. 222.
22. Cited by Marías, *op. cit.*, pp. 172–73. In his *De veritate fidei Christianae* Vives calls the reason "a certain ray of the divine light which shines in the upper part of the soul, by virtue of which we know and control ourselves. Man's excellence depends upon it." See J. Corts Grau, *Estudios filosóficos y literarios* (Madrid, 1954), p. 91.
23. Ed. Madrid, 1921, p. 3.

of the Good Life." [24] In the Middle Ages, philosopher-theologians like Scotus Erigena (d. 877?) devoted their lives to the search for God through an intellectual effort, seeking to analyze the creation and to prove by the authority of the Scriptures and of the Church Fathers the conclusions which were judged to be firmly established: one began by an act of faith, but it was by rational assurance that one realized all the nobility of human nature. [25] "When the thirteenth century discovered the glory of Aristotle, its greatest minds took delight in his belief that the life of intellectual contemplation was so far superior to all other earthly pursuits that it alone was worthy to be ascribed to God himself." [26] Hugues de Saint-Cher, for example, would not admit the existence in man of any faculty superior to the reason; this faculty, according to the Doctors of the Church, is queen of the kingdom of the soul. [27] St. Thomas showed that the path of reason, "though perilous, led to God as surely as the mystic's feeling, and that it has joys of its own beyond compare." [28] For Jean de Meun (d. 1305?), reason was "the very image of the mind of God." [29] In the seventeenth century, according to Herschel Baker, men "like Hooker, Shakespeare, Bacon, and the swarm of faculty psychologists clung to the old humanistic belief in the superiority of reason to will. . . . From Ficino the stream runs clear. . . . For him the will was clearly subordinate. . . . As Milton's Raphael explained [*Paradise Lost*, VII, 507 ff.], it was precisely because man was endued with the 'Sanctitie of Reason' that he could govern himself and all the lower creatures, and even claim a magnanimity to correspond to heaven's. To understand the variations on this theme is to know the greatest monuments of Renaissance literature." [30]

24. J. H. Randall, Jr., *The Role of Knowledge in Western Religion* (Boston, 1958), pp. 20–21.

25. Edgar de Bruyne, *Estudios de estética medieval*, trans. Fr. A. Suárez (Madrid, 1958–59), I, 362–63.

26. J. H. Randall, Jr., *The Making of the Modern Mind* (Boston–New York, 1940), p. 46.

27. D. Odon Lottin, *op. cit.*, p. 97.

28. Randall, *The Making of the Modern Mind*, p. 94.

29. A. F. Gunn, *The Mirror of Love: A Reinterpretation of "The Romance of the Rose"* (Lubbock, Texas, 1952), p. 150.

30. *The Dignity of Man: Studies in the Persistence of an Idea* (Cambridge, Massachusetts, 1947), p. 290. As the mention of Ficino suggests, this attitude can also be Platonic. León Hebreo writes in his *Diálogos de amor*: "so that with the eyes of the intellect we can see in one glance the supreme beauty of the First Intellect and of the

Among the faculties of the soul, reason has a rival: the will.[31] It will be remembered (see above) that whereas St. Thomas regarded synteresis as a habitus of the intellect, Franciscan thinkers tended to regard it as a quality of the will which inclined the latter to embrace the good. Indeed, it is a Franciscan who will give us our first statement of the voluntarist position — Fray Alonso de Madrid, whose *Arte para servir a Dios* (1521) was praised by St. Teresa of Avila: "The sixth Preliminary Consideration has to do with the power which we possess of working with the noblest instrument of the spirit, which is the will; that is, that we are able to wish or love, or to refrain from wishing or loving, anything that we wish, and as many times as we wish. . . . And this Consideration is necessary to us every instant of our lives, and we should be keenly aware of it, and especially as a means of combatting first impulses." [32]

Four years later, Vives wrote in his *Introducción a la sabiduría* (*ed. cit.,* pp. 42–43):

In order that we might escape sin and follow the true road of virtue, God endowed the superior part of our spirit with a virtue, a force or a faculty by whose use the spirit is enabled to understand, which is called *ingenium*, with which it discovers, examines and weighs the essence of every thing, and knows what is suitable for it and what is not. In addition to this, God gave to this same part the will, which by its nature tends to embrace the good which the *ingenium* discovered and which the judgment approved, and this will does not content itself with any ordinary good of the sort we usually esteem, nor is it sated or satisfied by the things we normally call goods: it flies higher than that. It rises toward its only, its unique, its supreme and true good, which is God; in whom it finds rest and outside of whom it never reposes. This faculty not only is free, but it is the mistress, the height and the depth of everything which exists in the spirit; it governs everything and brings everything under its sway. And if it wills (as it should) to guard and preserve its pre-eminence, its liberty and its rights, there will be no faculty in the spirit which would dare to oppose it, or could. Thus the *ingenium* discovers the truth, and if it does this as it should, and if it . . . receives education and doctrine, it finds

Divine Ideas" ("assí que con los ojos del entendimiento podemos ver en vn mirado la summa hermosura del primer entendimiento y de las Ideas diuinas" [*NBAE*, XXI, 427b]).

31. "The old Epicurean insistence on intellect alone as man's saving grace was exceptional. The Christian combination of divinity and free will and the juxtaposition, like Pomponazzi's, of free will and intellect are much more typical" (Abraham C. Keller, "Montaigne on the Dignity of Man," *PMLA*, LXXII [1957], 45–46).

32. *NBAE*, XVI, 600a.

light and clear knowledge of many things. . . . The will thereupon embraces and follows after the good which the intellect revealed to it, and by the exercise of following after and seeking it acquires virtue. . . ."

The task of the will, therefore, is neither strictly ethical nor epistemological, but theological: it is to lead the soul to find God and to achieve salvation. The Dominican Fray Luis de Granada explains this as follows in the Prologue to his *Guía de Pecadores*: "In order that we may tread the path to Heaven there exist also four very necessary virtues: the love of God, hatred of sin, hope in the divine mercy, and fear of His justice; in which virtues the sum total of our salvation consists. And these are called affective virtues; because they consist in the movements and the emotions of the will."

The Augustinian Malón de Chaide, in his *Conversión de la Magdalena*, declares that the will is "the mistress who commands the other faculties; love is called a unitive faculty, which joins the lover and the Beloved, drawing the lover out of himself and elevating him to the Object of his love, and there transforms the lover and makes him one with God."[33] In another place he explains that, in the case of things that are above us in value,

it is better to love them than to understand them, because loving them we become more perfect, since love unites us with its object; and when we understand them, it seems that they lose something of their being and their value, since we adjust and shape them to our understanding. But if they are of less value than we, it is better to understand them than to love them, because by loving them, we descend in the scale of being, since we take on their being and lose our own, and understanding them we improve them for the reason stated.[34]

Perhaps no one has better stated the case for a balance of will and reason than Fray Luis de Granada. "If all the dignity of man *qua* man," he wrote, "consists in two things, which are reason and free will, what is more inimical to the one faculty and to the other than passion, which blinds reason and drags will in its train? Wherefore you will see how injurious and harmful is any unduly violent passion; since it thus throws man down from the seat of his dignity, obscuring his reason and perverting his free will,

33. Ed. P. Félix García (Madrid, 1947), I, 69.
34. *Ibid.*, pp. 53–54.

without which two things man is not man, but a beast" (*Obras, ed. cit.*, I, 233).

Fray Juan de Pineda, in the Preface of his *Agricultura christiana*, points out that in the First Part of that work he speaks more to the intellect and in the Second Part, more to the will, since intellectual operations are prerequisite to movements of desire, just as operations of the senses are a necessary preliminary to intellective operations: in the same way that one does not love what he does not understand, he does not understand what he has not apprehended through perception.

Will and Reason: the Scholastic and the Platonic positions

It is frequently stated that the Middle Ages was the age of Aristotle and his interpreters; the Renaissance, the age of the newly discovered Plato. I shall here merely present three summaries: one setting forth the Aristotelian-Thomistic position, and the other two showing the thought of the great Renaissance Platonists, Marsilio Ficino and Giovanni Pico della Mirandola.

The Thomistic position gives pre-eminence to the intellect, and has been stated as follows: "Our extension in the world of being is measured, not by the narrow limits of our physical person, but by the vast horizon which is opened to us. Deprive us of thought and we are no better than the obscure beast content with a cave and an acre of forest; deprive us of all knowledge, and we are reduced to a fragile zero. We alone, of all nature, have the universe as our universe; the other conscious beings have only corners, and unconscious beings have no universe beyond themselves." [35]

Ficino (d. 1499) bases his doctrine of the soul and of immortality "not merely on knowledge as arrived at by logic, but to a much greater extent on the will, in other words on love." [36]

Pico (d. 1494) declares that "we are not angels, but beings composed of matter and spirit, and while we are in this world, hemmed in by the limitations of the world of sense, it is by love more than by reason that we can apprehend God. More than the efforts of thought, it is love that leads us to the frontiers of the divine.

35. A. D. Sertillanges, *Les grandes thèses de la philosophie thomiste* (Paris, 1928), p. 21.
36. F. Hermans, *Histoire doctrinale de l'humanisme chrétien*, (Tournai–Paris, 1948), I, 133.

More than by the wearying and faltering investigation of the reason, it is by love that we succeed in possessing God." [37]

Freedom of the will

I will treat the subject of freedom of the will in Chapter VI, but in reduced proportion it has a place here. If, for many of our thinkers, free will (rather than reason) was the foundation of man's nobility, we must know more about it and about their attitudes toward it. With Duns Scotus and William of Ockham, and, in general, with the rise of nominalism, reason (subordinated to will) was considered by many a human reality. God was no longer Supreme Reason but was all-powerful Will and Liberty, existing at an infinite distance from the finite reason of man. Thus man was considered to bear the image of God not as a rational spirit, but as a free creature: God can be intimately believed in, hoped for, and loved; He cannot be rationally thought.[38]

This problem of the freedom of the will is tremendously complicated and full discussion of it must be left for later. I shall here give three quotations from the sixteenth and seventeenth centuries, each separated by approximately fifty years from its predecessor. The first is from Hernán Pérez de Oliva:

For inasmuch as man contains within himself the nature of all other things, so he has freedom to become whatever he wishes. He is like a plant or a stone when he is in idleness, and like an animal if he gives himself over to bodily

37. *Ibid.*, p. 147.
38. Pedro Laín Entralgo, *La espera y la esperanza: Historia y teoría del esperar humano* (Madrid, 1957), p. 128–29. See Hardin Craig, *The Enchanted Glass: The Elizabethan Mind in Literature* (New York, 1950), p. 52: "The freedom of the soul, and hence of the will, was doctrinally so important, that even astrology had to admit that the stars incline but not compel. Nothing is more important than a knowledge of the doctrine held at any one time with reference to the immortality of the soul, because the conditions of its immortality often determine the degree of its freedom. If there is a warfare between reason and the will, it may take one of three forms: 1) the adversaries may be equal (a situation which may be disregarded); 2) reason may be superior, so that we may attain an Aristotelian peace in a life of contemplation; and 3) will may rule, with important results, for the supremacy of the will is the fundamental principle of Machiavellianism, Calvinism, Puritanism, and Stoicism. It is obvious that the status of the soul as regards this conflict between will and reason is important in literature, and that Shakespeare, Bacon, and Hooker occupy the second position." See Gérard Paré, *Le Roman de la Rose et la scolastique courtoise* (Paris–Ottawa, 1941), ch. III, the sections "Destin et Liberté" and "Liberté et Prescience Divine," pp. 87–88.

pleasure; if he wishes, he is an angel, created to contemplate the face of God; and he has the power to achieve such excellence that he may be counted among those to whom God said: "Ye are gods"; thus God placed man here on earth in order that he might first show what he wishes to be; and if he is pleased by vile and earthly things, in their possession he is lost and abandoned by God forever; but if reason lifts him up to heavenly things, or to the desire of these and the eagerness to enjoy them, there await him those places in Heaven which to you, oh Aurelio, seem so glorious.[39]

Our second witness is the Blessed Alonso de Orozco, in his *Victoria de la muerte*: "For inasmuch as the will is a queen in the soul, who commands (as a mistress) the other faculties (intellect and memory), love draws the intellect after it to contemplate what it loves, and does the same with memory to the end that it never forget; and this is the cause of our Redeemer's requirement, that we love Him with all our heart, which is to require of us all our love" (*ed. cit.*, p. 142).

Our third witness is Quevedo, who writes: "All sins are evil: that you confess; and you also confess, together with the philosophers and theologians, that the will desires that which is bad only when it is represented as a good; and that in order to commit a sin, we require not only the representation of anger or the awareness of lust, but the consent of the will. . . . When this is seen and understood, it is clear that whenever one of these sins is committed, the will consents to it and desires it. . . ."[40]

These statements will be better understood if considered against the background of the Thomistic position. It was the merit of St. Thomas, writes Dom Odon Lottin,

to have posed as a thesis that the will (a rational faculty) always follows that which (after deliberation) the reason has decided; if therefore there is liberty, it is in this decision . . . that it must be sought. . . . St. Thomas proves that every intelligent being is endowed with free will because it is the author of these practical judgments. . . . There is no doubt that the special turn of his thought is due to the axiom of Aristotle: *liberum est quod est causa sui.* . . . St. Thomas remains within the traditional formula, but, better than any other, he gave full expression to its content.[41]

39. *Diálogo de la dignidad del hombre, BAE, LXV,* 319a.
40. *Obras en prosa,* ed. Luis Astrana Marín (Madrid, 1932), p. 168b.
41. *Op. cit.,* I, 211–12.

Reason and faith

The function of reason "is the interpretation, and the logical ordering of the interpretations, both of sense experience and religious experience." [42] To discover God

is the function of faith. But reason, too, has its function in the religious sphere. It has to interpret to the intellect the discoveries of faith in the only possible way, by means of symbolic propositions; and also to ensure that these symbolic propositions are mentally consistent and fall into an ordered system. This is the truth of the medieval view that reason operates within the framework set by revelation. . . . This insight, correct in itself, is, of course, perverted when it is made to mean that what some book or organization has said is to be blindly accepted "on faith," without examination.[43]

The "insight" into the possibility of perversion, which Professor Stace sets forth in the last sentence quoted, was of course denied to all Christian believers during the period we are studying, whether Catholic or Protestant. For all of them the Scriptures were the ultimate source of authority: for the Catholics, that authority was supplemented by the authority of the Church, its saints, its councils, even its traditions. The number of genuine atheists (who would of course have denied the divine inspiration of the Bible) was negligible.[44] The Renaissance had ended before European thinkers accepted the idea that to believe "on faith" and "without examination" what the Bible declares to be true is a "perversion" of the Christian view that reason operates within revelation.

It must be remembered that we are tracing the intellectual history of a Christian people — of a people whose culture at no time ceased to be Christian. One is a Christian insofar as he hopes actively and confidently to possess eternal beatitude. But he cannot be content merely to live his hope: by the very nature of his faith

42. W. T. Stace, *Time and Eternity* (Princeton, 1952), pp. 145–46.
43. *Ibid.*, p. 152.
44. In later centuries, according to Paul Oskar Kristeller, it was possible to repel any intrusion of faith upon reason, or to reject revealed religion altogether. There is no evidence that the Renaissance Aristotelians were inclined toward the latter position. In the case of Bruno, it is hard to decide whether he was a heretical Christian or an outright unbeliever. It all depends on one's definition of religion. See "Changing Views of the Intellectual History of the Renaissance since Jacob Burckhardt," in Tinsley Helton (ed.), *The Renaissance: A Reconsideration of the Theories and Interpretations of the Age* (Madison, Wisconsin, 1961), pp. 43–44. We shall revert to this subject below.

— which is ever desirous of intellection, according to St. Anselm — he must to some degree understand that hope; he must be able to give an account of it, as St. Peter commanded (I Pet. 3:15): "Be ready always to give an answer to every man that asketh you a reason of the hope that is in you." Christianity consists not only in faith, hope, and conduct, but also in doctrine.[45]

Reason was not autonomous in the Middle Ages, which "could no more admit the complete autonomy of natural law than it could admit the autonomy of natural reason. Reason remains the servant of revelation. Its task within the realm of the mind is to lead to, and to help prepare the way for, revelation." [46] This statement applies, in Spain, not only to the Middle Ages, but to all periods before the eighteenth century. It is sin, we are told by Fray Hernando de Talavera, the first Bishop of Granada after 1492, to believe the things of the holy Catholic faith, not because God said them and commands that we believe them, but for natural reasons which apparently carry conviction, so that if the said reasons did not convince one, he would not believe. It is likewise sinful to seek and desire such reasons, if one's will is not prepared to believe as readily without them as with them. It is no less a sin to wish to prove or to affirm that one can fully prove the Catholic faith, even though, without those reasons, one be prepared to believe as he should.[47] Fray Luis de Granada, in his

45. Laín Entralgo, *op. cit.*, pp. 122–23. See José Ferrater Mora, *Diccionario de filosofía* (Buenos Aires, 1951), articles *Fe* and *Razón*; Virgilius Ferm (ed.), *A History of Philosophical Systems* (New York, 1950), Index, *s. vv.* "Faith and "Reason". No one until very modern times (not even the advocates of the "double truth") could have made a statement like this one by Stace: "Of the space-time world of appearance the naturalistic or scientific way of thinking will be one hundred percent true. Of the world of reality, which is outside space and time, the religious way of thinking will be one hundred percent true. This can never be proved by reason, but neither can it be disproved. For reason is itself a part of our mental structure which leads us to appearance, not reality. Reason, whether by way of proof or disproof, simply has no application to the real world" (*Religion and the Modern Mind* [Philadelphia, 1952], p. 196).

46. E. Cassirer, *The Philosophy of the Enlightenment* (Princeton, 1951), p. 241.

47. *Breve forma de confesar*, NBAE, XVI, 4a. In an allegorical Eucharistic work published nearly a century after Talavera's death by the poet and dramatist Andrés Rey de Artieda in his *Discursos, epístolas y epigramas de Artemidoro* (Zaragoza, 1605, fols. 121–25) we read this explanation of the roles of faith and reason: "the mystery of the Holy Sacrament is supernatural and inaccessible to the senses, except the ear which gives passage and opens the doors for Faith, which is the force that prevails and overcomes the difficulties of reason and of the senses. . . ." In this work, the allegorical personage *Philosophía* (i. e., human reason) loses the battle when she encoun-

Introducción del Símbolo de la fe, declares that it is not his intention "to prove the mysteries of the faith by human reasons, since the solidity of those mysteries is not founded upon such reasons but has its basis in the light of faith, by means of which the Holy Ghost moves and inclines our intellect to regard as true and infallible the articles of faith, . . . revealed by the First Truth, which can neither deceive nor suffer deceit." [48] "Reason and faith are not opponents, though faith is superior to reason," says Venegas in one of his chapter headings (*Diferencias de libros,* II, xi), and he goes on to explain: "What I mean is that reason should serve faith with her rationality and probability; and that faith should inform reason concerning her mysteries; because faith neither opposes reason nor does reason contradict the mysteries which faith preaches" (*ed. cit.,* fol. 203).

REASON, MYSTICISM, PHILOSOPHY

In his two books on the problems of religion and philosophy quoted earlier in this chapter, *Religion and the Modern Mind* and *Time and Eternity,* Stace considers the mystic experience as a source of one type of knowing which — while completely severed from philosophy as a series of propositions — is of value to philosophy in its effort to understand the totality of human experience. Usually the philosophical and the mystic approaches to truth are found separated in different individuals, but not always: Raimundo Lull, whose mystical *Book of the Lover and the Beloved* was considered by Menéndez y Pelayo as worthy of a place close to the works of St. Bernard,[49] believed that reason was capable of solving all problems, and that reason's conclusions, far from contradicting the Christian faith, could show with absolute certainty all the mysteries of religion.[50] Let us examine this position historically.

St. Bernard (d. 1153) was certain that no man in this life can

ters the lance-thrust of Faith. See Carlos Clavería. *Le Chevalier délibéré de Olivier de la Marche y sus versiones españolas del siglo XVI* (Zaragoza, 1950), pp. 132–34. We shall have other occasions to observe this continuity of Spanish thought (and its allegorical expression) from the early to the late Renaissance.

48. *Obras,* ed. Fray Justo Cuervo (Madrid, 1906–08), V, 6.

49. *Historia de las ideas estéticas en España* (Madrid, 1946–47), II, 80.

50. Frank Thilly, *A History of Philosophy* (New York, 1914), p. 207.

have a direct vision of God; yet he did grant to St. Paul, "caught up into the third heaven," the highest mode of vision humanly possible. In such moments of unexpected rapture, the human spirit departs from the things of the senses, and by a mystic flight reaches the heights, seeing more deeply into the things of heaven than is possible through the use of the creatures. This is the "knowing" of the mystic. Lower forms of what St. Bernard called "consideration" involve the use of the senses, and of things. Richard of St. Victor, a contemporary of St. Bernard, distinguished six kinds of contemplation: (1) through the imagination alone; (2) through the imagination but according to reason; (3) in the reason but according to the imagination; (4) in the reason and according to reason; (5) above but not contrary to reason; (6) above reason and beyond it.[51] The fourth form is the contemplation of the philosopher; forms five and six are the contemplation of the mystic.

It is because of the non-discursive character of forms five and six that mysticism presents difficulties to Church authorities concerned with orthodoxy. St. John of the Cross (d. 1591) speaks of the Dark Night of the Soul.[52] Francisco de Osuna (d. 1542?), the Franciscan whose teaching meant so much to Teresa of Avila, speaks of "our path, which leads from virtue to virtue, through the desert of withdrawal into the self," and of "the terrible solitude" of this withdrawal, and he prescribes Richard of St. Victor's fifth form of contemplation: "we must silence our intellect, by which I mean the speculative intellect, which is ever delving into the secrets of things: all of which should be left behind in order to come to know God by the negative way . . . , because St. Gregory says that whatsoever thing we see in our contemplation is not God, but that we understand the truth about Him when we fully realize that we can know nothing about Him." [53] The means of sudden and rapturous mystical experience is love. God is loved best, says the mystic, not by and through the creatures, but for Himself alone. Were we to take this negative way as the only way,

51. See Joseph A. Mazzeo, *Structure and Thought in the "Paradiso"* (Ithaca, New York, 1958), pp. 90 ff.
52. In *NBAE*, XVI, 391.
53. *Ibid.*, pp. 548–49, 562–63. See the entire Tratado XXI of his *Tercera parte del Abecedario espiritual* (pp. 558 ff.), which is an exposition of the *via negativa*, although not in its most extreme form.

such a virtual repudiation of the creatures would mean that the whole system of external, sacramental and historical religion would have to go, as so many stumbling blocks to the soul's advance. The Spanish mystics did not go this far; their mysticism remained active and practical; yet they taught that contemplation of the humanity of Christ was only for the lower stages of the mystical ascent. The mystic, in his ascent to God, leaves reason behind.

In philosophy and discursive theology (as against mysticism), reason is, of course, the bedrock upon which every structure is erected. "The great systems of scholasticism look upon it as their chief task to reconcile" revelation and reason "and to harmonize them according to their content." [54] "Men sought to arrange a compromise between what they wanted to believe and what they had to believe. They sought to make a truce between clay and fire, for most of them were unaware that there could never be a treaty between reason and faith." [55] St. Thomas, like Lull, believed that such a treaty could be made, and, for a brief moment, he succeeded in making it. When, in the sixteenth century, the authority of the fathers of theology and of philosophy seemed to be in danger of becoming disestablished, Melchor Cano and Francisco Suárez undertook the task anew.

In his *Theologia Naturalis,* Sabunde taught (with overconfidence) that the existence of God is demonstrable from his creation; that man inhabits a rational universe, created and sustained by the will of a rational God; and that it is man's privilege, through the use of his God-given reason and the gift of grace, to attain by an act of ratiocination (and of love) to the understanding of the truth and the contemplation of the good and the eternal. Though his book was placed on the Roman Index of 1559 (not the Spanish of that year), the theologians appointed by the Council of Trent limited the condemnation (1564) to the Prologue, whose intemperate rationalism did not extend to the book as a whole.[56]

54. Cassirer, *op. cit.,* p. 40.

55. Don Cameron Allen, *The Legend of Noah: Renaissance Rationalism in Art, Science, and Letters* (Urbana, Illinois, 1949), p. 174.

56. It is noteworthy that the rationalism that was feared was not scientific rationalism, but religous rationalism, which tended to minimize (but not destroy) faith; and that in general the Church feared not reason, but its opposite: any doctrine of interior prayer that might tend to make unnecessary the ministrations of the Church as an institution. See I. S. Révah, *Une source de la spiritualité péninsulaire au XVIe*

Vives lived without fear that faith might dull his reason (which would be equivalent to fearing that Nature could be diminished or weakened by Grace).[57] Reason, says Fray Luis de Granada, shows to man the goodness and the good order of nature; faith teaches the harmonious supernatural economy of the works of grace; and "these two lights together dispel all mists, remove all doubts, rise above all clouds, make level all roads, and cause us to embrace sweetly supreme truth."[58]

REASON AND EPISTEMOLOGY

Throughout this work there have been many references to Venegas and his *Differencias de libros que ay en el vniuerso*. It is now time to give a more complete picture of what those "books" were. Hugh of Folieto "makes the metaphor of the book a minor system of theology. According to him there are four books of life. The first was written in Paradise, the second in the desert, the third in the Temple, the fourth has been written from all eternity. God wrote the first in the human heart, Moses wrote the second on tablets, Christ the third on earth, and Divine Providence the fourth. He develops this further, in the course of which the stock phrase 'book of reason' appears."[59] The first of Venegas' "books" is the *Libro Original*, the book of God's essence. Of this we see only the cover. From it are derived the three books that we may open and study: (1) the *Libro Natural*, from which is derived the philosophy of the visible world; (2) the *Libro Racional*, that source of knowledge which comes to us from the office and use of reason; (3) the *Libro Reuelado*, which contains the authority and solid base of the Scriptures. Venegas sets forth an epistemological hierarchy: "Thus we see that the lowest level of knowing makes use of the corporeal creatures; the second level which rises

siècle: La "Théologie Naturelle" de Raymond Sebond (Lisbon, 1953), pp. 34–35; and my review, *HR*, XXIII (1955), 131–32.

57. José Corts Grau, in *Estudios de historia social de España*, II (1952), 65. See Vives, *Tratado del alma*, trans. Ontañón (Madrid, 1923), p. 103.

58. *Introducción del Símbolo de la fe*, I, 3. See Pedro Laín Entralgo, *La antropología en la obra de Fray Luis de Granada* (Madrid, 1946), p. 281.

59. Curtius, *European Literature and the Latin Middle Ages* (New York, 1953), p. 320.

above the first is the law of reason written and sealed in the hearts of men; and the supreme level is the revelation of the things contained in the Holy Scriptures" (*ed. cit.,* fols. 182v–183). When in this manner the light of reason joins the light of faith, says Fray Luis de Granada as he begins the Third Part of his *Símbolo de la fe,* "the soul receives from this union a great joy and consolation." [60]

REASON AND ETHICS

"If there is a rational science of the world, there will also be a rational science of man in his moral activity. For man forms part of the organized and intelligible universe. The individual also has natural laws . . . which direct him toward an end." [61]

"It is a common saying, both of philosophers and of theologians, that each human being contains within himself two men: one is called the interior man, which is reason, and the other is called the exterior man, which is sensuality; which two men, since they are different in substance, cannot live together in harmony, but are ordinarily engaged in desperate battle, so that no negotiation is possible, but rather it is necessary that one party must triumph and the other be subjugated. And for this reason philosophy admonishes us to control ourselves, so that thought (*consejo*) shall restrain our appetites and folly, and reason our wild impulses, which like furious horses seek to subjugate reason." So says Venegas in the prefatory pages of his *Agonía del tránsito de la muerte* (*ed. cit.,* p. 223b). Fray Luis de Granada says essentially the same thing in the first paragraphs of Part Four of his *Símbolo de la Fe*: "God gives to every Christian two lights whereby he may know Him; one is reason and the other, faith; the one is natural and the other supernatural; the one human and the other divine; but both are the daughters of God because both proceed from a single principle which is God himself — one by way of nature, the other by way of grace. All things which faith preaches about the mys-

60. Cited in Laín Entralgo, *La antropología* . . . , p. 271.
61. Paré, *op. cit.,* pp. 136–37.

teries of our redemption not only are not contrary to reason, but rather exist in the greatest conformity to reason." [62] Similarly, Malón de Chaide in his *Conversión de la Magdalena* declares: "There are three balances which serve for weighing. The first is unenlightened reason; this, says St. Paul to the Romans, is the balance of learned men puffed up with the folly of the world. It is a false balance, and it deceives. . . . The second balance is reason enlightened by the *lux naturalis*. This is the balance used by those who know what sin is, and know that they are wrong in doing what they do, but who are blinded by passion or lust so that they do not cease in their sinning. The third balance comes into use when sins are measured by the law of the Gospel — the plumb line that must determine the rectitude of men's lives, the rule and the level by which all must be judged." [63]

Reason and self-organization

The best statement of the principle that reason is the guide of life is perhaps a sorites placed by Venegas at the beginning of the Sixth Part of his *Agonía*: "Since it is the highest truth that every kingdom divided against itself must be laid waste . . . , it is true that the republic existing in the human body cannot be preserved without unity, and unity cannot be had without order, and order cannot be had without obedience, and obedience consists only in reason, and reason is the good stewardship which places and arranges things in their proper places, according to the law of order, from which it follows that in order for man to live like a man, he must take into consideration all the things that enter into his make-up, namely: body and soul, in order that he may place and employ each one of the things which he finds in his own person in the place which shall be most suitable for the preservation of the whole" (*ed. cit.*, p. 224a). The end of this self-organization is salvation. Venegas also says that the five senses were given to man "that by their means he might overcome the devil and obtain eternal glory, subjecting them to the control of reason . . . (*ibid.*, p. 140b).

62. Cited by A. F. G Bell, *El renacimiento español* (Zaragoza, 1944), p 29.
63. The translation is free but accurate (*ed. cit.*, II, 69–70).

LIMITS OF REASON

Sir Francis Bacon insisted that "we do not presume by the contemplation of nature to attain the mysteries of God." [64] Giordano Bruno (d. 1600) distinguished nine kinds of amorous blindness (e.g., "love is blind"), the ninth and highest being the sacred blindness produced by the immediate presence of the deity: "wherefore the most profound and divine theologians say that God is better honoured and loved by silence than by words . . . , and therefore the negative theology of Pythagoras and Dionysius is so celebrated and placed above the demonstrative theology of Aristotle and the Scholastics." [65] Among Renaissance theologians

it was almost a commonplace to say that the highest mysteries transcend the understanding and must be apprehended through a state of darkness in which the distinctions of logic vanish . . . ; "the portentous power of the negative" had been refined to a "learned ignorance" [Cusanus, d. 1464]. One did not need to turn to Pico's *Conclusiones* to learn of this particular principle. Any Platonist knew it as "the One beyond Being," to which Plato had pointed in the *Parmenides*. . . . Intellect excludes contradictions, love embraces them. It was thus that Lorenzo de' Medici [d. 1492] observed in *L'Altercazione* how his nature contracted whenever he tried to comprehend God through the understanding. . . . "Let us enter," Pico wrote, "into the light of ignorance and, blinded by the darkness of the divine splendor, exclaim with the Prophet: I fainted in thy halls, O Lord. . . ." In the famous handbook by Agrippa of Nettesheim [d. 1535], *De occulta philosophia*, Pico's conclusion was literally repeated with the marginal heading *Cur Amor caecus* (why Amor is blind); "Ideoque amorem Orpheus sine oculis describit, quia est supra intellectum." [66]

It is obvious that the Christian (and semi-Christian) thinkers do not agree in these matters. Western Christianity began with a complete identification of faith and reason, holding that every one of its ideas could be made the subject matter of rational knowledge; but the subsequent history of medieval rational theology was the gradual circumscribing of the "fields of truth" that could be proved by reason, "until by the middle of the fourteenth century they had reached the vanishing point with some of the

64. Herschel Baker, *The Wars of Truth: Studies in the Decay of Christian Humanism in the Earlier Seventeenth Century* (Cambridge, Massachusetts, 1952), p. 170.
65. Edgar Wind, *Pagan Mysteries in the Renaissance* (New Haven, 1958), p. 57.
66. *Ibid.*, pp. 57–60.

followers of William of Ockham." [67] The nominalists of the four-teenth and fifteenth centuries insisted on the irrationality of God, who is not supreme reason, but supreme liberty and power.[68] In the sixteenth century Luther declared that reason is "the pesti-lential enemy" of God.[69] Somewhat later Montaigne (d. 1592), arguing against those who claimed that Sabunde's arguments in the *Theologia Naturalis* are weak and unable to prove his case and who, as a result, made bold to attack religion on purely human grounds, said that the best means he could think of to combat these attackers was to tread under foot human haughtiness and pride, to make them feel the inanity and the vanity of man, to tear from their hands the feeble weapons of their reason, to make them bow their heads and bite the dust before the authority of the divine majesty.[70]

In the fifteenth century Fray Iñigo de Mendoza (d. 1490?), writ-ing of the mystery of the Eucharist, apprehendable only by faith (which is, after all, the firmest foundation), protests against those who would seek a rational explanation:

Human intellect — created,
Not creating — , I would teach you
To advance with bridled footsteps;
If without restraint you gallop
You'll cast your rider from the saddle.
Oh what folly for a creature
Formed of dust, yet full of pride,
To set his petty human limits
On the boundless power of God! [71]

Vives declared that original sin "covered our mind with great and dense mists." [72] In another place he explains that the faculties of the senses (both interior and exterior) in mankind are at the service of the mind, which, starting with an apprehension made

67. Randall, *The Role of Knowledge* . . . , pp. 48–49.
68. Laín Entralgo, *La espera y la esperanza* . . . , p. 151.
69. *Ibid.*, p. 162. See *Patrologia Latina*, vol. 219, p. 59: "Index De Ratione humana et eius excellentia, potentia et infirmitate."
70. *Essais*, ed. J. V. LeClerc (Paris, 1826), III, 21.
71. "Entendimiento criado, / lo que yo a ti te enseño / es que corras enfrenado, / que sy vas desatentado / despeñarás a tu dueño; / ¡o quándo [read quán] necio des-uarío / es, ombre fecho de lodo, / que con tu reposo y brío / al diuino poderio / pon-gas modo" (*Cancionero castellano* . . . , *ed. cit.*, I, 102).
72. *Tratado del alma, ed. cit.*, p 104

possible by the imagination, rises higher to a knowledge of spiritual things. But the mind, enclosed as it is in the dark prison of the body and surrounded by shadows, is deprived of the apprehension of many objects: it cannot gaze nor understand with the clarity that it would wish — which is to say that it does not grasp the essence of things which are themselves involved in matter, nor the quality of things immaterial, nor can it deploy its powers within such obscurity.[73]

In 1575 Juan Huarte de San Juan in his great book on vocational guidance, the *Examen de ingenios para las ciencias,* while expressing admiration for the reason as a noble faculty, insists on that faculty's frailty: "The intellect is man's most noble faculty, the one of greatest dignity; but there is none that can so easily be deceived in its effort to apprehend the truth." [74]

In 1583 the Augustinian Fray Luis de León expresses extreme disillusionment in regard to the human reason in the dedicatory letter that prefaces the Second Book of *De los nombres de Cristo*: men naturally desire their own good; sin is an evil; yet the enormous mass of human sin goes unrestrained. Even the thinkers of pagan antiquity, had they looked carefully into the matter, should have arrived at the conclusion of some essential human defect, some departure from the purity with which mankind left the hands of its Creator. How could a benevolent God place in charge of human conduct a reason so frail and so without doctrine as is ours at birth? Furthermore, the bestial desires awaken in us before we reach the age of reason. When we reach that age, the passions are already lying in wait for us, together with all manner of temptations, each one of which is able to obscure the nascent rational faculty. It was not God, but man's willful denial of obedience, that caused the disaster wherein *se conoce más claramente la miseria humana* — "the misery of the human condition is most obviously apparent."

73. *De anima et vita,* cited by Marías, *op. cit.,* p. 167. See *Introducción a la sabiduría, ed. cit.,* p. 43: "The glory of God is so great that he who rises to investigate His majesty cannot fail to go astray; and St. Paul commands us to know only what we need to know . . . and says that it is not licit for him to tell the secrets and mysteries that he beheld [in his mystical experience of being caught up into the third heaven]."

74. Cited by Mauricio de Iriarte, *El doctor Huarte de San Juan y su Examen de Ingenios* (Madrid, 1948), p. 237; cf. p. 256.

Skepticism

The skeptics, wrote Montaigne, *logeoient le souverain bien à la recognoissance de la foiblesse de nostre iugement* — "found that the *summum bonum* is the recognition of the weakness of human judgment." [75] These skeptics — Pyrrho of Elis, Timon of Phlius, Sextus Empiricus, and their continuators, Nicholas of Autrecourt, Vanini, Charron, Des Périers, La Mothe le Vayer, and Bodin [76] — had few spiritual brothers in Spain. [77] Though there are many expressions by Spaniards of their awareness of the inadequacy of human knowledge, of their sensitivity to dualism and contradictions, and of their concern with paradox as revealing the complexity of truth, the Spaniard of our period, when faced with the evidence that knowledge falters, turns back to the faith held by his culture and is not content with sole reliance on the "right life" as the only legitimate confidence known to man. [78]

The Spanish thinkers of the sixteenth century whose points of view illustrate the critical direction of thought are Vives, Francisco Sánchez, and Pedro de Valencia. Vives is a critical philosopher (though eminently Christian) in the true sense of the word. [79]

75. *Essais, ed. cit.*, III, p. 105. I will treat the subject of skepticism at some length, from the more technical standpoint of professional philosophy, in Volume III, Chapter X. My purpose here is merely to show the keen awareness, on the part of Spanish thinkers of various sorts, of the frailty of the reasoning faculty.

76. C. Michalski, *Les sources du criticisme et du scepticisme dans la philosophie du XIVe siècle* (Krakow, 1924); Allen, *op. cit.*, p. 16.

77. I know of no Spanish thinker of whom it might be said, as it was of Guido Cavalcanti (d. 1300), that "he held somewhat to the opinion of the Epicureans . . . that there was no God"; nor do I know of any intellectual circle in Spain in which skepticism was common, as it was in the highly educated class to which Guido belonged (see J. B. Fletcher, *The Religion of Beauty in Woman* [New York, 1911], pp. 77–78); there is only the case of the obscure Dr. Juan López de Illescas, who was tempted to entertain the thought that there was no God (see Angela Selke de Sánchez "¿Un ateo español en el siglo XVI? Las tentaciones del doctor Juan López de Illescas," *Archivum* [Oviedo], VII [1958], 25–47; especially pp. 29–32).

78. See Margaret L. Wiley, *The Subtle Knot: Creative Scepticism in Seventeenth-Century England* (Cambridge, Massachusetts, 1952), p. 59. Richard H. Popkin, in *The History of Scepticism from Erasmus to Descartes* (Assen, 1960), arguing that the French skeptics of the sixteenth and seventeenth centuries were attempting to discredit human reason in order to render untenable the Protestant claim that each individual should be his own interpreter of Scripture, causes Charron and many of the erudite *libertins* to appear "religiously much less suspect than many scholars, including Busson and Pintard, have thought" (see review by D. M. Frame, *RR*, LII [1961], 226 ff.). See also Allen, *Doubt's Boundless Sea.* . . .

79. Ferrater Mora, *op. cit., s. v.* Vives.

He writes in his *Introducción a la sabiduría,* so often cited in the present study: "Very little, very dark, and very uncertain is the sum total of what men in this life can understand; and our intellects, detained and shackled in the prison of this body, lie oppressed in a great darkness of ignorance; and the cutting edges of the mind are so dull that they cannot cut through or penetrate the surface of things" (*ed. cit.,* p. 51).

Sánchez published his *Quod nihil scitur* (*Nothing is Knowable*) in 1576. In his Introduction to the anonymous Spanish translation[80] of this work, Menéndez y Pelayo defines Sánchez's position: rational discourse cannot prove that the world is eternal, or that it had a beginning, or that it must have an end. Having declared in this manner the impotence of reason to solve the conflict, Sánchez takes refuge — apparently in all sincerity — in the testimony of faith. His position, according to Ferrater Mora, does not go beyond probabilism, which rises above radical skepticism but does not reach a criterion of truth even for the world of the senses. Sánchez' work is perhaps not an anticipation of that of Descartes but does prepare the way for it.[81] At the end of his famous book Sánchez announced his intention to write another book in which he would reconstruct philosophy on a sound basis — a critique of practical reason which never saw the light.[82] His position, in the book that he did write, is stated as follows: "if you except what is already within us or is done by us, the most certain knowledge is that which is arrived at through the senses, and the most dubious of all is that which is arrived at by rational discourse, since the latter is not true knowledge but a groping, a doubt, an opinion, a conjecture" (*ed. cit.,* pp. 116–17).

Pedro de Valencia (of whom so little is known that his name does not appear in Ferrater Mora's *Diccionario de filosofía*) in his *De judicio erga verum* (1596) addressed himself to a single problem: that of knowledge, as formulated by Arcesilaus and the New Academy. Admiring Valencia's skill in handling the technical terminology of Greek philosophy, Menéndez y Pelayo said that

80. *Que nada se sabe* (Madrid, n. d.).
81. Ferrater Mora, *op. cit., s. v.* Sánchez.
82. M. Menéndez y Pelayo, "De los orígenes del criticismo y del escepticismo y especialmente de los precursores españoles de Kant," in *Obras completas,* XLIII (Madrid, 1948), p. 135.

he knew of no monograph on a problem in the history of philosophy (before the great compilation of Brucker) that could compete with Valencia's essay: his discussion of the dispute beween Zeno and Arcesilaus, of the probabilist arguments of Antiochus and Carneades, and of Epicurus' analysis of the testimony of the senses "could not be improved upon in modern times." [83] (Valencia's work is not accessible to me.)

The Jesuit José de Acosta is known as a historian and also for his work in natural history,[84] yet in his *Historia natural y moral de las Indias* (1591) he expresses attitudes which make it necessary to mention him prominently in our examination of Spanish philosophical skepticism. Considering the force of magnetism, he writes:

What I will say is that I would gladly ask those college graduates who presume to know it all what this thing is; I would ask them to tell me the cause of this effect. For a small piece of iron, if rubbed against a lodestone, acquires a virtue of looking always to the North — and this with such powers of discrimination that it knows the climates and diverse positions of the world, where it should remain steady, where incline to one side and where to another — so great that there is no philosopher or cosmographer who knows it as well. If for these things that are part of our daily experience we can find no reason (so that they would surely cause in us great incredulity if we did not see them so palpably), who will fail to see how foolish and nonsensical it is to try to set ourselves up as judges, and subject sovereign and divine things to our reason? It is better, as the theologian St. Gregory says, for reason to be subject to faith, since the former does not know how to proceed even in the realms which are properly hers.[85]

One more text by Father Acosta needs to be quoted:

And thus it seems that this business must be attributed to its efficient superior and celestial cause, which can be no other than the sun, and the movement and influence of the heavens, which from different angles move and exert their influence in diverse ways. And since these principles of movement and influence are so hidden from men, and those forces in themselves are so powerful and efficacious, it was with great wisdom that the Holy Prophet David said: "He bringeth the wind out of his treasuries. . . ." Certainly these principles are rich and hidden treasures which the Author of All . . . brings forth for the punishment or the delight of men, sending His wind when He wishes. The beginning and origin of these winds are unknown to us, as are

83. "De los orígenes del criticismo . . . ," pp. 202–3.
84. J. R. Carracido, *El P. José de Acosta y su importancia en la literatura científica española* (Madrid, 1899).
85. Ed. Madrid, 1792, I, 55.

their duration, the place whence they came, or whither they go. But we do see their different effects, as the Author of Truth told us saying: "The spirit bloweth where it listeth . . . ," thus giving us to understand that, if we know so little in a matter so present and ordinary, we must not presume to know that which is high and lofty, such as the causes and motives of the Holy Spirit.[86]

REASON AND GRACE

Sabunde "showed what human reason can do with the aid of religion; Montaigne shows what it cannot do without it."[87] In his famous *Apologie* for Sabunde, Montaigne declares that true and essential reason is lodged in the bosom of God, where it has its dwelling place and its retreat. "It is from His bosom that reason issues forth, when it pleases God to grant us some gleam, some perception of reason's power."[88] "Montaigne's only denial of the possibility of knowledge is that of perfect knowledge . . . without divine grace."[89] Montaigne says: "All that we undertake without His assistance, all that we see without the lamp of His grace, is but vanity and folly; the very essence of truth, which is uniform and constant, when Fortune places us in possession of it, we corrupt and debase by our weakness."[90]

And what did Sabunde teach? In his Preface he says that God has placed the "book" of his creatures before us that we may read therein, each creature being as it were a letter, and that in reading we may achieve salvation; however, none can see by himself, nor read in this great book (though it is ever open before our eyes) unless he be enlightened by God and purged of the stain of original sin.[91]

Although it is general Christian doctrine that reason without grace is of no avail in human life or in man's striving for salvation,

86. *Ibid.*, p. 111.
87. Donald M. Frame, "Did Montaigne Betray Sebond?", *RR*, XXXVIII (1947), 317. "Sebond attempts a rational demonstration of Christianity; Montaigne insists that true belief is pure, obedient, and unreasoning" (*ibid.*).
88. *Essais, ed. cit.*, III, 207–8.
89. D. M. Frame, review of Hiram Haydn, *The Counter Renaissance*, in *RR*, XLI (1950), 287.
90. *Essais, ed. cit.*, III, p. 230–31.
91. *Op. cit.*, I, Preface.

such strong insistence upon the need of grace and the feebleness of reason is especially characteristic of currents of thought ultimately deriving from St. Augustine. When, almost in our own day, Cardinal Newman, "setting himself against the aggressive intellect of his impious age, declared that 'it is not a necessary mark of a true religion that it is rational in the common sense of the word,' he was in the main tradition of Christian apologetics."[92] The Reformation was essentially a restressing of the Augustinian position: "In the angry tumult of the real reformers, the correction of abuses was necessary but paltry; they wished to abandon the whole tradition of a rational theology and replace it—with violence, if need be—with a religion of Augustinian subjectivism and revelation. . . . Luther (and Calvin) could be satisfied only with a complete reversal of Thomistic rationalism" (*ibid.*, p. 266).

Though the Thomistic position (because of the course of the Counter Reformation in Spain) becomes characteristic, as we shall see, the essentially Augustinian stressing of grace is nonetheless an important factor in Spanish Renaissance thought. Our first testimony is from the *Amadís de Gaula*, 1508. The author pauses in his account of chivalric adventures in order to ponder the fate of men and nations: "And in this . . . you can see how insufficient is the force of human reason, when God Almighty, loosening the reign and raising his hand and withdrawing his grace, permits man's judgment to remain delivered to its own devices; wherefrom you will learn whether great states . . . can be won and governed by the discretion and activity of mortals; or whether, without God's divine grace, pride, covetousness, and armed force can maintain such a [political] state."[93]

In 1511 the Spanish pre-Reformation was moving forward at full strength. Spanish translators chose, as an aid to the spiritual life of their countrymen, to render in the vernacular a work, attributed to St. Augustine, entitled *Meditaciones, soliloquio y manual.* This translation, says Marcel Bataillon, is of capital importance, because it teaches a religion in which human pride is profoundly humbled in the presence of divine grace.[94] Chapter XV of the

92. Baker, *The Dignity of Man*, pp. 139–40.
93. Ed. Barcelona, 1847–48, II, 234.
94. *Erasmo y España* (Mexico City–Buenos Aires, 1950), I, 55.

Soliloquio bears the heading: "How man can do nothing by himself, without divine grace." [95]

In 1525 Juan de Valdés brought out his *Diálogo de doctrina cristiana*, an Erasmian (and Pauline) catechism. Its novelty consists in its insistence on man's nullity when left to his own devices — a nullity from which he can be saved only by divine grace. The just man is merely the sinner justified by divine mercy. Here, more explicitly than in the works of Erasmus, the soul is invited to confess its nothingness and to place all its hope in a supernatural intervention which will convert this nothingness into plenitude (*ibid.*, pp. 408–11).

In 1535 Fray Francisco Ortiz found a living faith necessary to combat our natural passions: "in such a temptation we are likely to forget that charity which God commands us to have toward our enemies, unless our soul is aided by celestial favor to help it to follow more the inclination of grace than of nature, which (corrupted by the fall) judges vengeance to be most reasonable." [96]

Venegas, in his *Agonía*, teaches that, as a result of the loss of our innocence (*la justicia original*) in Eden, our appetite is not restrained by reason, but like a lion tears to shreds not only natural reason but even the divine commandments, if divine grace does not come to our aid (*ed. cit.* pp. 133b–134).

Fray Luis de Granada wore the Dominican habit of the order of St. Thomas Aquinas, and perhaps for that reason, though he insists on grace, his figures of speech are less harsh, his hope brighter. He defines grace as "a participation in the divine nature, that is, in the sanctity, the goodness and the purity and nobility of God; by means of which man casts out the baseness and unworthiness that are his inheritance from Adam and becomes a participant in the holiness and nobility of God, stripping himself of his own nature and assuming the nature of Christ" (*Obras*, ed. cit., I, p. 157). The result is a "marvelous victory and liberty" which does not allow the passions to prevail against the reason (*ibid.*, p. 236). Grace is "a special light and wisdom which our Lord communicates to the just: to grace belongs the task of healing nature"

95. The date makes it obvious that this has nothing to do with the Counter Reformation.
96. *Epístolas familiares*, BAE, XIII, 260b.

(pp. 162–63). Grace, in an ineffable manner, "reforms and strengthens our virtues and all the faculties of our soul, enlightening the intellect, concentrating the memory, strengthening the free will, tempering our concupiscible inclinations and fortifying our irascible inclinations lest they grow weak and fearful in the struggle for the good" (pp. 160–61).

The Augustinian Fray Luis de León, in Part II of *De los nombres de Cristo*, teaches that, when touched by grace, the will becomes silent, the horrible fear of God's anger vanishes, and, in a secret and marvelous way, the kingdom of the soul is restored to peace, as will and reason, formerly at strife one with the other, are brought into harmony, and the body desists from its rebellion (*ed. cit.*, II, 165–67).

THE SCHOLASTIC TRADITION IN SPAIN [97]

Quevedo, citing as his authority the Jesuits of Coimbra (Collegium Conimbriense Societatis Jesu) and their course in philosophy, declared that it is not only by supernatural means that the faith is taught; some of the truths of the faith are accessible to natural reason.[98] Calderón, the last great figure of the Golden Age, presented "in his serious plays but one subject and one theme: man, subverting the order of natural values by his moral error and human frailty or, in the labyrinthine confusion of life, groping towards the light by the aid of reason and discretion."[99] Reason rather than passion should guide man's decision: when it does not, destruction and unhappiness follow, as in Calderón's *El médico de su honra;* when it does, man emerges victorious, as in *La vida es sueño.*[100] To Gracián, himself a Jesuit, reason is "Queen

97. In Chapter X of our Volume III there will be a section on the Spanish Neo-Scholastics.

98. Ernest Mérimée, *Essai sur la vie et les oeuvres de Francisco de Quevedo* (Paris, 1886), p. 259.

99. A. E. Sloman, *The Dramatic Craftsmanship of Calderón: His Use of Earlier Plays* (Oxford, 1958), p. 308.

100. Citing another dramatist, Juan Ruiz de Alarcón (d. 1639), we may point out that his heroes, and heroines also, "may be said to act on the basis of reason, reasonableness, or ratiocination," his ultimate solutions being set in a logical, reasonable frame well within the limits of dogma. See Alice M. Paulin (*read* Pollin), "The Religious Motives in the Plays of Juan Ruiz de Alarcón," *HR*, XXIX (1961), 39.

of Light, Mother of Awareness," and the judgment of the reason is "the most faithful friend that we have."[101] This attitude, rather than the Augustinian one that we found so well expressed in the first half of the sixteenth century,[102] seems native and natural in the country that produced the Society of Jesus and the triumph of the philosophy and theology of such Neo-Scholastics as Melchor Cano and Francisco Suárez.

Though St. Thomas said of God that the supreme knowledge we may have of Him is the awareness that He is above all our thoughts,[103] and although reason is used in theology not to prove the truths of faith (which are accepted on the authority of God) but to defend, explain, and develop revealed doctrines,[104] it is yet true that "the very *raison d'être* of Early and High Scholasticism" was to establish the unity of truth, and its task was "the writing of a permanent peace treaty between faith and reason."[105] Scholasticism taught that while the human reason cannot prove such doctrines as the Incarnation or the temporality of creation, it can, and does, elucidate or clarify these articles of faith (*ibid.*, p. 29). The "peace treaty" did not stay in force, however, and the mystics and the nominalists who succeeded St. Thomas abandoned the task of reconciliation. In the sixteenth century Luther expressed contempt for reason, and the Erasmists of sixteenth-century Spain developed an essentially anti-intellectual pietism which the Spanish Church felt it necessary to stamp out.

With the Counter Reformation there came a new intellectualism. Domingo de Soto (d. 1560) declared in his *De justitia et jure* that reason is an emanation of the Deity.[106] To reject reason as the Protestants do, said Cano (d. 1560), is not only folly but an act of

101. *El Criticón*, ed. Miguel Romera-Navarro (Philadelphia, 1938–40), I, 173–74.

102. The persecuted Erasmist Fray Bartolomé Carranza represented a pietistic current of thought which was opposed to the intellectualist current led by Melchor Cano. His *iluminismo* was an interpretation of Christianity which vigorously stressed the opposition between faith and reason and had little regard for the authority of theologians and philosophers. In short, it was anti-rationalism which came to be feared and persecuted by the ecclesiastical authorities. Cano was against 'interior prayer" and in favor of reason (Bataillon, *op. cit.*, II, 107, 325–26).

103. Sertillanges, *op. cit.*, p. 52.

104. *The Catholic Encyclopaedia*, art. Thomas Aquinas.

105. E. Panofsky, *Gothic Architecture and Scholasticism* (Latrobe, Pennsylvania, 1951), pp. 28–29.

106. Cited by Joseph Höffner, *La ética colonial española del siglo de oro: Cristianismo y dignidad humana*, trans. F. de Asís Caballero (Madrid, 1957), p. 339.

impiety, since God is truth.[107] Finally, Suárez (d. 1617) gave to this new Scholasticism a renewed vitalistic and dynamic character, mitigating its tendency to become extreme in its intellectualism.[108]

Reason and the Jesuits

It will be well to relate these various attitudes to the temper of the times as manifested in the teachings of the Society of Jesus. "As against Luther and Calvin, who never tire of repeating the despair-inspiring formulas of St. Augustine ('the virtues of the pagans are only vices in disguise,' 'Nature left to herself is incapable of any good'), the Jesuits, in accord with the Church Fathers and the theologians of Trent, maintain that Christianity does not destroy the natural virtues; it hierarchizes and harmonizes them." [109] It is not an abrogation of Nature's laws but a correction of her departures from truth and a fulfillment of her possibilities. There is thus no split between reason and revelation. "Ancient wisdom precedes in time and announces Christian truth; is, in fact, the preface to the Gospel. One can therefore imitate the pagans and 'take from them things good in themselves, i.e., such natural actions as honoring God, enacting laws to maintain justice, honoring one's father and mother . . . , or at the very least one can take from them things doctrinally indifferent, such as making statues and paintings and other things that the art of Nature teaches'" (ibid.).

It will be worth while to quote one more paragraph from Dainville's study of this subject:

with greater or less success [the Jesuit legislators] make it their business to safeguard total truth, to demonstrate the accord of faith and reason on the grave questions of the immortality of the soul, the plurality of souls, the creation, Providence, putting forth every effort to maintain or reestablish the equilibrium menaced by Protestantism (which preached a complete abandonment of the self to faith) and by the ever stronger party of the "atheists" and "libertines" . . . who wished to listen only to reason.[110] [The

107. Cited by José Gallegos Rocafull, *El hombre y el mundo de los teólogos españoles de los siglos de oro* (Mexico City, 1946), p. 183.
108. Mauricio de Iriarte, S. J., *El hombre Suárez y el hombre en Suárez* (Madrid, 1950), p. 34.
109. François de Dainville, *Les Jésuites et l'éducation de la société française* (Paris, 1940), I, 226. (Dainville's quotations are from L. Richeome, *Trois discours* [1597].)
110. I reserve the discussion of atheism for my chapter on the Spanish Renaissance in Volume III. It will here be sufficient to quote from Paul Oskar Kristeller, *The*

Jesuits] frequently succeeded. The conversion of the future Cardinal Du Per-
ron, brought back to the true Church by the study of St. Thomas' commentaries on Aristotle (which Father González, professor of philosophy at Pont-à-
Mousson [1574] had advised him to read "in order to fully dissipate his
doubts"), is surely not an isolated case. [Platonism] which had gone astray in
the matter of the soul, offered to [the Jesuits] a much-needed complement to
the faltering Aristotelian theodicy: the idea of a God who creates and is concerned with governing the destiny of men and things. Many pages of Seneca,
the *Dream of Scipio*, and above all the treatise *On the Nature of the Gods*
by Cicero, became the framework within which they developed their natural
theology.[111]

Francisco de Medrano (d. 1607?) was a Jesuit without call to be
a Jesuit, a victim of the disturbances in that Order that fill the
decade prior to 1593, a deeply religious[112] Jesuit who at length
left the Order. Dámaso Alonso's account of the "three currents of
thought and feeling" which dominated Medrano's life and work
is instructive for our present purposes: "In that sort of revival of
the Horatian atmosphere wherein Medrano, as man and poet,
moves and has his being, what perhaps strikes us first is the note
of Epicureanism;[113] but already in Horace himself this is fused
with certain Stoic elements, and other elements come to Medrano
from Seneca, Pliny, Boethius; still others come to him directly from
the Book of Job; so that it is Stoic thought which predominates,
with that special cast so characteristic of Spanish literature."[114]
This synthesis is well expressed by another intensely religious
Spaniard of the seventeenth century, Quevedo, who studied Hu-

Classics and Renaissance Thought (Cambridge, Massachusetts, 1955), ch. iv: The Renaissance "was a fundamentally Christian age"; "alleged cases of openly pagan or athe-
istic convictions are rare and dubious." (See my review in *RPh*, X, [1957], 281–82.)
"Serious skepticism," says Roland H. Bainton in an article entitled "Man, God, and
the Church in the Age of the Renaissance" (in *The Renaissance: A Symposium*, Metropolitan Museum of Art [New York, 1952], p. 59), "is scarcely discoverable prior to
the very end of the sixteenth century, in Bruno, Campanella, and Vanini, and they
expiated their temerity at the stake [or in the torture chamber] after the manner of
the High Middle Ages." Denys Hay, in *The Renaissance in its Historical Background*
(Cambridge, 1961), says that the alleged atheism of Poggio and Marsuppini has too
slender a basis for acceptance (p. 128) and regards Gemistus Plethon as "the one truly
paganizing figure of the fifteenth century in Italy" (p. 169).

111. *Op. cit.*, I, 238–39.
112. See the section entitled "Agonía del cristiano" in chapter x of Dámaso Alonso's
Vida y obra de Medrano (complete version) (Madrid, 1948–58), I, pp. 119 ff.
113. The Epicureans insisted on intellect alone as man's saving grace. See Abraham C. Keller, *op. cit.*, p. 45.
114. Dámaso Alonso, *Vida y obra de Medrano* (the short version read before the
Real Academia Española [Madrid, 1948]), p. 95.

manities under Jesuit masters: "Never keep far from your hand
the books of the Wisdom of Solomon; and the *Doctrine* of Epicte-
tus, the *Precepts* of Phocylides; and Theognis and the writings of
Seneca; and above all read with special care the books [sic] of
Job. . . . You will be a student and a good one if the reading of
St. Paul is your occupation, and the reading of the Saints your
task." [115]

REASON AND THE PASSIONS [116]

"All the evil that befalls us arises from the fact that we recognize
the voice of reason, yet follow where passion leads us," wrote Quevedo.[117] In our discussion of the limits of reason (see above) we
found frequent expression of the idea that the reason was ham-
pered by its association with the body and weakened by the inheritance of Adam's guilt. Peter Abelard (d. 1142), the precursor of
St. Thomas and of Scholasticism, claimed that man may, "by exert-
ing his God-given reason in avoiding the weaknesses of the flesh,
attain a good life," and that he achieves virtuous conduct "not
solely through the divine gift of grace, but also by regulating his
actions rationally." He asserted that "man's chief moral weapon
is his rational intellect. . . ." [118] Aquinas, in turn, taught that
intellect was superior to will because it sought truth, not the good;
that in both man and God the will was a faculty to implement the
dictates of reason (*ibid.*, p. 199). The reason is therefore a mover,
an agent; the will, a mobile, a patient.[119] Yet even Aquinas could
not overlook common human experience. The passions may over-
rule the will: "Since man's mind, because of original sin, with-
drew itself from obedience to God, it followed that not even the
inferior forces of our nature should be fully subjugated by reason;
which is the source of so much rebellion of the carnal appetite
against reason" (II-II, Q. 164, art. 1).

This is the situation as described by Milton (*Paradise Lost*, IX,
lines 1127–31):

115. *La cuna y la sepultura*, in *Obras en prosa, ed. cit.*, p. 915b.
116. See E. M. W. Tillyard, *The Elizabethan World Picture* (London, 1948), pp.
67 ff.
117. *Obras en prosa, ed. cit.*, p. 774a
118. Cited in Baker, *The Dignity of Man*, pp. 193–94.
119. D. Odon Lottin, *op. cit.*, I, 241.

> For Understanding rul'd not, and the Will
> Heard not her lore, both in subjection now
> To sensual Appetite, who from beneathe
> Usurping over sovran Reason claimed
> Superior sway. . . .

and by Shakespeare (Sonnet 151):

> Thou betraying me, I do betray
> My nobler part to my gross body's treason.
> My soul doth tell my body that he may
> Triumph in love, flesh stays no farther reason. . . .

"Here we see disaster as stemming, first of all, from the lover's adherence to a mutable good that betrays him by its false beauty. Loving this false-fair, he betrays his nobler part (his reason) to his body's desire. His soul furnishes his flesh a practical application of reason, which is as much as is needed to raise an action. . . . This theory . . . is subtler than the Stoic one. It seems, rather, to parallel that of Aquinas, who carefully distinguishes his own view from Stoic theory by tracing sin to an act of reason itself, which becomes corrupted by inordinate love of a temporal good, and then its corruption applies reason defectively in counselling appetite." [120] "If evil is desired, the cause of the desire is the goodness which seems to be (and is not) adjoined to it. Such a situation may arise from the claims of appetite. Sensible good is near-at-hand and potent, so that appetite is liable to be too strongly provoked. Sensible impression, especially when backed by custom, may prevail more than reasonable persuasion." [121]

In these contests the element of individual responsibility is not lost sight of. Boethius (d. 524) wrote that men's greatest bondage "is when, giving themselves to vices, they lose possession of their own reason." [122] Raimundo Lull stated in his *Blanquerna* that if the will inclines in a certain direction before the intellect has ruled on the wisdom of the choice, then the intellect is impeded

120. Roy W. Battenshouse, "Shakespearean Tragedy: A Christian Interpretation," in Nathan A. Scott, Jr. (ed.), *The Tragic Vision and the Christian Faith* (New York, 1957), p. 75.

121. Craig, *op. cit.*, p. 25. The idea that the body's appetites overpower the reason and suppress the natural virtues and affections of the soul is also characteristic of Renaissance Platonism. See E. F. Rice, *The Renaissance Idea of Wisdom* (Cambridge, Massachusetts, 1958), p. 87.

122. *De Consolatione*, V, ii.

in its task of understanding. Therefore, he who wishes light from the intellect, should be temperate in his acts of remembering, desiring, and understanding.[123] In another place (p. 170) he declares that "when man is unwilling to make use of reason because he desires to excuse himself from realizing his sinful state, God's justice may rightfully take from him his powers of discrimination and of conscience, so that he lives a reprobate among men."

The crucial danger lay in the role of the imagination: "Because it can misconstrue or distort the data of sensation, it can throw the whole response of the organism into disequilibrium." "As a mediate faculty lying between sense and reason, the will was particularly vulnerable; it could, and often did, let the objects of sense rather than the objects of reason determine its conduct, and when it did, the result was disastrous." "This is passion — the excessive physiological response to the externals of sense." [124]

The fifteenth-century Spanish moralist Fernán Pérez de Guzmán (d. 1440?) seems to be almost on dangerous ground when he writes:

Muy diffícil, digo yo,	I say it is very difficult — let him
diga imposible quien osa,	who dares say impossible — to
vencer la muy poderosa	overcome the powerful inclina-
natura que Dios crió.[125]	tions of Nature which God created [in us].

Not too many years later, Vives stated in his *Introducción a la sabiduría*: "Every perturbation darkens the clarity of the mind and dulls the judgment" (*ed. cit.*, p. 59).

The early lyric

It is because literature is so commonly an expression of human tensions that the motif of *reason pandering to will* is seen to be present in examples from all genres, from the lyric to the novel. The conflict between reason and desire (will) naturally has a prominent place in that great body of literature which has as its moving force the amorous passion. In Volume I, Chapter III, I have analyzed the part played by reason — as the power that inspires

123. Ed. Lorenzo Riber (Madrid, 1944), pp. 447, 181–82.
124. Baker, *The Dignity of Man*, pp. 283, 292, 286.
125. *Cancionero castellano, ed. cit.*, I, 579.

and controls the love of men and women — in the writings of the poets and prose writers of the courtly love tradition. Without repeating the texts cited in the earlier volume, I present here — in brief summary — what the lyric poets reveal to us of their conception of reason as a faculty of the soul.

Beauty is truth, truth beauty, and beauty is the cause of love. Fortune and Nature, also operative in love's ups and downs, are instruments of Providence. We would thus seem to be free from the *paradoxe amoureux* and love would appear to be the child of that noble faculty of the human soul, reason. In some few cases the poets so represent it: One surrenders his free will only to find that it is still free, that reason and attraction are compatible.

But the *paradoxe* returns. Other poets, in overwhelming number, represent love as the willful child of the appetitive faculty, the *voluntad*, ever at enmity with reason. Will desires self-indulgence, joys of the senses, happiness — forgetting all moderation, scorning fame and even health; reason is a great lady who loves honor and follows after virtue. Some poets find the tyranny of *voluntad* intolerable and declare death preferable to a life alienated from reason and goodness. In such extreme cases will succeeds in banishing reason.

In this conflict reason may, and on occasion does, have the better part, coming to the rescue — in an allegorical-psychological battle — of the faltering lover and relieving will of her subjection. But is not the will free? Being free, can it ever be placed in subjugation?

This involves what seems to be an ambiguity: reason may pander to will, may allow herself, in her encounters with sensuality, to be blinded — as in the allegorical battle just mentioned. When reason is bereft of her discerning power, the lover surrenders his freedom, loses the action of his free will, and is no longer his own master. Love becomes a triumph of sin, ruling and controlling the intellect and subduing all.

When one feels the heat of the fire of love, he should not allow it to gain headway by yielding to the enticements of desire. Victory through Divine Grace is always possible (if the sinner will but raise his hand to God's). Not to seek and accept God's help is a shameful defeat because, according to the teaching of St. Thomas, "the sensual appetite can never set in motion any motor impulse (if man is in his normal state and in perfect possession of his faculties) unless the will has deliberately given its consent." [126] Fray Luis de Granada points up the need for grace: "If you wish that your flesh should serve and be subject to the soul, see to it that your soul is subject to God. . . . God must control the reason; and the reason, the soul; and the soul, the body . . . ; but the body resists the control of the soul, if the latter does not submit to the control of reason and if the reason does not bring itself into conformity with the will of God." [127]

The Golden Age

Whether portrayed in John Gower's (d. 1408) *Confessio Amantis* [128] or in Shakespeare's tragedies,[129] the excesses of love — excusable or inexcusable [130] — arise from the fact that love has usurped dominion over reason. The insistence upon rational control has its origins, both for Elizabethan England and for the Golden Age in Spain, in centuries-old theological positions — theological sanctions reinforced by various pagan philosophies. In this respect, Christian doctrine and ancient philosophy combined to form a harmonious synthesis. The Church had very early felt the need to strengthen her doctrinal position by adapting and adopting concepts conceived in ancient Greece — concepts often made accessible by ancient Rome through such popular authorities as Cicero and Seneca.[131]

126. Thomas Pègues, *Commentaire français littéral de la Somme Théologique de Saint Thomas d'Aquin*, IV, *Traité de l'homme* (Toulouse, 1909), pp. 553–54.
127. *Obras*, I (Madrid, 1768), pp. 476–77.
128. "Gower, as well as another, is faced with this necessity of recantation. For him, as for Chaucer, the love which he celebrates is a sin, and in the lover Will has usurped dominion over Resoun" (C. S. Lewis, *The Allegory of Love: A Study in Medieval Tradition* [Oxford, 1936], p. 218).
129. "From this situation [physiology closely associated with morals and ethics] develops the clear-cut issue of passion versus reason, the terms in which Shakespeare invariably sees the tragic situation" (Patrick Cruttwell, "Psychology in Shakespeare's Age," *JHI*, XII [1951], 87).
130. St. Thomas taught that the "evil in the sexual act is neither the desire nor the pleasure, but the submergence of the rational faculty which accompanies them: and this submergence, again, is not a sin, though it is an evil, a result of the Fall (I-II, xxxiv, art. 1)." See Lewis, *op. cit.*, p. 16.
131. Here, again, I reserve full demonstration for the treatment of the Spanish Renaissance in Volume III. Margot Arce Blanco, in her "standard" book, *Garcilaso de la Vega: Contribución al estudio de la lírica española del siglo XVI* (Madrid, 1930), says (p. 53) that in Garcilaso de la Vega's poems there are but two concrete references

Garcilaso de la Vega. "With his return to Spain in the spring of 1530, the poet found himself once more a victim of his passion. The struggle through which he passed is portrayed in *Canción IV.* As a poem, the composition seems today oversubtle and artificial, with its allegory of the conflict of Reason and Desire. . . ." [132] Rafael Lapesa writes of the same *Canción* as a "renewed version of the conflicts between Reason and Desire, whose subject is the same as the Ladders, Wars, and other allegorical assaults in which the poets of the fifteenth century had caused Love to participate." The poet is a prisoner, led hither and yon by his wild thoughts: "Reason has tried to set up resistance 'with slow step and timorous heart' but has finally surrendered; the golden tresses are the net that encloses trapped Reason, caught 'in public adultery' with Appetite like Mars and Venus in the web spread around them by Vulcan." It is true that this theme in Garcilaso has a "strong medieval flavor" which might seem to have its source in the influence of Auzías March, as Lapesa believes; it is also true that the idea of the conflict, and its allegorical representation, will not disappear in Spain for many years: witness the *autos sacramentales.* [133]

Castillejo. Cristóbal de Castillejo (d. 1550) refused to follow Juan Boscán and Garcilaso in their adaptation of Italian lyrical

to Catholic-religious themes: one to the Protestant schism, and another to the martyrdom of St. Ursula. "The other manifestations which can be interpreted in the same sense are tinged, now with the doctrines of Plato, now with the philosophy of the Stoics, now with frank and conscious paganism." To write in this way is simply not to know the history of the Christian religion. Neoplatonic mysticism, as we have seen, is not remote from the Christian tradition by which it had long since been appropriated (Roland H. Bainton, "The Thirst for God in the Renaissance," *Renaissance News*, V [1952], 10). "Truth to tell, Stoicism was absorbed in . . . the Christian system" (R. M. Wenley, *Stoicism and its Influence* [Boston, 1924], p. 123). "Jerome was saturated with Cicero and Virgil. Cicero had much to do with giving direction to Augustine, and Virgil pervades *The City of God*" (*ibid.*, p. 127). Augustine himself had said: "The doctrine of the [Platonic] Ideas is so fruitful that without understanding it no one can become wise" (Sertillanges, *op. cit.*, p. 39; see also p. 12). Granada wrote in his *Símbolo de la fe*: "This was understood by that great moral philosopher Seneca, saying in a word a great part of what our religion teaches. . . . What more would this philosopher have said, if he had been a Christian? How great and how universal is the doctrine compressed in these brief words!" (*Obras*, ed. Cuervo, V, pp. 281–82).

132. Hayward Keniston, *Garcilaso de la Vega: A Critical Study of his Life and Works* (New York, 1922), p. 196.

133. Rafael Lapesa, *La trayectoria poética de Garcilaso* (Madrid, 1948), pp. 44, 68, 119–92. For the *autos, sacramentales*, see above, notes 16 and 100.

metres and strophe forms to Castilian poetry and, in his own way, offered opposition to the renovating tendencies. However, his attitude toward the love-reason conflict does not on that account differ from that of the majority of his predecessors and successors. He addresses Love:

Y pues de nuestra pasión	And since You are absolute king
eres absoluto rey,	of our passion, my suffering
mi penado coraçón,	heart, converted at last to your
tornado ya de tu ley,	banner, denies and renounces
reniega de la razón.[134]	reason.

Montemayor. Jorge de Montemayor's *Diana* was published in 1559. In it there are two kinds of love, true and false, which differ with respect to origin and object. Good love is born of reason, though not subject to it. This point is made in the paraphrase of León Hebreo's *Diálogos de amor* which provides the theoretical core of the *Diana*:[135] "Love is not of such a nature, oh lovely nymphs of the chaste Diana, that he who is in love can have any regard for reason, or that reason can cause a loving heart to depart from the path over which his fierce destiny guides him." [136] While good love aims at spiritual union with the beloved, false love springs from the base appetite and desires physical satisfaction.[137]

Si el mal de amor no fuera	If love's suffering were not con-
contrario a la razón, como lo uemos,	trary to reason, as we perceive it
quiçá que os lo creyera;	to be, I might believe what you
mas uiendo sus extremos,	say; but knowing its excesses,
dichosas las que dél huyr podemos.[138]	happy is the maiden who can
	avoid it.

Polo. Five years after the appearance of the *Diana*, Gaspar Gil Polo brought out his *Diana enamorada*, with a prologue in which he warns readers to avoid the bittersweet pangs of the "blessed suffering" of courtly love. "Love holds no sway over men except insofar as they, of their own accord, place themselves in its power."

134. *Obras,* ed. J. Domínguez Bordona (Madrid, 1926–28), II, 13.
135. See A. Solé-Leris, "The Theory of Love in the Two *Dianas*: A Contrast," *BHS,* XXXVI (1959), 65 ff.
136. Ed. M. Menéndez y Pelayo in *Orígenes de la Novela* (Madrid, 1905–15), II, 276.
137. Solé-Leris, *op. cit.,* p. 66.
138. *Ed. cit.,* p. 297a.

The freedom of the will is inviolable. The fatalistic view which makes love's power irresistible is attacked. "Only a free will can act according to the light of reason. . . . Once a man has surrendered his will to reckless appetite, his judgment is obfuscated: he becomes a prey to unreasoning impulses, which he cannot control," as reason panders to will.[139] True love, being spiritual, has its firm basis in unwavering and true reason, and causes one to follow after "virtues, skills, perfections, wisdom, and celestial things." The author's message to his readers is, therefore, that that courtly love [140] which "causes suffering and is symbolized by Cupid is desire in disguise and hence to be eschewed." "Suffering is the mark of *maligno amor*." Polo is thus the declared enemy of courtly love as transformed by the sixteenth century. The true lover, according to him, will "endeavour to rise from the direct contemplation of [the beloved's] beauty to that of its abstract image in his own mind, rising then still further from the love of the particular to that of universal beauty . . . until the ultimate mystical state of contemplation of divine beauty is reached. . . . Reason is only transcended by mystical contemplation." [141]

López Maldonado. Gabriel López Maldonado, a friend of Cervantes, published his *Cancionero* in 1586. In the following sonnet he renounces reason and embraces will:

> Through roughest wilderness and without guide,
> In darkest night, my heart worn out and weary,
> With stubborn mind and unretreating step
> I'm driven toward the brink by Imagination.
> Reason knows what's before me, but the foe
> Who holds her in subjection, ne'er relaxes.
> He is my Will, who o'er me now has power
> To usurp Reason's former government.
> And I, poor me! can only follow Will,
> With Reason gone completely from my sight —
> Unless to go on thus be reasonable!
> So be it! When the cause is such as mine,
> Let every man rejoice in his good fortune
> And deem his folly to be Reason herself.[142]

139. Solé-Leris, *op. cit.*, pp. 69, 71
140. See Volume I, Chapter III.
141. Solé-Leris, *op. cit.*, pp. 70–71, 75, 78.
142. "Por ásperos desiertos y sin guía, / en noche obscura y con coraçón lasso, / con

Espinel. Vicente Espinel's *Diversas rimas* appeared in 1591. In his *Eclogue,* addressed to Don Hernando de Toledo the Elder, he proclaims the sovereignty of reason:

> Do you not see him bursting into tears?
> Oh loving youth, so miserable and sad!
> Come with me, Urgenio, let us comfort him!
> For though his illness ever does resist
> And struggle against Reason, 'tis most clear
> That only in Reason does his cure consist.[143]

Alemán. Mateo Alemán's great picaresque novel, *Guzmán de Alfarache,* was printed in 1599. In chapter V of the third book of the Second Part (1604), the "speaker" of the action describes his falling in love at first sight—an emotional misfortune possible because the Fall left our human nature so upset and distorted that the human watch was left completely disassembled, without a fixed spring to move it. This sad state is the result of original sin, which brought about blindness in the intellect, guilt in the will, disorder in the appetite—a cruel squadron of highwaymen who beset the soul with false appearances and turn it from its true nature. So weak is the flesh that this condition of disorder is almost natural to man. Great indeed is the strength of him who can defeat these enemies, because of the infernal war that ever exists between reason and appetite. The latter presents itself under the disguise of the good, whereas the reason is like a cruel schoolmaster, rod in hand, so that we, like children, flee from school, and leave our father's house to live with an aunt or grandmother. Although every one knows that reason retains its ancient and pre-eminent place in the scheme of things, appetite with the blinding flash of the appearance of a desirable (and desired) good, can abduct (*robar*) the will, and the two together can produce any effect they please. This is the

ánimo seguro y largo passo, / me lleua a despeñar mi fantasía. / La razón bien lo entiende, mas porfía / quien la sojuzga y la detiene el passo. / La voluntad es ésta, que en tal caso / quitó el gouierno a quien regir solía. / Todo es ya voluntad quanto yo sigo, / sin quedar de razón señal ninguna, / si no es razón seguir por tal camino; / mas por tal ocasión, conozco y digo / que seguir cada qual tras su fortuna / más es buena razón que desatino" (ed. facsimile [Madrid, 1932], fol. 84v).

143. "¿No veis cómo soltó la rienda al llanto? / ¡O tierno joven, miserable y triste! / Vamos, Vrgenio, a consolarle vn tanto. / Que aunque esta enfermedad siempre resiste / y opuna a la razón, es cosa cierta / que su reparo en la razón consiste" (*Diversas rimas,* ed. D. C. Clarke [New York, 1956], p. 109).

explanation of love at first sight: it happens when reason is not given time to estimate values and to make a choice — as it were by a "confrontation of the blood," to which we are moved by a particular influence of the stars. This is but a repetition, on the individual scale, of what happened in Eden when our first parents surrendered their prerogatives in exchange for the object desired by appetite. The "speaker" accepts full responsibility: "I sought only delectation. . . . Nor did I allow reason to advise me concerning things . . . that I was unwilling to hear; I closed my eyes; I sent reason away. . . . Driven by desire, I obtained an evil desired as a good (*un mal bien deseado*)." [144]

Cervantes. The *Exemplary Novels,* a collection of twelve tales, appeared in 1613. In one of them, *La Gitanilla,* the protagonist, a *puella senex* — a young person old in wisdom beyond her years — says that she knows that "the amorous passions in persons who have recently fallen in love are, as it were, heedless impulses which unhinge the will; which faculty, brooking no interference, foolishly rushes on in the wake of its desire, and thinking that it will obtain the apple of its eye, falls into the inferno of its regrets." [145] Later on in the same story, the discreet heroine explains that in her opinion "jealousy never leaves the intellect free to judge things as they are," and she begs her beloved to proceed in this and in everything that concerns their relationship wisely and discreetly (*ibid.,* p. 794). In another one of these tales, *El casamiento engañoso,* the speaker confesses that appetite (*gusto*), me tenía echados grillos al entendimiento — "had shackled my intellect" (*ed. cit.,* p. 992). In *El coloquio de los perros,* Cervantes presents one of those pathological cases resulting from long-continued indulgence in sin. The victim regards herself as incorrigible and incurable: "I have one of the souls that I have pictured to you; I see and understand everything, and since delight has placed shackles on my will, I have always been and shall always be bad" (*ed. cit.,* p. 1017). With all this burden of sin, she knows "that God is good and merciful and that He knows what shall become of me," and that God is waiting — "for no other reason than his divine mercy" — to help her soul to rise (*ibid.*).

144. Ed. Madrid, 1926–36, V, 52–57. This is greatly condensed.
145. *Obras completas,* ed. Angel Valbuena Prat (Madrid, 1956), p. 782.

True love, according to Cervantes, is based on and controlled by reason. He says in the *Trabajos de Persiles y Segismunda* (1616): "Arnaldo said this in order to show Auristela and Periandro, and all other persons who knew of his desires, how adjusted to reason were all his inclinations and emotions" (*ed. cit.*, p. 1566). In the same novel we read: "thus lascivious desires flatter the will, thus imagined delight deceives the understanding, thus sweet imaginings draw into their train those who do not set up resistance in their amorous encounters" (*ibid.*, p. 1591). And still farther on we find a statement of the essential paradox: love dominates reason, though reason should dominate love: "they again heard about the treacherous designs of Policarpo; but these designs did not appear to them so treacherous that they could not find an excuse for them in the fact that they had been born of love — an excuse sufficient even for greater errors, for when the amorous passion takes possession of a soul, there is no human discourse that can cope with it successfully, nor is there any reason that can withstand it" (p. 1617). Américo Castro in *El pensamiento de Cervantes* has brought together other examples, of which this one is perhaps the most significant: "The amorous passion is mastered only by fleeing from it, because divine strength is needed to overcome its human power" (p. 149, n. 4; see also p. 146, n. 1). Yet Cervantes insists on the autonomy and the freedom of the individual will: "for when it comes to changing the will, unseating it from its foundations, inasmuch as this would be counter to the freedom of the will, there is no science that can achieve it, no virtue, no [magic] herbs that can accomplish it" (*ed. cit.*, p. 1595).

Céspedes y Meneses. The *Poema trágico del español Gerardo y Desengaño del amor lascivo* of Gonzalo de Céspedes y Meneses was published in two parts, in 1615 and in 1617. One brief quotation will suffice: "Don Fernando's heart was suffering from his blind passion; and thus, although his clear intellect could have prevented the greater evil, the incentive of his will, impeding the free use of the reason, of the faculties, and of the senses, hastened his decision. . . ." [146]

146. *BAE*, XVIII, 262a.

Soto de Rojas. The *Desengaño de amor en rimas* of the Gon-
gorist poet Pedro Soto de Rojas was published in 1623. In a sonnet
which bears the heading "Love born of reason is not mitigated by
possession," he wrote:

> Fear not that dark and unbecoming passion
> Can ever touch my love, which follows reason,
> Drawn to that path by my unfaltering star —
> My love, of reason born, not appetite.[147]

The theme is derived from León Hebreo's *Diálogos de amor.*[148]

Quevedo. Quevedo presents both faces of the medallion. In
Sentencia 346 he presents the following sorites: "When a passion
takes possession of the soul, pleasure is the bait of the senses; the
senses become slaves of desire; the latter becomes a conflagration
in the heart; the heart has vital spirits of great power; these latter
cloud the intellect and cause it to idolize the object of the passion." [149] In his *comedia, Cómo ha de ser el privado,* the King
soliloquizes:

No debo poco a ser rey;	I am a king and must live the
con mis afectos batallo;	part; I struggle against my emo-
los ojos quieren mirar,	tions; the eyes insist upon look-
la razón los ha enfrenado.	ing, but the reason has restrained
Ojos, no habéis de vencer.	them. Eyes of mine, you shall
(Discuidéme y vila. ¡Ay, Cielos!)	not win! (Alas, failing in my dili-
Venzamos, razón, venzamos.[150]	gence, I caught a glimpse of her!)
	Reason, help me! We must con-
	quer!

Gracián. We have already quoted from Baltasar Gracián's *El
Criticón,* to the effect that reason is Queen of Light, Mother of
Awareness, the most faithful friend that man has; but Gracián,
too, reveals the reverse of medallion. In Gracián's world, only
man is vile, and the cause of that vileness is original sin, sin pur-

147. "No temas que el deleyte obscuro, reo, / mi amor ofenda, pues razón le
obliga: / y firme estrella, a la razón le llama: / hijo suyo es mi amor, no del deseo"
(*Obras,* ed. Antonio Gallego Morell [Madrid, 1950], p. 116).
148. See above, the discussion of Montemayor.
149. *Obras en prosa, ed. cit.* It is not certain that the *Sentencias* are rightly attributed to Quevedo. The presumption is that they are. But our quotation would be just
as valuable should they prove to have been written by someone else.
150. *Obras en verso,* ed. L. Astrana Marín (Madrid, 1932), p. 616.

sued and embraced through all generations. The world is out of joint. Some blame Fortune; others, the rebellion of Lucifer; some even blame Woman. Gracián says that the culprit is man, one man being sufficient to turn a thousand worlds topsy-turvy. "And the most noteworthy thing is that man, being a rational creature, proceeds with all haste to make his reason the slave of bestial appetite" (ed. cit., I, 211). This is, of course, not true of all men. Even those who are born humpbacked (so that we expect their intentions to be twisted); those who are hollow-chested (so that we fear that there are cavities in their spirits); those who have a cast in an eye (whom we do not pity as we do blind men, but rather suspect of being easily blinded by passion); the lame and halt (whom we suspect of stumbling on the path of virtue); the one-handed (who would seem to be of necessity imperfect in any task undertaken) — all of these can overcome their disability by the use of reason: "Reason, in wise men, corrects all these sinister prognostications." [151]

SUMMARY

In our consideration of reason we have come a long distance and it will be well to survey in restrospect the ground traversed. Reason, whether "pure" or "practical," — whether the upper portion of the soul whose business is knowledge and contemplation, or the lower portion whose task is to govern conduct — is always considered by the Spaniards of our period as a positive, a creative, force. Though as pure reason this faculty has been left to feel her way in darkness as a result of the Fall; though as practical reason she is subject to enslavement by a capricious will (whose freedom enables her to flout reason's teaching and to ignore reason's protests); though she herself may pander to will, presenting as a good that which is in reality an evil; though she is not autonomous and must move within the limits of a doctrine which she receives from above as set forth in the "book" of the Scriptures and in the declarations of the Church — in spite of all these qualifications, reason is one of the two highest gifts of God to man, by some held to be nobler than her sister, the will. Human faculty though she be, she has it in her

---

151. Ed. cit., I, 267. See O. H. Green, "Juan Ruiz de Alarcón and the topos Homo deformis et pravus," BHS, XXXIII (1956), 99–103.

power—in ways that to us remain mysterious—to watch against temptation, to guard the paths of virtue. The witch in Cervantes' exemplary tale, *El coloquio de los perros*, confesses:

the habit of vice easily becomes second nature, and thus my habit of being a sorceress is converted into flesh and blood, and in the midst of its ardor (which is great), it carries with it a cold which it infuses into the soul in such a way that it cools off and dulls faith, producing a forgetfulness of the interests of the self, so that the soul neither remembers the fears with which God threatens it nor the glory to which He invites it; and indeed, since this is a sin of the flesh and involves pleasure, it cannot fail to deaden all the senses, to fascinate and entrance them, so that they cannot perform their office as they should; and thus the soul, in this useless, weak, downcast condition, cannot raise itself up to have even one good thought; wherefore, allowing itself to remain sunk in the deep pit of its misery, it refuses to raise its hand to the hand of God, who is offering it His own as a pure act of grace, in order that the soul may rise.[152]

I wonder if this description and exposition of reason's defeat by willful passion may not have some well-known theological source — perhaps St. Augustine; I wonder, also, if Michelangelo did not have such a theological text in mind when he painted Adam with his finger almost joined in contact with the finger of the Creator. Whether any such source exists — and Cervantes' passage is so striking that it seems difficult to think of a layman as its sole author — it remains true, for our Spanish thinkers, that reason (with its sister faculty, will) constitutes the best of man. Without grace, she is of course unreliable, as St. Thomas taught, since man may use his reason to commit sin. But when the human finger stretches out to receive the grace of God, when reason watches against temptation as it is her duty to do, she cannot possibly be a dangerous guide. One of her tasks is to find out the truth; the truth being one (*veritas una*), reason cannot lead us except to a closer perception of Ultimate Reality. The other of her tasks is to distinguish the ethically good from the bad, and (again provided she lift her hand toward God's) that which is approved by "right reason" cannot fail to be salutary for mankind.

Fray Luis de León, in the chapter of *De los nombres de Cristo* entitled *Rey de Dios*, sets forth the difference between Christ and other ethical legislators. There are two types of law, one which

152. *Ed. cit.*, p. 1017.

instructs the intellect, and another which wins the heart, that is to say, the will. The first consists in commandments, the second in a quality of celestial health that heals the will and restores the taste for the good, which was lost in Eden. In respect to both these laws, the sin of our first parents left us miserably weak, darkening our intellect and injuring our will so that it longs for that which is most injurious to it. Because of this we have need of the two laws: one of rational commandments for the "blind" intellect, the other of spirit and right inclination for the perverted will. The first law, with its commandments, may actually stir us to rebellion since things forbidden are rendered attractive by the prohibition; but the second, the law of love, cuts the plant of evil and pulls it up by the root, because it makes attractive and desirable that which is necessary for our salvation. This second law is the *ley de gracia y de amor* — the law of grace and love. This law of grace is sweet in the extreme; like an expert grafter, it grafts upon us a desire and a fondness for the good. This law is perfect because it carries with it the perfection of itself. It is by reason of this law of grace that the New Testament constitutes a new dispensation, that Moses is superseded by Christ.[153]

It was in connection with the first of these laws that the teachings of the ancient sages — of whatever philosophical school — could be grafted onto Christian teaching, enriching it and giving it an appeal especially suited to the intellectually inclined. And even in regard to the second, Plato, Cicero, Seneca, and others succeed in making virtue attractive — intellectually — to those who find a reward in being virtuous. At all times, throughout the period we are studying, reason (understood as "right reason," illumined by grace) was regarded as a noble thing — the best friend we have, as Gracián said. The Spanish Church had no fear of science, of knowledge, since God's truth is one.[154] The Church's fears were two: heresy, the elaboration of mistaken dogma by the "blind intellect"

153. Ed. Clásicos Castellanos (Madrid, 1914), II, 102–5. Fray Luis' source is Augustine's *De Littera et Spiritu.*
154. This had not always been so. The Council of Sens in 1210 prohibited university study of Aristotle's works on natural science; in 1215 the Pope renewed the prohibition *donec corrigantur.* The decree was renewed in 1263; yet in 1255 the University of Paris was prescribing virtually all of Aristotle. See G. G. Coulton. *The Medieval Scene* (Cambridge, 1959), pp. 109–10; J. V. Langmead Casserley, *The Christian in Philosophy* (New York, 1951), pp. 71 ff.

(without grace); and certain types of mysticism — those that seemed to lead either to quietism or to a disregard for the Church's ministrations, as each man tended to become his own priest. In general, it may be said that, within the limits that the ecclesiastical authorities could conceive — and it was only after Galileo's invention of the telescope that the Copernican theory came to appear dangerous — the authorities feared not reason but its opposite. As for science, Spanish thinkers would conclude, with Calderón's English contemporary Samuel Butler, that "man spends too much time numbering the hairs in the lion's mane." [155] With Milton they held that "the validity of intellectual inquiry ceased at the point beyond which its findings contributed nothing to the execution of the divinely enjoined requirement that fallen man work out his salvation in the imperfect world to which his initial defection consigned him."[156] Venegas wrote: "If we but stop to think, human faith will teach us how much better it is to believe than to prove and to experiment. . . . It is an infallible truth that 'an evil and adulterous generation seeketh after a sign.' " [157] It is this Biblical attitude toward science that prevails. St. Thomas of Villanueva, the last Father of the Spanish Church (d. 1555), wrote that to know oneself is more important than to know "omnes scientias mundi et omnes bibliothecas" — all the sciences and libraries in the world.[158] Like Pascal, like Milton, [159] like Bacon — though without Bacon's hesitations [160] — Calderón died (1681) believing in a Ptolemaic, a geocentric, universe,[161] governed by a rational God to whom man's

155. They disregarded the fact that by the third quarter of the seventeenth century the hairs were being counted and man was now trying to add up the atoms in the universe. See Allen, *The Legend of Noah*, p. 36.

156. E. L. Marilla, "Milton on 'Vain Wisdom' and 'False Philosophie,' " *Studia Philologica*, XXV (1953), 4.

157. *Agonía* . . . , ed. cit., p. 265ab. Venegas' quotation is from Matt. 12:39.

158. *Opera omnia*, I (Manila, 1881), pp. 89–90.

159. In *Paradise Lost* Raphael pauses in his discussion of the solar system to state that it does not matter whether Ptolemy or Copernicus is correct. See Allen, *The Legend of Noah*, p. 38.

160. Arthur O. Lovejoy, *The Great Chain of Being* (Cambridge, Massachusetts, 1950), pp. 110, 126. In the age of Queen Elizabeth and of King James "the Ptolemaic cosmology, in spite of Kepler and Copernicus, was still the cosmology of most educated Englishmen" (Don Cameron Allen, *The Star-Crossed Renaissance* [Durham, North Carolina, 1941], p. 169).

161. Pedro Simón Abril, in his MS *Filosofía natural* (ca. 1589), comments upon Copernicus' theory and, without even thinking of the religious and philosophical reasons for not accepting the new theory, he clings to the traditional one "as commonly

reason gave him access. He did not share Pascal's sense of desolation in infinity: *nous sommes si terriblement petits*. Between the years 1140 and 1681 the alliance of faith and "right reason" is not disrupted in Spain.

received doctrine." (See our Chapter II, especially notes 65 and 66.) But compare what happened in England: "To a greater extent than he realized, John Donne [d. 1631] was present at the death of a world. Gabriel's trumpet had sounded. *Sex millibus annorum stabit Mundus*, declared *Elia Propheta*. Luther and many other chronologists had predicted that the last thousand years would not be completed; the world would end before its appointed time. Luther and the chronologists were right. The world created four thousand years before the birth of Christ did perish seventeen centuries after that event. The world of Aristotle, of Ptolemy, of Augustine and Dante, of Shakespeare, was gone. In its place was only a lesser planet, taking its orderly way among other planets, moving about the Sun that had usurped the 'proud Center' that for centuries had been the world of Man" (Marjorie Nicolson, *The Breaking of the Circle: Studies in the Effect of the "New Science" upon Seventeenth-century Poetry* [New York, 1960], p. 122).

VI · Free Will[1]

The most unrelenting fate,
The most violent inclination,
Or the most sinister planet
Can but incline man's free will,
Never can they overcome it.[2]

Calderón

Fortune has much in common
with the stars: both are subject to movement and both influence the human body but
cannot affect the soul.[3]

Quevedo

FREE WILL AND ASTRAL INFLUENCE

The quotations chosen as epigraphs for our consideration of free will are both from the seventeenth century — the last of the five surveyed in the present work. All responsible thinkers in Calderón's or Quevedo's generation would have agreed with Chaucer's lines:

O influences of thise hevenes hye!
Soth is, that under God, ye ben our hierdes.[4]

In *Life is a Dream* (II, 14) Calderón declares that

What the Heavens have determined,
And what God's eternal finger
Has written on the starry tablet

. . . .

Of the skies' vast blue expanse

1. See Alberto Bonet, *La filosofía de la libertad en las controversias teológicas del siglo XVI y primera mitad del XVII* (Barcelona, 1932).
2. "porque el hado más esquivo, / la inclinación más violenta, / el planeta más impío / sólo el albedrío inclinan, / no fuerzan el albedrío" (*La vida es sueño*, Act I, Scene 6).
3. *Obras en prosa*, ed. Luis Astrana Marín (Madrid, 1932), p. 805a.
4. "Oh, influences of these heavens high! / True is it that, under God, you are our shepherds" (cited by T. O. Wedel, *The Mediaeval Attitude Toward Astrology, Particularly in England* [New Haven, 1920], p. iii).

Cannot possibly deceive us;
The deceit is born of evil
In some man's twisted intention,
Reading for his evil purpose
Starry letters etched in gold.[5]

God's designs, written with golden letters on the blue parchment
of the firmament, are thus declared to be infallible and irresistible. The Creator reserves for Himself knowledge of the future
(hence judicial astrology is a vain pseudoscience), but He leaves to
man's free will the faculty of acting ethically at every moment and
in every circumstance — a thought implicit in this drama and in
all Calderón's theater, and explicitly stated in Calderón's *auto
sacramental,* also titled *La vida es sueño.*[6] Man is a whole and
harmonious creature, exercising an enlightened and rational
choice and controlling his faculties if he so chooses. The stars
incline, and wise choice is difficult; but the choice is free.

Quevedo is very specific:

The first cause is God, and the secondary intelligences [i.e., angels] are the
executors of His Providence. Human happiness and misery depend on the
First Order [Providence]; at one remove, they depend on the stars; ultimately,
on the human will, which is moved by impulse. To say that the heavenly
bodies are causes is like saying that the fire and the hammer are causes of the
sword (who would venture to subordinate the artificer to his instrument?).
Man's will is not subject to the stars directly, but by accident, in so far as the
body receives celestial influence (like man's animal spirit and his four humors);
and although man's rising upward usually proceeds from his will and his
virtues, yet (since man is more indulgent with his sensuous than with his
rational nature), we must say that one's star affects the body and hence affects
the soul indirectly, as a predisposing agent; one's guardian angel operates as
a persuasive agent; God, as the physical motive force."[7]

Cervantes causes a character of his *Persiles* to explain (in accordance with commonly accepted doctrine) that "all souls are equal,
being created separately and individually by their Maker from
one single substance; yet, depending on the character of the en-

5. "Lo que está determinado / del cielo, y en azul tabla / Dios con el dedo escribió, /
de quien son cifras y estampas / tantos papeles azules / que adornan letras doradas, /
nunca engaña, nunca miente; / porque quien miente y engaña / es quien, para usar
mal dellas, / las penetra y las alcanza."
6. Tomás Carreras y Artau, "La filosofía de la libertad en *La vida es sueño* de Calderón," *Estudios eruditos in memoriam de A. Bonilla y San Martín,* I (Madrid, 1927),
57.
7. *Obras en prosa, ed. cit.,* p. 786b.

casing body and its balance of humors, some seem more or less intelligent than others, and take interest in and seek to know those sciences, those arts or those skills to which the stars most incline them, for which reason it is said that poets are born, not made." [8]

We shall quote one more bit of testimony from the generation of Cervantes. Mateo Alemán puts these words on the lips of a character in *Guzmán de Alfarache*: "You were given free will whereby to govern your actions. Your star does not force you, nor can you be forced by the entire firmament and all the stars therein. You compel yourself to depart from the good and to exert yourself in doing evil. . . ." [9]

Such, then, was the state of belief in the century of Cervantes and Calderón: the stars affect the body, not the soul; they incline, but do not force, the will; they are the agents of God's Providence; God's decrees and dispositions are infallible and irresistible, except in the realm of human action, where, by reason of their permissiveness, the divine dispositions allow for their own abrogation, and God's will can be defied by the free will of the sinner. With this cross section of seventeenth-century doctrine as a preamble, we shall return to the Middle Ages and trace chronologically the history of these ideas.

St. Augustine (d. 430), in an early treatise entitled *De divinatione Daemonum*, crystallized the doctrine of the early Church regarding the divinatory powers of demons and the possibility of astrological prognostications, concluding that "when astrologers give many wonderful answers, it is to be attributed to the occult inspiration of spirits, not of the best kind, whose care it is to creep into the minds of men, and to confirm in them false . . . opinions concerning the fatal influence of the stars, and . . . it is not due to their inspecting of horoscopes, according to an art which in reality has no existence." [10] Astrology, thus denied recognition as a science, lived under this stigma until the thirteenth century, when the diffusion of Arabic interpretations of Greek science forced a revision of the Church's verdict. Strangely enough, St. Augustine had himself

8. *Obras completas*, ed. Angel Valbuena Prat (Madrid, 1956), p. 1564.
9. Ed. Clásicos Castellanos (Madrid, 1926–36), III, 12.
10. Wedel, *op. cit.*, p. 23. In summarization of the early church's attitudes toward astrology, I follow Wedel (pp. 24–41, 50–58, especially) rather closely.

left the door open for compromise, for in his *De Civitate Dei* he admitted that it is not altogether absurd to say that certain sidereal influences have some power to cause differences in bodies alone. The tides of the ocean, and other things such as oysters and sea urchins, he said, increase or diminish in size as they are affected by the waxings and the wanings of the moon; what does not follow, he insisted, is that the wills of men are subject to the configuration of the stars. The fact that canon law classed astrology among the diabolic arts became a matter of consequence only when in the twelfth-century the Church was again called upon to deal with astrologers in the flesh. Even before the arrival of Arabian science in the schools of Europe, the literary revival of the twelfth century, especially in the School of Chartres, produced an awareness of classical fatalistic doctrines. In Bernard Silvestris (*ca.* 1150) medieval astrology had one of its champions; he was attracted by the philosophical astrology of the Neoplatonic commentators Chalcidius and Macrobius. By the time of John of Salisbury (*ca.* 1159), the influence of the astrological treatises of Ptolemy and Albumasar was beginning to find its way into the schools of France and Italy — opening a new chapter in medieval philosophy.

Astrology and astronomy were at this time again united. Herman of Dalmatia's translation of Albumasar (1143) did more than any other textbook to make astrology acceptable to the thirteenth-century Church. Gerard of Cremona, a contemporary of Herman, made translations of Ptolemy's *Almagest* and of Aristotle's *Meteorologica* and *De Generatione et Corruptione*. With the spread of knowledge of these works, the stars came to be thought of as spherical bodies, endowed with a perpetual motion which is circular like that found in the sublunary sphere, and cyclical, as is the alternation, below the moon, of growth and decay. The cause of the cycles here below is none other than the eternal circular motion of the stars. The uniform motion of the fixed stars is interpreted as a principle of permanence; the irregular motion of the planets ("wandering stars") becomes a principle of change. All that is born and dies on earth depends on the motion of stars and constellations; to the "wandering stars" belongs the care over the details of earthly life. By observing the diversity of planetary motions, one can comprehend the unnumbered varieties of change in the sublunar world. All of this points the way to the compromise between Christianity and astrology effected in the thirteenth-century writings of Albertus Magnus and St. Thomas Aquinas. In their elaboration of theories, the *arbitrium animae* remains free, unimpelled by necessity either this way or that.

By the fourteenth century no scholastic theologian any longer dared question the Peripatetic teaching that the processes of earthly growth and change depended for their existence upon the stellar spheres. Christian theologians, in welcoming Aristotelian cosmology, were inevitably impelled to offer a favorable reception to astrology as well. Albertus Magnus took for granted that the stars govern the material elements, the *anima vegetabilis* of plants and the *anima sensibilis* of animals. The Church thus accepted astrology as a science, at the same time saving appearances by rejecting fatalistic theories of the human soul and all attempts to establish an arbitrary art of divination.

Indirectly, however, and by accident (as stated above in our long quotation from Quevedo), the influence of the heavenly bodies does affect the intellect and will, since both of these faculties are intimately connected with corporeal organs. Yet predictions of man's future actions *per certitudinem* are still condemned as the work of demons. Indeed, Cecco d'Ascoli, professor of astrology at Bologna, was burned as a heretic in 1327 for having dared to determine, by astrological methods, the date of the birth of Christ.[11]

For Dante, the influence of the heavenly bodies upon human life was an awe-inspiring fact: "To the heavens the First Mover has delegated the power to mould the destinies of the world; they are the hammers, earth the metal; they are the seals, and earth the wax. Were it not for the influence of the stars, children would be exactly like their parents" (cited *ibid.*, p. 80). So long as the cosmology of Aristotle and the geometric astronomy of Ptolemy held, a refutation of these doctrines was impossible. With the acceptance of the new astronomy of Copernicus, refutation became unnecessary. No astronomer of note, down to Johannes Kepler (d. 1630), questioned the reality of astrology. Even Galileo (d. 1642) wrote horoscopes for the Medicean court (*ibid.*, pp. 88–89)

11. His execution (*ibid.*, p. 77) forms an almost isolated instance in the history of the Inquisition.

Before turning from the history of astrology to its treatment in Spanish literature, one final observation is necessary. It has to do with human responsibility. Lactantius and Augustine do not doubt the influences of the stars, but they believe that man's free will, aided by Divine Grace, can overcome them. Since, according to the doctrine of predestination, man's salvation or damnation depends exclusively on the eternal decision of God, many thinkers see in the inevitable constraint of the stars merely an evidence of that doctrine. The most liberal view is that the will and the power of the Almighty — his immutable decrees — are revealed to man through the intermediary of the planets and constellations. St. Thomas admits that the stars determine, at least physically, individual character; and since most men follow their passions, that is to say, their physical appetites, it is really the stars that incline them to sin. Dante on this point follows St. Thomas faithfully: while recognizing the freedom of the will, he admits also the effects of cosmic influences on the soul:

> Heaven starts your inclinations, though I say
> Not all; but ev'n supposing that I did,
> Light has been giv'n to you for good and evil,
> With Free Will, which, if it endure fatigue
> In its first fights with heaven, will afterward,
> If duly nourished, conquer everything.[12]

Astrology in the Middle Ages

There is a fine example of the use of these doctrines in Spain's first novel, the *Libro del Cauallero de Dios que auia por nombre Zifar (ca.* 1300). In chapter 130 — one of those chapters in which the King of Mentón instructs his sons *de cómo siempre fuesen nobles,* i.e., how they should conduct themselves so as to maintain their nobility untarnished — there is intercalated the *exemplum* of Filemón,[13] a philosopher who arrived at a certain city and set up a

12. "Lo cielo i vostri movimenti inizia, / non dico tutti; ma, posto ch' i' 'l dica, / lume v' è dato a bene e a malizia, / E Libero Voler; che, se fatica / nelle prime battaglie col ciel dura, / poi vince tutto, se ben si notrica" (*Purgatorio,* XVI, lines 73–78; Langdon's translation). See Jean Seznec, *La survivance des dieux antiques* (London, 1940), pp. 42–43, 47.

13. I assume that this Filemón is Philemon (or more properly Polemon), the physiognomist. See Polemon, *De physiognomonia liber Arabice et Latine,* ed. Georgius Hoffman, in Richard Foerster (ed.), *Scriptores Physiognomonici* (Leipzig, 1813), I, 93–

school of philosophy. A man whose enmity he had incurred gathered a number of Filemón's pupils and asked them to state the character traits of a man showing such-and-such facial characteristics — forehead, eyes, eyebrows — and they replied that such a man would be envious, lascivious, and deceitful. The evil-minded man then told them that, were they to analyze the features of their mentor, they would find that he showed the characteristics specified. Troubled, the pupils referred the matter to their master, courteously saying that, though the physical traits were present, the character traits were not.

Filemón . . . replied: "My sons, those things which my face reveals are things that I still covet and are dear to my heart; but I force my heart in such a way that I do not experience in the slightest those things which the nature of my body covets, and I constantly struggle to aid and strengthen my soul so that it may fulfill such possibilities for good as it may have. And that is why I am as you see me, in spite of the fact that my countenance reveals the traits you mention. And be advised that a wise man, when asked about the phases of the signs of the zodiac and their ascendancy, said that in every phase there rise above the horizon many figures of many sorts, and that the first phase, which is the ascendant, is always desired and loved by man, more than anything else. And you must know that in the phase of my ascendent there appeared two small black men, and that consequently there is nothing in this world that my will so greatly desires to see daily; and, since I regard this as wrong and unfitting, I forced my will and gave orders that no black man should enter my house or appear in my presence." [14]

Filemón continues, saying that another wise man, when asked if a murderer or rapist whose horoscope had predicted that he would commit one or the other of these crimes should be punished (inasmuch as he apparently had no responsibility), replied that the freedom of the will makes just the punishment of the evildoer. "How can a man so unfortunately born have free will?" Filemón's pupils ask. The wise man refuses to answer, but the author of the *Caballero Zifar* answers for him:

Heavenly bodies act on elemental bodies, which, being soul-less, are no more to be esteemed than mud. The soul is a spiritual entity, the element of life

294. For an elucidation of this passage (unnecessary here) we shall have to await the publication of the late Charles Phillip Wagner's *Notes* to his edition (Ann Arbor, Michigan, 1929) of *El libro del Cauallero Zifar*. Professor Wagner died in 1964.

14. From *Libros de caballerías españoles*, ed. Felicidad Buendía, (Madrid, 1954), p. 173.

which God instills in the bodies of men that they may live; and the union of body and soul produces man, a living, reasonable, and mortal creature; and without this union human life is impossible. Since the soul is spiritual, and the body composed of the four elements, the soul has the power to govern the body; and although the constellations exert certain influences on the birth of a man, his soul has power to defend him from those influences, if he so wishes; since the soul is spiritual and higher than the stars and more worthy than they. . . . So say the astrologers, and this proves that it is in the power of man to do good or to commit evil, and this decision should receive reward or punishment. Therefore you should know, my sons, that man has it in his power to resist the inclinations of his flesh, and to give strength to the goodness of his soul; for this free will is given to him in order that he may do good or commit sin and receive rewards and penalties.[15]

We now pass to the year 1343, the date of completion of the definitive version of Juan Ruiz's *Libro de Buen Amor*. It too contains an astrological *exemplum*, introduced (in MS S, *copla* 123) by this heading: "Here [the poet] speaks of the constellation and the planet that form the horoscopes of men, and of the judgment which the five scientists made concerning the birth of the son of King Alcaraz." It tells the story of a prince whose father, before the child's birth, summoned his astrologers to learn from them the prince's destiny in life. The reports were frightening: one foretold his death by stoning, another by fire; the third declared that he would die by being cast down from a great height; the fourth, that he would die from suspension; the fifth, that he would be drowned. The king, incensed, flung the soothsayers into prison. One day the son, now grown to young manhood, begged his father to let him go hunting, and a day was chosen for the expedition. While the party was in the forest there came a great hailstorm, and the young man's mentor, remembering the prognostication of years past, urged that they take shelter. Spurring his horse as they crossed a bridge, the prince was struck by lightning, the bridge was shattered, the prince fell from its height, the skirts of his tunic catching in a tree on the bank so that he was suspended with his head in the water and perished. The king released the astrologers and bade them continue their studies.

The interesting history of this tale and its analogues in folklore and in medieval literature has been traced by a number of scholars;

15. I have condensed this long passage; see *ibid.*, pp. 173–74.

what concerns us is, rather, the astrological doctrine, in which some scholars have thought they perceived Oriental fatalism.[16]

Juan Ruiz's exordium refers to astrology as "a good science" that judges the course of a man's life by the zodiacal sign at the time of his birth. The second stanza (124) quotes Ptolemy and Plato and "many other masters who agree with them" to the effect that man's fate (fado) is determined by the ascendancy of the planet that presides over his entrance into the world, i.e., by his horoscope. Many men, the poet says, spend time and treasure in order to become monks, but fail: "their fate guides them"; non pueden desmentir a la astrología — "they cannot gainsay the decrees of astrology." Similar failures occur in other professions. How can this be? Creo ser verdaderos,/ segund natural curso, los dichos estrelleros — "I believe that the astrologers, insofar as they deal with physical nature, tell the truth" (125–27). Stanza 140 reads:

> I hold that all astrologers, guided by nature's course,
> Inform us of the truth; but that a greater Force,
> God's heavenly Providence, that all the stars created,
> Can overrule the stars: this by the Church is stated.[17]

The doctrinal exposition continues. An earthly king, we are told (coplas 142 ff.), has the power of declaring laws within his kingdom, and these he causes to be codified into books. In this kingdom it may happen that a servitor of the king commits an act of treason, for which he should suffer the established penalty. But the king's counselors, moved by pity, beg the king to pardon the offender, and the monarch, remembering past services, grants

16. See Américo Castro, España en su historia (Buenos Aires, 1948), p. 408, n. 1. This long note is transferred to the body of the text in the English translation of this work, The Structure of Spanish History, trans. Edmond L. King (Princeton, 1954), p. 446. In the second edition in Spanish, La realidad histórica de España, published in Mexico City in 1954, neither the note nor the paragraph of text is present. Félix Lecoy, in Recherches sur le Libro de Buen Amor (Paris, 1938), p. 193, said that "Juan Ruiz shows himself to be closer to the common people than to the learned." Julio Puyol y Alonso, in El Arcipreste de Hita: Estudio crítico (Madrid, 1906), pp. 111–12, says that Ruiz "professes a certain easy-going fatalism." Pierre Le Gentil, in La poésie lyrique espagnole et portugaise à la fin du moyen âge, Première Partie: Les Thèmes et les Genres (Rennes, 1949), p. 361, n. 79, goes so far as to say that Juan Ruiz "fait abstraction du libre arbitre." Our exposition of the matter should make it clear, however, that Ruiz's position is orthodox and in accord with what was taught.

17. "Yo creo los estrólogos verdad naturalmente; / pero Dios, que crió natura e açidente, / puédelos demudar e fazer otramente, / segund la fe cathólica: yo desto so creyente" (ed. J. Ducamin [Tolouse, 1901]).

the request. Thus the maker of the law temporarily and in a special case abrogates it: *Quien puede fazer leyes, puede contra ellas yr* — "He who makes laws can go against them." In similar fashion, the Pope can set aside his decretals, granting dispensation. Neither of these actions, so common in ordinary experience, nullifies the law. Exactly so our Lord, when He created the heavens, placed therein signs and planets and granted them powers of determination — *Sus poderíos çiertos e juyzios otorgó* (148) — , but retained even greater power for Himself. Therefore a Christian, by means of such "good works" as fasting, almsgiving, and prayer, and by serving God with great contrition, can overcome the baleful sign of his constellation: the power of God miraculously removes his tribulation (149).

This does not mean that the astrologers are liars; they judge according to natural evidence by *sus cuentos fermosos* — "their beautiful calculations." They and their science are reliable and not subject to doubt; but they do not have power to oppose God's will in any given case or at any given moment (150).

The Archpriest of Hita then makes his playful application of the doctrine to his own situation. Many men are born under the sign of Venus; their whole life is devoted to the love of women, yet they fail of success in their quest. The author of the *Libro* believes himself to be in that category: his sign is as described; he is an unsuccessful lover of women:

> Though man taste not the yellow pear, though he ever hungry be,
> To stand beneath the pear-tree's shade seems wonderful to me.[18]

At this point Juan Ruiz drops the subject of horoscopes and passes to other matters, but he twice returns to the idea of fate in later portions of his poem. So, in stanzas 692–93:

> How many times Dame Fortune, with all her power and force,
> Compels men to abandon the better for the worse!
> 'Tis for this reason that the world goes ever up and down,
> But God and human effort can baleful Fate uncrown.

> Fortune aids her favorites, and whom she doesn't love
> To him in her contrariness she gives a hostile shove;

18. "Aunque ome non goste la pera del peral, / en estar a la sonbra es plazer comunal" (154 *cd*).

> Fate and human effort may work to a single end,
> But unless God is willing, no good can they portend;[19]

and again in stanza 793d:

> God's help and your great effort can overcome all fate;[20]

and in 803d:

> God and God only knows what's held for us in store.[21]

We may well pause here to analyze the doctrine contained in the two literary texts from which I have drawn my illustrations. In the first, the *Caballero Zifar*, we are told, quite simply, that the stars affect the body but cannot touch the soul since its spiritual essence "is higher than the stars." Man is a free moral agent, responsible for his acts, who by those acts earns rewards or punishments. St. Augustine could scarcely disagree with this point of view. In the second work, the *Libro de Buen Amor*, the doctrine is more complex, but just as orthodox as that of Jean de Meun in *The Romance of the Rose*.[22] Looking back over the lines quoted, we note, in the last example, that judicial astrology is a vain error: only God knows man's future.[23] In the other quotations the doc-

---

19. "Muchas vezes la ventura con ssu fuerça e poder / a muchos omes non dexa su propósito fazer: / por esto anda el mundo en levantar e caer; / Dios e el trabajo grande pueden los fados vençer. / Ayuda la ventura al que bien quiere guiar, / e a muchos es contraria, puédelos malestorbar; / el trabajo e los fados suélense acompañar; / pero syn Dios todo esto non puede aprovechar."

20. "Dios e el uso grande fazen fados bolver."

21. "Solo Dios e non otro sabe lo porvenir."

22. G. Paré, *Le Roman de la Rose et la scolastique courtoise* (Paris–Ottawa, 1941), p. 89: "Les philosophes chrétiens n'enseignent pas autre chose"— the Christian philosophers do not differ. See Leo Spitzer, "Zur Auffassung der Kunst des Arcipreste de Hita," *ZRPh*, LIV (1934), 255: "Tacke hebt den 'echt mittelalterlich scholastischen Zug' in Juan Ruiz's Auffassung der Wirkung der Sterne auf das Menschenschicksal hervor" (i. e., Otto Tacke, in "Die Fabeln des Erzpriesters von Hita . . . ," *RF*, XXXI [1912], 550–705).

23. The fifteenth-century Fray Martín de Córdoba, in his *Compendio de la Fortuna*, ed. P. Fernando Rubio Alvarez, O.S.A. (El Escorial–Madrid, 1958), pp. 30–34, says: it is permissible to consult the stars to ascertain the proper time to plant crops or to go fishing; it is licit to do so when the purpose is medical (i. e., physical, as in bloodletting); but when the operations concerned depend entirely on man's will (business deals, marriages, battles, journeys), any appeal to astrology is superstition and therefore to be condemned. It is even permitted that a captain have an astrologer with him when on campaign as a means of keeping up his men's morale, but the captain himself must not believe that the prognostications are valid. On the need for the physician to know astrology, see Dr. Diego Cisneros, *Sitio, naturaleza y propriedades de la ciudad de Méjico* (Mexico City, 1618). This book stresses the need to know the constellations over Mexico if one is to practice medicine there. See Bartolo-

trine is no less Catholic: the stars incline, and the operation of their inclination on the body can be calculated in much the same way that eclipses can be foretold. Man's resistance against astral inclination can be successful through the action of Divine Grace,[24] not passively accepted but actively sought by means of "good works," fasting, and prayer. Without this intervention of Grace, the man who opposes his horoscopal tendencies in his desire to become a monk will fail to learn theology.[25] The Catholic striver, hoping for Divine aid, does not surrender to his "fate"; he struggles against it. This is the essence of the Christian doctrine of free will.[26] The sixteenth-century Alejo Venegas, whose *De las differencias de libros que ay en el vniuerso* has been cited so often in the present work, makes clear the orthodox position: "although we accomplish something by virtue of the *arbitrium animae*, the Grace of God is the chief instrumentality that operates in us." [27]

With Juan Ruiz's merry application of the doctrine of astral influence to his own unsuccessful love-making (he was born under the sign of Venus . . .), we are brought down from the level of the serious inculcation of accepted beliefs to the level of "literature as entertainment." This is a truancy on Juan Ruiz's part (see Vol. I, Chs. II and VII). It is exactly what happens in John Fletcher's (d. 1625) *Love's Cure,* where we meet a character, "one Aguazier, who insists on the virtues of free will, but . . . elects to use his free will to follow the inclination of his stars." [28]

About a century after the Archpriest of Hita completed his *Libro*

mé Jose Gallardo, *Ensayo de una biblioteca española de libros raros y curiosos* (Madrid, 1863–89), II, cols. 466–67.

24. In an early seventeenth-century work on Christian physics, *De universitate et rerum conditarum originibus* (Langen, 1610), Andreas Libau (Libavius) declares that God may have created cause and effect, but he is not controlled by them and his Providence governs all alterations. Libau is an opponent of astrology. Alexius Göckel, an advocate of astrology, in *Acroteleution astrologicum* (Marburg, 1618), takes a position very similar to that of Juan Ruiz (D. C. Allen, *The Star-Crossed Renaissance* [Durham, North Carolina, 1941], pp. 93–96).

25. According to the author of the *Sententiae Divinitatis*, free will remained after the Fall, but so weakened that without Grace it can do nothing (Dom Odon Lottin, *Psychologie et morale au XII⁰ et XIII⁰ siècles*, (Louvain–Gembloux, 1942–60), I, 27.

26. Juan Ruiz's perfectly regular position is analyzed by Angel Benito y Durán, *La filosofía del Arcipreste de Hita* (Alcoy, 1946), p. 64.

27. "y aunque hazemos nosotros algo por virtud de la libertad del libre aluedrío, la gracia de Dios es la que principalmente obra en nosotros" (Salamanca, 1572, fol. 26b).

28. Allen, *op. cit.,* p. 184.

de Buen Amor, Don Enrique de Villena (d. 1434), grandson of King Enrique II of Castile and translator of Cicero, was composing his *Libro de astrología*.[29] Though he was considered a dabbler in the black arts,[30] and for centuries was the personification and symbol of the occult sciences,[31] his teaching in the *Libro de astrología* appears perfectly acceptable: "The human body is affected by the behavior and the complexion of the seven planets and takes its vital spirit from the order of the firmament, which is the eighth sphere, and takes its knowledge of good and evil from the Lord our God."[32] Astral influences cannot touch the soul, which is not derived from the *hyle* or prime material, but is created anew by the Almighty *non sometida a natura* — free of natural influence. His position is, then, the classical one among Christian authors. He insists that there is no real conflict between "los santos Padres et doctores" and "los astrólogos" (*ibid.*, p. 13).

Contemporaneous with the treatise just analyzed is the work entitled *Arçipreste de Talavera*, commonly known as the *Corbacho* (1438), of Alfonso Martínez de Toledo. The Third Part of this work "treats the complexions of men and of the planets and signs, qualitatively and quantitatively." Chapter I of this Part concludes: "certain it is that the celestial bodies give to the bodies below them their influences and affect them to a greater or lesser degree."[33] Over against this undeniable *inclination* he sets two *rrespuestas*, or "replies": God with his almighty power can grant dispensation against the "quality" of any person, for He desires not the death of the sinner (*ibid.*, p. 245); God gives to each human

29. This work, unknown to Menéndez y Pelayo when he composed his *Heterodoxos*, was studied in 1943 (from a manuscript of the year 1438) by José María Millás Vallicrosa. See his article, "El *Libro de astrología* de don Enrique de Villena," *RFE*, XXVII (1943), 1–29.

30. Fernán Pérez de Guzmán said of him (*Generaciones y Semblanzas*, cited by Menéndez y Pelayo in *Historia de los heterodoxos españoles* [Madrid, 1947–48], II, 437–38) that "he allowed himself to take up certain vile and worthless arts of divination and interpretation of dreams and sneezes and omens" and that he "gave himself over greatly to astrology. . . ." King Juan II ordered Fray Lope de Barrientos to examine his books, with the result that some were burned and some were kept (and utilized) by the examiner, who defended the right of the learned to read such books and to make use of them "for the defense of the faith . . . and the confusion of idolators and necromancers" (*ibid.*, p. 440).

31. His treatise on the evil eye "shows clearly the influence of Moors and Jews on the forbidden arts in Castile" (*ibid.*, pp. 437, 444).

32. Millás Vallicrosa, *op. cit.*, p. 12.

33. Ed. L. B. Simpson (Berkeley, 1939), p. 206.

being intellect and judgment to discern good and evil; to each
He gives free will to act in accordance with that discernment;
furthermore, He gives to each a Guardian Angel to sound a warning when passion perturbs [34] the will and blinds it so that it cannot
see, or when it is "induced" by Satan or other enemies such as
the world, property, bodily delight. These things being so, can
any sinner deny that his sinning is his own doing, and not the
doing of his "constellation and planet and sign, or of the admixture of humors in his body?" *Por cierto non lo faze otro synon tú
mesmo que lo asy quieres frazer* — "surely none is responsible
except yourself, because you are determined to sin" (pp. 245–48).

About the year 1440 Alfonso de la Torre composed, at the request of Don Juan de Beamonte, Prior of the Order of St. John
of Jerusalem and tutor of Prince Carlos de Viana, his *Visión delectable de la philosophia e de las otras sçiençias*, which was printed
about 1480 and in several subsequent editions in Castilian, translated into Catalan in 1484, into Italian in 1556, and translated
back into Castilian from the Italian in 1623.[35] Divining by means
of the stars, said La Torre, *licito es si es a buen fin* — "is permitted
if its purpose is good," and the good astrologer "may make an
image in the sign of the Scorpion to cure men of snakebite . . .
or an image to drive away wolves or locusts from the land." [36] The

34. *Tractado que fizo . . . el Tostado . . . por el qual se prueba por la Santa
Escriptura cómo al ome es necessario amar e que el que verdaderamente ama es neces-
sario que se turbe* (ed. A. Paz y Mélia in *Opúsculos literarios de los siglos XIV a XVI*
[Madrid, 1892]).

35. J. W. Crawford, "The Seven Liberal Arts in the *Vision Delectable* of Alfonso de
la Torre," *RR*, IV (1913), 59 ff.; *idem*, "The *Vision Delectable* of Alfonso de la Torre
and Maimonides' *Guide of the Perplexed*," *PMLA*, XXVIII (1913), 188 ff.; *idem*, "The
Seven Liberal Arts in Lope de Vega's *Arcadia*," *MLN*, XXX (1915), 13 ff. (in which he
shows that La Torre was the source for Lope). Crawford inclines to see no merit in
La Torre's work, based on the *Anticlaudianus* of Alanus de Insulis, on Isidore of Seville's *Etymologiae*, Al-Ghazzāli's *Makā-sid al-Falāsifa*, and Maimonides' *Guide of the
Perplexed*. M. Bataillon, working from manuscripts that give a purer text than the
printed editions, sees in La Torre "a curious link between the Judeo-Arabic thinkers
of the Middle Ages and Spinoza because of his taste for an ethic demonstrably more
geometric" (*Collège de France. Résumé des cours de 1950–1951*, pp. 7–11). Menéndez y
Pelayo (*op. cit.*, II, p. 452) finds in La Torre's work "doctrines which we could call
spiritistic," involving spirits of the air, fire, etc., concerning which "it is not permitted
to speak."

36. Cited *ibid.*, p. 453. According to Lord Bacon, the new astrology "may be applied
confidently to predictions and cautiously to elections" (Allen, *op. cit.*, p. 152; see also
pp. 149, 151).

astral bodies, La Torre taught, are "like causes through which Providence accomplishes all that is to be accomplished, and these planets or signs have no other office than that of major-domos or treasurers, because they bring to pass in Time that which Providence ordered before Time was, and this consideration is called Fate,[37] which is to say a bond of causation."[38]

Very close in time to La Torre's *Visión delectable* is the *Laberinto de Fortuna* of Juan de Mena (*ca.* 1440), in which the burning by royal order of Enrique de Villena's books (see above, n. 30) is deplored, and their author is eloquently praised as "illustrious, wise, and very learned."[39] According to this widely-read poet, sidereal influence on mankind is a very real force: one must know that "each one of the seven planets exerts its perfect operational power . . . , to the glory of the Eternal," and that in this way "all persons are inclined and disposed according to the virtues of the material that forms each sphere."[40]

A transitional figure between the Middle Ages and the Renaissance in Spain is Hernán Núñez, known as El Comendador Griego from the double circumstance that he was a knight-commander of the Order of Santiago and a leading figure in Greek studies in the Peninsula. He lived a long life (1475?–1553) and in his youth published a lengthy, erudite commentary (1499) on Juan de Mena's *Laberinto* together with an edition of the poem. This work went through some fifteen editions in a relatively short space of time, some of them printed abroad (Antwerp, Paris, Lyon, Basel), and was still being reprinted in the seventeenth century. To Núñez, the claims of judicial astrology are impossible: "of the future we

37. See the chapter on Fortune and Fate, below.
38. "como causas, por las quales hace la Providencia todo lo que se ha de hacer, y aquestos planetos [sic] o signos no tienen oficio sino de mayordomos o tesoreros, ca ellos hacen por los años et tiempos aquello que la Providencia ordenó ante todos los tiempos; y aquesta consideración es llamada fado, que quiere decir ligamento de causas" (*BAE*, XXXVI, 360b–61a).
39. Cited in Menéndez y Pelayo, *op. cit.*, p. 439.
40. "que cada qual de las siete planetas / sus operaçiones ynfluyen perfetas / a cada qual orbe por gloria yneterna" (stanza LXVII); "e todos de todas por esta manera / son ynclinados a disposiçión / de las virtudes e costelaçión / de la materia de cada vna espera" (LXVIII). Hernán Núñez's interpretation of these lines in his commentary (1499) is reproduced by J. M. Blecua in his edition of *El Laberinto* (Madrid, 1943), p. 40, n. 67. It coincides with the interpretation here given.

mortal men have no knowledge at all because the presence [*read prescience*] of what is to be is found only in God, whose inscrutable judgments cannot be understood by the human mind" (ed. Antwerp, 1552, p. 130). Yet man's mind has a power of its own that can defy the physical heavens. Commenting on Mena's treatment (stanzas CCLXV–CCLXVI) of the breaking and tearing down by his enemies of a statue which the ill-fated Don Alvaro de Luna had erected to mark the place of his own future burial, Núñez explains: "Here the poet says that just as lions, when forced by great hunger, return to a former kill when they are unable to catch fresh meat to eat, so the constellations and planets, when they find resistance on the part of a person on whom their influence would otherwise have been imposed, transfer their action to some likeness of that person, as in the case of this statue of the Condestable. A beautiful simile, worthy of the grace and keen intellect of Juan de Mena" (*ed. cit.*, p. 522).[41]

Astrology in the Renaissance

During the Renaissance the stars and other semi-deterministic forces are given an ever greater place in the literature of the imagination as poetic, that is to say, decorative, elements of style. They are cited as the determining factor in love or friendship, enmity or hatred, success or failure, in countless poems, plays, and novels, and they are prime-movers in serious dramas such as Juan Ruiz de Alarcón's *El dueño de las estrellas* and Calderón's *La vida es sueño*. Chaucer had made free use of such devices; in his *Troilus and Criseyde*, necessity, destiny, the Fates, Fortune, Nature, Providence, and astral influence give emphasis to the idea of the irresistibility of love. Nearly two centuries later, in Cervantes' novelette *La Galatea* (1585), as in almost all literature of the Golden Age, Fortune appears identified, mingled, or confused with the related ideas of Fate, the stars, the heavens, Providence.[42] In the last analysis, all these agents are referred back to the source

41. Núñez believes that the geographical location of one's birth affects (through the stars) one's character, and that comets foretell political disasters. See below.

42. F. López Estrada, "Sobre la Fortuna y el Hado en la literatura pastoril," *BRAE*, XXVI (1947), 436; O. H. Green, "Sobre las dos Fortunas: de tejas arriba y de tejas abajo," *Studia Philologica: Homenaje ofrecido a Dámaso Alonso* (Madrid, 1960–63, II, 145. See Chapter VII below.

of all power in the universe — God — and Calderón entitles one of his dramatic works *No hay más Fortuna que Dios* — *There is no Fortune except God's Will*. Yet with great frequency both the stars and Fortune are conveniently thought of as secondary instruments for the carrying out of the divine decisions. Bernardo de Balbuena, in his *Bernardo o Victoria de Roncesvalles* (1642) — an epic, rich with the tropical splendor he had known in Mexico and Puerto Rico, in which he endeavored to nationalize the legend of Roland and Charlemagne — expressed the prevailing state of opinion:

> God seldom intervenes directly in our affairs,
> Yet life and death are far from being haphazard.[43]

To pass from the consideration of such purely rhetorical uses of astrological lore to a study of the conscious use of the astrologer's doctrine as an explanation of the relationship between man and his cosmos or as an apology for man's character and activities, is, as Don Cameron Allen points out, "to realize the amazing currency of this type of learning in Renaissance England." In Renaissance Spain no less than in Britain, "the notion of a general celestial influence on man and his world is a part of most literary men's philosophy." In both countries, "the literary men knew . . . the whole infallible chain of logic. The planets influence the elements and in this way come to the sovereignty of the [bodily] humors; the resulting complexion establishes the character of the star-cursed man." This idea was basic in the psychology of Siglo de Oro, no less than in Elizabethan and Jacobean, authors. When one studies the rhetorical language of plays and poems and works of fiction, "he notices that there are many adjectives, many epithets

43. "Que ni es todo milagros celestiales / ni todo caso y muertes no entendidas" (Canto IX, stanza 44; cf. stanzas 38–46). "This theory is stated even more explicitly in the *Alegoría* attached to Canto VII, where Balbuena, discussing the influence of the stars or of Fate on men, states that this influence is not sufficient to overcome free will, but is very strong in minor matters. . . . Fate he defines as the disposition of the sign of the Zodiac under which one is conceived." His authority is St. Thomas. See John Van Horne, *El Bernardo of Bernardo de Balbuena: A Study of the Poem with Particular Attention to its Relations to the Epics of Boiardo and Ariosto and to its Significance in the Spanish Renaissance* (Urbana, Illinois, 1927), p. 121; Frank Pierce, "L'allégorie poétique au XVIe siècle," *BHi*, LI (1949), 381–406, and LII (1950), 191–228; *idem, La poesía épica del Siglo de Oro* (Madrid, 1961); W. J. Entwistle, "The Search for the Heroic Poem," University of Pennsylvania Bicentennial Conference, *Studies in Civilization* (Philadelphia, 1941), pp. 89–103.

which suggest that for men of this age the force of the stars was ineluctable"[44] — ineluctable, that is, if man is left to his own devices, but resistible with the aid of Grace."[45] Sir Walter Raleigh (d. 1618) believed the stars to have complete power over all reasonless things in the inferior world, and a definite influence on the disposition of men; he admitted that their force could be counterbalanced by prayer and education, but held that they presided over the fates of most sublunar things. Richard Burton (d. 1640) confessed: "If thou shalt ask me what I think, I must answer . . . they [the stars] do incline, but not compel; no necessity at all: *agunt non cogunt*: and so gently incline, that a wise man may resist them; *sapiens dominabitur astris*: they rule us, but God rules them."[46] Many other examples could be cited to show that "belief in astrology was not confined . . . to the ignorant and credulous."[47] Even the possession of a theological degree "was no bar to the practice of astrology." In the Renaissance, astrological learning was a part of any national culture (*ibid.*, p. 170).

Astrology as science. Dante (d. 1321), in his *Convivio*, held that man, "by reason of the nature of his mixed body . . . loves the season of the year wherein he was generated" and "feels best physically when he is in the place of his birth, and at the time of year he was conceived." Marsilio Ficino (d. 1499) and Paracelsus (d. 1541) were convinced that without astral knowledge no physician could know or cure the human body.[48] La Torre in his *Visión delectable* explains that men conform naturally to the "complexions and climates and places and lands and influences wherein or whereunder they are born, the inhabitants of some lands being affable and kind, while those of another region may be malicious, thieving fellows, and still others proud and daring or timorous

44. *Op. cit.*, pp. 159–61; see also pp. 28, 181–82.
45. Here I speak for Spain only.
46. Cited in Allen, *op cit.*, pp. 153–54. "Like his earth, man was governed by the planets and stars. Saturnine or jovial, martial or mercurial, he was what cosmic forces had made him. 'A star danced,' laughed Beatrice, 'and under that I was born.' 'Saturn was the lord of my geniture,' said the Anatomist of Melancholy" (Marjorie Nicolson, *The Breaking of the Circle: Studies in the Effect of the "New Science" upon Seventeenth-Century Poetry* [New York, 1960], p. 15).
47. Allen, *op. cit.*, pp. 60, 69; see also pp. 81, 100.
48. J. A. Mazzeo, *Structure and Thought in the "Paradiso"* (Ithaca, 1958), p. 54; see also Allen, *op. cit.*, pp. 7, 9, 11, 13 ,16, 18–19, 43, 48 ff., 52, 60–61, 63, and 99–100.

and cowardly" (*ed. cit.,* p. 370b). Some fifty years later Núñez, in his commentary on Mena's stanza LIII, says of Sardinia: "There are in this island cities and many towns and villages teeming with people, who, because of the grouping of the stars above, are more inclined to evil than to good conduct" (*ed. cit.,* p. 123). Pedro Mexía, in his *Silva de varia lección* (1540), speaking of the influence of each man's horoscope, declares that those born under the sign of Pisces will, by accident (i.e., by this accident of birth), be good swimmers.[49] This physical force, he explains in another place, is a secondary cause or instrument whereby God is pleased to work His will in terrestrial bodies (*ibid.,* p. 172). Even the great longevity of Old Testament worthies such as Methuselah can be scientifically explained by the more benign aspects of the stars and planets when the world was young (*ibid.,* p. 17).

The study of these matters is a respectable science, says Pedro Ciruelo in his *Reprobación de las supersticiones y hechicerías* (1539). The true scientist can tell, with all propriety, "if a child will be well-endowed, or dull, for the study of letters or for other arts or exercises . . . and this astrology is a licit and true science like natural philosophy or medicine." Mistaken prognoses may be attributable to the difficulty of the special case or to the incompetence of the scientist.[50]

In 1553 Alonso García Matamoros composed a manifesto proving Spain's right to consideration in the world of letters, and in it he calls for an improvement on the part of writers of medical treatises. They should, he insists, follow Pythagoras, Democritus of Abdera, Apolonius of Tyana, Ficino, and many Arabic physicians and compose their works in accordance with the laws of astronomy; they will be better physicians, or better practitioners of animal husbandry, if they investigate the nature of earthly creatures, the forces of the heavenly bodies, and their reciprocal attractions.[51]

In 1559 Fadrique Furió Ceriol in all seriousness cites the influence of his star as justification for venturing to write a book on

49. Ed. La Sociedad de Bibliófilos Españoles (Madrid, 1933), I, 143; cf. p. 135.
50. Ed. Salamanca, 1539, fol. xxiii v.
51. *Pro adserenda hispanorum eruditione,* trans. J. López de Toro (Madrid, 1943), p. 231.

statecraft, *El concejo y consejeros del Príncipe*: "I am not held back by the fear that many will accuse me of temerity for presuming to treat so arduous and difficult matters, because the influence of my star guides me and practically forces me to do it; and thus, following so excellent a guide, I have always busied myself from my early years in analyzing and understanding forms and means of good government." [52]

So taken for granted was the belief in these influences that, even in a trivial matter like the composing of a dedicatory letter to the Duque de Feria to accompany his novel *El español Gerardo* (1615), Gonzalo de Céspedes y Meneses relates "the natural inclination of all persons to be, or to appear to be, devoted to Your Excellency" not only to the latter's heroic virtues and generosity of spirit, but also to *secreta felicidad de estrellas* — a secret affinity of their stars with his. [53]

Such felicity of constellation is extended on occasion to the entire Spanish nation. Fray Bernabé Moreno de Vargas, in his *Discursos de la nobleza de España* (1621), states that it is natural that Spaniards should be second to none in asserting their sense of honor, "since they have been regarded as noble from ancient times, and they are descended from all the noble nations of the earth [Romans, Goths, etc.] who, when once they had settled in Spain, received from its sky a new value, which is Spanish." [54]

In his personal correspondence Quevedo expresses the belief that his condition of disease or of health is related to his location on the earth, near or removed from the stars that presided at his birth: "The physician who is treating me . . . insists that I give up the idea of going to Andalusia and return to Toledo, since the trip is shorter and the road better, and the sky, though not as sunny as that of Granada, is more suited to my constitution; he judges by the air of Madrid, where I was born." Quevedo expresses a similar concern over the children of a friend: "God knows that I would like to see the sons of Your Excellency removed from so hot a climate and enjoying the sea wind, for they were engendered and

52. *BAE*, XXXVI, 319.
53. *BAE*, XVIII, 117.
54. Cited by Albert A. Sicroff, *Les controverse des statuts de "pureté de sang" en Espagne du XVe au XVIIe siècle* (Paris, 1960), p. 291, n. 111.

reared in a cold region which is just the opposite of where they are."[55]

In a book of poems printed in 1623, Pedro Soto de Rojas applies astrological science to his own particular case as an *amant désespéré*. According to his psychology, every instinct clamors for that particular form of expression that was assigned to it by the stars at the moment of birth. A man's star inclines him to arms, to the chase, to the plow, or to the helmsman's wheel. Yet Nature's law has its one exception: the poet, born to love, derives only sorrow from the exercise of his instinctive drive:

> Every instinct demands the full expression
> Of the inclination of the star that guides it,
> And finds therein fulfillment, rest, and joy.
> And yet, alas for me! though I love ever —
> Driven by the cruel star that watched my birth —,
> No rest is mine, no joy, no hope, no comfort.[56]

For a summary of this section we may well turn to Alonso de Acevedo's epic of the Creation, *La Creación del Mundo* (1615):

> If there's no lightning flash in heaven above
> That on the spheres beneath casts not its spell —
> Producing change, contraction, or expansion
> In response to the brightness from on high —
> Surely we must believe that every planet
> Exerts on us some secret natural virtue,
> Product of its attraction or repulsion.[57]

The same poet, describing the Ninth Heaven (the "waters" that are above the Heaven of the Fixed Stars), explains that those heavenly waters were placed there by the Creator to control the exces-

55. *Epistolario completo de D. Francisco de Quevedo Villegas*, ed. Luis Astrana Marín (Madrid, 1946), pp. 487, 493.

56. "Acude todo instinto al exercicio / a que la estrella en que nació le influye, / y alcança en él descanso y alegría; / de mí solo, que asido al duro oficio / de amar nací por fuerte estrella mía, / el alegría y el descanso huye" (*Obras*, ed. Antonio Gallego Morell [Madrid, 1950], p. 44).

57. "Luego si en el Olimpo no hay centella / que en los círculos ínfimos no influya / mudanza alguna con su lumbre bella, / que las cosas augmente o disminuya; / está claro que a cada errante estrella / también sobre nosotros se atribuya / alguna natural virtud secreta / que influya desde el círculo el planeta" (*BAE*, XXIX, 266a). The fact that the poet, interpreting the work of the six days of Creation, should call the firmament *Olimpo* need cause no surprise. See my article, *"Fingen los poetas*: Notes on the Spanish Attitude toward Pagan Mythology," *Estudios dedicados a Menéndez Pidal*, I (Madrid, 1950), 275 ff.

sive heat of the luminous bodies, so that the various stars might exert the influence ordained by Divine Providence (see Ch. II, n. 46).

Omens and portents. In his *Tesoro de la lengua castellana,* Covarrubias defines *agüero* (omen) as "a kind of divination by the flight of birds and by their cries, or by the way in which they peck at the grain or the crumbs that were cast to them, in order to conjecture future events, good or bad; the word is extended to any sign or happening that can announce good or ill success. All of this applies to gentiles and barbarians, not to Christians." He gives various examples of worthies of antiquity who were willing to say *defy such signs,* and adds a final remark: "Some families are famous for having certain omens, but, thanks to God, this is gradually being forgotten. Since it is all a matter of impertinent curiosity, I refrain from citing omens of good and disastrous events." He refers the reader to Alexander ab Alexandro and Guillaume Budé.

As we shall see when we examine the practically unanimous condemnation of judicial astrology with its claim to reveal secrets of the future which belong only to God, the act of divination,[58] whether by means of omens, signs, portents, or otherwise, was regarded as sinful. Further light will be shed on this in our discussion (below) of "Divine foreknowledge," since any determinism bears on the problem of predestination. Furthermore, inasmuch as many of the signs are astronomical (e.g., comets), they constitute a sort of extension of the idea of astrological influence.

Belief in omens was condemned by the ecclesiastical authorities. Fray Hernando de Talavera (d. 1507) wrote in his *Breve forma de confesar: Item [pecan] los que creen a los sueños o a abusiones y agüeros de diez mil maneras que desvariadas personas se hallan —* "No less guilty of sin are those who believe in dreams or the misuse of words and the omens of ten thousand different sorts that unstable persons are constantly inventing."[59] The condemnation

58. José Amador de los Ríos, "De las artes mágicas y de adivinación en el suelo ibérico: Su influencia en las costumbres," *Revista de España,* XVIII (1871), 1–26, 321–48.

59. *NBAE,* XVI, 23a. The same Fray Lope de Barrientos who was commissioned by Juan II of Castile to burn Don Enrique de Villena's books on astrology (see n. 30) was also ordered by that king to compose a *Libro del dormir y despertar, y del soñar y adivinar agüeros y profecías* (MS V, 157 [old style] of the Biblioteca Nacional in Madrid). See Gallardo, *Ensayo,* II, *Apéndice,* p. 14.

is repeated by Juan del Encina; in his *Cancionero* (1496) he warns against giving heed to flying birds, croaking ravens, barking or howling dogs, or the lowing of larger animals: death comes to each man when God so wills; the hour is known only to Him and to the person to whom God chooses to reveal it. Others can only watch and pray.[60] Similarly, Cristóbal de Villalón (d. 1581?), in his *Diálogo de las transformaciones*, declares that animals are guided by instinct only and therefore cannot foretell the future; he who believes in omens will never accomplish anything worth while, since he will always wait to see if the auspices are favorable, or he will be led astray by the devil. God may even punish those who offend in these matters by permitting the disaster to occur as foretold, though the foretelling (and hence all thought of necessity) was false.[61]

But the matter was far more complicated. It will be remembered that in the quotation of Encina just cited reference was made to the possibility of special revelation by God, to a chosen human being, of a future event. In a curious manuscript by Christopher Columbus entitled *Liber sive manupulus de auctoritatibus circa materiam . . . inventionis et conversionis insularum Indie*, addressed to Ferdinand and Isabella, the navigator declares: "I say that the Holy Spirit operates in Christians, Jews, and Moors and in others of other sects, and not only in the wise, but also in the ignorant . . . ; and I say that not only does the Holy Spirit reveal future events to rational creatures, but also that He reveals them to us by means of the signs of the heavens, of the air, and of animals, when it pleases Him so to do. . . ."[62] Núñez expresses faith in the baleful announcements of comets: "Among these stars, those that are called comets, with rays like hair and of bloody color, whenever they appear in the sky, signify that there will be in the kingdom above which they appear, some royal death or the demise of a great lord, or some other calamity."[63] His authorities are Aristotle, Albertus Magnus, and Seneca. Somewhat earlier, Pero Díaz de Toledo, in his *Dialogue . . . on the Death* [1458] *of the Marqués de Santillana*, explains the death-song of the swan as an

60. Ed. facsim. (Madrid, 1928), fol. Aii verso.
61. Ed. M. Menéndez y Pelayo in *Orígenes de la Novela* (Madrid, 1905–15), II, 115b.
62. Cited by Gallardo, *Ensayo*, II, col. 504.
63. Commentary on Mena's stanza CLXIV, *ed. cit.*, p. 375.

act of Divine Revelation to men to the end that they too may learn
to receive death bravely and with dignity: "I hold it true that, just
as God and Nature gave awareness to certain animals to prognosti-
cate certain coming events (as I remember having read in Lucan
about a fish called the dolphin and a bird that is called the gos-
hawk, and the crane, which foretell and reveal to men, by God's
permission, the storm and tempest that will soon burst upon the
sea), so it appears that God and Nature chose to endow the swan
with this gift and grace, in order that it should teach men to receive death with a strong and happy heart." [64]

In his *Historia natural y moral de las Indias*, the Jesuit José
de Acosta presents the two aspects of the problem — the Christian
prohibition against believing in omens as the Romans did, and
the obvious fact that the Bible itself contains numerous examples
of not dissimilar portents: "Although the Holy Scriptures forbid
us to lend credence to omens and prognostications, and Jeremiah
warns us to fear nothing from the signs of the heavens as the Gentiles do, nevertheless Holy Scripture itself teaches that in certain
universal changes [e.g., the death of Christ] and in certain punishments which God wishes to impose, signs, monsters and prodigies
are not to be scorned, for they actually occur with frequency, as
Eusebius points out." There follow two full pages of documenta-
tion of these statements, and chapter 23 of Book VII is entitled:
"Concerning the strange forewarnings and prodigies which oc-
cured in Mexico before that Empire came to its end." [65]

The evidence of belief in such signs could be multiplied from
all sorts of serious works.[66] I shall give one Spanish and one Italian
example. In his report on the political uprisings in Aragon in 1591
and 1592, Don Francisco de Gurrea y Aragón, Conde de Luna,
writes of a great resplendent light that appeared one night above
the Cathedral of Nuestra Señora del Pilar in Saragossa, causing
terror in some and encouragement in others. He continues: "The
Justiciary of Aragon was imprisoned on the twentieth of Decem-
ber, three days after the two glowing lights that appeared miracu-

64. Paz y Melia (ed.), *op. cit.*, p. 269. On Nature as *Natura naturans*, see above,
Chapter III.
65. Ed. Madrid, 1792, II, 203 ff.
66. One cannot possibly subscribe to the statement of Miguel Herrero García, in his
study on astrology in the Spanish theater of the Golden Age (*RFE*, XXVI [1942], 18),
that "Renaissance rationalism is decidedly opposed to the acceptance of auguries."

lously, and amazing and novel judgments were rendered." [67] The Italian example is a century earlier. In his *Storia d'Italia* (1494) Guicciardini states unequivocally that "the calamity of Italy was pronounced both by man and by the heavens. . . . In Apulia by night three suns were seen in the skies. . . . In Arezzo for many days there passed through the air great numbers of armed men riding on huge horses. . . . In many places in Italy the images and sacred statues were seen to break into a sweat. Many monsters were born among men and animals. . . . The people were filled with an incredible fear." Referring to Guicciardini and Pontano, Myron P. Gilmore observes: "They both emphasize how much the course of history lies hidden from human eyes. . . . They believe in historical miracles . . . and they also believe in miracles in the conventional sense. They report prophecies and prodigies." For them the determinisms of human history are inscrutable.[68]

Similar determinisms are frequent in Spanish literature,[69] appearing both as mere superstition[70] and as perfectly acceptable Divine interventions. Dreams are discredited in the *Amadís de Gaula* (1508), but are nonetheless employed as a literary device: "And one of these, named Ungán el Picardo, who was the best informed, replied: 'Sire, dreams are a vain thing and should be regarded as such; but, since you desire that some importance should be given to this dream of yours, grant us some time to examine its significance.'"[71] The Pythoness, or soothsaying woman, had both Biblical (Acts 16:16) and classical antecedents; she is very common in the romances of chivalry,[72] as well as in the drama.[73] In Andrés Laguna's *Viaje de Turquía* (ca. 1557), the interlocutor Pedro tells

67. *Comentarios de los sucesos de Aragón*, ed. el Duque de Villahermosa (Madrid, 1888), p. 251.
68. "Freedom and Determinism in Renaissance Historians," *Studies in the Renaissance*, III (1956), 55–56.
69. See L. L. Barrett, "The Omen in Guillén de Castro's Drama," *Hisp.*, XXII (1939), 73–75; *idem*, "The Supernatural in Juan de la Cueva's Plays," *SP*, XXXVI (1939), 147–68; and the article by Herrero García referred to above. Barrett is not concerned with Christian doctrine. M. N. Pavia, *Drama of the Siglo de Oro: A Study of Magic, Witchcraft, and Other Occult Beliefs* (New York, 1959), should be used with caution.
70. *Poema de Mio Cid*, line 11; *Leyenda de los Infantes de Lara* (2d ed.), ed. R. Menéndez Pidal (Madrid, 1934), p. 227.
71. Ed. Barcelona, 1847–48, I, 25.
72. *Amadís, ed. cit.*, I, 25.
73. E.g., Tirso de Molina's *Amazonas en las Indias*.

how, on his departure from Constantinople, the first thing he encountered as the city walls fell behind, "was a white dove which gave me the greatest encouragement in the world," so that he said to his companions: "I believe that with God's help we shall make this journey in safety, because this dove assures us of it." One of the companions asked in surprise: "And if the dove had been a crow, would you have turned back?" To which Pedro replied: "Do not think that I pay attention to omens; the appearance of the dove is a confirmation of hope, but the flight of a crow would have no significance for evil." [74]

Céspedes y Meneses, in *El español Gerardo*, causes a character to give a plus-minus, or rather a minus-plus importance to omens: "I omit telling of certain omens which I had on that day, because I have never been fearful of such things; but I assure you that if I had heeded them, and that if, when my horse stumbled in the center of a flowery meadow as I left town, dumping himself and his rider on the ground, I had really turned back as I was tempted to do, I should never have fallen into the cruel hands of my enemies" (*ed. cit.*, p. 137b).

Whether or not the omen is a trap for the unwary, involving in sin him who heeds it, or is, on the contrary, a salutary warning from On High, depends on whether or not God is interfering: a dove and a rainbow were meaningful signs to Noah on Mt. Ararat, and the young Samuel was called by a Voice. Very interesting as an example of the divinely inspired omen is the device, common in the Spanish *comedia* but utilized also in other genres (e.g., in *Don Quijote*), known as *kledonomancy* — the interpretation of words overheard by chance as applying to a given critical situation of which the speaker of the words has no idea. "The protagonist may be aware of the 'voice from heaven,' or it may be only the public that is conscious of it, in which case the dramatic effect is . . . more intensely felt. An upright man may perform a noble action that nevertheless brings about his downfall [e.g., in Lope's *El Caballero de Olmedo*], and the mysterious presage of evil that is to befall him (in this case never understood) aids admirably to impress upon the audience the inexplicable ways of God, who thus

---

74. *NBAE*, II, 62b. It will be remembered that the dove brought a message of hope to Noah in the Ark.

deliberately afflicts his own, the inscrutability of God's motives being a point that the dramatist Mira [de Amescua] is very fond of bringing out." [75]

Antonio Mira de Amescua is by no means the only dramatist to use this device, which is world-wide. Tirso de Molina employs it, along with other heavenly presages, for example, in *La elección por la virtud*, in *El Burlador de Sevilla*, and in other plays. [76] A poignant passage in *Don Quijote* involving its use would appear to be secular in character, except for the fact, not stated but implicit, that God is leading the erring hero home, to recognize his error with an act of thanksgiving to his Maker, and to prepare his soul for Heaven. As Don Quijote approaches his village for the last time, unable now to accomplish the disenchantment of his lady Dulcinea, he overhears the voices of two quarreling boys, one of whom shouts: *No te canses, Periquillo; que no la has de ver en todos los días de tu vida*— "Stop your nonsense, Pete; you'll never see it [i.e., her] again, as long as you live" (Part II, ch. 73). The reference is to a cage of crickets, but the feminine pronoun *la* suggests, to Don Quijote's depressed mind, the enchanted lady of his thoughts. Sancho upbraids his master for making so superstitious an interpretation, reminding him that the village curate condemned as silly all Christians who pay attention to such trifles (*ibid.*, pp. 247–48). The prudent safeguard seems scarcely necessary; the reader sees deeper than Sancho and realizes that Don Quijote is being led and admonished by a genuine Voice from Heaven.

Kledonomancy in Spain had also its darker, its illicit, side, Ciruelo in 1540 attacked it as an evil. In the thirteenth century, Alfonso the Learned had condemned to death persons found guilty of practicing this type of divination, which, however, refused to be stamped out: Juan II in 1410 and Felipe II in 1598 penalized officers of justice who failed to prosecute violators of the old law, which was now required to be read publicly on one market day of each month (*ibid.*, p. 249).

When, on the other hand, the omen could be interpreted as an

75. C. E. Anibal, *"Voces del Cielo*: A Note on Mira de Amescua," *RR*, XVI (1925), 58. See the series of articles, a sort of "dialogue" between Anibal and A. H. Krappe, on this subject, in vols. XVII, XVIII, XIX, of the same journal.
76. Anibal, "Another note on the *Voces del Cielo*," *RR*, XVIII (1927), 251.

act of God or of his heavenly ministers, it was perfectly acceptable.
Anibal wrote: "Most interesting is the quite extraordinary moral
note, and this is what should be borne most deeply in mind, as
being . . . highly characteristic of the theologian Mira at his
best. . . ." 77

When considered as acts of God, all sorts of omens are permissible in the theater. One example will suffice. In Tirso de Molina's
Todo es dar en una cosa, the young Francisco Pizarro, known, historically, to have been fond of bowling, is made to contend physically with Hernando Cortés for the possession of a wooden bowling
ball. The sphere splits in two, one half remaining in the hands of
each contender. The symbolism is obvious: the two shall divide
between them a New World.

The legislation of three Spanish kings, from the thirteenth to
the sixteenth century, is most clearly a *Non*. For a *Sic* — i.e., for an
acceptance of omens by an author treating one of the most sacred
of subjects, the work of the Six Days — let us turn again to Acevedo
and his *Creación del mundo*. Omens, he says, may be meteorological, as they have been in the past:

> Ere Alaric, king of the Goths, first came
> To Italy, the darkling sun its splendor
> Hid behind densest clouds from pole to pole;
> Hail smote the fields, and in the heavens the Bear
> Trailed in the path of a most hoary comet.78

Or they may be ornithological, even in the present:

> The croaking owl, perched on his lofty cliff,
> Announces doom to an unhappy nation;
> The cackling goose upward directs our gaze
> To where blood-dripping and death-bringing clouds
> Veil the bright sun, foretelling treachery,
> As wild storms beat upon the waters' breast
> And Ocean trembles to its lowest depths.79

77. "*Voces del Cielo*," p. 57.
78. "Primero que Alarico, rey de godos, / viniese a Italia, el sol con negro manto /
triste escondió sus resplandores todos, / escuro el cielo de uno y otro canto; / y de
grandeza en excesivos modos / derramó el aire con temor y espanto / granizo espeso,
porque a la Osa fría / un crinito cometa el paso abría" (*ed. cit.*, p. 254b).
79. "El buho anuncia desde la alta peña / al triste pueblo los futuros daños; / con
su graznido el ánsar nos enseña, / que con bañados y funestos paños / cubren las
nubes la dorada enseña / que sacó el sol, descubridor de engaños, / y levantando negras tempestades / tiemblan del Ponto las profundidades" (*ed. cit.*, p. 273a).

Free Will vs. the stars. Américo Castro, after a detailed study of the many references to astrology in Cervantes' works, ends with a quotation from the play *La Entretenida* to the effect that astrology is mere triviality — not in its role as a science, but because simple souls dabble in it without study or experience — and arrives at this conclusion: "it is prudent to conclude . . . that Cervantes was not entirely free from the interest in this matter which was common to his century, and that the folly and false prognostications of the astrologers were attributable, in his mind, to their ignorance and their evil character, not to the falsity of the science which they professed." [80] Cervantes' inveighings against false astrologers and against all attempts to force the human will we shall leave for our section on the opponents of astrology. As a child of his century, he naturally shared the *preocupaciones comunes de su siglo.*

Cervantes, like his contemporaries, is at any time willing to cause a fictional character to cry out against his "unlucky" star, as Aurelio does in *El trato de Argel,* using the words *destino, fuerza insana de implacable hado, estrella, suerte, fortuna, sino* — "destiny, blind force of implacable fate, star, luck, fortune." Aurelio is answered by Saavedra — a *figura* of his creator:

> Oh bitter, dire, inexorable star,
> How have you brought and dragged me miserably
> To the cruel pain by which I'm overcome! [81]

This is mere rhetoric. These stars, this fortune, and this fate have no transcendence. Their value for defining attitudes and ideas is nil. Their ornamental literary use will be better understood when we have studied Fortune and Fate in a later chapter. They are the fortune and fate "of daily circumstance," of the ups and downs of man's earthly struggle with the perversity of inanimate objects or of his fellows. They are *de tejas abajo* — not *de tejas arriba* — and they hold sway from the roof downward. They are not the instruments of God's Providence, the means of His ultimate disposition of the lot of every man. They are like the rhetorical appeals to the irresistibility of love: *sin poderse resistir, le había entregado el alma (señal que una misma estrella predominaba en la inclina-*

---

80. *El pensamiento de Cervantes* (Madrid, 1925), p. 101.
81. "¡Ay dura, inicua, inexorable estrella! / ¡Cómo de los cabellos me has traído / al fuerte dolor que me atropella!" (*Obras, ed. cit.,* pp. 116–17).

ción de entrambos) [82] — "unable to resist, she had given him her heart (a true sign that a single star determined the inclination of both)." In all such cases, author and reader knew that the human soul could resist, that these outbursts were not to be taken as definitions of the soul's capabilities, or as human judgments of God's government of His universe.

Disregarding, therefore, mere exclamations and laments against the heavens, we may believe that Cervantes agreed with Don Quijote's acceptance of astrology as a science — *esa ciencia se llama astrología* — the kind of dependable knowledge that enables a man to sow barley rather than wheat in one year, chickpeas and not barley in another, or to foretell that the crop of olive oil will be abundant (*Don Quijote*, I, 12).

In the realm of human character and conduct, Cervantes believed, with his contemporaries, that the stars incline. In *La Galatea* Silerio tells how he sought the friendship of Timbrio, "I know not whether because of his many sterling qualities, or because of the action of the stars, which inclined me so to do" (*Obras, ed. cit.*, p. 647a). In the *Persiles* he states the doctrine of the essential equality of all souls, created by their Maker from a single substance, and of the accidental differences arising from the accidental nature of the body that encloses them, so that they devote themselves to the skills or arts or sciences to which their stars incline them.[83] His insistence that the stars act on the body, that is to say, on the admixture of the bodily humors that determine the temperament of each person, and his eloquent defense of the absolute freedom of the will, are in full agreement with the doctrine of the Christian humanist Juan Luis Vives in his *De anima*: the heavens, made of inanimate substance, are controlled by necessity, whereas man's will is immaterial and free.[84]

In regard to judicial astrology and its claim to clairvoyance, Cervantes, like the author of the first book ever written on differen-

---

82. Juan Pérez de Montalbán, *Sucesos y prodigios de amor* ([1624], ed. La Sociedad de Bibliófilos Españoles, [Madrid, 1949]), p. 225.

83. "porque las almas todas son iguales, y de una misma masa . . . formadas por su Hacedor, y, según la caja y temperamento del cuerpo donde las encierra, así parecen ellas más o menos discretas, y atienden y se aficionan a saber las ciencias, artes o habilidades a que las estrellas más las inclinan" (*Obras, ed. cit.*, p. 1564b). See Carlos Castillo, "Cervantes y Pero Mexía," *MPh*, XLIII (1945–46), 98–99.

84. Carreras y Artau, *op. cit.*, p. 153.

tial psychology and vocational guidance, Juan Huarte de San Juan (cited *ibid.*, p. 152), was inclined to admit, with a reasonable man's caution, the possibility of partial or occasional success. Chapter XVIII of Book I of the *Persiles* bears the heading: "Wherein Mauricio learns by means of astrology of a misfortune which befell them at sea." In chapter XIII this same Mauricio tells how he was led to the study of astrology by the normal human desire to know everything, past, present, future. Having lost — and seeking to recover — his beloved daughter, he observed the stars and planets, indicated their points and "houses" to the end that his work should correspond to his desire, "because no science, qua science, ever deceives; the deceit lies in the man who does not know the science, especially the science of astrology, because of the velocity of the heavens, which whirl the stars along with them so that they do not exert the same influence in all places; and thus the judicial astrologer, if he at times is successful in his predictions, succeeds by reason of the fact that he has based his judgment on the probable, in the light of long experience." [85] In chapter XVIII of Book III we meet another judicial astrologer named Soldino, who says with the reasonableness that characterizes Cervantes: "I am not a magician nor a seer, but a judicial astrologer, which science, if it is well mastered, teaches one almost to foretell the future" (*ibid.*, p. 1678a). In both of these statements Cervantes seems to be following Ciruelo's *Reprobación de las supersticiones*:

> Inasmuch as the skies and stars, affecting and altering the air and the earth, affect also men and the other animals . . . , the true philosopher who knows the virtues and properties of the stars can by their means know the aforesaid effects on the elements and on men, birds, and beasts. . . . And although these good astrologers are not always correct in their judgments, we should not be surprised, for two reasons. The first is because of the science itself, which treats of lofty matters, difficult to know because of their great diversity. The other reason has to do with the astrologer, who often does not know his science as fully as he should.[86]

Since this matter of foretelling the future — like the doctrine of Divine foreknowledge (see below) — is, as it were, an ever present

---

85. *Obras, ed. cit.*, p. 1557a Mauricio recognizes the limits of his sciences; when asked from what direction the threatening danger would come, *respondió que no lo sabía*—"he replied that he did not know" (p. 1563a; cf. p. 1563b).

86. Cited by Castro, *El pensamiento* . . . , pp. 104–5.

cloud (hand-sized, to be sure) that threatens the clear formulation of the fundamental doctrine that man is a free moral agent, it will be well to place beside Cervantes' text one from Venegas' *Agonía del tránsito de la muerte*:

Astrology differs from astronomy, for astronomy is a sure and true science, whereas astrology fails on many occasions, because it has for its basis effects not yet produced, which are uncertain because of the uncertainty of the disposition of the four elements. Animals are directly affected, for all animals are mere bodies; but men are affected only by indirection, since the movement of the firmament has nothing to do with rational souls: a body cannot produce its effects on the spirit. This is the cause of the wild errors of the astrologers when they cast judgments on persons.[87]

Lope de Vega's bewildering treatment of the many aspects of astral influence in his plays and non-dramatic works has led to the belief that he was credulous and superstitious in these matters.[88] More thorough study, however, has shown earlier judgments to have been superficial: Lope adhered closely to authorities;[89] he held very definite and unequivocal beliefs;[90] a careful weighing of the evidence indicates that his sustained thesis is that free will intelligently applied by wise men can and will alter any natural inclination of the stars:[91]

87. *NBAE*, XVI, 290b.
88. See the Bibliography in Frank G. Halstead, "The Attitude of Lope de Vega toward Astrology," *HR*, VII (1939), 205–7; E. S. Morby, "Levinus Lemnius and Leo Swabius in *La Dorotea*," *HR*, XX (1952), 110, n. 6.
89. "Lope has characteristically adhered to his model so closely as to translate" (*ibid.*, p. 113).
90. Halstead, *op. cit.*, p. 207.
91. I am not satisfied with Halstead's insistence on two exceptions which he supposes Lope (and Tirso — see below, n. 97) to have supported, namely: that lovers and persons of royal blood (as well as great captains) are not able to resist the stars (p. 208, and nn. 26, 27). Halstead's chosen texts do not support his contention and, concerning love, Halstead himself notes "at least four occasions when Lope reverses himself and writes that the stars cannot force the free-will to love" (n. 26 at the end). Lope, himself an erring lover, in the sonnet-palinode quoted in our Volume I, Chapter VI (*En el último punto de mi vida*), exonerates the stars and accuses himself: *No por causa fatal, influjo o suerte / sino por pasos de mi mal gobierno* — "Not through the influence of stars or fate, / But by successive steps of willful folly." In the play *El alcalde mayor*, Lope causes Beatriz to ask: "If Venus should force me, could I resist?" She is answered that the evil can be escaped, but such an achievement is difficult: "Si me forzara a querer / podríame resistir? — El mal, bien se puede huir, / mas es difícil de hacer" (N. Acad., XI, 215). As for kings, princes, captains: in the play *Lo que ha de ser* (N. Acad., XII, 399b–400a) Lope causes Leonardo, a person of royal blood, to declare: "Since the wise man and the strong / Is lord of the constellations, / Though

God has given to mankind
The gift of free will, whereby
Wise men have the obligation
To struggle against misfortune,
Bravely resisting its blows
Before misfortune can strike;
Let not the fact that opinions
Declare that all is determined
At the moment of man's birth
Cause men to adjust their conduct
To what has thus been foretold.[92]

In the last analysis, Lope's knowledge of astrology was a scientific one. He believed, with his contemporaries and his intellectual peers, that "the will is the best key": happy is the man who, by exercising prudence, can overcome his condition.[93] But — one may ask — are all men prudent and strong-willed? Does not the New Testament contain the parable of the foolish virgins? The way of the foolish is hard: *liberum arbitrium tanto liberius, quanto a peccato remotius* — "free will is freer in proportion as it is farther removed from sin,"[94] and sin is avoided by the exercise of prudence and reason. Even so, we are not too far removed, in this matter of weakness, from the grim doctrine of predestination. Fray Luis de Granada explains:

This appetite [sensuality] is one of the principal tyrants to which the wicked are subject and, as St. Paul says, enslaved. The Apostle calls such

they seek to impose their law / I can with my own free will / Enjoy my lordship in freedom / And deny them all obedience. / For the cause of all their power / Is the weakness of each man, / Who offers token resistance / To that which they would effect" ("porque si el sabio, el que es fuerte, / es señor de las estrellas, / aunque me lo manden ellas / puedo yo con mi albedrío / gozar de mi señorío / y dejar de obedecellas. / Por lo que tienen poder / es por la flaqueza humana, / que hace resistencia llana / a lo que quieren hacer"). In this play the prognostication, by a freak and as a result of uncontrolled anger, comes true; but the subject matter is not Christian and the plot is a *raro suceso que escriben / las historias africanas* — "a rare event reported by African histories" (*ibid.*, p. 408b).

92. "Dios ha dado a los hombres / libre albedrío, y con éste / deben los cuerdos varones / prevenirse a las desdichas / y resistir a sus golpes / antes que a sus puertas lleguen, / que no porque hay opiniones / que está el fin determinado / al punto que nace el hombre, / es justo que se remita / a lo que así dispone" (*El animal profeta*, cited by Halstead, *op. cit.*, pp. 207–8).

93. See the sonnet from *El Duque de Viseo* cited by Halstead, pp. 209–10: "Dichoso aquel que con prudencia sabe / vencer su condición y ser bien quisto, / que es la voluntad la mejor llave." See also *ibid.*, p. 214.

94. D. Odon Lottin, *op. cit.*, I, 32.

sinners slaves, not because they have lost through sinning the free will with which they were created (for this was neither lost nor will it ever be, as far as its essence is concerned, no matter how great the number of sins), but because sin so weakened a part of this free will (while the appetite remained so strong), that for the most part the strong prevails against the weak, and the rope breaks at the point where it is most frayed.[95]

In the matter of judicial astrology, Lope "takes occasion to lampoon astrologers in several passages ranging from the humorous to the scathing." Only God has foreknowledge.[96]

Tirso de Molina's attitude toward astrology also has been studied by Halstead,[97] who finds that the dramatist possessed the technical knowledge, both of this pseudoscience and also of the true science of astronomy, which characterized the well-educated layman in his day. Tirso holds that the stars bestow on each individual his own separate personality: this is why they are so varied. The astronomical Prime Mover is translated into its Christian counterpart of omniscient intelligence and design; it exercises a physical influence on physical bodies on earth, and upon organic bodies, man in particular, as taught by all the medieval interpreters. Man's will is free — *Vir mediante Deo sapiens dominabitur astris*:

> Man's soul, which is pure spirit,
> Unlike his body, is not
> Subject to the conjurer's art,
> Nor to the witch's concoctions;
> Its substance being so perfect
> That wise men without exception
> Regard it as free, contradicting
> Your astrological predictions,

95. "Pues este tal apetito [sensualidad, carne o concupiscencia] es uno de los más principales tyranos a quien están los malos sujetos y (como dice el Apóstol) vendidos por esclavos. Y llámalos aquí vendidos como esclavos, no porque por el pecado perdiessen ellos el libre alvedrío con que fueron criados (porque ni se perdió ni perderá jamás quanto a su esencia, por más pecados que se hagan), sino porque por el pecado quedó por una parte este libre alvedrío tan flaco, y por otra el apetito tan fuerte, que por la mayor parte prevalece lo fuerte contra lo flaco, y quiebra la soga por lo más delgado" (*Obras*, I [Madrid, 1768], 221).

96. This will be treated below. See Halstead, *op. cit.*, p. 206; Morby, *op. cit.*, p. 110.

97. *HR*, IX (1941), 417–39. Halstead in this article makes the same mistake as in his earlier article on Lope, claiming that Tirso denied free will (against astral influence) to lovers and to the nobly born. Again, his own chosen texts do not bear him out (see below).

Since all omens and all influences,
Though they may incline, force not.[98]

Any human being may be saved by grace. When God created man,

He gave him the gift of free will,
And he gave him human frailty
Both of body and of spirit;
But to him he also gave
The right and the power to ask
For the gift of God's great mercy,
A gift to no man denied.[99]

As for lovers, Tirso says that it is the folly (*desvarío*) of astrologers that assumes (*adivina*) that celestial influences incline the free will to love.[100] As for kings and nobles, they are indeed more subject to the influence of their horoscopes than are ordinary mortals (only kings' deaths are foretold by comets, etc.). But the texts do not say that rulers are totally controlled by such influences:

Princes, who from their birth
Have a delicate complexion,
Pure blood and unsullied humors,
In their lives are much more subject
(If we listen to astrologers)
Than the folk to astral influence.[101]

The if clause sounds a warning against assuming that astral control is absolute.

Tirso, like Lope, lampoons judicial astrologers and all persons who practice divination as a technical and exact science (*ibid.*, pp. 427–28).

98. "el alma espíritu puro, / ni a las hierbas ni al conjuro / como el cuerpo se sujeta; / su substancia es tan perfecta / que por libre la reputan / los sabios, con que confutan / tus astrólogas violencias, / porque agüeros e influencias / si señalan, no ejecutan" (*Amazonas en las Indias*, cited *ibid.*, pp. 425–26).

99. "Dióle Dios libre albedrío, / y fragilidad le dió / al cuerpo y al alma; luego / dió potestad con acción / de pedir misericordia / que a ninguno negó" (*El Condenado por desconfiado*, cited *ibid.*, p. 456). This is a much clearer statement than any I know of from Lope that no one is denied the gift of grace.

100. "y el desvarío / del astrólogo adivina / que es fuerza de astros que inclina / a amar el libre albedrío" (*La elección por la virtud*, cited *ibid.*, p. 430). See also p. 433, where another text shows that the will of the lover is free ("sin que los astros lo obliguen").

101. "Los príncipes que nacieron / desde sus reales principios / de complexión delicada, / sangre pura, humores limpios, / siempre viven más sujetos / (si a astrólogos dais oídos) / que el pueblo a las influencias / de las estrellas y signos" (*Privar contra su gusto*, cited *ibid.*, p. 436).

Calderón "defends the doctrine of free will from a position which is absolutely orthodox." [102] Man is a being endowed with liberty, which manifests itself in his power to choose, by use of his natural reason and his will, either good or evil (*ibid.*, p. 206). In the *auto sacramental* (not the drama) *La vida es sueño*, the Holy Ghost (Amor) requests of the Father (Poder) that he create man,

> Giving him freedom of will
> Whereby to choose evil or good.[103]

In an invocation to Night in the *auto, Lo que va del hombre a Dios*, the stars are seen as a pattern of good and of evil influences:

> Night, burnished and luminous background
> On which the sun's track or the moon's fair wake
> Trace the characters which form
> Dissimilar fortunes for us,
> Patterns of evil or good.[104]

In another invocation to Night, this time in *El verdadero Dios Pan*, the arbiter of happiness or of misfortune is not the inclining pattern of the stars, but the will, free in all mortals:

> Yet leaving always the will
> In every mortal man,
> Sole arbiter of every good or ill.[105]

This is also the thesis of the drama (as against the *auto*), *La vida es sueño*: "the final outcome is not determined, but is whatever Basilio and Segismundo make of it." [106] Segismundo overcomes the fate foretold by the astrologers as he applies his free will to the achieving of virtue. All the action, in the play, takes place in this world and involves, not the salvation of the soul, but a literary equivalent: virtue.[107] A comparison of this drama with its

---

102. Eugenio Frutos, *La filosofía de Calderón en sus autos sacramentales* (Zaragoza, 1952), p. 214. See also p. 197.

103. "dándole un libre Albedrío / con que use del mal y del bien" (cited *ibid.*, p. 208).

104. "Noche, lámina bella, / en quien esculpe la dorada huella / ya del carro del sol, ya de la luna, / caracteres que lee nuestra fortuna, / siendo sus desiguales / astros padrón de bienes y de males" (cited *ibid.*, p. 209).

105. "bien que dejando siempre al albedrío / en todos los mortales / árbitro de los bienes y los males" (cited *ibid.*, p. 209).

106. Peter N. Dunn, "The Horoscope Motif in *La vida es sueño*," *Atlante* (London), I (1953), 196.

107. Frutos, *op. cit.*, p. 210.

corresponding *auto* affords a striking example of "the skill with which Calderón has deepened an idea already once developed, by endowing the incidents of his original treatment with a richer, symbolical meaning. Segismundo becomes the symbol of mankind, created in God's image and born to rule the earth, but destined to fall through pride to the snares of the tempter and have his former glory dimmed by the shadow of sin. He then returns to his prison only to be redeemed by grace through the sacrifice of God-made-Man on the Cross."[108]

I conclude this section by citing the *locus classicus* for an understanding of the problem of human freedom in Calderón — the scene between the Devil and Justinia in *El Mágico prodigioso*:

> Free will would not be free will
> Should it ever yield to force.[109]

Opposition to astrology. We may apply to the Golden Age in Spain Don Cameron Allen's findings with respect to Elizabethan and Jacobean England. During the sixteenth and seventeenth centuries astrology was often attacked and often defended:

Most of the opponents of astrology were as ready to admit the reality of an *astrologia naturalis*[110] as they were to grant that of a *magia naturalis*. The stars, they said . . . , have some sort of occult influence on the sublunar world. The force of the astral rays is perhaps undefinable; it is also, without doubt, unpredictable; and it may certainly be opposed by the more dominant forces of mind and spirit. These are the attitudes of the opponents of judicial astrology, for there were no opponents of natural astrology, no deniers of the general influence of the heavens.[111]

108. Ramón Silva, "The Religious Dramas of Calderón," in *Spanish Golden Age Poetry and Drama*, ed. E. Allison Peers (Liverpool, 1946), p. 148, n. 3.
109. "No fuera libre albedrío / si se dejara forzar" (Act III, sc. vi). On the theological mysteries of Calderón's *autos*, see Alexander A. Parker, *The Allegorical Drama of Calderón* (Oxford–London, 1943); reviewed by H. A. Hilborn, *HR*, XII (1944), 75–78.
110. Cristóbal de Villalón, in his *Ingeniosa comparación entre lo antiguo y lo presente* (1539), attributes the flourishing or the decline of humanistic and other studies to astrological causes. In a given region, one type of doctrine can at one time be popular and later be the object of contempt "because of contrary planets" (ed. Bibliófilos españoles [Madrid, 1898], pp. 135–36). A century later, Céspedes y Meneses writes in his *El español Gerardo*: "we embraced, for our . . . friendship demanded even greater expression: so powerful is, at times, the sympathy of the stars, which others call confrontation of the blood" (*ed. cit.*, p. 125a).
111. *Op. cit.*, p. 148. These statements apply to men of letters. For the two dominant views among astrologers themselves, see *ibid.*, pp. 148–49; and Craig, *The Enchanted Glass: The Elizabethan Mind in Literature* (New York, 1950), pp. 40–41.

In seventeenth-century Spain, judicial astrology was forbidden by the Inquisition, though it was possible for a practitioner of the art to claim ignorance of the prohibition and, surprisingly enough, to have his case dismissed.[112] In Lope de Vega's *La Dorotea,* César offers his unconditional friendship to Fernando: "Wherein can I serve you?" He is told to "erect a figure" whereby the outcome of present events may be determined. César replies that interrogations may not be made, and that their prohibition is very proper. Nonetheless, he has already made a *figura* of Fernando's horoscope; all that remains is to judge it; he will bring it the coming afternoon, or next day. He explains that in his youth he studied with the famous Portuguese cosmographer and mathematician Juan Bautista Labaña, and that sometimes, out of mere curiosity, he casts a horoscope; but he never answers *interrogaciones* concerning future events, since the free will cannot be subject to the stars. Professor Morby, in his annotated edition of *La Dorotea,* points out that both types of inquiry (horoscope and interrogation) were forbidden although the laws were not always rigorously enforced.[113] We shall now go back to the fifteenth century and provide samples of opinion on these matters among Spanish writers.

Pérez de Guzmán (d. 1460?) speaks of *la incierta y variable astrología* — "the uncertain and variable science of astrology" — and puts these words on the lips of Christ: *non vos es demanda honesta / saber tiempos e momentos del Padre* — "is is not proper for you to ask concerning the time and the moment determined by the Father" —, adding that what is predestined will surely be fulfilled.[114] In another place he declares that the true friend of God has no confidence in planets, stars, or signs, and that he fears neither Fortune nor comets.[115]

In the sixteenth century Vives condemns judicial astrologers in his *Introducción a la sabiduría:* God has reserved for himself

112. See M. Menéndez y Pelayo, *Heterodoxos,* IV, pp. 382–87 (note B). The year is 1605.

113. *La Dorotea,* ed. E. S. Morby (Berkeley–Los Angeles–Valencia, 1958), p. 412, n. 93, and p. 433, n. 146

114. *Cancionero castellano del siglo XV,* ed. R. Foulche-Delbosc (Madrid, 1912–15), I, 616–17.

115. "Aquel a Dios ama que en las planetas, / estrellas nin signos non ha confiança, / nin teme fortuna, ni de las cometas / entiende que puede venir tribulança" (*ibid.,* p. 630).

knowledge of the future; [116] and Ciruelo sets forth orthodox doctrine in his *Reprobación de las supersticiones y hechicerías*: (1) Judicial astrology is false because it claims to determine by studying the stars things which cannot be the effect of astral influence, such as whether one will fall on one's head on the way to the market or find a sack full of ducats — things which, according to Aristotle, are determined by chance, not cause. Hence one should not ask an astrologer about the success of a projected journey, or possible earnings at the gambling table. What the astrologer says on such matters he derives from diabolical inspiration. (2) The secrets of the heart and will of men cannot be determined, because of human fickleness — they are known only to God, and it is diabolical astrology to promise one a good reception in his audience with the king, or to tell one that his wife will be true or false, since loving or not loving a person depends on man's will, not on the stars.[117]

In 1589 Pedro Simón Abril in his *Filosofía natural* gives no credence at all to astrological propositions.[118] In the same year a Spanish translator of Ovid's *Metamorphoses*, Pedro Sánchez de Viana, commenting on Cristoforo Landino's earlier annotation of Ovid, reports character traits supposedly attributable to persons born when Mercury's position is unfavorable, and adds: "Landino might [better] have omitted these details, and thus I consider them to be false, or else they must be interpreted . . . with due allowance for free will." [119] Even when other writers have given due weight to free will, Sánchez de Viana finds the details of horoscope "so individual and particular that, since I regard them as vain, I refrain from enumerating them here" (*ibid.*, fol. 55 r. and v.). In yet another place, reporting the belief of astrologers that those who are born when Draco is setting, or is in the West, are likely to be bitten by some poisonous animal, Sánchez adds: *Créalo quien quisiere* — "Let him who will believe it."

Passing now to the seventeenth century, we shall consider first a pure work of history. Bartolomé Leonardo de Argensola, in his *Primera Parte de los Anales de Aragón* (1631), writing of Magellan's friend Ruy Faleiro and of his failure to be taken into

116. Cited in Carreras y Artau, *op. cit.*, p. 153.
117. *Ed. cit.*, fols. xxxi verso and xxiii verso to xxiv.
118. M. Morreale de Castro, *Pedro Simón Abril* (Madrid, 1949), p. 157.
119. Salamanca, 1589, *Anotaciones*, fol. 63 v.

the service of the king as astrologer, comments: "as if the job of
erecting figures were of some consequence to a king (and especially
in the case of a king so given to the observance of ecclesiastical doctrine), these figures being most frequently ridiculous, or open to
suspicion, and a matter of dangerous curiosity. Furthermore, there
were not lacking persons who said that Faleiro did not know this
science, and that it was dictated to him by a demon who, without
having studied it, knew it better than its very teachers. Or perhaps
it was a matter of defamation that he knew no astrology and was
accused of having a compact with the devil." [120]

Two points in this quotation should be emphasized. The words
most frequently are an admission that in some respects the future
can be foretold; and the words *dangerous curiosity* suggest the
pact with the devil hinted at immediately thereafter. Ciruelo admits that physical matters can actually be predicted: astrologers
announce on what day sick persons will die or recover, and fore-
cast the crises of their diseases. This is possible, first, because these
are bodily matters, and second, because the devil knows all science
and communicates it to his votaries. In his belief that the devil
interferes in human affairs Ciruelo would have been contradicted
neither by Martin Luther nor by the American colonial preacher
Jonathan Edwards (d. 1758).

Quevedo calls judicial astrology a false testimony raised by badly-
occupied men against the stars of heaven; strange cases of predic-
tion he leaves in the realm of doubt.[121] Mira de Amescua, in the
comedia entitled *Adversa Fortuna de Don Alvaro de Luna*, allows
an astrologer to predict accurately that Don Alvaro will die on
the scaffold, but causes another character to protest:

> What that astrologer said
> Is mere folly, a mere whim
> A product of the man's humor.[122]

The younger Argensola in one sonnet asserts that human destiny is
determined by the light or the error of the human will, and in another admonishes a foolish astrologer to live by the light of reason
and of justice, though the celestial orbs fall in ruins from their lofty

120. Zaragoza, 1631, fol. 134 r. and v.
121. *Obras en prosa, ed. cit.*, pp. 610ab–11a .
122. *NBAE*, IV, 288b–89a.

spheres.[123] We may conclude with Hardin Craig: "It was not that anybody doubted that there might be significance in the behaviour of the stars, but that everybody knew that many astrologers were imposters; and yet the impression one gets from Renaissance literature is not prevailingly adverse to astrology" (*op. cit.*, p. 41).

FREE WILL AND PREDESTINATION: THE PROBLEMS

In Spain there had existed, from remote times, a keen interest in the theological problems of predestination. In the fifteenth century this subject became a topic of the day, occupying the minds and pens of several poets of the *Cancionero de Baena (ca.* 1445) and inspiring the composition, at some time between 1453 and 1473, of a learned treatise on predestination — *Tratado sobre la predestinación* — in the vernacular, by the Augustinian Fray Martín de Córdoba.[124] This interest continued to manifest itself, and to affect the handling of human problems in literature, to the very end of the seventeenth century. Kant declared that freedom is an idea "the possibility of which no human intelligence will ever fathom, but the truth of which . . . no sophistry will ever wrest from the conviction of even the commonest man." [125] The question of predestination is not a simple one of orthodoxy against heterodoxy, and throughout the centuries Christian controversy revolves about the question of the soul's activity or passivity in meriting or simply receiving the gift of Divine grace.

The dogma of predestination will always be a mystery of Divine mercy and Divine justice, inaccessible to human reason. It is stated clearly in the heading of St. Augustine's *City of God*, XIV, i: "That the inobedience of the first Man had drawne all mankind into the perpetuity of the second death, but that God's grace hath freed many from it." [126] That predestination exists is, among Catholics,

123. "Que a la luz o al error del albedrío / se elige o se fabrica nuestra suerte"; "Vive tú a la razón i a la justicia / i caigan rotos los celestes orbes" (*Rimas de Lupercio y Bartolomé L. de Argensola*, ed. J. M. Blecua [Zaragoza, 1950–51], II, 224 and 235).

124. See Fray Martín Alfonso de Córdoba, *Un tratado del siglo XV sobre la predestinación en castellano*, ed. with preliminary study by Aníbal Sánchez Fraile (Salamanca, 1956), p. xxxv, n. 3.

125. Cited in W. T. Stace, *Religion and the Modern Mind* (Philadelphia, 1952), p. 197.

126. Ed. London, 1620, with commentary by Vives. Cf. Córdoba's *Tratado, ed. cit.*,

an article of faith; it is set forth with the greatest clarity in the Scriptures: "For whom He did foreknow, He also did predestinate to be conformed to the image of His Son." [127] The existence of reprobation—predetermined Divine condemnation to eternal punishment—is also an article of faith: "Then they said unto Him, Lord, are there few that be saved? And He said unto them, Strive to enter in at the strait gate: for many . . . will seek to enter, and shall not be able;" "I know not whence ye are . . . depart from me, ye workers of iniquity." [128] Yet, according to the teaching of St. Augustine as accepted and modified by St. Thomas, the doctrine of reprobation does not deny human freedom.[129] In some way which is beyond human understanding, in some men it is fitting that God show his Divine justice; it is equally fitting in other cases that He show his Divine mercy.[130] Fray Martín addresses himself to these and similar problems in the fourteen chapters of the *Tratado*, whose analysis would extend and complicate unduly our present treatment. The rational conflicts are insoluble: if, in the relationship of God and man, the action of God is predominant, human action suffers detriment; if the latter prevails, there seems to be produced a detriment of the power and sublimity of God. The argument extended into the seventeenth century. Between the purely theological position of Saints Augustine and Thomas on the one hand and, on the other, the more psychological, rational

p. 70: "Since we all come from that damaged prime material, let no one complain if he is stiff-necked and hard of heart; let no one complain of the punishment, which is his due, though he himself have committed no personal sins."

127. Rom. 8:29; cf. Rom. 8:30; 11:2; Eph. 1:5; 1:11. See the Introduction by A. Sánchez Fraile to Fray Martín de Córdoba, *op. cit.*, p. xcviii.

128. Luke 14:23–27; cf. Matt. 25:41, Psalm 68:29 (Vulgate numeration), and *Tratado*, p. cxxii.

129. See St. Thomas, I, q. xxiii, a. iii, ad 2um (cited by Sánchez Fraile [ed.]), *Tratado*, p. cxxi, n. 1, which concludes: "Sed culpa provenit ex libero arbitrio ejus qui reprobatur et a gratia deseritur." Fray Martín translates: *Dios es cabsa . . . de la pena; porque esto es bien de justiçia, que al malo sea dada pena: pero Dios no es cabsa de la maliçia, salvo nuestro albedrío* — "God is the cause . . . of the punishment, because this is an attribute of justice, that the wicked man should receive punishment; but God is not the cause of evil, but rather our own free will" (p. 84).

130. "Necesse est autem quod divina bonitas, quae in se est una et simplex, multiformiter repraesentetur in rebus. . . . Voluit igitur Deus in hominibus quantum ad aliquos, quos praedestinat, suam repraesentare bonitatem per modum misericordiae, parcendo; et quantum ad aliquos, quos reprobat, per modum justitiae, puniendo — "es conveniente que en algunos paresca la divinal Justiçia, e en algunos su ynfenida Misericordia" (I, q. xxiii, a. v, ad 3um; *Tratado*, p. 66).

and human position of Luis de Molina [131] (d. 1600) and the followers of *congruismo*, there are many shadings in the emphasis
that each system gives to the two elements of the problem; but all
systems arrive ultimately at the exclamation of St. Paul: "Oh the
depth of the riches both of the wisdom and knowledge of God!
How unsearchable are his judgments, and his ways past finding
out!" [132] All of these speculations are acceptable to the Church provided two principles remain intact: Divine love is the cause of the
goodness of things; Man is a free agent who can be saved by Divine
Grace.[133]

Another problem is that of Providence and Divine foreknowledge. If God knows what the destiny of each man is to be,[134] can
any man be truly free? A modern writer has explained the affirmative answer as follows: "It's like a man standing on a railway bridge
watching an express train coming down the line and a cow cross-
ing a field toward the line. The man knows that the cow will be
killed, but the cow has still the free will to turn aside and not
be killed, although the man also knows that the cow is too stupid
to use her free will and turn aside and not be killed." [135] Pedro
de Cartagena (d. 1492?) used a different analogy: "As in a ball
game, a spectator realizes that one of two contenders must lose, so
God foreknows events. I, who realize that one of the players is

131. See J. Ferrater Mora, *Diccionario de filosofía*, art. *Molina (Luis de)*, and J.
Gallegos Rocafull, *El hombre y el mundo de los teólogos españoles de los siglos de oro*
(Mexico City, 1946), p. 90.

132. Rom. 11:33; see *Tratado*, p. lxiv.

133. See *Tratado*, p. 20; "Man is created for an end so greatly exceeding his natural
capacity that it is necessary for God to give him special help through the agency of his
grace." Also, p. 18: "So that you may be saved, it is necessary that God extend His
hand to help you; for you to be damned, it suffices that you neglect to ask Him to give
you His grace, having no regard for it." See also p. lxv, and p. 18, n. 7. The controversy
is clearly set forth by Martín Ortúzar, O. de M., "*El Condenado por desconfiado*
depende teológicamente de [Francisco] Zumel*," in *Estudios* (Madrid), IV, núm. 10
(1948), especially p. 26. See below, our analysis of Tirso's *El condenado*.

134. We may recall the words of the witch in Cervantes' *Coloquio de los perros*,
quoted in Chapter V, above: "in spite of all this I know that God is good and merciful
and that He knows what is to become of me" (*Obras*, ed. *cit.*, p. 1017b). This is the
problem of Tirso de Molina's *El Condenado por desconfiado* (*The Doubter Damned*);
see below.

135. Bruce Marshall, *The World, the Flesh, and Father Smith* (New York, 1960),
p. 11.

less skillful than the other, know that the former will lose, but his defeat is not caused by me."[136]

In the Middle Ages and in the Renaissance, similar arguments are used. Córdoba repeats the analogy with human memory: "As you by means of memory recall things past without compelling them to have occurred as they did, and as you did not yourself commit or do all the things whereof you have recollection, so God knows the sins we will commit before we commit them but He is not their cause."[137] "If someone should say that Pharaoh could not turn from his evil purpose because God already knew that he would not turn from it, I reply that the foreknowledge of God does not compel man to be as he is to be in the future . . . since Pharaoh was not the way he was because God already knew his destiny; rather, because he was to be such as he was, God knew it without forcing him to be so; but left by God in his freedom, Pharaoh did what he did. Thus God foreknows who are to be sinners, though He does not cause them to fall into sin."[138]

These truths, though they have no doctrinal solution, should not move us to despair, but rather to humility, fear of God, and piety, and should stir us to diligence, so that we may direct our life wisely. They err who say that the running of the runner is not of his doing, nor the wishing of the wisher (since none can resist God's will); they err who ask: why should a sick man seek medi-

136. *Cancionero castellano*, ed. *cit.*, II, 509–10: "Como quando acá entre nos / conosce alguno mirando / qual ha de ganar de dos / a la pelota jungando, / bien assí contesce a Dios: / yo que miro desde acá / que el vno sobra en saber / al que maña no se da, / conosco que perderá, / mas no le hago perder."

137. *Tratado*, p. 76, and p. cviii, where this text is quoted in Latin from *De lib. arbitrio.*

138. *Tratado*, p. 76. Córdoba is thus in agreement with Catholic dogma and tradition: "Placed by grace in a certain state, man, if he remains in that state, deserves eternal life; God knows and wills, from all eternity, the destiny of each one; justification and predestination present themselves to the theologian as facts to which Scripture and Tradition bear witness, at the same time that they give testimony of the fact of liberty accepted *a priori*, namely that the Creator has decided to make rational creatures participants in His beatitude. One does not deduce these things; one does not reduce them to an interplay of rational necessities; all is given. The theologian reconciles for himself the given articles of faith and organizes them in a form which claims to show a certain rationality" (Paul Vignaux, *Justification et prédestination au XIVᵉ siècle* [Bibliothèque de l'Ecole des Hautes Etudes. Sciences Religieuses, vol. XLVIII], Paris, 1934, p. 178).

cines, the farmer plant wheat? In the practical and ascetic order, as against the doctrinal, each man should seek to merit predestination to eternal beatitude by means of fasting and prayer, relieving the sick and performing other good works. God's will concerning each person is a secret. What, then, should a man do? St. Augustine, says Fray Martín, gives the answer: *qui videtur stare, videat ne cadat* — "let him who thinketh he standeth, take heed lest he fall" (*op. cit.*, ch. IX and p. cxxvii).

The conclusion of our fifteenth-century theologian in respect to Divine foreknowledge is thus strongly reminiscent of that of the fourteenth-century Archpriest Juan Ruiz in respect to astrology; fasting, prayer, good works, openness to the gift of grace — these constitute the means whereby the Christian, through the exercise of free will, offsets (with a greater or a lesser degree of optimism according as he regards the power of human decision to have been more or less seriously damaged by the Fall) the darker aspects of the pseudoscience of astrology and of the dogma of his religion; that is to say that by exercise of Christian virtues each man counterbalances influences which, because of an accident of birth and the original sin of his first parents, have combined to render his salvation difficult. In no case may he address a complaint to the forces that have formed him and that threaten to undo him. "He who says that [predestination] is unjust," warns Córdoba, "let him hear the words of the Apostle: 'O man! Who art thou that repliest against God? Shall the thing formed say unto him that formed it, Why hast thou made me thus? Hath not the potter power over the clay, of the same lump to make one vessel unto honor, and another to dishonor?' "[139]

There remains one final question: Could God have made the world better than it is? Córdoba replies in the affirmative. "If therefore anyone ask: Could God have made the world better than he made it? I say yes, in view of his absolute power; but he made it with the exact proportions which his wisdom imposed on his power."[140]

139. *Tratado*, p. 71; for corresponding texts from Augustine, see p. cxxvii.
140. *Ibid.*, p. 86. Alfonso de la Torre, *Visión delectable* (1436), has a section "On the Goodness of God, wherein are set forth remarkable things, why God did not make things better than they are." Even men's sins are needful, because man must have freedom to chose the good and to abhor evil (*ed. cit.*, pp. 356a–357a).

Medieval answers

In the *Cancionero de Baena* (compiled *ca.* 1445), along with
things infinitely less lofty, questions of Catholic dogma are debated
in a considerable number of poems by writers who at times confess that their preoccupation with these problems amounts to
a wound of the heart.[141] Along with difficulties having to do with
Fate and Fortune, with the apparent worldly success of the wicked,
and with the nature of the Trinity, there is a surprising concern
for the problems of predestination, reprobation, and free will.
The formulators and answerers of the questions are both laymen
and ecclesiastics, and sometimes exception is taken by the latter
to the treatment given to these themes by "poets." Thus Fray
Lope de Barrientos writes to Juan II of Castile, in answer to the
king's request for a doctrinal exposition of the theological problem of Fortune: "although certain modern poets have informed
you somewhat in these matters, it might be that their knowledge
is insufficient to expound the matter perfectly . . . for lack of
study in books of philosophy, and even though they had read
these, lacking a knowledge of philosophical principles, they could
not satisfy your inquiry. . . ."[142]

The initiator of the questions and answers on predestination
and free will was Ferrán Sánchez Calavera in a *Question,* "very
subtly and learnedly conceived," which he addressed to Pero López
de Ayala "and to many other very learned scholars of this kingdom
who replied to it, as will be seen in subsequent pages of this
book."[143] The questioner asks for the balm of certainty for his
uncertain heart. God knows the past, present, and future (he
writes), and this implies that He knows, before each man's birth
and the creation by God of each individual soul, who will be
saved and who will be damned. Does not this make it seem that
God is pleased to create a human being who, He knows, is already
condemned to Hell? If by God's grace, and by that means only,
men are protected from Hell, it would appear useless to fast and

---

141. The actual time of this poetic debate was before 1407, the date of the death of
El Canciller Ayala.

142. Cited by Sánchez Fraile in his edition of *Tratado,* p. xxxix.

143. *El Cancionero de Juan Alfonso de Baena,* ed. P. J. Pidal (Madrid, 1851), no.
517, pp. 549 ff.

to give alms; one's fate is already sealed. This leads to an ugly conclusion: God appears to be the source of cruelty, of evil. The poet says that he has consulted learned men about this and that they have told him that God gives free will to all men and gives them also reasoning power to the end that they know that they will be judged by their works; hence it is an error to think that God is the cause of evil: God does not take pleasure (*non es plazentero*) in the soul's damnation, though He foreknows it. It is unwise, the poet has been told, to inquire into such matters. God's ways are inscrutable. All of this brought some relief, but some of the pain remains in the questioner's heart, since the problem of foreknowledge and responsibility is not settled. God knows of the reprobation before He gives to any individual reprobate his free will (p. 551). Many learned men desire to know the solution; the poet's desire is to stir discussion but not to create doubts or cause error. The next thirty pages of the *Cancionero* are filled with the various replies.

López de Ayala's reply (no. 518) is conventional. Men cannot judge these questions, and St. Paul's *Oh altitudo* is repeated.[144] The unguent to be applied to the heart's wound is that of belief and penitence. The supreme authority is the Church. No just man will be damned, no evil man saved. A more authoritative reply is made in poem 519 by the Master in Theology Fray Diego de Valencia, who cites Alexander of Hales (d. 1245), Peter Lombard (d. 1164?), and St. Thomas (d. 1274) on this "matter . . . of foreknowledge and predestination" and argues against the conclusion that foreknowledge is equivalent to condemnation before sin. If the questioner's wound still smarts, there are two unguents. The first is that good works count with God, that rewards and punishments correspond to merits and demerits; the second, that free will was given to man to increase his goodness, not to limit God's power. Foreknowledge does not constitute necessity. Fray Alfonso de Medina, in poem 520, defends the justice of Providence and argues against any thoughts of determinism or of quietism: society itself would be impossible if the concept of the sinner's responsibility were denied. To receive God's grace, the sinner has only to "open the door." If a room remains dark because of closed

144. See above, note 132

shutters, the darkness cannot be attributed to the sun. With God's help even reprobates can be saved.

Francisco Imperial in poem 521 admits that the questioner's wound is — temporally — incurable, so deep and dark is this matter. He introduces an argument not heard before: With God, Time does not exist. Past, present and future are but one. Saints and reprobates were not born at one time to die at another: before and after simply do not exist with God. This relieves God of the charge of creating a soul after deciding that it is destined to be damned.

Number 522 — *mirabile dictu!* — is composed by a Moor, "un moro que desían Maestro Mahomat el Xartosse," physician to the Almirante Don Diego Hurtado de Mendoza. The doctrine in question is inscrutable, he says — "non a prosas / nin testo onde ello bien cabe" — but God is just. García Alvarez de Alarcón in the next poem defends God's omniscience; man cannot know God's secrets; the will is free; quietism is to be eschewed, prayer and good works are necessary; St. Paul is again quoted. In poem 524 Ferrant Manuel de Lando declares this to be the best of possible worlds — "que la mejor vía es ésta en que estamos" — and argues that foreknowledge does not constitute necessity: Judas was created as free from sin as was St. Augustine. Prayer and good works are necessary; grace will save us.

The final poem in the series is number 525, by the original questioner, Ferrán Sánchez Calavera. He has profited by the exchange and his heart is at peace. God is timeless; He does not force reprobates into sin; man's will is free; foreknowledge is not necessity; each soul is created innocent; grace is at all times available but must be actively sought; the arbitrary saving of certain ones from among the totality of underserving mankind is not an act of injustice; the judgments of God are pure and righteous altogether.

There is an interesting sequel. The heading of poem 528 explains that it is composed by Fray Diego de Valencia to convey advice to Sánchez Calavera. The advice: *que vos alongués de la theología* — "that you stop worrying about theology." [145] In spite

145. See E. Gilson, "Libre arbitre et liberté chrétienne," in *L'esprit de la philosophie médiévale* (Paris, 1944). The bibliography on this subject is large. On God's foreknowledge, see Fray Martín de Córdoba, *Compendio de la Fortuna, ed. cit.,* pp. 22–25.

of this advice, for two centuries Spanish theologians and moralists, novelists, poets, and playwrights will continue to worry about the doctrine of free will.

Renaissance answers [146]

The sixteenth century. The subject of free will and predestination, apparently so successfully settled by the poets and novelists of the fifteenth century, continued to interest the public to so great an extent that Diego Sánchez de Badajoz (*fl.* 1525) composed a theatrical work entitled *Farsa racional del libre albedrío*; it is not, however, a significant document in the history we are tracing, except, perhaps, for these two lines:

> No, no, no! for man's free will
> Is never subject to force.[147]

The question of predestination continued to challenge Spanish minds in the pre-reformation of Cardinal Cisneros. Spanish translators, wishing to make the Church Fathers available to the untrained public, did not always choose wisely in what they rendered from Latin into Spanish. An example of the type of material often translated is the apocryphal *Meditaciones, soliloquio y manual* (1511) [148] attributed to St. Augustine. In it predestination is strongly upheld. The elect are so guarded by the hand of the Almighty "that all things which they do are transmuted into good, even the sins they commit." On the other hand, for reprobates "prayers become sins that are held against them." [149] In 1534 an otherwise unknown Juan del Castillo confessed to the Inquisitors in Toledo his belief in a certain universalism: all men will be saved, whether sinners or not, good works are useless, and other heresies. In 1548 Ignatius de Loyola advised preachers against

146. See Charles Trinkhaus, "Renaissance Problems in Calvin's Theology," *Studies in the Renaissance,* I (1954), 59–80.

147. "No, no, no, que al Albedrío / nadie le puede forzar" (*Recopilación en metro,* ed. J. López Prudencio [Badajoz, 1910], I, 339).

148. There were five reprintings in the sixteenth century.

149. Bataillon, *Erasmo y España* (Mexico City–Buenos Aires, 1950), I, 55–56. William of Ockham (d. 1349) had taught that even such sins as hatred of God, theft, adultery, "must not be regarded as contrary to the allegedly rational and preëxisting disposition of things; they can only be relative to God's volition, which is itself contingent on nothing. . . . They may even be meritoriously performed by man if they fall under divine precept . . ." (Baker, *The Wars of Truth* [Cambridge, Massachusetts, 1952], p. 142).

raising questions of such great delicacy as predestination, faith, or grace. Some thirty years later (*ca.* 1575) Benito Arias Montano, in his Biblical commentaries, deplored his contemporaries' curiosity and audacity in matters relating to God's foreknowledge and predestination. Similarly, in a work published in 1576, Fray Diego de Estella repeated Loyola's injunction that preachers discuss no metaphysical questions, such as predestination.[150]

Alfonso de la Torre, in his much cited *Visión delectable,* had declared: "And you will know from me a secret, how our free and voluntary acts of choice are not understood in the way that most men think; and this causes most of those who write or compose great books on predestination to fall into error" (*ed. cit.,* p. 356a). In the sixteenth century many books did indeed continue to be written on this problem. As an example of these *grandes libros de predestinación,* I cite Diego de Cabranes' *Spiritual Key to Open the Great Mystery of Predestination.* [151]

In 1527 Francisco de Osuna issued his *Tercer abecedario espiritual,* with its Erasmian overtones. Good works by themselves are no justification, he writes, but they prepare the sinner for the justification which comes from above, from God. Just as it is necessary to open the eyes to receive the benefit of the sun — it being the sun and not we ourselves that infuses this benefit —, so must we prepare our hearts by good works to receive the Sun of Justice which is Christ. The will is impotent without grace; with grace and the exercise of the will, all things are possible.[152]

In the *Segunda comedia de Celestina* (1534) by Feliciano de Silva, a very secondary writer who composed his sequel in order to exploit the popularity of the masterpiece by Fernando de Rojas, the old bawd Celestina is resurrected from the dead to continue her exceedingly earthy existence. People seeing her going about her business with swishing skirts remark: "It would surely seem that this is a case of predestination, since God chose to bring her back from hell to do penance for her sins." [153] This is an early indi-

---

150. Bataillon, *op. cit.,* II, 63, 358, 372, 377.
151. *Llave espiritual para abrir la alta materia de la predestinación* (Toledo, 1529). I have not seen this work.
152. Bataillon, *op. cit.,* I, 218–19, especially n. 52.
153. Ed. J. A de Balenchana (Madrid, 1874), pp. 90–91.

cation that the humble folk for whose spiritual safety St. Ignatius de Loyola expressed such concern were not strangers to the great theological problem of their century.

Formulated in the 1520's, though first published in 1548, rules 14a and 15a of St. Ignatius' *Spiritual Exercises* prescribed: "Although it is true that no man can be saved without being predestined and without possessing faith and grace, great care should be had in discussing these matters. We should not speak much of predestination in the ordinary way; but if in some way and at some time the subject is to be discussed, let it be so that the humble and the ignorant shall not fall into any sort of error, as sometimes happens, when they say: 'If I am foredestined to be saved or damned, everything is set for my glory or condemnation and cannot be otherwise'; in this way they become sluggish in performing the works which conduce to the spiritual health and profit of their souls."

Alejo Venegas defines predestination in chapter ix, of his *Diferencias de libros que ay en el vniuerso*. After quoting St. Augustine on the salvation of him who is saved, and the reprobation of him whom God permits to die in the mortal sin for whose delights the sinner chose to leave God, Venegas explains: "the perdition of him who is damned consists in closing the door of his soul to the infusion or inspiration of grace — *a la infusión o inspiración de la gracia* — and the cause of reprobation is the personal and voluntary guilt of the sinner — *la propria y voluntaria culpa del pecador*." A full account of predestination, he warns, cannot be given.[154] Free will, according to Venegas is like the opening of a window; grace is like the light of the sun; each is necessary for the illumination of a room or the salvation of a soul (*ed cit.*, fols. 28b–29).

The reader may remember Venegas' description of the "first" or "original book," which (unlike the "books" of nature, of Scripture, and of human introspection and reason) may not be opened: this is the book of God's secrets; we perceive only its closed covers.

154. Ed. Salamanca, 1572, fol. 27. The case for freedom of the will is argued starting with fol. 11.

In a striking metaphor Venegas says that on the cover of this "original book" we read the words predestination and reprobation — not clearly, but by the indications which our sense of conjecture can penetrate — for which reason this subject should not be suppressed from our discussions, but should be talked about and preached.[155] Herein he differs, of course, from St. Ignatius.

Venegas is bold in his affirmation of free will and in his attempt to argue out of existence the idea of reprobation (which he does not properly explain). The heading of chapter v, Book I reads: "Wherein it is shown that in addition to the above, free will is a reply applicable to all questions concerning salvation or damnation."[156] Saint Paul's words ("them he did predestinate") are applied by Venegas to all men. The thought that they apply only to a portion of mankind is, he says, an illusion or a temptation. If one is so persuaded, the remedy is at hand: each one should act as if he were predestined to glory. The heading of chapter xiii reads: "It is in the power of each man to make certain — hazer cierta — his predestination by righteously carrying out the commands of God." Such fear as we may have must be sunk and drowned out in the confidence we have in God's infinite mercy. The next chapter heading reads "Confidence in God accompanied by performance of His commandments is the most certain assurance (prenda) of salvation which men can have." Since salvation depends only secondarily on works (dependent on man's free will) and primarily on grace (dependent on the will of God), man's predestination is not in his own power, though his salvation is. This is the same solution that Juan Ruiz offered in connection with the horoscope of the son of King Alcaraz in the Libro de Buen Amor: prayer and good works. Possessing such hope and such expectancy, man will do what he can and as a consequence will attain to glory: y por consiguiente alcançará la gloria. God, Venegas says by way of illustration, chose to light the world by means of the sun; He could have lighted it otherwise. Good works

155. "Que en la enquadernación del libro diuino se lee la predestinación y reprouación de los hombres: no claramente, sino por las señales que la probabilidad humana puede alcançar, por lo qual no es razón que se calle" (fol. 21b).

156. "Que demás de lo sobredicho el libre albedrío es vna respuesta común de todas las preguntas que cerca de la saluación, o condemnación de los hombres se pueden hazer" (fol. 12v.).

are as the sun and man is as the terrestrial globe; the light which comes through good works is salvation (fols. 34v–35v).

Divine foreknowledge does not constrain or force free will, as we read in the heading of chapter xii of Book I. There is no time in eternity; with God, all time is but an instant (fol. 33v). From all eternity God willed that good works should be the instrumentality (the secondary causes) of human salvation. God aids the free will to perform good works, yet leaves the will free to perform bad works, should the sinner in his willfulness so choose (fols. 29r–32v).

At the Council of Trent (1545–63) it was inevitable that the varied positions of the opposing theological schools regarding human freedom and Divine grace should be argued. In the matter of justification there was no hesitation, but the explanation of that doctrine brought forth passionate, even violent, discussion. The question was destined soon to create a major division among the adherents of Spanish Baroque Scholasticism. Is free will inert, or can one accept or reject the gentle action of grace? The successors of St. Ignatius, Diego Laínez (d. 1565) and Alfonso Salmerón (d. 1585), held — with the majority — that the action of grace is to perfect, not annihilate, the power of each man to decide his fate.[157]

Martín de Azpilcueta's *Manual de confesores y penitentes,* in its edition of 1567, takes into account the decrees of the Council of Trent. He declares that it is mortal sin to hope to gain salvation without personal merit, or with only those merits which, without the grace of God, one stores up through the action of free will. Both of the extreme positions are condemned. It is likewise mortal sin if one despairs of the mercy of God, assuming that God will not or cannot pardon his sins. This in itself is a sin against the Holy Ghost which, like the other sins in the same category, "will not be forgiven in this or in the other world," according to St. Matthew. One sign, Azpilcueta points out, that the sinner's will did not consent to this blasphemy, is that he has doubts concerning it, and another is distress at being beset by

157. F. Cereceda, *Diego Laínez en la Europa religiosa de su tiempo* (Madrid, 1945–46), I, 236–38.

such temptations, since doubts and feelings of guilt indicate that the temptation was born of the sinner's sensual rather than his rational nature—*en la sensualidad, y no en la razón.*[158] In summary: the will is not inert but must gladly receive God's grace and actively engage in meritorious works.

In 1575 and in 1594 Dr. Juan Huarte de San Juan issued the original and the corrected editions of his *Examen de ingenios para las ciencias,* to my knowledge the first book on vocational guidance ever written. Huarte's theories were based on a differential psychology the determining force of which was the ever-varying admixture of the traditional four humors in the human body. He was primarily a Galenist, believing with Galen that human vices and virtues could be controlled by medicine, that is to say, by altering the "temperament," the relative proportions of the elements earth, water, air, and fire which are the building blocks of man's physical frame. At times he stresses so strongly the dependence of the higher faculties on their bodily base that he would seem to be preaching physiological and psychological determinism.[159] The book went through five Spanish editions before the Inquisition placed it on the Index (1583). The corrected edition of 1594 was never mentioned in any Spanish Index. We cannot here examine the reasons (some of them personal) for the denunciation, or collate the two texts.[160] Huarte's ideas, sincerely expressed, were not intended to shock ecclesiastical opinion.[161] In the corrected edition of 1594 [162] he reaffirms Galen's teaching on the four humors and their influence, but within the limits of the official dogma of free will: the humors incline but do not compel. As proof he adduces the case of St. Paul, with his figura-

---

158. Ed. Barcelona, 1567, fols. 442 and 505.

159. Mauricio de Iriarte, S.J., *El Doctor Huarte de San Juan y su "Examen de ingenios"* (Madrid, 1948), p. 242.

160. See the notes of the work's modern editor, R. Sanz, to ch. V in vol. I of the edition of Madrid, 1930.

161. Of his teaching on the subject of grace, Father Iriarte remarks: "this he supposed to be the doctrine of the Church." And in another place: "He did not always hit upon the right expression of his conceptions, which were without doubt orthodox." See *op. cit.*, pp. 243 and 242.

162. It is saddening to note that this Spanish edition was printed after the author's death, *ca.* 1591. See Father Iriarte's chapter II, "Historia del libro," for an account of editions made in Spain and in the Low Countries, as well as of translations (French, Italian, English, Dutch, German, Latin).

tive "thorn in the flesh": "whereby we may conclude that Galen was right when he said that it was the physician's task to render a sinner virtuous, and that the moral philosophers were negligent in not taking advantage of the data provided by medicine." [163] The historian of Spanish medicine, Antonio Hernández Morejón, after examining the evidence, declared (and Father Iriarte agrees with him against Sanz) that the book suffered no essential mutilation at the hands of the Inquisitors.[164] The two texts are interesting, however, as an indication of the caution that was necessary, in the latter part of the sixteenth century, when writing on subjects that impinged on accepted doctrine.

Pedro Malón de Chaide's *Conversión de la Magdalena* (1588) is a classic of Castillian prose and also of Spanish devotional literature. Its treatment of the doctrine of predestination is typical of that in works written in the vernacular and intended for the instruction of the lay public. Its author, an Augustinian, held, with the earlier Venegas, that for the simple reason that *esta materia es peligrosa* — "this is a dangerous subject" — it should be explained so that all might understand it. It is frightening, he admits, to find — over against assurances of the infinite mercy of God — passages in the Scriptures which imply that the sinner's guilt may cause God to close the door to the evildoer, to harden His heart toward him, and to consign him to damnation. His first answer is that in the Scriptures all harsh passages must be interpreted as merely allowing the sinner, by the exercise of free will, to condemn himself, as when Jesus said to Judas Iscariot: "Do quickly what you are determined to do" (John 13:27). Any portion of the Divine Word which seems to limit God's mercy must be interpreted symbolically (*por figura*).[165] In another connection (*ibid.*, p. 213), Malón de Chaide quotes St. Jerome, who said that though the heat of the sun, being constant, softens wax but hardens clay, in accordance with the varying natures of the receiving substances, so God, with one and the same light, blinds the eyes of him whose soul is unfit to see the light (*al que tiene enfermos los ojos del*

---

163. Ed. Sanz, p. 85.
164. *Historia bibliográfica de la medicina española*, vol. III, cited by Iriarte, *op. cit.*, p. 94.
165. Ed. P. Félix García (Madrid, 1947), I, 207–11.

alma), that is to say, whose desire and intention are disinclined to accept the good, and illumines the man who is rightly inclined.

In the second volume of the *Conversión* (*ed. cit.*, pp. 23–24) Malón de Chaide returns to the case of Judas. It is the end that counts. God knows what our end shall be, though we ourselves will it. So it was with Judas: God knew that he would reject grace and hang himself, though Jesus had received his kiss of betrayal with the loving words: "Friend, wherefore art thou come?" (Matt. 26:50).

Another argument is that of *nil frustra* — God creates nothing in vain. How, then, could reprobation of the innocent be possible when God has placed in all men an inclination to be joined with Him? Experience proves it: though men be wicked and given over to violence (*desalmados, desuellacaras*), they long (*querrían*) to be saved and to enjoy God, as St. Augustine has said: "Thou has made us for thyself, and our hearts are restless till they rest in Thee."[166]

The subject of Malón de Chaide's book — the conversion of Mary Magdalene — lent itself especially to a consideration of the problem of God's apparently arbitrary calling of certain chosen souls, and of the different responses made by these souls to the Divine summons. Why should God have called Mary Magdalene with all her burden of lust? Why St. Matthew, a money changer (which is to say, a cheat: *trampeador*)? Why Zaccheus, a publican and a tax-gatherer? Why should Jesus have said to the Pharisees that those who hear God's word belong to God, but that they, the Pharisees, heard it not for they were not His? Here the human understanding fails, says Malón de Chaide. Not even St. Augustine has the answer. "I confess without shame," says our Spanish author, "that I do not understand it . . . , and I rejoice to have a God so great that His mysteries are beyond my grasp" (*no quepan en mi entendimiento*) (*ed. cit.*, II, 61–65).

That there is a difference in souls — like the differences in the ground that received the seed in the parable of the sower — is undeniable. Saints Peter and Andrew responded to a single word, leaving all and following their Lord; so it was with Saints John

166. *Ed. cit.*, II, 56. Cf. p. 57: "and you experience this every day in yourselves when, because you wish to do it, you commit sin, seeing that you are doing wrong and that you are able to refrain, and yet you do it and persist in doing it."

and James. St. Matthew was attracted merely by a glance — one of the greatest proofs, says Malón de Chaide, of Christ's divinity. But St. Paul had to be struck down and blinded on the road to Damascus. And finally, there was St. Augustine, almost dragged by the hair to compel him to a knowledge of God. These favors are rare, and bestowed on few. They are special mercies which God owes to no one and seldom grants. But all are at all times invited by His *llamamientos generales,* his call to all mankind. Why should God have said to Moses: "I shall have mercy on whom it please me, and to whom it does not please me I shall deny it?" These words must apply to the special mercies, to a St. Matthew, a Zaccheus, a Mary Magdalene. St. Augustine said: "Seek not to penetrate the mystery, if you would not go astray" (*ed. cit.,* II, 57–65).

In the same year that Malón de Chaide's *Conversión* became available to the layman, the great debate on grace and predestination at the ecclesiastical level was given tremendous impetus by the publication of the first of the commentaries on St. Thomas by the Dominican Domingo Báñez and of the *Concordia Liberi Arbitrii cum gratiae donis, divina praescientia, providentia, praedestinatione et reprobatione* by the Jesuit Luis de Molina.

Báñez (d. 1604), confessor (1561–67) and friend of St. Teresa of Avila, in his commentaries set forth a concept of predestination which he modestly called Thomist but which his opponents, more accurate in this than he, called Bañecian. With an argumentation which has been compared, in its massiveness, to a block of granite, he passionately exalted God as Universal Cause in a way unequalled, perhaps, since St. Augustine.[167] In the beginning was God, he taught, whose utterly free will decreed — because God so willed — that certain men should be saved, and arranged events so that this decree must inevitably be obeyed. God decreed that those forming this body of the elect should participate in His glory, and this decree had nothing to do with any possible foresight that the elect would by their conduct deserve election. These souls have no part in the Divine decision, as they have no part

167. J. M. Gallegos Rocafull, *El hombre y el mundo de los teólogos españoles de los siglos de oro* (Mexico City, 1946), p. 68.

in the reason for their existence. The good display goodness because God has chosen them to be good. God does not foresee their acts, He foreordains from all eternity that those who are to be saved shall choose the good. Men do not know God's designs, nor do they perceive that they are of the elect. On the contrary, they have the conviction that they act with free will, and indeed this is so; for this Divine action, coming from God, neither restrains their will nor destroys their freedom (*ibid.*, p. 71). Báñez uses the example of St. Paul to press his point: by giving more to some than to others, God establishes differences between men (p. 73). The gift is, of course, the gift of grace. St. Paul is an example of effective grace (*la gracia eficaz*). Usually without the startling accompaniment of outward events that attended St. Paul's conversion, this type of extraordinary grace cannot fail to have its effect: it is, in fact, a Divine determinism.

Yet it is no less true that God desires the salvation of all men. Consequently, he gives to every man born into the world grace sufficient for his salvation. However, distinctions must be made between one form of grace and another. That ordinary grace which God grants to all men is designated sufficient (*gracia suficiente*), whereby men are enabled to act so as to merit salvation. Still another distinction is necessary: it is one thing to be able to act (as all men are), and another really to act rightly (as few men do). For sufficient grace to operate in the supernatural order it must be aided by effective grace, in which case we have the miraculous conversion of a St. Paul or a St. Matthew. The human will is forcefully and inevitably moved toward the act which gives salvation. It would seem that Alain Guy is right in saying that Báñez, in these special cases, reduces the act of man *jusqu'au néant* — "to nothing." [168]

Molina (d. 1600), on the other hand, insisted on effective human liberty and proclaimed that it had a part in determining the effectiveness of grace applied to human salvation. It would be most difficult, perhaps profitless, to analyze here the distinction between Divine Knowledge, Knowledge of Vision, and Intermediate Knowledge (*Scientia media*), this last being considered a neces-

---

168. See Gallegos Rocafull, *op. cit.*, pp. 71–72; A. Guy, *La Pensée de Fray Luis de León* (Limoges, 1943), p. 58.

sary concept by some theologians, but not by all. Molina, in opposition to the doctrine of Báñez (as well as to pure Thomism and extreme Augustianism), declared that the human will is not completely determined for either good or evil, but that it can, in the last analysis, decide whether or not a given act of choice is to be made; it is aware of exercising or of not exercising the corresponding faculty of decision.[169] In his *Concordia* he made *Ciencia media* one of the fundamental bases of his doctrine, in which he was opposed not only by Báñez but by the Mercedarian Francisco Zumel. Molina's doctrine is one of optimism and is pervaded by a sense of human dignity.[170] We shall have to return to a consideration of this controversy when we study Tirso de Molina's *El Condenado por desconfiado — The Doubter Damned.*

Between these contending extremes it was possible to take a less exaggerated view, and this was done in 1589 by Fray Juan de Pineda, whose Franciscan background — love as the basis of piety — perhaps made it easier for him to lay stress on man's voluntary contribution to his soul's health. He wrote in his *Agricultura christiana*: "and I say further, that not only the substance of predestination [to glory] depends on the works of the predestined soul, but that it is affected also by the prayers of other persons for that soul's salvation."[171] He is even more explicit: "If you live well to the end of your life, you are predestined; and if you do not live well until death so that you end in a state of grace, you are not predestined; from which we conclude that the end of your predestination depends on you, just as its cause (which is the gift of right inclination and Divine grace) depends on God. . . . Christian doctrine teaches that to no one who does his best will God deny His grace and the aid necessary for salvation" (*ed. cit.,* fol. 35). This is, of course, the doctrine of sufficient grace, which to Friar Pineda seems the one thing needful.

Seventeenth-century writers. We now pass to the seventeenth century. In 1602 Fray Diego de la Vega preached a Sermon on

---

169. Ferrater Mora, *Diccionario de filosofía,* art. *Molina (Luis de)*; see also arts. *Ciencia Media* and *Futurible.*

170. See Pedro Laín Entralgo, *La espera la esperanza: Historia y teoría del esperar humano* (Madrid, 1957), pp. 152–53.

171. Ed. Salamanca, 1589, fol. 34v.

St. Joseph, the husband of Mary, bringing in the arduous question of predestination and reprobation — quite unnecessarily it seems — by way of illustration. Developing the thought that Joseph was a just man, the preacher associates that kind of justice with the idea of maintaining a just measure in everything, and cites Isaiah 11:5: "And righteousness shall be the girdle of his loins, and faithfulness the girdle of his reins." He urges his parishioners to be just in this sense, as against the looseness symbolized by the un-girded shepherd from the Asturian hills, whose flapping garment scarcely covers him, whose loose sandals carry along a "basketful" of earth and stones. A man of the court, on the other hand, goes about well-girded and cannot tolerate the smallest pebble in his shoe. The preacher then speaks of the girded and the ungirded in the spiritual sense. The ungirded wear loose sandals on the conscience and tolerate no restraint of raiment, and these are the *gente villana y rústica, que está prescrita para el Infierno* — "rustic folk from the village, predestined to Hell." Set over against them are the girded ones — *gente ilustre, criada para el Cielo* — "men of nobility, created for Salvation." These are they whom God has predestined for His glory; these can endure no manner of looseness, and the weight of a hair on their consciences is unbearable. These are the "courtiers of heaven" — *cortesanos del Cielo.*[172] This preacher is addressing, most assuredly, the elite of the King's capital city. Perhaps all are so well educated that the grave problems then engaging the best talents of Báñez and Molina were not, for them, *materia peligrosa* — "dangerous matter." We can only note the fact: this Franciscan friar brings in the subject of predestination to glory and fore-damnation to Hell as the most natural thing in the world, as a bit of decoration for his sermon, and flattering, no doubt, to his aristocratic hearers who may have forgotten that Jesus found disciples among humble fishermen, assuredly poorly "girded." We conclude that the subject of God's inscrutable will did not always inspire an overpowering awe of the impenetrably sacred.

It was some two decades later (*ca.* 1621) that Tirso de Molina brought this subject to the theater in a play which has been called

172. M. Herrero García (Comp.), *Sermonario clásico* (Madrid, 1942), p. 29.

the best religious drama ever written but which assuredly deserves no more than the assessment of Américo Castro: it possesses elements of greatness.[173] It is the drama of two men, one of whom leans excessively on his belief in the efficacy of good works (though the spirit of true charity be lacking), while the other, a criminal, attains (precariously) to final salvation because he believes that man is justified by God's mercy (though there is a minimum of good works: the criminal knows filial piety).

Like Tirso's other great play of sin and eternal punishment, *El Burlador de Sevilla,* which gave to world literature the figure of Don Juan, *El Condenado por desconfiado* is based on legendary material. It is a combination of two folk tales: one of the sinner who is saved through Divine grace, and the other, of the hermit who renounces faith when he beholds the salvation of a thief.

The first legend is of great antiquity, having its origin in an Indian tale concerned not with grace and hope, but with the transmigration of souls. This tale, which, because of its simplicity, appealed to Mohammedans, Jews, and Christians, is an interesting example of the way in which homiletic material passes from one religion to another.[174] It appeared originally in *The Mahabharata,* reached the ears of Greek Christians in the fourth century, was utilized by the Mohammedans in the seventh century, and from them passed to the Jews living in Mohammedan territory. A later version is one told by a Spanish Morisco[175] and taken over by the Jews of many nations, including those of Spain. In all these tales the principal motif is filial piety, a virtue which, for all its humility, may be superior to religious asceticism; in them is a second element also of capital importance in our play: the contrast between a man's infamous crimes and his one filial virtue. Variants of these tales appear in the *Vitae Patrum* (mentioned as a source by Tirso). In the simplest of them, a hermit learns from a tanner no other lesson than humility.

In a fourth-century version, the story of the humiliated hermit

173. See Castro's edition (Madrid, 1919, pp. 5–6). On the attribution of the play to Tirso, see S. G. Morley, "The Use of Verse-Forms (Strophes) by Tirso de Molina," *BHi,* VII (1915), 406–7. Morley concludes that it is unlikely that Tirso was the sole author of the play.

174. See R. Menéndez Pidal, *Estudios literarios* (Madrid, 1920), pp. 9–100; G. H. Gerould, "The Hermit and the Saint," *PMLA,* XX (1905), 529–45.

175. A Moor converted to Christianity.

is carried much further in the account of St. Paphnuthius' confrontation of a thief, who is led to adopt the monastic life. A still later version of this in the fourteenth-century *Conde Lucanor* of Don Juan Manuel, son of the Infante of Castile, is so close to *El Condenado por desconfiado* that it may have served, in part, as a direct source for Tirso. In it we have the prayer of the hermit asking God to show him the glory reserved for him in Heaven; the revelation that the hermit is to share the destiny of a despicable man; the inability of the hermit to accept the Divine will; and his rebellion, whereby he sets foot upon the road to his denial of God's mercy, and his own damnation. On the other hand, Don Juan Manuel's version does not furnish an important element used by Tirso: the hermit's failure to admit the possible salvation of the evildoer, his own immediate plunge into despair, and his decision to enjoy sin inasmuch as he is to be punished for it.

In Act II Tirso restores to the legend an element which it had lost in the versions of the desert Anchorites: Enrico's solicitous regard for his aged father is astonishingly close to the tale told by the Spanish Morisco, in which we find, likewise, Enrico's declaration that he hopes to be saved not because of merits which he does not have, but through God's grace. In both the play and the Morisco's tale, the sinner is saved through parental mediation.

Paulo's end (in our play) is very different, and here we find another legend, that of the hermit who becomes an apostate on seeing the redemption of a thief. Examples of this tale are found in collections of medieval homilies. A Catalan example was published in 1923.[176]

Tirso's Paulo is thus more than an argument personified. He is a figure born of Buddhism and adapted by three other religions. His drama possesses human significance apart from its theology: he is a victim of moral ambitions, unsanctified by charity, which carry him to perversity and crime; and he would penetrate the secrets of Heaven, and by Heaven he is crushed. But the main interest of *El Condenado* is theological and cannot be understood apart from Augustinian teaching.[177]

176. J. Pijoán, "Acerca de las fuentes populares de *El Condenado por desconfiado*," *Hispania*, VI (1923), 109.

177. The play was translated into French and published in Paris in 1863. In 1869 George Sand published in the *Revue des deux mondes* an adaptation entitled *Lupo Liverani*.

In the opening scene of *El Condenado por desconfiado* we behold Paulo, who for ten years has mortified his flesh in the desert and who "tempts" God by insisting that he be shown his future destiny (supposedly glorious). Punishing this act of temerity, God allows the Devil to deceive Paulo, just as Job was tempted by the same enemy of mankind. The Devil (revealed to the audience as such but disguised as an angel) tells the hermit that he must go to Naples where he will encounter a certain Enrico. Whatever Enrico's fate is, that shall be the fate of Paulo also. Of course this prophecy, being diabolical, is not carried out; Enrico the criminal is saved while Paulo in his despair goes to eternal damnation.

The poet presents the position of God in all fairness. In order to offset the effects of the temptation (the first, diabolical, vision), a genuine angel is sent disguised as a shepherd who descends the mountain weaving a crown intended for the just man, singing, as he goes, of the mercy of God and of the ease with which God pardons repentant sinners. He chides Paulo — now, in his despair, a bandit — for his distrust, and proves with arguments that one should never despair of salvation. Paulo hesitates for a moment, and even goes so far as to wonder whether he has made a terrible mistake, but he again falls into his temptation:

> Surely both of us must go
> To eternal punishment.[178]

God has thus extended His hand to the sinner, and the sinner has rejected it by an act of that free will which God gave to all those whom He created in His image.

St. Augustine, in his sermons and his commentaries on the Psalms, has given an exposition of the mental processes of the sinner in the clutches of despair. Once a desperate sinner makes up his mind that nothing can save him, he readily commits whatever sin appeals to him at the moment; he loses all self-control and acts without constraint of anything save his own despair. Believing himself doomed to Hell, he decides to grasp what the world has to offer. Recognizing the evil of his course, he yet willfully persists in following it, knowing that he does so freely. He seeks no excuse: *Cur non impleam, quantum possum, quaecumque desideria, si post haec non restant nisi sola tormenta?* The robber

---

178. "Ya no hay más remedio / que el condenarnos los dos" (*ed. cit.*, p. 113).

becomes a murderer and finally yields to his despair, the worst of all possible sins. On the other hand, the sinner who turns his back on despair and heeds God's voice may be regenerated and returned to His friendship. *Hac voce audita et credita . . . ab illa altissima et profunda voragine, qua submersi fuerant, emergunt.*

Enrico, Paulo's foil, for all his wickedness is not guilty of the sin of presumption which St. Augustine discusses in his *Tractatus.* Enrico does not assume that God is too merciful to punish the sinner even when he flouts God's justice.[179] Enrico is humble: God knows him, God knows his end, and whatever that end is to be, God is good. When Paulo greets Enrico with the words *Alabado sea el Señor*—"God's name be praised"—Enrico the malefactor replies: *Sea por siempre alabado*—"May His name be praised forever." Enrico, however, is so hardened in crime that he requires the extra gift of effective grace:

> May just Heaven punish me,
> For although I would repent
> The power to do so is not in me.[180]

This is the extra gift of grace that saved St. Paul with the violence of a fulmination on the road to Damascus. Enrico's spiritual condition is exactly the same as that of the witch in Cervantes' *Coloquio de los perros*: sin has become so ingrained that the witch cannot lift her hand up to God's, though God is extending His hand downward in mercy; yet God is good, and knows what end is reserved for her.[181]

Over and over again Enrico repeats his confidence in God's goodness and mercy; he even preaches to Paulo, warning him of his guilt of despair.[182] Finally Enrico repents and—as the light of understanding and reason at last dawns for him—asks the Virgin to tell her Son that he would prefer a thousand deaths to the memory of having offended his Lord; and he cries out:

> Oh Lord, have mercy upon me!
> More than this I cannot say.[183]

179. See Sister Rose Bernard Donna, *Despair and Hope: A Study in Langland and Augustine,* Catholic University of America (Washington, 1948), pp. 30–31.

180. "Vénguese en mí el justo cielo; / que quisiera arrepentirme, / y cuando quiero, no puedo" (*ed. cit.,* p. 122).

181. See above, summary of the chapter on Reason.

182. *Ed. cit.,* pp. 136–39, 166, 174, 176.

183. "¡Gran Señor, misericordia! / No puedo deciros más" (*ibid.,* p. 175).

Paulo, on the other hand, rejects all thought of salvation:

There's no mercy for such men.[184]

As the eternal destiny of the two men is made clear, the Judge exclaims: *Misterios son del Señor*—"These are God's mysteries."

There is another play by Tirso, *El mayor desengaño (The Greatest Disillusion)*, in which the sin of presumption rather than of despair is the cause of a soul's condemnation. The play tells the story of the founding of the Carthusian order by St. Bruno. Of all the disillusions that lead Bruno to abandon the world, the last comes through a miraculous revelation. The canon Dion, Bruno's master, dies, and the populace regards his body as a sacred relic; but Dion's own voice is heard, miraculously proclaiming that he has been damned by God's just decree:

By God's just and righteous judgment
I am damned.[185]

The crowd is dumbfounded and the Queen, in her terror, flees. The King exclaims that God's secrets are inscrutable. One of the characters present, Roberto, explains that pride had wrought Dion's undoing, just as it destroyed Lucifer. For before his death Dion had been heard to say that he expected from God no mercy; on the contrary, he willed (*quiero*) to be judged with all the rigor of Divine justice on the basis of his virtues and his sufferings:

In this last moment I wish
That God judge me without mercy,
By applying to my case
All the rigor of his justice,
Granting me the seat in Heaven
That by my virtues and sufferings
I have gained.[186]

In both of these dramas commonly attributed to Tirso, we have examples of "fierce resistance to the influence of Divine grace." A theologian who expresses himself in such terms is far from attrib-

184. "Pero no con tales hombres" (p. 192).
185. "Por justo y recto jüicio / salgo condenado" (*NBAE*, IV, 115b).
186. "No quiero que en este paso, / según su misericordia / me juzgue Dios, porque aguardo / que por rigor de justicia / me dé el cielo que han ganado / mis virtudes y paciencia" (*ibid.*, p. 116a).

uting to human liberty the fruitful initiative that the Jesuit Molina had assigned to it.[187] The effectualness of grace depends not merely on the human will, but on the intrinsic quality of the Divine gift; the effectualness of condemnation does depend, however, strictly on the human will. We thus have a denial of what is called "negative reprobation" — condemnation without demerits — and an assertion of God's will that all sinners who will accept salvation be saved. It is here that the influence of Francisco Zumel — the Mercedarian — is most apparent, and Tirso is shown as participating in the theological controversies of his time (*ibid.*, p. 333).

Tirso magnifies God at the expense of man. The latter is indeed free, but weak:

> God gave man freedom of will,
> And with it He gave him frailty
> Of body and of spirit.[188]

God's loving pursuit of the lost sheep, Enrico's died-in-the-wool habit of sinning, his final yielding to contrition, and his acceptance of pardon; Paulo's continued defiance of God, his proud insistence that there is no hope — the acceptance of grace by the one and its rejection by the other are magnificently presented. On the other hand, Enrico's boastful listing of his crimes at times seems childish. The author would have done better had he presented his malefactor as possessing at all times the dignity of a St. Paul. We return to the estimate of Américo Castro: the play possesses elements of greatness.

SUMMARY

The study of free will that has occupied us in this long chapter has shown, not only the centuries-old preoccupation with the problems of salvation (man's struggles to aid or annul the influences that would condemn or save his soul), and the expression of this preoccupation in works both doctrinal and literary; it has shown also that the easily-formed assumption that all Spanish literature is an exaltation of human dignity and of the individual's clearly-defined power of choice to control his destiny is

187. See Father Ortúzar, in the second installment of his study on *El Condenado por desconfiado* (*Estudios*, V [1949], 321–40). See n. 133, above.
188. See text and reference in note 99 above.

a concept too easily formed. When the forces of the anti-Protestant Counter Reformation were most powerful, there were theologians in Spain who exalted God while they assigned to his chief creature an Augustinian frailty—though the infinite value of this creature was never questioned. Other theologians insisted on man's near autonomy, his all-but-sovereign will to work out his destiny with the aid of that minimum of grace which was called sufficient. While the main stream of doctrine, as set forth in treatises, sermons, poems, and plays, was fundamentally against determinism — *agunt, non cogunt*[189] —, there were other works which showed extreme cases of conversion in accordance with God's secret mysteries, by means of an extraordinary application of effective grace to accomplish Divine purposes into whose reasonableness the mind of man may not inquire. (Cases of reprobation, on the other hand, were "positive"; i.e., they were clearly on the basis of sin committed.) St. Augustine has been called the most Protestant of Catholic Saints. The Augustinian order flourished in the Golden Age of Spain and many of Spain's greatest writers — including one of the very greatest — were Augustinians; opposing them were others who were Molinists or Bañecians. *Sic et non.*

Such a concern with the great questions of religion was not a characteristic solely of Spanish Renaissance literature. "With whatever spiritual hosts the aggregated traditions of human imagination may have peopled all the vast world," writes Hardin Craig, "the significant fact remains that theology had given to man a soul, and soul is spirit. The life of the soul is the religious life, and in that life resided the deepest interest of the age. So all-important was the subject of religion that those who seek to know the sources of Elizabethan thought must turn to it. The most fateful questions concerned the soul. . . . The freedom of the soul, and hence of the will, was doctrinally so important, that even astrology had to admit that the stars incline but [do] not compel" (*op. cit.*, pp. 49-52). In these momentous matters Spain is clearly in the tradition of Western Europe.

189. "By and large, it is the old, formal, and peaceful religion which is usually to be found in both the learned and the literary works of the [Renaissance]" (Craig, *op. cit.*, p. 52).

VII · Fortune and Fate

*The fate assigned in the cradle
lasts forever.* . . . This proverb
is very suitable for tragedies,
and for persons who perceive only
what befalls one from the cradle.
By attributing everything to the
will of God one avoids getting involved with so great a superstition.
                    Juan de Mal Lara [1]

Fate is subject to variation, for
it is an order of secondary
causes whereby Providence produces
its outward effects.
                    Fray Martín de Córdoba [2]

Above the main door was a sign
which said: "Dwelling Place of
Fortuna, to Whom by God's Permission many Bodily Things are Subject."
                    Antonio de Torquemada [3]

A mere glance at the index of Howard R. Patch's *The Goddess
Fortuna in Mediaeval Literature* [4] will show that in the Middle
Ages Fortune was thought of as a multiform goddess or power. In

1. "*Quien hadada males en la cuna, siempre le dura.* . . . Este refrán es muy
proprio para tragedias, y personas que no tienen ojos para mirar más de lo que viene a
la persona desde la cuna: con darlo todo a la voluntad de Dios, están fuera de tan
gran superstición" (*Filosofía vulgar*, ed. A. Vilanova [Barcelona, 1958–59], IV, 12).
In another connection Mal Lara writes (*ibid.*, p. 59): "To discuss Fortune is not my
intention; the matter has been treated by both ancient and modern authorities. The
question of whether she exists, as the poets imagine her, is in itself a foolish question,
since it has fallen into the hands of poets."

2. "Fado es variable, ca es una orden de causas segundas por la cual la prouidencia
faze los efectos exteriores" (*Compendio de la Fortuna*, ed. P. Fernando Rubio Alvarez,
O.S.A. [El Escorial–Madrid, 1958], p. 38). Providence, he says, is immutable.

3. "Tenía encima del arco de la puerta principal una letra que decía: 'Morada de
la Fortuna, a quien por permissión divina muchas de las cosas corporales son sujetas' "
(*Coloquios satíricos*, in *Orígenes de la Novela*, ed. M. Menéndez y Pelayo [Madrid,
1905–15], II, 571a).

4. Cambridge, Massachusetts, 1927, p. 208, *s. vv.* Fortuna, Fortuna Barbata, Functions and Cults of Fortune.

St. Augustine's day "the special fidelity to Fortuna Muliebris, Fortuna Dux, Fortuna Barbata, and the like, was still alive" (*ibid.*, p. 15). During the Middle Ages, we are told, "the populace . . . never abandoned faith in one or more powers, occult and irresistible, distinct and separate from the divine will, and variously designated, as the case might be, by the name of destiny, fortuna, or astrological influence."[5] That the Spanish populace was guilty in these matters is of course evident from the amount of preaching and discussion that was devoted to the combatting of such errors: a certain degree of cosmic insecurity is clearly apparent. But our texts will show, in the final analysis, that there are but two Fortunes: what I have elsewhere called *Fortuna de tejas arriba* and *Fortuna de tejas abajo* — Fortune above and Fortune below[6] the roof tiles. The first is in the final analysis equated with God's will: *No hay más Fortuna que Dios*, wrote Calderón.[7] The second is a personification of the disorder, the vicissitudes, the ups and downs of human life, equated with human prudence during the up periods and with human stupidity or passionate willfulness during the down periods.

For the sake of clear exposition, Fortune and Fate must be given separate divisions in this present chapter — a procedure not strictly justified by the nature of the concepts, which were often confused. Fate was more easily identified with God's will, as when Milton causes the Creator to say of Himself:

> . . . Necessitie and Chance
> Approach not mee, and what I will is Fate.[8]

Fate was also more obnoxious to theologians, who often objected to the interposition of a symbolic figure between God and his human creatures. The Spanish Inquisition deleted a fatalistic reference to predestination in a poem of Torres Naharro in its expurgated edition of 1573 of that author's *Propalladia*, and the Portuguese Inquisition (always more strict than the Spanish) elimi-

5. A. Graf, *Miti, leggende e superstizioni del Medio Evo* (1892); cited by Patch, *loc. cit.*

6. "Usually . . . Fortune's powers have to do with more secular matters, and we find her particularly associated with the world (which, adopting her qualities, becomes more than ever 'mundane') and the court. Both the world and the court are fickle" (Patch, *op. cit.*, pp. 58–59).

7. See the edition of this *auto* by A. A. Parker (Manchester, 1949).

8. *Paradise Lost*, VII, lines 172–73.

nated all references to Fate in Cervantes' *Galatea* (1585). Typical
of the Portuguese attitude is the censor's remark in connection
with Corte Real's *Sucesso do segundo cerco de Diu*: "we indicate
some words which affect the decorum of the poetry, such as *fate,
fortune, destiny*, which should be taken in a Catholic and Christian sense, leaving freedom to the will and taking into account
Divine providence, to which all things are subject; which truth
the author himself in many passages of this work expresses clearly
and in Christian fashion, with pious and religious words." [9] As
we shall see in due time, Fate, when consciously and seriously
analyzed, becomes a mere name, an outmoded manner of speaking,
since it is God who grants life and status in the world; it is a syno
nym for *mutability*; a creative force not unlike Nature (hence
God's deputy); it is God's own immutable will; and also the
mutable determination of the stars. At times the phrase *Dios y sus
hados* — "God and his fates" — appears in a poem of religious intent, showing that the word *hados* — "fates" — meant God's ministers, the intermediaries (whether astral or simply causal) between
the will of the Almighty and its execution.

"The idea that the gods are ill-disposed, that they are well-dis-
posed, that they are indifferent, all find expression in *King Lear*,
and in other plays as well." [10] This shifting of concept or viewpoint
— from the roof-tiles upward or downward — will characterize our
findings in this chapter. This is, of course, not surprising. Petrarch
(d. 1374), in his *De Remediis utriusque Fortunae* (*Remedies
against Good and Evil Fortune*), at times accepts the general, non-
philosophical meaning of *fortuna*, as found throughout Latin
literature; at other times he uses the word fate in its philosophical
sense. (Cicero had done the same before him, though Cicero, since
he did not have to fit Christian Providence into his thinking, is
less inconsistent.) Thus Petrarch sometimes spoke as a pagan,
sometimes as a Christian. "His mood determined his attitude, and

9. *Propalladia and Other Works of Bartolomé de Torres Naharro*, ed. J. E. Gillet
(Bryn Mawr, Pennsylvania, 1943–51), I, 71; F. López Estrada, "Sobre la Fortuna y
el hado en la literatura pastoril," *BRAE*, XXVI (1947), 435–36; I. S. Révah, *La censure
inquisitoriale portugaise au XVIe siècle* (Lisbon, 1960), p. 31.

10. Alfred Harbage, *As They Liked It: An Essay on Shakespeare and Morality* (New
York, 1947), p. 150.

he was a man of many moods." [11] Most of our Spanish literary men, like Petrarch, write with literary ends in view: when they philosophize, they are moralists, not logicians. The theological and non-literary moralists whom we shall quote will naturally, in their capacity as such, be relatively consistent; yet even a rigorously trained theologian will (if he is a poet and if it suits his mood) employ the concepts of Fortune and Fate (in a sonnet, for example) in a way that is impossible to justify if we apply his own enunciated precepts.

Enrique Moreno Báez, in his study of Mateo Alemán's *Guzmán de Alfarache* (1599), finds that the Scholastic, the pagan, and the Stoic-Christian ideas of Fortune alternate in this book without any seeming sense of conflict; yet Alemán's serious declarations are always orthodox: "I cannot say that my unlucky star caused it, but that the loss occurred because of my long-enduring shamelessness. The stars do not compel, though they incline." [12]

Gonzalo Sobejano, reviewing Klaus Heger's *Baltasar Gracián . . .* (Heidelberg, 1952), finds a similarly bewildering constellation of concepts: "The name *Fortuna* serves in *El Criticón* as a term to bring about a certain focusing within the multitude of functional perspectives which characterize Gracián's thought regarding man's uncertain lot." Though Fortune is the agent of Divine Providence and hence the arbiter of the human and of the divine world, her characteristics are variability and inconstancy. They vary in meaning and condemn to failure all effort to systemize them. Such a perspectivism is not a destructive procedure, but rather a method of syncretic acceptance of tradition.[13]

11. B. L. Ullman, reviewing Klaus Heitman, *Fortuna und Virtus: Eine Studie zu Petrarcas Lebensweisheit* (Cologne, 1958), in *Speculum*, XXXIV (1959), 661. In the year 1360 Petrarch, having sought to console King John of France by attributing his troubles to Fortuna, was challenged to give his opinion about the goddess, since the mention of her name had disturbed the audience, and was later visited in his chamber by three *dottori* who had a long talk with him on the subject. "Five years later Petrarch wrote a letter to a friend on the whole problem. In this he takes the orthodox position of the Church Fathers, denying the existence of the goddess" (Patch, *op. cit.*, p. 21).

12. *Lección y sentido del Guzmán de Alfarache* (Madrid, 1948), pp. 146–51.

13. "Nuevos estudios en torno a Gracián," *Clavileño*, V, núm. 26 (1954), 23–32; see especially pp. 27–28. On Gracián's meaning when he speaks "seriously and as a Catholic," see below. Discussing Gracián's views on the nature of truth, and his use of the words *mundo, hombre, mujer, amistad, vida, fortuna, muerte*, John T. Boorman declares that "Gracián defies paraphrase and exposition." See his review of Hell-

Petrarch, Shakespeare and Milton, Alemán and Gracián, all used inherited pagan material for artistic purposes, within an accepted framework of moral and (in the cases of the Italian and of the Spaniards) religious responsibility. The three Latins, at least, would have accepted Calderón's phrasing of the solution: *There is no Fortune except God.* We may believe that all five would have agreed with Jacques Bossuet (d. 1704): "Let us speak no more of Chance or of Fortune, or let us speak of the latter as if it were but a name whereby we cover up our ignorance." [14]

FORTUNA IN SPAIN: A SAMPLING OF DEFINITIONS

Probably the earliest Spaniard to offer a definition of *Fortuna* is St. Isidore of Seville (d. 636). He merely presents her among the gods of the gentiles (*Etymologiae*, XI, 94), flanked by the Parcae and the Furiae: "*Fortuna* derives her name from *fortuitus*, since she is a goddess who makes sport of human affairs by reason of the fortuitousness and varied character of her action; for which reason she is said to be blind, since she at times favors certain men without examining their merits, and visits both the just and the unjust. The ancients distinguished between Fate and Fortune, since the latter comes without cause or antecedents, while Fate is determined and certain." [15] *Fortuna* is not said to be a dangerous or a sinful symbolization, nor is she said to be non-existent. St. Isidore's description of her seems purely archaeological, one might even say "paleontological."

By the time we reach the *Arçipreste de Talavera* of Alfonso Martínez de Toledo (1438), things appear less simple. The wordly

mut Jansen, *Die Grundbegriffe des Baltasar Gracián* (Geneva–Paris, 1958), *BHS*, XXXVIII (1961), 170.

14. Cited by Pedro Laín Entralgo, *La espera y la esperanza: Historia y teoría del esperar humano* (Madrid, 1957), p. 144. This statement might be questioned in regard to Shakespeare, and I therefore quote from Harbage (*op. cit.*, p. 146): "The enemy is not God but human unkindness. . . . The enemy is always unkindness behind the familiar visage of one of the seven deadly sins." See also *ibid.*, p. 151.

15. He is cautious in what he says about Fate, which he deprives from *fando*, "speaking." He says: "If this name of Fate were not commonly applied to something else, which we would like to guide men away from, we could reasonably use that word to designate the speaking (or speech) of the gods." (*Etimologías*, trans. L. Cortés y Góngora [Madrid, 1951], pp. 209–10). For the very early centuries, see Menéndez y Pelayo, *Historia de los heterodoxos españoles* (Madrid, 1947–48), VIII, 403.

man not only disrespectfully questions God's judgments, he does worse: he believes *ser asy que fados, planetas, e fortunas son las cosas que dan ser e non ser, e fazen las criaturas rricas e pobres, dolientes e sanas* — that Fate and planets and Fortune determine existence and non-existence, poverty and riches, sickness and health — whereas it is God who gives to all things *ynfluencia, ser, rregir, e cursar* — their influence, being, ruling power, and determined course. All the astral movements proceed from God; without His will they would have no force as they are but intermediaries. To believe anything else is mere vanity of vanities: there are no Fortunes, no gods of fate or of good luck, no gods of nature, or of signs or planets — concepts (all of them) which are mere lies and deceits.[16]

In another place Talavera insists that the soul and the mind of man are supercelestial and hence not subject to planet, sign, Fate, or Fortune, since they are subject to God alone. Such influence as the stars may have (if they have any) is limited to the body; if there is any such corporeal influence, it is insufficient to give being or non-being to a man, to bestow upon him good or evil, to kill him or preserve him from death — all of this belongs to God alone (*ed. cit.*, pp. 301–3).

The Media Parte of this same book is given over to a discussion of the "common manner of speaking of Fate, Fortune, signs and Planets," and contains a long "Allegory of Fortune and Poverty" derived from Boccaccio's *De casibus virorum illustrium* (*On the Fall of Famous Men*), III, i.[17] Here Fortune claims that all things are *a mi rregimiento* — "under my control" — but she is rebuked by Poverty for not knowing herself: she is *engañadora, ynica e traydora* — "a cheat, an iniquitous betrayer." Poverty with her natural powers of reason has overcome Fortune: *mi juyzio natural venció a ti, burladora.*

Fortune, in the allegory, is identified with the world, in the sense of enemy of the soul: *todas estas cosas ynconuenientes e lazos del falso mundo.* The two personifications come to grips and Fortune's head is struck violently on the ground. She begs for mercy, and repents. Poverty delivers a sermon: let no one trust in power,

16. Ed. L. B. Simpson (Berkeley, 1939), pp. 263–64.
17. See Patch, *op. cit.*, pp. 72 ff., and his Plate 3, which pictures Poverty vanquishing Fortuna.

wealth, favor, force, or estate; justice must in the end prevail. Poverty then imposes sentence: since Fortune has dared to call herself *del vniuerso mundo deesa* — "goddesss of the universe" — and since she has claimed power to give and take away being and non-being without interference from free will — *voluntad e libre e franco aluedrio* — she must henceforth be bound by chains. Hereafter no man or woman may ascribe what befalls him or her to Fortune or Fate (for they are identical: *que vna cosa son*); the responsibility rests with the individual who willfully releases Fortune from her chain. The final chapter of this Media Parte draws the moral: *que solo Nuestro Señor es el que faze e desfaze, e da ser e non ser* — "only God makes and unmakes, gives being and non-being." All things are in God's power, and every human creature may, with his gift of free will, do what it pleases him to do.

The important points established are two: there is no other Fortune than God; Fortune, as popularly conceived, is identified with "the world" and is personified as a fickle and evil woman.[18]

Contemporaneous with Martínez de Toledo was Alfonso de la Torre. In his *Visión delectable*, this fifteenth-century moralist affirms that, although "the opinions of the people" are not true, they contain *alguna parte de verdad* — some element of truth. It is not true, he says, that all things happen by Chance, arbitrarily — *sin regimiento ninguno*. But there are certain things which are subject to Chance and to *Ventura*.[19] Nor is it true that all things were ordered by God *ab eterno* — *eternalmente ordenadas por Dios* — for God does not determine how many times a man shall blink his eyes. But it is true that all things that happen in the world have known causes, though these causes be hidden to us. The hidden causes are known to God — *a él son ciertas* — and He ordains them, making such provision as is needful — *et provéelas según la provisión necesaria a ellas*.[20] In an earlier passage (*ed. cit.*, p. 353a) La Torre causes Wisdom to say to her attending damsels: "Since the Understanding is inclined to disputation, . . . we shall first prove to him that God exists, and shall show him how God is the

18. She is often called a harlot. See Patch's section on Fickleness, pp. 49 ff. Dante wrote: "In the beginning she is admirable . . . , at the end she is fetid and horrible" (cited *ibid.*, p. 68).

19. On *Ventura*, see Patch, Index.

20. *BAE*, XXXVI, 359b.

ruler of the world, and thus any notion that Fate, Chance, or Fortune exist will be destroyed." [21]

The fifteenth century was rich in treatises and statements on Fortune. The Augustinian Fray Martín de Córdoba, whose study of
Predestination [22] proved so useful in our preceding chapter, wrote
also a *Compendio de la Fortuna*, in which he treats of Fortune as
a natural, as a practical, and as an ethical concept.[23] In his dedica-
tion of this work to the favorite of King Juan II of Castile (d. 1454)
he offers the fruit of his labor to the powerful politician and gives
thanks for whatever success he may have had in treating the problem "to the God of the mighty and inscrutable Fortuna" — *al Dios
de la alta e inescrutable Fortuna.* Fray Martín's long treatment is
summed up in a single sentence: "Now we know what Chance and
Fortune are; they are accidental causes operating on things which
happen for some purpose at rare intervals." [24] That purpose is
God's will; Fortune is *ancilla Dei.* We are thus brought back to
Bossuet, whose warning was quoted earlier: "let us speak of [For-
tune] as if it were a name whereby we cover up our ignorance."

In the humanistic commentary (1499) of Hernán Núñez on
Juan de Mena's *Laberinto de Fortuna* there is a long dissertation
on Fortune. After many quotations from the ancients and from
Augustine, the great Professor of Greek at Alcalá and Salamanca
concluded: "we must therefore hold it certain that there is no
such thing as Fortune, but that all is subject to the will of God
and that He determines in this world the estate of all men, and of
all other things, as is pleasing to His high and divine Providence.[25]

Another humanist, Herán Pérez de Oliva (d. 1531?), author of
the earliest version of Sophocles in any modern language, in his
Diálogo de la dignidad del hombre [26] eulogizes man's free will
which enables him to free himself from the insults of Fortune,
and declares that he who suffers at Fortune's hands brings the suf-

21. On Fortune's non-existence, see Patch, p. 16.

22. *Un tratado del siglo XV sobre la predestinación en castellano,* ed. Aníbal
Sánchez Fraile (Salamanca, 1956).

23. See the second of the three quotations with which this chapter opens and note 2.

24. *Ed. cit.,* p. 8; see pp. 10–13, 16, 18–19; see also *idem, Tratado . . . , ed. cit.,*
p. xxxix.

25. This is, of course, pure Scholastic doctrine. See ed. Antwerp 1552, p. 8.

26. Modeled on the famous oration of Pico della Mirandola, but with far greater
regard for the Christian basis of man's dignity. *BAE,* LXV.

fering on himself—*él mismo se le dió*. This is Fortune identified with the "world" rather than with the "heavens," and her presence among us should serve principally to undeceive the discontented: "She declares herself by means of many examples, and she is not responsible for the ills that befall her pursuers; the responsibility belongs, rather, to him who through carelessness or blindness gives no thought to her evils. More blameworthy still is he who follows after her, all the more since we are at all times very close to death, beyond which the goods of this world cannot be carried" (*ed. cit.*, p. 359a).

Much less secular in tone is the statement of the Christian humanist Vives: "We must be certain that God's will or command is the law established in the world, that this is its proper law, identical with the law which we call natural, whereby all things are ruled, and that there is no such thing as Chance, Fortune, or Luck; we must believe that everything which this law does is done with infinite knowledge and justice, though this be along paths which our eyes cannot perceive." [27]

Pedro Simón Abril's manuscript *Filosofía natural* (ca. 1589) has more than once been cited in preceding chapters of this study. His treatment of Fortune occupies somewhat over one printed page in the *Apéndices* of Margherita Morreale's *Pedro Simón Abril*. The ancients, he says, philosophized erroneously about Fortune, as they did about other matters having to do with religion. In philosophy, he explains, Chance or Fortune is the rare coming together of two causes possessing entire independence of each other. For a man to walk along a road is a voluntary act; for a bolt of lightning to descend to earth is "natural violence." That the stroller should happen to be at the point struck by the flash is "fortune." Such fortune can be good or evil, according as it benefits or harms a man. Other examples are cited, such as the damming of a valley by an earthquake to form a lake: the current of the river and the upheaving of the earth are natural independent phenomena of rare occurrence. Simón Abril states that if the two actions are accomplished by inanimate forces, the conjunction is called chance (*caso*); if one or both of the actions depend on a human will, their coincidence is called fortune (*fortuna*). He concludes

27. *Introducción a la sabiduría*, Spanish trans. (Madrid, 1944), p. 62.

that neither chance nor fortune is a cause; in every case, the phenomenon so considered is a coincidence, and it is always rare. If, he adds, there is any cause, it is supernatural — which is to say that there is direct intervention of God's Providence. Within the law of nature there is nothing that can properly be called the cause of these rare conjunctions.[28]

A special place among sixteenth-century works concerned with Fortune is occupied by Juan Huarte de San Juan's *Examen de ingenios para las ciencias* (first ed. 1575). This work had immense influence, in Spain and in Europe generally. Its thesis is that human conduct and achievement depend on physical factors: the proper (or improper) admixture in a given human body of the humors that correspond to the four elements. Huarte says flatly (as did Calderón years later) that there is no other Fortune than God: *no hay otra fortuna sino Dios.* Operating at a lower level, however, there is another force which leads to a false belief in Fortune. This is human cleverness joined with human enterprise: *la buena diligencia del hombre.* Peripatetic and Stoic philosophers, Huarte says, dreamed up — *fingieron* — the idea of the existence, parallel to the Supreme Cause and Supreme Wisdom, of another cause called *Fortuna,* not only irrational and brutish, but inclined to favor base and perverse persons. This conception, he says, is wrongheaded — *ruin y perversa.* If the children of darkness prevail over the children of light, if the former are more, and the latter less, prosperous in the world, it is because the prosperous ones are more *ingeniosos,* more imaginative, and are endowed with an intellectual quickness which is both sagacious and abundantly cunning.[29]

28. Madrid, 1949, pp. 238–39. A sidelight on this philosophico-scientific point of view is afforded by J. C. Scaliger's commentary on Aristotle's *History of Animals.* The creative force that generates animals and men, all of it, "must indeed derive from one beginning, which is God, whose will is called Fortune and whose power is Nature." See John E. Hankins, "Howlet's 'God Kissing Carion': A Theory of the Generation of Life," *PMLA,* LXIV (1949), 510.

29. See Mauricio de Iriarte, *El Doctor Huarte de San Juan y su "Examen de ingenios"* (Madrid, 1948), p. 217. On the meaning of *ingenio* and *ingenioso* as used by Huarte, see my article, "El *ingenioso* hidalgo," *HR,* XXV (1957), 175–93. Huarte would appear to have been influenced by Aristotle. Francisco Sánchez de las Brozas (*el Brocense*) wrote in his commentary on the second stanza of Mena's *Laberinto de Fortuna:* "If Fortune exists or not, and what Fortune is, would require a long dissertation. . . . Aristotle in his *Greater Ethics* says that where there is knowledge and understanding there is little fortune, and where these things are lacking there is much fortune . . . " (Mena, *Las obras,* ed. Francisco Sánchez de las Brozas [Salamanca, 1582]).

As we pass into the seventeenth century we find the lexicographer Sebastián de Covarrubias in his *Tesoro de la lengua Castellana* (1611) completely unconcerned about Fortune. As St. Isidore had done in the seventh century, Covarrubias presents Fortune (aside from the ordinary meaning of luck in one's daily affairs) as a goddess of the gentiles, to whom statues were raised and whom Juvenal ridiculed: *Nullum numen habes*. As to the related words *ventura, suerte, caso, ocasión*, only the latter is recorded as having a meaning other than the ordinary one. *Ocasión* was "una de las deidades que fingieron los gentiles" — one of the deities dreamed up by the gentiles. He refers to her statue by Phidias, to an epigram by Ausonius, and to an emblem by Andrea Alciato. That is all.

This does not mean that interest in Fortune as a power had subsided. Men still wrote books on the subject: Gutierre Marqués de Careaga's *Desengaño de Fortuna* (Madrid, 1612) shows by its title that it argued a case against Fortune. The same is true of Jerónimo de Molina Lama's *Vivir contra Fortuna: Escuelas politicas de Séneca* (Murcia, 1652), whose subtitle: *para hacer rostro a los trabajos y estar consolados entre las miserias del tiempo* — "wherein we may learn to face hardships and find consolation amid the miseries of time" — indicates that the writer belongs to the line of authors of "consolations." [30] The Senecan tradition becomes very strong, no doubt in part through the influence of Justus Lipsius,[31] and a relatively new element comes to the fore: the political, as a reaction against the writings of Niccolò Machiavelli.[32] Machiavelli's Fortune, unacceptable in Spain, must be stripped of her irrational (and hence non-Providential) attributes (Maravall, *op. cit.*, p. 309). Such irrationality as she retains is merely what Bossuet

30. I have not seen either of these books.

31. C. Nisard, *Le triumvirat littéraire au XVIᵉ siècle: Juste Lipse, Joseph Scaliger et Isaac Casaubon* (Paris, n. d.); Jason L. Sanders, *Justus Lipsius: The Philosopher of Rennaissance Stoicism* (New York, 1955). Lipsius' influence in the Spanish Peninsula was strong. He appears as an interlocutor in the *Hospital das letras* of Francisco Manuel de Melo (d. 1666).

32. J. A. Maravall, *La philosophie politique espagnole au XVIIᵉ siècle* (Paris, 1955), pp. 308 ff. "In general, writers seek to transform into a Christian value this powerful historic factor so emphasized by Machiavelli." The main points of interest in Machiavelli's writings are *virtù, fortuna, necessità, libertà, Stato*. See J. A. Hexter, "*Il Principe* and *lo Stato*," *Studies in the Renaissance*, IV (1957), 114.

called "our own ignorance," our inability — as finite beings — to know the mind and the designs of the Infinite.

Baltasar Gracián, in the tenth and eleventh *Primores* of *El Héroe* (1637), expounds a bit of practical political or military advice: the Great Man, when faced with any sort of Rubicon, will do well to know first how he stands with Fortune. If he be her favorite, let him boldly take the decisive step; if not, caution is called for. Let no one, drunk with past successes, fail to govern himself when Fortune beckons — *si [le] está bailando el agua la fortuna*. When Charles V was forced to raise the siege of Metz in 1553, the Marqués de Marignano consoled him by saying that Fortune shows not only the fickleness of a woman but the recklessness of a flirtatious girl: *liviandad de joven en hacer cara a los mancebos*. All of this seems pagan enough and suggests Phidias' statue of Occasio, or Opportunity, with her inviting forelock. Gracián does not wish to be so interpreted and in the next sentence declares: "But I say that these ups and downs are not mere feminine whims; they are the alterations of a most just Providence" (*Primor* XI). A few pages earlier (*Primor* X) he had given his definition: "Fortune, as famous as she is misunderstood, is none other (speaking seriously and in accordance with Catholic doctrine) than that great Mother of Contingencies and great Daughter of Providence who ever assists the latter in her work of causality, now requiring, now permitting. She is that sovereign Queen, inscrutable, smiling on some, receiving others either as mother or as stepmother, not out of partiality but in accordance with judgments utterly beyond our grasp." [33]

Gracián will speak quite differently of human Fortune, as we shall see, but when he is speaking *a lo cuerdo y aun católico* — seriously and as a Catholic — he agrees with Calderón, who in his allegorical drama *There is no Fortune but God* meant to show that "men reject God's Justice and follow human Fortune because they cannot understand the Cross." [34] Calderón brings this play to a close with a final repetition of the refrain:

> Love the God whose love enfolds thee.
> Smiling Fortune, gracious Fortune,

33. *El Héroe. El Discreto* (Buenos Aires–Mexico City, 1939), pp. 30–33.
34. Parker in the Introduction to this play, *ed. cit.*, p. xxv.

Is no goddess, is no deity,
But God's Justice is.[35]

FORTUNE IN SPANISH LITERATURE

Fortuna, or *Ventura,* appears in all her guises in works of polite literature. Sometimes the poet or dramatist or novelist will choose to indicate that she is subject to God's control, but to explain this dependence was no more necessary than it is in the case of a modern clergyman whose nearest approach to blasphemy is "Confusion take the luck!" Thus Fray Luis de León, in *La perfecta casada* — his book of doctrine for the Christian wife — cautions that the woman who has many servants in her charge should remember that they and she "are of a single substance, and that Fortune, who is blind, and not careful Nature, has caused the differences that separate them . . . and that they all are destined to have an identical end, and that they go through life seeking identical blessings. If they only would realize that tomorrow the air may change so that masters may become servants, . . . as happens every day; in short, we all . . . serve the same Lord, who will measure unto us with the same measure that we ourselves use." [36] This *Fortuna ciega,* this Blind Fortune, is no pagan deity in the mind of this Augustinian moralist; it is simply that he recognizes that, "after the fall, the blows of circumstance [began] to fall at random." [37] Blind Fortune is thus *una manera de hablar,* a figure of speech.

35. "Ama a un Dios que te ama, / que, hermosa y gentil, / no es deidad la Fortuna, / no, no, la Justicia sí." Cf. his *La exaltación de la Cruz,* I, 12: "No hay más fortuna que Dios. . . . / Viene el mal como castigo, / viene el bien como regalo" (There is no Fortune but God; evil and good come as punishment or reward). Human Fortune, says Calderón, "Is of so confused an aspect, / Of a countenance so doubtful, / Is so treacherous in her dealings, / Is in every way so fickle, / That, to him who looks upon her / She appears to be making faces" ("es de aspecto tan confuso, / de tan dudoso semblante, / de tan engañoso trato, / y de condición tan fácil, / que, a quien la mira, parece / que diversos rostros hace" [*Saber del bien y del mal,* I, 12]).

36. "son de un mismo metal, y que la fortuna, que es ciega, y no la naturaleza proveída, es quien las diferencia, y que . . . han de tener un mismo fin, y que caminan llamadas para unos mismos bienes; y si considerasen que se puede volver el aire mañana, y a los que sirven agora servirlos ellos después . . . como cada día acontece, que al fin todos . . . servimos a un mismo Señor, que nos medirá como nosotros midiéremos" (ed. Madrid, 1917, pp. 114–15).

37. Nathan A. Scott Jr. (ed.), *The Tragic Vision and the Christian Faith* (New York, 1957), p. 46.

We shall now go back to the fourteenth century and see how the various conceptions of Fortune, as symbol either of Providence or of simple contingency, are utilized in literary works.

Juan Ruiz

In our chapter on Free Will we cited Juan Ruiz's *Book of Good Love*, with its horoscope of the son of King Alcaraz. In stanzas 692 and 693 he makes the following pronouncement about Fortune, mistress of man's ups and downs:

> Full many a time does Fortune, with her resistless power,
> Prevent a man from rising to a high place from a lower;
> She makes this poor old world of ours toss like a cockleshell,
> But Providence and human work she never can compel.
> Dame Fortune lifts whome'er she please, and others she casts down,
> But luck and effort go together, they our success may crown —
> If, when we undertake a thing, we trust in God's design
> And know that if He be displeased our fortune must change sign.[38]

Ruiz's position on this is no less orthodox than his exposition of the doctrine of Free Will was found to be.

Bernat Metge

In the year 1381 this Catalan[39] harbinger of the Renaissance in Spain[40] composed a poem of 1194 lines entitled *Libre de Fortuna e Prudència*. It belongs to medieval "vision" literature. The poet, on awaking one morning, is beset by chest pains and walks

38. "Muchas vezes la ventura con ssu fuerça e poder / a muchos omes non dexa su propósito fazer: / por esto anda el mundo en levantar e caer; / Dios e el trabajo grande pueden los fados vençer. / Ayuda la ventura al que bien quiere guiar, / e a muchos es contraria, puédelos malestorvar; / el trabajo e los fados suélense acompañar; / pero syn Dios todo esto non puede aprovechar." (Words meaning fortune and fate are here used indiscriminately; in 693c *fados* must mean "good luck").

39. I find it advisable at times to overstep the limits of the subtitle of *Spain and the Western Tradition*. Regretfully, but of necessity, I have found it necessary to omit Catalonia and Portugal from my survey of Spanish intellectual history. I have on occasion utilized, however, important texts from the Catalans Raimundo Sabunde and Raimundo Lull, the Valencian Auzías March, and others who were not Castillians and who did not write in Castilian (e.g., the use already made, and still to be made, of Martorell's novel of chivalry, *Tirant lo Blanc*) as well as from the Catalans (e.g., Boscán) and the Portuguese (e.g., Montemayor) who did write in Castilian. My criterion in all cases is the usefulness of any given example for the purposes of my exposition. Bernat Metge's poem on Fortune and Prudence is useful at this point.

40. Martín de Riquer, Metge's modern editor, commentator, and translator, finds that the Latinisms in the early work we are considering are characteristically medieval, in contrast to the humanistic Latinisms of Metge's later prose works (*Obras de Bernat Metge* [Barcelona, 1959], p. 29).

down to the sea seeking relief. He meets a naked old man wearing a hempen hat and seated near a small boat and is enticed into entering the boat, whereupon it is launched violently and he is carried out to sea. At length the boat touches a rocky shore and he steps out, thinking that his *Ventura* has brought him there to die. It is a cruel place, and he comes to the conclusion that neither God nor Nature exists, since he sees no sign of order or of reason (*ed. cit.*, p. 39).

Climbing up the rock, he spies a walled castle, surrounded with horrible filth. Before him there appears an unspeakably disgusting woman,[41] advancing with imperial solemnity. One of her arms exceeds the other in length, and in one hand she carries a great wheel which she whirls ceaselessly and with great noise (*ibid.*, p. 47). She identifies herself as *Fortuna*. The poet accuses her of having caused his misfortune but is told that only fools can blame her. All men are born naked; how can they blame her if she gives them nothing, or takes away what she once gave? The poet continues to revile her and she answers: blame not her who does what she ought. Giving and taking away, she says, is her business (p. 61). The poet replies defiantly and is hurled violently from the castle. He falls senseless.

Recovering his senses, he sees a woman, as agreeable as the other was horrid, accompanied by seven damsels. She is Prudence and the damsels, the seven liberal arts. Prudence tells him he is in danger; his infirmity is ignorance. He is ignorant, since he believes that Fortune can bestow good or evil. All that occurs in the created world is done with God's permission, and God — though he permits evil and suffering — permits nothing to be done without reason (p. 69). Ultimate rewards and punishments will set all to rights; God is the only Judge and, what is more, Fortune herself is always Good Fortune. She is God's agent; he created her to test or punish, to recompense or correct good men and bad, according to their deserts. And further: Fortune is even subject to the human will. Every man possessed of good judgment and natural reason has his fortune in his hand.[42]

41. The author follows the *Anticlaudianus* of Alanus de Insulis. See the editor's note, *ed. cit.*, p. 45.

42. "E podets-los dir, certamen, / que Fortuna tostemps sta / en la ma de tot hom qui ha / bon seny a rayso natural" (*ibid.*, p. 86).

With gentle courtesy Prudence leads him back to his boat and makes him enter it. In a moment the vision — along with the boat — disappears and he is back at his starting point in Barcelona. May God bless his listeners and admit them to Paradise (p. 88).

The doctrine is derived not only from Alanus de Insulis, but also from Jean de Meun's *Romance of the Rose* and from *On the Consolation of Philosophy* by Boethius: *In uestra est enim manu, qualem uobis fortunam formare malitis,* wrote Boethius — "what kind of fortune you wish for yourself is in your own hand." The central theme of the poem, says Riquer, "is not presented in the form of a dream . . . but in the form of a fantastic incursion by a being of flesh and blood — Bernat Metge — into a world which for him is no longer legendary in the strict sense of the word, but literary, purely and simply bookish. It is a fantasy of the scrivener of the Duke of Gerona who, under the impulse of his persecution complex, lets his imagination fly through the world of books . . ." (p. 26). The saving idea that man's fate is in his own hand is rare in the Middle Ages, we are told, but is renewed in the Renaissance.[43] We shall meet it over and over again in Cervantes.

The "Cancionero" poets

The Stoic idea that the "goods of Fortune" have nothing to do with the inner self is expressed by the poet Soria:

que ni son bienes ni males lo que la Fortuna ordena, antes son obras yguales.[44]	What Fortune gives is neither a good nor an evil, but rather indifferent.

The thought is often repeated, for example by Juan de Andújar:

Puede la Fortuna los bienes mundanos dar et quitar segund su plaser, pero las virtudes no son en sus manos nin dellas vos pudo desnuda faser.[45]	Fortune can give and take away earthly blessings according to her whim, but to bestow or take away virtue is not in her power.

The Marqués de Santillana (whom we shall soon study more in detail) represents Fortune as lumped together with Fate and as

43. See R. C. Cochrane, "Bacon and the Architect of Fortune," *Studies in the Renaissance*, V (1958), 180. Bibliography in n. 14.

44. *Cancionero castellano del siglo XV*, ed. R. Foulché-Delbosc (Madrid, 1912–15), II, 260.

45. *Cancionera de Stúñiga*, eds. Marqués de la Fuensanta del Valle and Sancho Rayón (Madrid, 1872), pp. 192–93.

questionably responsible for the disappearance of the illustrious dead of the *ubi sunt* theme:

O muy transcendentes poetas limados,
yntrínsicos, sabios, discretos, letrados:
dezid, ¿quién los roba, Fortuna o sus fados,
que de aquestos ninguno non veo? [46]

Oh polished and transcendental poets, Hermetic, wise, discreet, and learned, tell me who steals them away; is it Fortune or her fates, for none of these is visible to me?

Francisco Imperial regards her as an arbitrary force, claiming power to upset even the influence of the planets, which she apostrophizes:

A guysa de dueña que está sobre sy,
con buenandança e presentuosa,
començó Fortuna su rrazón asy;
"Vuestras influencias syn mí non val cosa,
ca yo en el mundo so más provechosa,
muy más amada que vos todas siete,
ca lo que [a] alguno se da o promete,
non le aprovecha, si d'él so enojosa. [47]

Like a most self-possessed great lady, presumptuous in her worldly success, Fortune began to speak: "Your influences without me are worthless, for I in the world am more esteemed than all seven of you, and accomplish more. Whatever is given or promised to a man is a dead letter if I am displeased with him."

Garci Sánchez de Badajoz points to the general confusion of names and gives an orthodox definition:

De mil nombres me han nombrado . . . ,
vnos, Ventura [48] y Fortuna;
otros, Dicha e Suerte e Hado.
So vn efeto sin substancia
    de ocasiones
como quando entre dos sones
se causa la consonancia.

I have been given a thousand names . . . ; some have called me Ventura or Fortune; others, Happiness or Luck or Fate. I am a substanceless effect of two things chancing to come together, as when harmony is produced by the sounding of two musical notes.

As we saw earlier in Metge, man may dominate Fortune:

Este caualga sobre la Fortuna,

46. *Pregunta a nobles* in *Cancionero de Roma*, ed. M. Canal Gómez (Florence, 1935), II, 80.

47. *Cancionero de Baena*, ed. F. Michel (Leipzig, 1860), I, 206.

48. "*Ventura*, or *Aventure*, is a name that at one time threatened to replace the name Fortuna. . . . Ventura receives a treatment similar to that of Fortuna herself . . . she turns a wheel, and exalts or debases; she guides; and she is confused with Fate or Destiny" (Patch, *op. cit.*, p. 39). This verse quotation is from the *Cancionero castellano* . . . , II, 649.

"This man rides astride of Fortune," wrote Mena in his *Laberinto* (stanza 235a).[49] In Mena we are confronted with the concept of the two Fortunes, inasmuch as he himself (as we shall see in a moment) defines Fortune also as Providence, a force infinitely above all conceivable human domination. Gómez Manrique makes the same identification:

y ésta que nos llamamos Fortuna, es la prouidencia del alta tribuna, aunque los vocablos traemos mudados.[50]	And this so-called Fortune is the Providence of Him who sitteth upon the throne, though we confuse the words.

In his *Laberinto de Fortuna,* Mena begins by berating *Fortuna* for her inconstancy, and asks to see the "house" [51] where the goddess has her wheel (stanza 12). He is caught up in Belona's chariot and sees a vision of Divine Providence. Surely, he says, this palace must obey her, not Fortuna. She tells him to come and see; she will show him

aquello que puede
ser apalpado de vmano ynteleto, (stanza 26)

—all that the human intellect can grasp. The solution given is the orthodox one, "in its most general lines": *Fortuna* "is none other than the servant of Providence, the true arbiter of blessings and misfortunes." Thus Mena, "not without literary skill," presents his concept of *Fortuna* as developing in the course of the poem. Beginning with the conventional attitude of complaint (*mudable Fortuna*), he next defines her as the essence of arbitrariness, and at last proclaims her to be *divina ordenança.*[52] In addition to the decisive passages, there are others throughout the poem in which Fortuna reappears in what Patch would call her incidental "pagan guise"—ever useful to poets. In stanza 188 she is called "perfidious"; elsewhere, "cruel" and "blind" (stanzas 188, 267).

49. "The idea of man as master of Fortune appears long before the Renaissance — e.g., in the works of Gower — and is an outgrowth of the classical idea that Fortune aids the brave" (Patch, *op. cit.,* p. 23, n. 4).

50. The names, the *vocablos,* the author explains in a prose commentary, are inherited (*quedar*) from the gentiles; the ups and downs of life come to us by God's secret disposition — *por permisión de Dios, cuyos secretos son ynotos (Cancionero castellano . . . ,* II, 58).

51. "The first actual account of the house of fortune was given in the twelfth century by Alanus de Insulis in his *Anticlaudianus"* (Patch, *op. cit.,* p. 126; see p. 140, and Plate 7, after p. 130).

52. María Rosa Lida de Malkiel, *Juan de Mena* (Mexico City, 1950), pp. 20 ff.

She is identified with Fate (174, 226), and also as the author of all that happens in the world (142). It is even she who brings the winds (169).[53] (It is of course true that the winds obey the Lord's will, and that all that happens in the world is divinely — providentially — ordained; here indeed Fortune is the servant of Providence.) It is the relapses into the other, the "vulgar," conception that bring us back to the concept which is the thread of this part of the present chapter: there are two Fortunes, one earthly and one divine.[54]

CONFUSION WITH OTHER TERMS AND CONCEPTS

Before proceeding to an examination of how this double aspect is treated in two poems by Santillana, it will be well to give an exposition of other ways in which the poets viewed Fortuna.

Nature

First, there is her confusion or identification with Nature, or her presentation as Nature's co-adjutor. In the thirteenth century Frère Laurent, in his *Somme des Vices et des Vertus*, "sets forth the gifts of God as divided into those of nature, of fortune, and of grace. Nature bestows the properties of the body — fairness, strength, prowess, nobility, eloquence; and the properties of the soul — clear intelligence and subtle wit." Fortune gives, on the other hand, lofty position, honors, riches, delights, and prosperities. Frère Laurent's drawing of this distinction is the beginning of a steady tradition.[55] I shall not dwell here so much on Fortune's gift-giving as on her sharing with Nature some of the power of *Natura naturans*,[56] the creative force. In a lyric poem by Mena, *Natura* creates the lovely creature; *Fortuna* endows, organizes, and forms her.

Desde niñez en la cuna,	Since your childhood in the
cobrastes fama, beldad,	cradle you received fame and
con tanta graciosidad	beauty, with all the charm show-

53. Malkiel, *op. cit.*, p. 23, n. 12.
54. See Pierre Le Gentil, *La poésie lyrique espagnole et portugaise à la fin du moyen âge, Première Partie: Les Thèmes et les Genres* (Rennes, 1949), p. 353, n. 56.
55. Patch, *op. cit.*, pp. 65–66
56. See above, Chapter III, *Natura naturans*.

que vos dotó la fortuna,
que assí vos organizó
y formó
la composición humana,
que vos soys la más loçana
soberana
que la natura crió.[57]

ered upon you by Fortune, who
so organized and formed your
human portion that you are the
most lovely and queenly creature
that *Nature ever created.*

Similar poems, by Gómez Manrique (nos. 334 and 359) and by Tapia (no. 791), are found in the *Cancionero castellano del Siglo XV.*

Love and the Stars [58]

I spoke in Volume I of the courtly idea that love was regarded as a sort of feudal quest, as something unalterably reserved for a certain *caballero* and for no other. It was said of Amadis of Gaul that for him and him alone it was given — decreed — that he should love so lofty a person as Oriana. A determining power could easily be — and was — attributed to Fate; such power was also an attribute of *Fortuna.* "Fortuna," writes Patch, "sends what is due from her — failure as well as success — in her special functions as goddess of love, war, and so on" (*op. cit.,* p. 66). Among the "cults" that he enumerates in medieval times, Patch gives first place to the Fortune of Love (*ibid.,* p. 89). He even goes so far as to say that Amor, or Cupid, was not "entirely supplanted by Fortune" (p. 90); and he adds that sometimes it seems "as if Fortune got her power in love affairs, not by replacing the God of Love, but by bestowing or withholding her gifts of riches and glory which would bring the lover to his lady more easily" (p. 90). At all events, as early as the eleventh or twelfth century "the similarity between Fortune and Love had been recognized in a poem by Hildebert de Lavardin, *De Infidelitate Fortunae et Amoris Mundi*" (*ibid.*). Both Fortune and love are faithless, Hildebert said; neither deity is true. Some men are broken by one, some by the other (p. 91).

57. *Cancionero General* (comp. Hernando del Castillo), ed. Bibliófilos Españoles (Madrid, 1882), I, 114. See also my article "Courtly Love in the Spanish *Cancioneros,*" *PMLA,* LXIV (1949), p. 292 and n. 158. This will be abbreviated hereafter as "*Cancioneros.*"

58. "Amor, que está sujecto al tiempo y a la fortuna . . . " — "Love, who is subject to time and fortune" (Montemayor, *La Diana,* ed. F. López Estrada [Madrid, 1946], p. 69).

Fortune and the stars are linked together as cocauses by Lope de Stúñiga. His sufferings, he complains, were determined before his birth by the stars in the ascendant at the fatal hour,

e la rueda de Fortuna,	and Fortune's wheel, with the
con el signo más esquiuo,	most baleful zodiacal sign and
con la más menguante luna	the most unfavorable moon fated
me fadaron en la cuna	me in the cradle to be your cap-
para ser vuestro captiuo.[59]	tive.

The idea was popular in Spain. I shall give here but one additional example: *Ordenó mi ventura que me enamorase de Laureola* — "My Fortune ordained that I should fall in love with Laureola," declares the lover in Diego de San Pedro's *Cárcel de amor* (1492).[60]

Fortune and mutability: Time [61]

When Shakespeare in *The Rape of Lucrece* (lines 947 and 952) states that it is Time's function

> To feed oblivion with decay of things
>
> . . . .
>
> And turn the giddy round of Fortune's wheel,

he is utilizing a tradition with very ancient roots. The powers of Chance and Time were linked in the thinking of the Greek school of atomistic philosophers. The myth of Saturn, devouring and vomiting up his children, was an allegory of Time, which devours all things and makes them rise again.[62] John Lydgate (d. 1451?) made Fortune the incarnation of mutability, and throughout his epic, *The Fall of Princes*, the *Ubi sunt* melody haunts the reader.[63] Edmund Spenser's (d. 1599) "traditional complaints against the ravages of Time . . . owed less to science than . . . to received medieval thought." [64] Gracián in *El Criticón* (*Crisi* X) pictures personified Time as a traveler carrying a pair of cloth saddlebags

59. *Cancionero castellano* . . . , II, 593. Mario Equicola, in his *Libro de natura d'amore* (1525), accuses Fortune of causing unworthy lovers to be loved, and vice versa. See "*Cancioneros,*" p. 292, n. 155; see also Volume I, p. 89.

60. "*Cancioneros,*" p. 292; see also Volume I, p. 90.

61. See note 58 above; see also *La Diana, ed. cit.,* p. 273.

62. E. R. Curtius, *European Literature and the Latin Middle Ages,* trans. Willard R. Trask (New York, 1953), p. 443.

63. W. F. Schirmer in *English Studies Today,* ed. Wrenn and Bullough (Oxford, 1951), p. 107.

64. Samuel I. Mints in *JHI*, XII (1951), 155.

over his shoulder, one to the front, the other to the rear. The world's successes and reverses are the result of Time's shifting his burden, the rear bag to the front, the front bag to the rear. Fortune even borrows the hourglass of Father Time.[65]

Time, Fortune, Mutability, all of them agents of change and insecurity, are symbols for the expression of the philosophy of contempt for the world, and they are utilized as such across the centuries. Pedro Salinas, in his book on Jorge Manrique, has shown vividly how Spanish literature in the fifteenth century "takes possession of this dialectic theme, with ever greater insistence, and charges it with poetic forces. Flying on the wings of verse, the theme emerges from the cocoon of ascetic meditation and, now a butterfly, soars on its own power . . . , gliding through the air of pure creation. In this stripping away of man's transitory goods there enters another important factor. Gómez Manrique, in his poem to the Condesa de Castro, speaks of the brief duration of the things of the world." And Salinas quotes two lines from the poem (which I shall later need to reproduce in greater fullness). "There thus enters upon the stage," Salinas continues, "another most active collaborator of Time and Death. . . . The number of faithful servants — all three of them indefatigable — is now complete. For if Time never taries in its course, if Death never rests, the wheel of Fortune never ceases in its whirling." [66]

The poem of Gómez Manrique (*La péñola tengo con tinta en la mano*) is interrupted, every few stanzas, by a prose commentary. After a poetic definition, in perfectly orthodox terms, of Fortune as Providence, with its explanation in prose, the author quotes and expounds Job 14:1 — "Man that is born of woman is of few days, and full of trouble" — and proceeds to develop this theme in four stanzas. Man's struggles bring him suffering and tears, an inheritance that we all must pass on to our posterity, just as we received it from those who went before. The oars of our ship are no stronger than theirs, its sails are composed of a fabric no less frail. All earthly pomp and prosperity last no longer than the shining dew of morning: *no duran más que el blanco roçio*:

> For never does Fortune permit their retaining
> Their bright pristine substance, in spite of your cries —

65. Patch, *op. cit.*, p. 89. See his section "The Fortune of Time," pp. 155 ff.

66. *Jorge Manrique, o tradición y originalidad* (Buenos Aires, 1947), pp. 96–97.

Fortune, to whom the God that you worship
Has given the power to favor the rise
Of him who mounts upward, and then to cast down
The man whose possessions to other hands flee.
To witness this truth I summon fair Athens
Whose history lies open for all men to see.[67]

The Marqués de Santillana, Gómez Manrique's uncle, in his *Comedieta de Ponza* has an equally eloquent section on Fortune and Mutability, beginning with stanza 108. *Fortuna* announces herself as the agent to whom God has entrusted the control of the world and the motion of the firmament, the distribution of crowns and tiaras, the transfer of riches from the great to the lowly, the bestowing of happiness and sadness at the proper time — *a tiempo*. Since she is God's Providence, she claims powers that are really those of *Natura naturans*: "Of all that's engendered, the author am I." She produces all corruption, she distributes every bane and blessing; she controls the heat and the cold of the seasons; the sovereignty of states and nations is in her hand. She even has the gift of prophecy.[68] Though personified Time is not mentioned in these stanzas, Fortune's ruling of the firmament — *revuelvo las ruedas del gran firmamento* — and her controlling of the seasons, converting summer's heat into winter's snow and ice — *por tiempos en aguas, e nieves e frios* — are functions properly belonging to Time.

Finally, we come again to the greatest poem of the declining Middle Ages in Spain, Mena's *Laberinto de Fortuna*, so often referred to in the preceding pages. Guided by Providence, the poet sees not only Fortune's Mansion, but also the Wheels of the Past, the Present, and the Future. In each cycle are seven circles, those of the planets that govern human destiny. "The tradition of Fortune was naturally part of Mena's literary heritage," writes Florence Street. "He does not claim to be writing anything new, but simply 'what should be familiar ground to the learned.' Yet he is not content with the more ordinary forms of the allegory, and tries to give it universal significance by combining it with the other great topics

---

67. "Ca nunca los dexa estar en vn ser / esta Fortuna de quien vos quexays, / la qual por el Dios en quien adorays / le es otorgado bastante poder / para de pobres muy ricos fazer, / e grandes riquezas tornarlas agenas, / de lo qual testigo podrá ser Atenas, / si su gran cayda quisiéredes leer" (*Cancionero castellano* . . . , II, 59; see also p. 58).
68. *Cancionero castellano* . . . , I, 473–74.

popular in the Middle Ages, the influence of the planets and the fleetingness of Time; or, as Salinas has it, the 'famous instrument of Fortune now consists of three wheels, that of the past, the present, and the future, a curious instance of the dovetailing of the topics of Fortune and of Time.' " [69]

THE TWO FORTUNES

Bías contra Fortuna

In the poem *Bías contra Fortuna* Santillana — a poet who shared with his contemporary Mena the desire to ennoble Spanish poetry by giving to it a richer, a more learned, and a loftier tone and form worthy of the tradition of antiquity and of the example set by Dante and Petrarch — sought to console by means of philosophical moralizing a cousin of his, the Conde de Alba, who in 1448 found himself in prison. The poem therefore extols the Graeco-Roman ideal of the Stoic *sapiens*, as well as the chivalric ideal of a lettered *caballero* of the Spanish fifteenth century.

Previously, in *La comedieta de Ponza*, Santillana had presented Fortune as the delegate of an all-governing Providence; here, the goddess appears as a blind and arbitrary power that can be vanquished by adjusting one's life to Stoic reason.[70] Bías, one of the "seven wise men" of Greece, can with all propriety express Stoic sentiments which are incompatible with Christianity; indeed, he praises suicide as a means of putting an end to human misery. His treatment of the abode of the blest is, in its general lines, suggestive of the pagan concept of the rewards and punishments alloted to the famous dead. But Santillana allows himself an anachronism: as through a glass darkly, Bías has inklings of the Christian paradise (as well he might, according to the interpretation of Graeco-Roman antiquity as a divinely ordained way station considered as a *figura*

69. "The Allegory of Fortune and the Imitation of Dante in the *Laberinto* and the *Coronaçion* of Juan de Mena," *HR*, XXIII (1955), 5. We find Time and Fortune frequently linked together in the imagination of Golden Age writers: "All men, great and small, are vassals of Time and of Fortune" (Quevedo, *Obras en prosa*, ed. Luis Astrana Marín [Madrid, 1932], p. 732).

70. See Rafael Lapesa, *La obra literaria del Marqués de Santillana* (Madrid, 1957), pp. 215, 217, 219–20; O. H. Green, "Sobre las dos Fortunas: de tejas arriba y de tejas abajo," in *Studia Philologica: Homenaje a Dámaso Alonso* (Madrid, 1960–61), II, 143 ff.

of, and a preparation for, Christianity). Unwilling to leave unaltered the pagan conception of the Elysian fields as a region of flowery meadows enlivened by knightly exercises and noble arts, the poet imagines a *morada superior*, a higher abode, free from change, where the souls of the blest enjoy pure beatitude, singing. Rafael Lapesa, studying this problem, remarks that the poet does not say that he is thinking of the Dantesque Paradise, "without doubt because he does not wish to break the line of thought of a poem which he had tried to keep within the framework of Classical conceptions." This *morada superior*, this higher dwelling place, however, did not need to be proclaimed as the Christian abode of the blest; informed contemporaries must at once have recognized it as the Christian Empyrean. Bías knows — anachronistically of course, since he enjoys Santillana's own knowledge — that through the Harrowing of Hell the souls of the just who lived before the Redemption will be redeemed from Limbo, and he sees before him the road to Christian beatitude:

> Along that road I too shall pass,
> When my last days shall come,
> In spite of your protests, Fortuna,
> To the Blessed Saints' abode;
> And there
> I shall dwell rapt in joy and song,
> Forever untouched by change.[71]

Forever untouched by change — The men of the fifteenth century needed only this to identify the Christian Empyrean. "The Empyrean does not move; it imparts permanence and constancy to things, against the whirling of the other spheres," wrote Venegas. It is "the palace of God and his elect," wrote Fray Luis de Granada. It is a concept altogether unknown to the pagan philosophers, known only through Christian theology, we learn from Calepinus' *Dictionarium* and from Fray Juan de Pineda's *Agricultura christiana*. Mena's anonymous continuator in his *Adiciones al Laberinto de Fortuna* also insists on this quality of fixity and permanence:

71. "Este camino será / aquel que faré yo, Bías, / en mis postrimeros días, / si te plaçe o pesará, / a las bienaventuranzas; / do cantando / viviré, siempre goçando, / do çessan todas mudanzas" (stanza CLXXIX).

Oh lovable God, as we learn in our creed!
No words can suffice, no tongue can express
How You give motion to all things created
Though You yourself are forever unmoving.[72]

It is now clear why Bías says he will spend eternity *goçando* and *cantando* — rejoicing and singing — and it is also clear what he will sing. In the Empyrean he could sing only praises to the Most High.

Let us pause a moment to sum up: Santillana, in the *Comedieta*, had already presented Fortuna as subject to the God of the Christians, with no other power than that which she exercised as the delegate of Providence. Here, in his Stoic poem *Bías contra Fortuna*, he chose to limit himself — by a conscious act of will and for literary reasons — to a consideration of the arbitrary willfulness of the "other" Fortune, Fortune from the roof tiles downward, and only at the end of his poem has he enabled us to perceive that that is not all; that, indeed, there really is "no other Fortune than God."

Tirant lo Blanc

These two Fortunes, as we now know, are found in all Spanish literature, both medieval and classical, though they are often confused with other concepts: Fate, the stars, Heaven, Providence.[73] In general, this confusion of terms gave no cause for concern, even though the rigoristic Portuguese Inquisition did eliminate the concept Fate from Cervantes' *Galatea*. Only a sense of proportion and a consideration for the length of this chapter place a limit on the

72. "O Dios adorable, según nuestro credo! / Cierto, no bastan las lenguas agudas / decir el modo en que vuelves y mudas / todas las cosas estándote quedo!" (stanza XVI of the *Adiciones* to the *Laberinto*). For other references, see Green, "Sobre las dos Fortunas. . . . "

73. "Cervantes had a basis and source for the use of the [confused] terms here referred to: it is found in the scientific or learned books of the period, in its varied aspects. I have searched for it, especially among the texts whose date of publication is closest to [Cervantes'] *La Galatea* (1585), and in one of them (*Repertorio del mundo particular de las Spheras del Cielo y Orbes elementales y de las significaciones y tiempos correspondientes a su luz y mouimiento*, Madrid, 1584) I have found the following chapter, which gathers up into one harmonious and orthodox exposition the various terms mixed by Cervantes in his novel: Fate-stars-heaven-power of the planets-free will-Providence" (F. López Estrada, *op. cit.*, p. 436). See also Fray Martín de Córdoba, *Compendio de la Fortuna*, ed. cit., *passim*.

marshaling of quotations from Siglo de Oro literature which show the coexistence of the two Fortunes.

Let us remain for a while longer in the fifteenth century. Martorell's *Tirant lo Blanc* (so enthusiastically admired by Cervantes) was published in 1490. In chapter CXVIII of Book III the Emperor speaks: "No one in this life should complain of the things which are ordained and permitted by the Divine Wisdom, especially as Fortune administers them, because no human discretion can guard against future reverses, which come in many and diverse ways, and virtuous men should be patient in their adversities" [74] On the other hand, the Princess laments: "Oh monstrous Fortune, with variable and diverse faces you ceaselessly move your restless wheel . . . , envious of the brave and enemy of the weak!" (*ibid.*, p. 1713a). In other passages, which are numerous, the use of the name Fortune is neutral, meaning scarcely more than "the course of events": "And since my fortune has not allowed me to speak to you . . . " (*ibid.*, p. 1709b).

Amadís de Gaula

The Amadís de Gaula, in the form we know, was published by Rodríguez de Montalvo in 1508. Here, Fortune often means simply "luck." Oriana speaks to her lover: "I assure you that if Fortune or my intelligence does not provide us with some means of relief, my fearful daring will find a way" (*ibid.*, p. 441b). Or Fortune may be an arbitrary force, friendly or hostile. Mabilia speaks to the Queen: "And though you now feel the sting of this great blow of your contrary Fortune, you should remember that that same Fortune placed you in a position of great height and power, intending that you should enjoy it for only such time as her fickle will should decide . . . she always takes delight in trying her hand at such upsets" (p. 812a). Against her, strong language may be used, as when the Queen complains to Don Grumedán: "Deceitful and frightful Fortune, hope of the wretched, cruel enemy of those who prosper, upsetter of all worldly things, how can I praise you?" (p. 1039b). She may be the very antithesis of Providence, aiding and abetting sinners. A damsel writes to King Lisuarte: "and so,

---

74. See Castilian translation in *Libros de caballerías españoles*, ed. F. Buendía (Madrid, 1954), p. 1447a; see also p. 1261b.

after winning this fearful battle, you placed me in liberty and in all good fortune; for you, sir, having entered my castle, it so happened that, either as a result of my own beauty, or because Fortune so decreed, I (smitten by love of you), under that lovely rose arbor, lost the symbolic rose which until then I had kept entire, conceiving in my womb that youth who, to judge by his goodly presence, may be called a beautiful fruit of that act of sin, so beautiful, indeed, that God will pardon us." [75]

But Holy Fortune, Fortune as Providence, is also present in this novel and indeed determines its denouement. King Lisuarte, Oriana's father, had been during many years a "favorite son" of Prosperous Fortune, to so great an extent that he allowed himself to be blinded by his successes and to fall into the sin of pride or *hubris* (it is this that brings about the catastrophe). The author explains, with insistence, the nature and the consequences of that sin in chapter LXXX of Book III: "But neither she, nor the grandees of the kingdom, nor others of lesser station could divert the king from his purpose, and it was for this reason that Fortune, angry and tired of having placed him in such an eminence and bestowed upon him so many blessings (as a result of which he was become much more subject to attacks of anger and pride than formerly), determined, more for the good of his soul than for the sake of his honor, to turn about-face and be contrary to him, as in the fourth book of this great history will be related . . ." (p. 794a).

This Fortune, the personified power who — in the *Amadís* — for the good of a wayward man's soul — *por reparo de su ánima* — brings upon him all manner of disasters, is the same Power that governs human events — both prosperous and adverse — in Santillana's *Comedieta de Ponza*; the same Power that causes Bías, the Greek wise man, to foresee the seat that awaits him in glory, in the Christian Abode of the Blest, in the motionless Empyrean where all is permanence: *do çessan todas mudanças*. And the other Fortune, the blind, fickle, and disgusting woman, is the power which controls the ordinary ups and downs of life — those events in which Providence is not directly concerned, events which are so often the result of human error and depravity, or of irrational forces that chance to coincide. The temporary "fall" of King Lisuarte is divinely

75. See *ibid.*, p. 665a, or Green, "Sobre las dos Fortunas . . . ," p. 153.

caused by the former (in *Amadís*); the ordinary "falls of princes," product of the interaction of a personality and its "circumstance," are the work of the latter. It is the lower Fortune who threatens the bodily comfort, and endeavors to upset the peace of mind, of Santanilla's Bías. Both Fortunes will continue to play their unchanged roles in the sixteenth and seventeenth centuries.

The sixteenth century

Fortune appears constantly as the personification of life's vicissitudes. Don Pedro Manuel Ximénez de Urrea writes in his *Cancionero* (1513): "one should not blame anyone but Fortune who, for every estate, and without ever ceasing, keeps causing events whose origin is not based on reason: and therefore I would not complain or be cast down if in this matter I have had Fortune against me, since she never gave anyone a passport of safe-conduct." [76]

Fickle and deceitful Fortune enters upon the stage in a religious play of about 1520, and those who drew her chariot sing:

> This is the crazy bastard woman,
> This is the falsifying cheat,
> Fickle, giddy, light as a feather,
> False and lying, unstable as the weather. . . .[77]

In another religious play of approximately the same date, the *Auto de los Desposorios de Isaac*, we are told that the patriarch Abraham is feeling better:

> He had feared the turns of Fortune,
> Viewing her wheel with concern,
> Believing Isaac would marry
> A Canaanite, but now we learn
> That things have taken a better turn.[78]

Obviously, if the popular (non-theological) conception of Fortune were in this case looked upon as something other than a decorative

---

76. "no se deue ni puede dar la culpa sino a la sola Fortuna, que, por todos los estados, de contino sin cansar va causando cosas que su nacimiento no está fundado sobre razón: y assí yo no quiero quexarme, ni entristecerme, si en esto a la Fortuna por aduersaria he tenido, pues a nadi a dado saluo conducto" (ed. Martín Villar [Zaragoza, 1878], p. 57).

77. "Esta es la loca mestiza, / trapaçerona, falsaria, / varia, movible, boltaria, / mentirosa, antojadiza" (*Auto del Rey Assuero quando ahorcó a Amán*, in Rouanet, *Colección de autos, farsas y coloquios del siglo XVI* [Barcelona–Madrid, 1901], I, 283).

78. "El temía los rrodeos / de fortuna con cuydado, / y temía ver casado / a Isaac entre Cananeos, / pero ya está sosegado" (*ibid.*, p. 85).

element of speech or a convenient manner of expressing a shallow thought, these lines would not have been incorporated into *autos* composed for the religious stage. In these instances, Fortune is simply not given her divine meaning of Providence.

This worldly Fortune is, of course, extremely useful to the lyric poets. Garcilaso employs the common figures of speech:

> But Fortune, ever eager for my ruin,
> Gives me no rest, and heaps up trial on trial;
> Now from my home, now from my love she takes me,
> Testing my constancy in countless ways.[79]

This is the Fortune to which the stoically fortified heart can offer resistance and to which all manner of reproaches may be directed. She may appear at any time, in any writer. The other Fortune, a mere name for Providence, is also likely to appear at any time, in any place, as in Pedro Mexía's miscellany, *Silva de varia lección* (1540): "I have gone to some length to explain a thing which, since it is nothing, has no value at all. But I chose to do so in order that the ignorant mass of men, and ignorant Christians, may lose the unfortunate custom of complaining against, or of praising, Fortune; because there is no Fortune, and they should understand that everything comes from God, and that to him alone should they address their petitions in time of trouble." [80] In this attitude Mexía is seconded by Antonio de Torquemada who, in his *Coloquios satíricos* (1553), recognizes that, by Divine concession, many events of the physical world are controlled by Fortune, and causes Fortune herself to cite this Divine permission in self-defence: "Do not be surprised, or blame me, or address me in such harsh and offensive terms, for after all I do as I am commanded, I have a Superior to obey, and by His will I govern and control my actions." [81]

The Christianized Stoic attitude toward Fortune is expressed, at about the same time, by Cristóbal de Castillejo (d. 1550):

> Nor, to be brief, is there left to me
> More than my soul to lose;
> And it, Fortuna, is safe from thee,

---

79. "Mas la fortuna, de mi mal no harta, / me aflige, y de un trabajo en otro lleva; / ya de la patria, ya del bien me aparta, / ya mi paciencia en mil maneras prueba" (*Egloga III*, lines 17–20).

80. Ed. Bibliófilos Españoles (Madrid, 1933), I, 449.

81. *Ed. cit.*, p. 573b; see also the third quotation at the opening of this chapter.

Nor canst thou its freedom abuse,
For thy jurisdiction must ever be
Subject to God. . . .[82]

Jorge de Montemayor—no rejector "of the austere and other-worldly Christian ideals," as Gilbert Highet assumed[83]—makes literary use of Fortuna as a means of plot development and de-nouement in his *Diana*. In Volume I of the present work we saw that in the novelistic genre prior to the advent of the pastoral, plot development required—in contrast to the static quality of courtly *amor purus*—the passage from lyric adoration to dramatic touch, and, very frequently, to intercourse (*amor mixtus*) in clandestine marriage, the final unraveling being provided by a public marriage. The problem of settling the ultimate relationships of various pairs of lovers in the ethereal setting of the pastoral required a different solution. In order not to fix the individual forever in an unchanging vital attitude, it was necessary to adapt Neoplatonic psychological attitudes to the dynamics of the novel. The solution of the romances of chivalry being unsuitable, Montemayor had only one recourse: an appeal to the supernatural, that is to say, to the magic of Felicia's "enchanted water" in matters of love, to For-tune in other matters. We have noted above that the Portuguese (not the Spanish) Inquisition deleted references to Fate in Cer-vantes' pastoral, *La Galatea*. In the preliminary pages of Gonzalo de Saavedra's imitation of the *Diana*, *Los pastores del Betis* (1633), the author's son and editor shows a slight theological concern, say-ing of his father: "during his lifetime the author . . . always in-sisted that the words Fate, Chance, Fortune, Luck, gods, and others like them, were words taken from the language of pagan pastoral literature . . . , since everything in the book is subject to the cor-rection and censure of the . . . Church." Juan Bautista Avalle-Arce, who studies these matters, finds this attitude "very character-

---

82. "No me queda, en conclusión, / sino el alma que perder, / do no basta tu poder; / que de tu jurisdición / la quiso Dios defender" (*Obras*, ed. J. Domínguez-Bordona [Madrid, 1926–28], III, 51).

83. See Highet's treatment of Pastoral and Romance in *The Classical Tradition: Greek and Roman Influences on Western Literature* (New York–London, 1949), p. 169. Highet is unaware that Montemayor, in his *Cancionero espiritual* (1554, 1558) and in his *Exposición moral del Salmo 86* (1548) was the first Peninsular poet who felt the majestic music of the Psalms and sought to express it in the new Italianate hen-decasyllable verse introduced by Boscán. See Bataillon, *Erasmo y España* (Mexico City–Buenos Aires, 1950), II, 208; and our Volume I, Index, *s. v.* Montemayor.

istic of the seventeenth century, when the concept of Fortune was either denied outright, or was replaced by that of Providence."[84] The evidence presented in this chapter shows, I believe, that while at times there was indeed a certain *gêne* or uneasiness in these matters, and some writers like Mexía would have wished to deflect the attention of the masses from the thorny problems of Providence, the concepts here specified by Avalle-Arce are "characteristic," not only of the seventeenth, but of the fifteenth and sixteenth centuries as well.

In *Don Quijote* (I, ix), Cervantes seems to equate the terms "Heaven," "Chance," and "Fortune": "although I know well that if Heaven, Chance and Fortune had not helped me, the world would have been deprived of the pleasure and the pastime" of the story (contained in Cide Hamete Benengeli's "manuscript account"). In Cervantes' play *La Entretenida*, composed at approximately the same time, Nature appears to be identical with Fortune:

> It was Nature that determined
> The fate of every mortal
> Compounded of bane and blessing . . . ;
> He who wept yesterday laughs today;
> He who once laughed, his tears cannot stay.[85]

In his poetic epistle to Mateo Vázquez, composed during his captivity in Algiers to urge that the Spanish King undertake the capture of that city, Cervantes refers to his own *implacables hados* — implacable fate — which caused him to fall into the enemy's power and, in his direct appeal to the royal Secretary, he dwells on the latter's merits, the gift not of Fate or earthly Fortune, but of personal integrity and worth:

> Neither the false, unresting wheel of Fortune,
> Nor planetary sign, nor star, nor yet Ventura,
> Nor luck of any sort, raised you to greatness. . . .[86]

That all the serious references to Fortune and Fate stand for Providence is clear from other statements scattered throughout

---

84. *La novela pastoril española* (Madrid, 1959), pp. 68–69, 194.

85. "Naturaleza compuso / la suerte de los mortales / entre bienes y entre males. . . . / Ayer lloraba el que hoy ríe, / y hoy llora el que ayer rió" (*Obras completas*, ed. A. Valbuena Prat [Madrid, 1956], p. 478).

86. "Ni la inconstante rueda presurosa / de la falsa fortuna, suerte o hado, / signo, ventura, estrella ni otra cosa, / dice que es causa que en el buen estado / que ahora poseéis os haya puesto . . . " (*Obras, ed. cit.*, pp. 58–59).

Cervantes' works. Reverting to *La Entretenida*, we find Don Antonio correcting a reference to "ever unstable Fortune" and replacing it by "el cielo firme"—the firm design of heaven.[87] In the *Persiles* (IV, xiv) we read: "those unaccountable changes fall under the power of her who commonly is called Fortune, though she is none other than the unchanging will of Heaven."[88] The two Fortunes are defined in a single conversation between Don Quijote and his Squire. The latter, one day when he is in a philosophical mood (*muy filósofo*) and is able to find words for his thoughts (*muy a lo discreto*), declares that, if his memory serves him, he has heard it said that "she whom people call Fortune is a drunken and fickle woman, and above all blind, so that she does not see what she is doing any more than she knows whom she is exalting or casting down"; to which Don Quijote replies: "I can assure you that there is no fortune in the world, and that the good and evil things that happen in the world do not come by chance, but by special design of Heaven."[89] Although the word fortune is not mentioned, it is appropriate to end our discussion of Cervantes with these words pronounced by the semirepentant witch in *El coloquio de los perros*: "All the misfortunes which come to people, to kingdoms, to cities, and to nations; the sudden deaths, the shipwrecks, the falls, in short, all the evils called evils of injury, come from the hand of the Most High and from His permitting will; and the evils and disasters called evils of guilt come from and are caused by ourselves" (*Obras, ed. cit.*, p. 1017a).

By the year 1588, three years after the publication of Cervantes' *La Galatea*, Lope de Vega had made himself the foremost dramatist of Madrid. The national drama that he created and his followers developed made much use of Fortune as a literary theme, even in the titles of plays: *Próspera* (or *Adversa*) *Fortuna de D. Alvaro de Luna*; *Próspera* (or *Adversa*) *Fortuna de don Bernardo de Ca-*

87. "¿No es locura / hacer caso de honra los sucesos / varios de la fortuna, siempre instable, / o por mejor decir, del cielo firme?" (*ibid.*, p. 466).
88. "estas mudanzas tan extrañas caen debajo del poder de aquella que comúnmente se llama Fortuna, que no es otra cosa sino un firme disponer del Cielo" (*ibid.*, p. 1713).
89. II, 66. On Cervantes' favorite concept, that each man may be the maker of his own *ventura*, see A. F. G. Bell, *Cervantes* (Norman, Oklahoma, 1947), p. 217. See F. López Estrada, *op. cit.*, pp. 431 ff., and "La influencia italiana en la *Galatea* de Cervantes," *CL*, IV (1952), 161–69. For Calderón's use of *ventura* to mean gamblers' luck, see below, note 133.

brera; La rueda de la Fortuna. This is the worldly Fortune, the symbol of mutability. Lope's concept of Fortune and Fate in his dramatic works has been studied by Miss Helen L. Sears in her unpublished doctoral dissertation (UCLA, 1949). "Lope de Vega," she concludes, "inherited from earlier periods two concepts of Fortune: an independent power of pagan ancestry, which is often associated with human iniquity and seems to act in opposition to the divine will; and the Christian Fortune, a minister who carries out the divine providence. In the latter concept, Lope confuses Fortune and Fate and identifies both with divine determinism; Fortune becomes an allegorical figure which, like other allegorical and mythological characters, assists in fulfilling the divine predestination." [90]

In 1596 Alonso López Pinciano published his exposition of Aristotle's *Poetics*, the *Philosophia antigua poética*, in which he gives considerable attention to Fortune, declaring "that if Fortune is a cause without a reason, and if God is the cause of all that exists, then everything is guided by reason and Fortune has no existence at all." But he adds: "with respect to men, Fortune does exist in the manner explained, which is a cause without any reason and purely accidental." Or, as another of the interlocutors expresses it: "when wise men are concerned there is little Fortune; when God is concerned, there is none, because He is the supreme wisdom who, with cause, moves everything; for which reason some concluded that Fortune did not exist, since everything was guided by the Divine reason." [91] This summary meets with favor: "Bien estoy con esse dicho."

The seventeenth century

A similar argument appears in *El Bernardo* (1624) of Bernardo de Balbuena. Various learned men, the poet says, seeing that the world of mundane events was, as they thought, deistically dissev-

90. See Green, "Sobre las dos Fortunas . . . ," p. 152, n. 36.
91. "si la fortuna es causa sin razón, y, de todo quanto ay, es Dios la causa, luego todo es guiado con razón; luego nada es la fortuna"; "acerca de los hombres, ay fortuna de la manera que es dicho, que es vna causa sin razón alguna y accidental"; "acerca de los sabios ay poca de fortuna, y acerca de Dios, ninguna, porque es la summa sabiduría que, con causa, lo mueue todo; atendiendo a lo qual dixeron algunos que no auía fortuna, porque todo era guiado con razón diuina" (ed. Alfredo Carballo Picazo [Madrid, 1953], I, 108; see also p. 106).

ered from "the holy Heaven" and without law or dependency in its government, conluded that this was the cause of mankind's floundering in a world of blessings and disasters, Fortune having been entrusted with the shaping of events, as "the clock of the en-tire divine order." But this is not true; there are

> natural laws
> Which shape the natural course of human life;
> Not all takes place by heavenly miracle,
> Nor yet by chance or luck inscrutable[92]

—for the simple reason that many ills have their origin in the human will. There are also cases in which prudence cannot possibly prevent trouble. In such cases luck does play a part: the matter being uncontrollable by the human will, one man may succeed where another may fail; indeed, one may

> Find life when all he wants to find is death.[93]

Quevedo shares the common interest in, and concern about, the two Fortunes. He presents *Ocasio* as the servingmaid of Fortune and bids all to listen to her words. *Ocasio* speaks: "If fools let me pass, why am I to blame for having passed? . . . If they know [that the wheel of my Mistress] is a wheel, that it rises and falls, that it falls in order to rise and rises in order to fall, why do they ride on it? The sun has been known to stop, Fortune's wheel, never. . . ."[94] But Quevedo often adopts the theological interpretation: "Life is not subject to the varied movements of Fortune, nor does it depend on chance; rather, it is governed by the ineffable providence of the Lord, with which He disposes and governs all things."[95]

Gracián knows the two Fortunes. Worldly Fortune's house, he says in *El Discreto*, has two doors, and all mortals enter through

92. "modos naturales / con que sus cursos corren nuestras vidas, / que ni es todo milagros celestiales / ni todo caso y suertes no entendidas" (ed. J. Van Horne [Urbana, Illinois, 1927], Book I, lines 40–43).

93. "Hallar la vida por buscar la muerte" (*ibid.*, line 46).

94. "si los tontos me dejan pasar, ¿qué culpa tengo yo de haber pasado? . . . Si saben que [la rueda de mi ama] es rueda, y que sube y baja, y que por esta razón baja para subir y sube para bajar, ¿para qué se devanan en ella? El sol se ha parado; la rueda de la Fortuna, nunca. . . ." (*Obras en prosa, ed. cit.*, p. 228b).

95. "La vida no está sujeta a los movimientos varios de la fortuna, ni depende de caso; antes es gobernada de la inefable providencia del Señor, con la cual dispone y gobierna Su Magestad todas las cosas" (*ibid*, p. 839a).

one of them; "but there is an inviolable and inexorable law that he who enters through the one must emerge by the other; so that no man may issue forth through the door whereat he entered, but through its opposite: he who entered through pleasure must depart through pain; and he who entered by the gate of pain emerges invariably by the gate of pleasure." [96] In *El Criticón*, Time actually rides on the *Rueda de la Ocasión*, the wheel of *Ocasio*. Yet in *Primor* X of *El Héroe* we have the classic Christian definition of Fortune as outlined in the introductory pages of the present chapter.

We shall end by recalling the simplest statement of all, that of Calderón: "There is no Fortune but God."

SUMMARY: FORTUNE IN OTHER COUNTRIES AND IN SPAIN

In a chapter entitled "The Concept of the Renaissance," in Frederico Chabod's *Machiavelli and the Renaissance*, the author asks:

How, then, is it possible to reconcile all these divergent forces — man, nature and God? The answer is never clear. Instead, we are confronted with a vacillation between one or the other of the terms of the problem, or with the intrusion of ambiguous notions like that of Fortune. . . . "Fortune" is very hard to define. At one moment, in conformity with the Christian adaptation of the ancient concept, it appears in the guise of an *ancilla Dei*. At another, it resumes its ancient character of a blind, uncontrollable fate. Now it becomes a magic influence radiating from the stars, now the natural consequence of preceding events, though it always defies precise analysis. And we find phrases and similes of a naturalistic or positively medical character creeping into political treatises and histories. . . .[97]

Don Cameron Allen, treating of astrology in fifteenth-century Italy, finds that:

The nature of fortune and the remedies for fortune were two major questions of the Renaissance, and the humanistic treatises on these problems are many. Poggio . . . advises one not to seek after the external goods of fortune, but to cultivate a . . . tranquil mind. Coluccio Salutati, who . . . believed like Pico in free will, identifies fortune with providence and believes in a sort of predestination. Alberti . . . urges the life of contemplation as an anodyne for

96. Cited by M. Romera-Navarro in his edition (Philadelphia, 1938–40) of *El Criticón*, I, 313, n. 162.
97. Cambridge, Massachusetts, 1958, pp. 189–90.

the blows of fortune. Enea Silvio Piccolomini says . . . that a tranquil mind
can endure the jests of fortune, but . . . [he also urges] men to follow fortune
and points out that men are miserable only when they fly from the fickle
goddess. Pico . . . mentioned this matter in the *Disputationes*. Ficino . . . finds
a certain irrationality in the cosmic process, the uncaused cause. Providence,
he thinks, can overcome fortune, and so can wisdom. Pontano . . . [concludes
that] the true Christian is satisfied that the decisions of God are just; he does
not ask for reasons. God . . . is a delegator of duties. Some of these duties are
assigned to Fortune. . . .[98]

In England, according to E. M. W. Tillyard, the moving forces
in the time of Elizabeth were Providence, fortune, and human
character:

For the sway of fortune the image of the wheel is presented both in literature and in picture; and at times it is presented with such concrete circumstance as both to risk absurdity and to turn the spectator's or the reader's
thoughts from the stars with their subtly penetrating influences. There are
those grossly physical pictures of human beings, realistically dressed, clinging
or tied to what seems a large cart wheel, in process of being turned aloft or
hurled in undignified somersault onto the ground; or there is this from Hamlet: "Out, out, thou strumpet, Fortune.[99]

John Calvin (d. 1564) was "concerned to refute the false interpretation that men placed upon the chaotic character of historical
events and personal destinies. Even when God seemed to be operating in an arbitrary and capricious way through fortune, order
prevailed."[100] As Calvin explained: "the chaunces as well of pros-
peritie as of aduersitie, the reason of the flesh doeth ascrybe to fortune. But whosoeuer is taught by the mouth of Chryst, that all the
heares of hys hed are numbered, will seke for a cause further of[f],
and wyll fyrmelye beleue that all chaunces are gouerned by the
secrete councell of God."[101] In another place he declared that we
must not interpret this Divine regulation of all things as either
Stoic fate or mere chance, since what we call chance is that "with
the reason and cause of which we are not acquainted."[102]

98. *The Star-Crossed Renaissance* (Durham, North Carolina, 1941), pp. 40 ff.
99. *The Elizabethan World Picture* (London, 1948), p. 48.
100. Charles Trinkaus, "Renaissance Problems in Calvin's Theology," *Studies in
the Renaissance*, I (1954), 65.
101. Cited by H. Baker, *The Dignity of Man: Studies in the Persistence of an Idea*
(Cambridge, Massachusetts, 1947), p. 230.
102. H. Baker, *The Wars of Truth: Studies in the Decay of Christian Humanism
in the Earlier Seventeenth Century* (Cambridge, Massachusetts, 1952), p. 14.

Sir Thomas Browne, who died in 1682, one year after Calderón, in the following quotation expresses perfect agreement with Calderón's doctrine: "Let not Fortune, which hath no name in Scripture, have any in thy Divinity. Let Providence, not Chance, have the honour of thy acknowledgements, and be thy Oedipus in Contingencies. Mark well the paths and windings thereof. . . . The hand of Providence writes often by abbreviations, hieroglyphics or short characters, which, like Laconism on the Wall, are not to be made out but by a hint or key from that Spirit which indicted them." [103]

From this quick survey it appears that the Spanish solutions generally coincide most closely with the solutions provided by non-Spanish Europeans of deep religious persuasion: Calvin, Browne, and — as we saw earlier — Bossuet.

FATE

Fate, too, is a name.[104] The semimystic poet Francisco de Aldana (d. 1575), in a poetic epistle to Arias Montano, "On the Contemplation of God, and the Preparation therefore," does not hestitate to preface the expression of his aspirations to union with the Godhead with a listing of his complaints against Fate, which is here indistinguishable from Fortune:

> I am a man, alone and unprotected,
> Exposed to Fate's rude blows; a withered leaf
> Shaken by cruel winds; a human being
> Whose life in Time is like a cruel inferno
> Of harsh events; of good bereft, by evil
> Beset at every turn.[105]

103. Cited by Baker, *ibid.*, p. 18.
104. "The distinction between Fortune and the Fates . . . or . . . Destiny is . . . difficult to settle. The abstract word 'fate' as embodying the will of God was in the earliest medieval times accepted by the philosophers and the Church Fathers; but as early as Boethius Fate tended to become a changeable, almost a whimsical, force, and to approach Fortune in manner if not in figure. Medieval writers never seem to be quite clear about the distinction between Fate and Fortune. . . . But . . . Fortune was not lost among the Fates; rather, the Fates submitted to her" (Patch, *op. cit.*, pp. 78–79).
105. "Yo soy un hombre desvalido y solo, / espuesto al duro hado, cual marchita / hoja al rigor del descortés Eolo; / mi vida temporal anda precita / dentro el infierno del común trafago / que siempre añade un mal y un bien nos quita" (*Poesías*, ed. Elias L. Rivers [Madrid, 1957], p. 57). See also pp. 109, 115, 120, 121, 132. "Through Provi-

Aldana is "alone and unprotected" only in his *vida temporal*, his life in Time. The *duro hado*, Fate, merely symbolizes the "blows of circumstance" which, ever since evil obtained a foothold in the world, have fallen at random in the "rough injustice" of common experience.[106] It is in this sense that Erasmus (d. 1536), who devoted his life to the cause of restoring Christianity to a state of purity and simplicity worthy of its Founder, wrote to Servais Roger: *vellem eam mihi vitae libertatem fata sinerent natura quam contulit* — "I would that the Fates would allow to my life that liberty which Nature [*Natura naturans*] conferred upon it."[107] Fate here is a mere figure of speech, as in these lines from a Spanish religious *auto* (ca. 1520) based on the story of Jacob's flight to the land of Aram. In it a shepherd says to Rachel: *Dios la dé muy buenos hados* — "God grant that Fate smile upon you." It is almost like wishing someone good morning.[108] Other views of the problem could be less lighthearted. We have already seen how Isidore of Seville in the seventh century, like Pedro Mexía in the sixteenth, preferred to keep such thorny questions out of people's heads.[109]

Fate as a problem

Menéndez y Pelayo, in his *Historia de los heterodoxos españoles* (*ed. cit*, I, 408), cites particularly uses of the feminine word *fadas*, a derivative of the Latin plural *fatum*, and quotes texts of fatalistic tendency from Juan Ruiz's *Book of Good Love*, from the anonymous *Poema de Alfonso XI* (1348), and from popular proverbs. Ruiz wrote: *Que las mis fadas negras non se parten de mí* — "I can't escape from my unlucky Fate" (*copla* 824d).[110] These expressions may be regarded, as Menéndez y Pelayo suggests, as intrusions into learned works of popular superstition.

dence," says Ficino, "the soul is above Fate; but through nature, the body is subordinate to fate" (cited in Allen, *op. cit.*, p. 57).

106. E. LaB. Cherbonnier, "Biblical Faith and the Idea of Tragedy," in Scott (ed.), *The Tragic Vision . . .* , p. 46.

107. Cited by Lucien Febvre, *Le problème de l'incroyance au XVIᵉ siècle* (Paris, 1947), p. 333.

108. *Aucto de cuando Jacob fue huyendo a tierras de Aran*, cited by Edward Glaser, "El patriarca Jacob, amante ejemplar del teatro del siglo de oro español," *BHi*, LVIII (1956), 7.

109. See above, note 80 and text.

110. It is equally easy to cite old texts showing the masculine form, *fados* or *hados*; see José María Aguado, *Vocabulario sobre Juan Ruiz* (Madrid, 1929), under the words in question and also under *fadar*.

The same manner of speaking is found in the *Cancionero de Baena*, as in the following lines by "un bachiller en artes de Salamanca:"

> Nor would I, believe me, ever think of daring
> To flatter you in anything I write,
> Since such an abundance of gifts and fair graces
> Upon you were showered by your planet and fate.[111]

At about the same time, Mena apostrophizes the Fates:

> O unrelenting, pestiferous error,
> O proud, cruel Fates, like ravening wolves,
> You who take from us the best and the truest,
> Permitting long life to the basest of men![112]

On this passage, Hernán Núñez in his edition and commentary on the *Laberinto* wrote: "Seneca says in his first tragedy: unjust Fortune rarely spares men adorned with great virtues, and Statius in the last *Sylva* of the second Book, in which he deplores the death of Lucan, complains of the Fates . . . and sets up Lucan as an example, because he died very young. . . . Likewise Lactantius Firmianus in Book III of his *Diurnales Institutiones* writes that in war the bravest and most valiant are wont to perish."[113]

Essentially contemporaneous with our "bachelor in arts from Salamanca" and with Mena is the *Arçipreste de Talavera* or *Corbacho* of Alfonso Martínez de Toledo. The *Media Parte* of this work treats, as we have seen, *del común fablar de fados, fortuna, sygnos, e planetas* — of the expressions "Fates," "Fortune," "signs and planets." All of these words the author equates with "Necessity" (*ed. cit.*, p. 244). Against such personifications of determinism he argues for free will, aided by Divine grace: the saints in their successful contending with evil influences "do not pray to signs or planets, to Fate or Fortune, but to God Almighty" (*ibid.*, p. 249). There is no necessity; the will is free (p. 250). If fate (*mal sygno, planeta, o fado*) existed, there could be no Divine justice (*ibid.*).

---

111. "Nin yo, bien creades, que fuesse osado / de lisonjar en los mis sermones, / pues tan perfeto de graçias e dones / a vos costelaron planetas e fado" (ed. P. J. Pidal [Madrid, 1851], p. 92).

112. "¡O porfioso pestífero error! / o Fados crueles, soberuios, rabiosos, / que siempre robades los más virtuosos, / e perdonades la gente peor" (*Laberinto* . . . , stanza 198).

113. *Ed. cit.*, p. 406. I abbreviate the commentary.

Persons who are not theologians should not worry or dispute concerning these matters: *dexarse dello sabyeza es* (p. 251). The arguments and examples which he gives are Augustinian: *E esta tal nescesydad de ser o non ser . . . se rrefiere a la diuinal prouidencia de Nuestro Señor* — God's providence rules over all (p. 254).

In all of this there is more than a mere matter of figures of speech, says the Archpriest of Talavera: "the worst part, and the most sinful aspect of it, is that they believe that this is really so, and have faith in their assertion" — for example, that a child's death is caused by his Ventura. And this sin is not taken seriously: *e por nuestros pecados . . . este pecado en vso de las gentes que ya non es tenido en nada.* Even great men and learned ones say these things no less than *synples ynorantes* (p. 255). As proof, he cites the last of the Decretals, *On Customs*: "Established usage" does not minimize the sinfulness of the practice (or belief); let no one appeal to Fortune or Fate (p. 257).

Yet the use of the condemned figures continued. At times they carried with them a sufficient suspicion of belief for action to be taken. In its expurgated edition of Torres Naharro's *Propalladia* (1573) the Inquisition deleted "a fatalistic reference to predestination," [114] an action very exceptional in Spain. Definitions and explanations of fate, on the other hand, were repeated with some frequency.

We shall consider some of these expositions of the problem. Alfonso de la Torre's *Visión delectable* belongs to the same period as the text just quoted (*ca.* 1440; first ed. *ca.* 1480). Chapter XIII treats of Providence, Fate, and Fortune, and "declares marvelous secrets." After discussing the Three Fates (the Parcae of the ancients) and the idea that not even God's providence could alter the course of events as determined by Necessity, the author points out that this doctrine renders useless all human action, all exercise of virtue. The hanged man did not need to be a thief; he would have been hanged anyway. The next chapter "declares the true belief in the Providence of God." The planets are merely God's servants, His "treasurers," who at all times carry out His will, or His express bidding. In so far as they execute in Time what God determined

114. *Ed. cit.*, I, 71. On the general leniency of the Inquisition in its treatment of the *Propalladia*, see pp. 68 ff.

before Time was, they are called *fado*, Fate, which signifies a concatenation of causes.[115]

In the early sixteenth century we have the exposition of Vives in which two types of "fate" are described: one, God's immutable will;[116] the other, the mutable determination of the stars — mutable in the sense that God, in response to the individual's efforts and attitude, may change the course of events as astrologically determined.[117]

Antonio de Torquemada represents opinion at mid-century. According to the scholar who has studied this matter most closely, Torquemada's conception of fortune and chance, fate and free will, nature, the supernatural, and astrology, amounts to this: the basis of his philosophical concepts is complete subservience of all to God. "Nothing can be conceived as operating distinctly from Him; all power is inherent in Him. Luis Zapata [d. 1595], in one sentence, expressed not only his own opinion, but Torquemada's too, when he said: *Fortuna, suerte, ni destino, ni hado, no hay otro sino la diuina voluntad* — 'Fortune, luck, destiny, fate, all are merely expressions signifying the Divine will.'"[118]

To Juan de Mal Lara, whose *Filosofía vulgar* was published in 1568, *hado* is "a manner of speaking used by the gentiles, like others that have remained in our language and are passing out of use."[119] Fray Juan de Pineda, in his *Agricultura christiana*, treats the subject from three points of view: that of the philosophers, that of the poets, and that of the theologians. The ordinary language of the poets recognizes three Fates — the Parcae. Catullus

115. "y aquestos planetas o signos no tienen oficio sino de mayordomos o tesoreros, ca ellos hacen por los años et tiempos aquello que la Providencia ordenó ante todos los tiempos; y aquesta consideración es llamado *fado*, que quiere decir ligamiento de causas" (*ed. cit.*, p. 360a; see also p. 359a). The Augustinian teaching on all these matters is expounded in various chapters of Córdoba's *Compendio de la Fortuna*.

116. "Fate considered in regard to second causes is changeable, but as subject to Divine Providence it derives a certain unchangeableness" (St. Thomas, *Summa*, I, q. 116, art. 4).

117. See Vives' "Vigilia al margen del 'Sueño de Escipión,'" in *Obras completas*, trans. L. Riber (Madrid, 1947–48), I, 644b–45a.

118. James H. Elsdon, "Aspects of a Study of the Life and Works of Antonio de Torquemada" (unpublished thesis, University of California, 1934), p. 49. The reference is to Zapata's *Miscelánea*; see the ed. of Pascual de Gayangos (Madrid, 1859), p. 298.

119. "En lo que dixe *viniese su hado*, es manera de hablar de los gentiles, como han quedado otras que ya se van desusando" (*ed. cit.*, III, 211). See also the quotation from Mal Lara that is one of the three epigraphs introducing our present chapter.

calls them "old," and "we read almost the same designation in our romances of chivalry."[120] What the poets call Fates, the philosophers call *Fatum* or *Hado*. Among learned men who know Latin, it is an eloquent way of expressing oneself to say, of someone who has died: *concessit fatis,* he has yielded to the fates. Pineda, a theologian, now gives his own definition: "Fate . . . is nothing other than the fatal necessity emanating from the eternal law by means of the order and concatenation of second causes, which concur to produce effects in accordance with the decrees of the First Cause, which is God Almighty."[121] In other words, Fate means only "the necessity which all things have to obey the Divine will, from which no escape is possible" (*ibid.*).

Fray Juan defines the concept even more explicitly: "Fate is nothing other than an order and an everlasting interconnection of of things whereby the universe is maintained in the order which God gave it; and Seneca . . . defines it as the necessity according to which all things proceed, without possible deviation, and this is simply God's will" (*ibid.*). He reconciles this Fate with Free Will and advises against the use of the term, for such language is frivolous: *tal lenguaje quán friuolo sea, y quán engorroso de entender, todos lo entendéis* (fol. 271v). Theologians could well be satisfied with the things already said on this subject, but it is desirable to corroborate this with the authority of *sanctos y grandes theólogos*: St. Augustine condemns the use of the word *Fatum*; St. Thomas identifies it with providence — *lo que se llama 'hado,' bien entendido de los cathólicos, es parte de la diuina prouidencia* (*ibid.*). Fray Juan concludes: "providence is in the mind and will of God, and Fate resides in the created causes which produce the foreordained effects."[122] It thus appears that the noun *hado* and the verb *hadar* are permissible when used as theologians use them. It is permissible to say that Tom, or Dick, or Harry was happily- or ill-fated in his affairs, for, although we refer all creatures to God and His providence, when we refer to the interrelationships be-

120. Ed. Salamanca, 1589, fol. 269v.
121. "Hado . . . no es otra cosa que aquella necesidad fatal emanante de la ley eterna, mediante la orden y trauazón de las causas segundas, que concurren a la produción de los efectos, conforme a la disposición de la causa primera, que es Dios omnipotente" (*ibid.*, fol. 270v).
122. "la prouidencia está en Dios, y el hado en las causas criadas que produzen los efectos hadados" (*ibid.*, fol. 272).

tween creatures as they are acted on by natural causes and effects, this is where Fate comes in.[123] We are thus brought back to the position of Vives: Fate is both God's immutable intention and the mutable influence of the stars, alterable by prayer, faith, good works, and the gift of grace.

In 1635 Antonio López de Vega published his *Paradoxas racionales*, in which *hado* signifies the human condition: "and that other idea of Seneca, that by taking thought (*dum putas*) a prudent man can and should make his pains tolerable, applies to troubles not brought upon oneself through one's own fault [*por elección del desvarío*], but to those that come to man through mortality or what people call fate." [124]

Fate in Spanish literature

We have already given some examples of the use of the word *hado* and its congeners in early literary texts, through the fifteenth century. In the religious drama of the sixteenth century there are two distinct attitudes toward "fate." Diego Sánchez de Badajoz (*fl.* 1525–47) in his *Farsa de la Fortuna* attacks the belief that there is any "fate" but God. The Knight speaks to the Shepherd:

> *Caballero.* — In what you have said about fate
> I am bound to undeceive you,
> For being and life and estate
> Are assigned by none other than God. . . .
> *Pastor.* — Now I understand your meaning:
> There is no good, no evil fate.[125]

In *Las Cortes de la Muerte*, by Micael de Carvajal and Luis Hurtado de Toledo (1557), *hado* is merely a word, an expression signifying providence or God's will: Death, in broadcasting the

123. "por lo qual se dize que Hulano tuuo buen hado o mal hado en sus sucessos, porque referirse a solo Dios las criaturas, es de la diuina prouidencia, mas el referirse vnas a otras según la orden y dependencia entre causas y efectos naturales, éste es el punto del hado" (*ibid.*).

124. "i essotro de Séneca, que con la opinión [*levem, dum putas, facies*] se puede i deue hazer el prudente tolerables los dolores, se entiende de los que no vienen por elección del desvarío, sino de los que trae la mortalidad, o lo que llaman hado" (ed. E. Buceta [Madrid, 1935], p. 68).

125. "Deso que dizes del hado / yo quiero desengañarte, / que Dios es el que reparte / el ser y vida y estado." "Ya yo entiendo la historia, / que no ay bueno ni ay mal hado" (From *Recopilación en Metro*, facsimile ed. of the Academia Española [Madrid, 1929], fol. ciii r and v).

call to the "Court of Death," expresses the hope that all who voice petitions there may have their wishes fulfilled:

> And may God and his fates grant
> That you obtain your heart's desire.

Some pages later, the Poor Man tries to encourage his fainting children:

> Let your hearts be lifted up,
> Knowing that God and his fates
> Chose to give us holy poverty.[126]

In early secular drama, the situation is very similar. In Gil Vicente's (d. 1563?) play *Don Duardos*, based on a popular novel of chivalry, the "divinity that shapes our ends" is spoken of in one breath in the language of pagan mythology, and in the next as *Dios*, the Christian God. Don Duardos soliloquizes:

> And you, unworthy eyes of mine,
> What fates sent you
> (Since you're surely not divine)
> To look upon the loveliest orbs
> That the great gods did incline
> To make of clay? [127]

Two pages farther on he says that while other great ladies are but shadows, mere tapestry figures, the ladies he is addressing were formed with special care by the Creator: *y tales os hizo Dios.*[128]

For all the advice against the use of the word *Fatum* that St. Augustine and his Spanish interpreters in our period dispensed, the word was regularly used in devotional poetry. The Portuguese André Froes de Macedo published his *Amores divinos*, in Castilian, in 1631 at Lisbon. In it are two sonnets "that stir in one the love of God," as the headings indicate. In this first, the object of contemplation is a tomb, which the beholder is expected to take as a symbol of the ephemeralness of life and of all earthly glory:

> If you, amazed, should doubt, if in your ignorance
> You know not how this change has come to be,

126. "Y ¡Plega a Dios y a sus hados / que alcancen lo que pidieren"; "Procurá ir regocijados, / pues que Dios quiso y sus hados / darnos la sancta pobreza" (*BAE*, XXXV, 4a, 14a).

127. "Y vos, mis ojos indinos, / ¿cuáles *hados* os mandaron, / siendo humanos, / ir a ver los más divinos / que los dioses matizaron / con sus manos?" (ed. Dámaso Alonso [Madrid, 1942], p. 60).

128. *Ibid.*, p. 62. We find the same use of the concept a century later in Calderón.

> Know that relentless Fate, like a vast sea,
> Engulfs and humbles human arrogance.

In the second sonnet, the mariner is urged to remember, when the sea is calm, the reversals brought by sudden, violent change:

> If in the supreme peace of quiet seas
> You think yourself beyond the reach of waves,
> You'll see that every beach this ocean laves
> Can wreak Fate's vengeance; that ruin follows ease.[129]

This same year, 1631, saw the death of Bartolomé Leonardo de Argensola, Canon of the Cathedral of La Seo in Saragossa. In 1610 he had composed an elegy for the consolation of his (and Cervantes') patron, the Conde de Lemos, who had not been able to master his grief over the loss (in 1608) of a brother, the Conde de Gelves. The deceased was stricken, the poet says, by *accidente*, by a sudden physical reversal,

> que anticipó los términos del hado

— which cut him off before his time, shortening the life span set by Fate. As wild winds tear leaves from a tree,

> So do the unkind Fates with absolute power
> disturb the order of things subordinate,
> exacting tribute, heeding not the hour.

All is mutability: even tombs erode in time, even they are subject to Fate:

> Los sepulcros también sienten sus hados.

Not all is lost, however; above the world of mutability is the changeless Abode of the Blest:

> Think how the light of true philosophy
> Guides us by paths propitious and benign
> To that fair region where all blessings be;
> Where every building, by God's great design
> Houses, on golden streets, celestial choirs
> And souls elect Hosannas sing divine —
> Oh glorious home! Oh end of our desires! [130]

129. "Si dudas admirado, si ignorante / la causa del fatal cruel desuío, / sabe que en el rigor del hado impío / acaba humilde todo lo arrogante"; "Si en la bonança del lugar supremo / seguro de las ondas te imaginas / verás, que de los hados las ruinas / te bueluen de vn extremo en otro extremo" (ed. facsim. publ. by Antonio Pérez Gómez [Valencia, 1959], pp. 32–33).

130. "que anticipó los términos del hado" (line 2); "assí los hados turban absolutos /

This poem, full of classical allusions, gave no offense when published in 1634 with the rest of the author's *Rimas*. The various meanings of *hado* which it presents have already been documented; we shall encounter them again, as we review now their use in other writers and in other genres.

Garcilaso de la Vega. In her book on Garcilaso de la Vega, Margot Arce Blanco wrote: "In Garcilaso there is no vacillation; he is absolutely pagan, Stoic and fatalistic. Destiny — Fate — has for him an unquestionable reality." [131] Such a statement appears very questionable today.[132] Garcilaso's use of Fate, Destiny, Luck, *Ventura*,[133] Heaven, is not only indiscriminate, as Margot Arce Blanco says (*op cit.*, p. 57); it is by now thoroughly familiar to us in all its semantic uncertainty. His poetry is largely a poetry of unsatisfied love. Fate — *hado* — is a normal symbol in poetry of this type throughout the centuries we are studying: *el hado, / acerbo, triste, airado* — "bitter, sad, and angry Fate" (*Egloga* II, lines 1248–49). The theme of love by destiny is thoroughly familiar to us from our study of the courtly tradition in Spanish love poetry: the lover is predestined to love a certain lady. Garcilaso, exactly like Amadis of Gaul, suffers such a destiny, determined by his star:

> Not by my will's election did it happen.
> From my first tender years the stars above me
> Inclined me toward that love; my baleful star,
> My destiny drove me onward to my ruin.[134]

There is no need to belabor the point: such expressions are found

el orden de las cosas tributarias, / i dilatan o cobran sus tributos" (lines 40–42); "los sepulcros también sienten sus hados" (line 226); "Mas la luz de más fiel filosofía, / por otros más seguros y propicios, / a la región de la verdad nos guía; / entre cuyos lucientes edificios / forma el número electo de las almas / estruendo de triumfales exercicios. / ¡O eterna pompa, o incorruptibles palmas!" (*Rimas de Lupercio y Bartolomé L. de Argensola*, ed. J. M. Blecua [Zaragoza, 1950–51], II, 342–52).

131. *Garcilaso de la Vega: Contribución al estudio de la lírica española del siglo XVI* (Madrid, 1930), p. 62.

132. See my article, "The Abode of the Blest in Garcilaso's *Egloga Primera*," *RPh*, VI (1953), 272–78, and the pages devoted to Garcilaso in Chapter IV of Volume I of the present work.

133. *Ventura*, in Calderón's *El gran teatro del mundo*, is used to signify gamblers' luck (line 44); see A. A. Parker, *The Allegorical Drama of Calderón* (Oxford–London, 1943), p. 165.

134. "Ni fué por elección de mi albedrío. / Desde mis tiernos y primeros años, / a aquella parte me inclinó mi estrella, / y a aquel fiero destino de mis daños" (*Egloga II*, lines 164 ff.).

everywhere in literature which has for its subject the unhappiness
of the *amant désespéré* — in the courtly verses of the *Cancionero*
poets, in the sentimental novels, in the novels of chivalry, in pastoral novels or eclogues, in the Middle Ages, the Renaissance, and
the Post-Renaissance. I take as an example these lines from an
unknown poet whose use of the Italianate metre marks him as a
follower of Garcilaso:

> It was my eyes, it was my Fate that brought me,
> Led on by every enticement that Love knows
> To this dark cavern of oblivion.[135]

Castillejo. Garcilaso's opponent in the matter of metrical reform
in the sixteenth century, Cristóbal de Castillejo, expresses his distress in identical terms though with infinitely less poetic efficacy:

> It was my luck — no, no, my Fate! —
> Inseparable Nemesis of love,
> That overcame my will and forced me . . .
> Ever to gaze on and desire
> That which evermore must give me
> Vastly more torment than pleasure.[136]

Herrera. Especially illuminating is Fernando de Herrera's (d.
1597) elegy on the death of Don Pedro de Zúñiga. It is, says the
poet, sinful to lament his departure, since his spirit dwells in the
Realm of joy.[137] He cries out against the sorrows of this world —
nuestra mísera vida (line 64); we never raise our eyes to Heav-
en — *nunca alçamos los ojos en el cielo* (line 70); we are enemies
of the glory of that Supreme Abode — *de aquel supremo asiento
soberano* (line 75). Hunger, fear, war, and other ills beset us.
And now! Adverse Fate has taken from us this heroic youth. Happy
he who, caught up to Heaven, joyfully sees the shining stars, and

135. "Mis hados y mis ojos me lleuaron / con el más dulce cebo que amor tiene /
asta el lóbrego centro del olvido" (*Poesías barias y recreación de buenos ingenios*, ed.
J. M. Hill, *Indiana University Studies*, X [1923], 86).

136. "Fué mi suerte, fué mi hado / dolencia casi contina / de amor a mal de mi
grado, / de mi natura forçado, / que, sin yo querer, me inclina / a querer / y a no
poderme abstener / de mirar y desear / lo que sé que me ha de dar / más tormento
que placer" (*Obras*, ed. J. Domínguez Bordona [Madrid, 1926-28], II, 206).

137. "Y culpa si su espíritu desierto / lloro, que en la región del alegría / está,
dexando en tierra el cuerpo muerto" (*Rimas inéditas*, ed. J. M. Blecua [Madrid, 1948],
p. 170; see also p. 168 and note).

before the Kingly Throne seeks remission of the sins of those he left behind![138]

The Pastoral — Montemayor's "Diana." The *Diana* of Montemayor has as its subject *el fino amor* of the courtly tradition, modified by the Neoplatonic interpretations of León Hebreo. The shepherds consider the "blessed sufferings" of love as so many claims to, or titles of, honor; the honor is in proportion to the suffering.[139] We have seen in earlier pages that courtly loves are often poetically spoken of as fated, as determined *ab initio* by an overruling Power. This "irrational" character of love, as seen in the *Diana*, has been overstressed by critics.[140] It is indeed true that the "wise" Felicia says: "Although perfect love is born of reason, it is not governed by it." [141] The more perfect love is, she insists (*ibid.*, p. 196), the greater the psychological upset. These amorous upsets affect most violently persons of noble birth: "In these cases of love . . . the generous spirit and the perceptive intelligence . . . have a great advantage. . . . For since love is virtue, and virtue lodges in the best possible place . . . , persons of high birth will be the best lovers" (p. 170). When asked to explain, Felicia continues: "This advantage resides solely in the individual virtue of the man, that is to say, in having keen judgment, one's thought inclined to lofty things, and other virtues which are born with him." [142] The remedy which Felicia applies to the "disturbed" lovers is a sleep potion. "The philter of the wise Felicia," writes Gustavo Correa, "is not the *deus ex machina* that it has been thought to be. It consists in the deepness of the sleep in which the shepherds and shepherdesses are

138. "Entonces (¡o dolor!) el ímpio hado / arrebató aquel ioven animoso" (lines 82–83); "Dichoso tú, que al çielo arrebatado, / alegre reluzir ves las estrellas / . . . / y ante el immenso Rey esclareçido / que al alto çielo rige y pone freno / al mar, que no se estienda enbraueçido, / . . . / ruegas por nuestras culpas . . ." (lines 139–49).

139. Gustavo Correa, *El Templo de Diana en la novela de Jorge de Montemayor*, (Bogotá, 1961), p. 16.

140. E. g., by A. Solé-Leris, "The Theory of Love in the two *Dianas*: A contrast," *BHS*, XXXVI (1959), 76: "Montemayor's theory is defined by the distinction between *buen* and *falso amor*. The difference betwen the two theories [of Montemayor and of Gil Polo] is obvious on the points of free will and jealousy. . . . For Montemayor, it is of the very essence of true love to be irrational."

141. *Ed. cit.*, p. 197; see also p. 271.

142. "No está en otra cosa sino en la propria virtud del hombre, como es en tener el juyzio vivo, el pensamiento inclinado a cosas altas y otras virtudes que nacen con ellos mismos" (p. 170).

plunged."[143] This remedy is more powerful than the normal action of time (which weakens the memory of the object desired) and is necessary in *enfermedades grandes* — extreme cases of lovesickness. So it is that the "fate" (or the "fortune") that controls the lives of Montemayor's lovers is not an absolute fate. Its effects can be set at naught by means which, though presented as supernatural and magical, are in effect natural.[144] Love, in the *Diana* of Montemayor, is "irrational" in that it produces *turbación*, but this irrationality is relative and temporary. The best lovers, says Montemayor, possess perceptive intelligence and a judgment ever on the alert (*ed. cit.*, p. 170). When love's *turbación* has gone too far, the state of suffering is simply brought to an end. By having experienced it, the lovers attain to a higher level of virtue and worth. Montemayor uses the natural (disguised as supernatural) for artistic, that is to say, literary purposes. He is not expounding an irrationalist conception of human existence. Indeed, it is a condition imposed by Felicia that entrance into the Temple of Diana (the goddess, not the shepherdess of our tale) is limited to those who have remained chaste and faithful to their true loves — a stipulation unthinkable if love (as conceived by Montemayor) were really "irrational" (see p. 165).

The "Diana enamorada." Gaspar Gil Polo's continuation (1564) of Montemayor's novel is much more didactic than the original. The author is unwilling to concede that the *turbación*[145] of traditional chivalric love is a source of virtue,[146] and in his Epistle to the Reader he warns that it is important to guard the soul against such perturbations.[147] There follows "a reasoned criticism aimed at lovers rather than at love, on the ground that the lovers themselves, by surrendering to passion, are responsible for their own sufferings." The whole speech points up the inviolability of the

143. *Op. cit.*, p. 19, n. 15.
144. Correa refers to H. Azima, "Sleep Treatment in Mental Disorders," *Diseases of the Nervous System*, XIX (1958), 523–30; see his note 15.
145. See my *Courtly Love in Quevedo* (Boulder, Colorado, 1952), pp. 41–42; and Gillet–Green, *op. cit.*, pp. 355 ff.
146. In the opinion of Chaucer's Troilus, "the bliss and pathos of a gravely conducted amour are the finest flower of human life" (C. S. Lewis, *The Allegory of Love: A Study in Medieval Tradition* (Oxford, 1936), p. 191).
147. Solé-Leris, *op. cit.*, pp. 66–67.

free will. If love has any power, it is because men make a cult of it, meekly surrendering their heart and their liberty: *ofresciéndole sus corazones, y poniendo en sus manos la propria libertad (ibid., p. 67).* The *sabia* Felicia here attacks the fatalistic view with a direct, didactic appeal for the exercise of will power:

> Your sufferings should serve you, and all those who hear about them, as a lesson to be more on the watch, so as to live more wisely and thus avoid the troubles in which you have floundered so many years. And although by curing you I have given evidence of my science and have gained fame, I would have preferred that you had lived so discreetly that you would have had no need of my services. You lovers will say that it is not in your power not to be overcome by Cupid and become his slaves. To me it appears that whoever serves him becomes his servant and submits to him voluntarily, for there is no human spirit that is not master of its liberty.[148]

We are thus brought back once more to a conclusion by now quite familiar: what seems pagan in these works of literature is not really so. Fate surrenders to the Christian Free Will, by implication in Montemayor (who stresses the upsetting factor of the inevitable *turbación*); directly in Gil Polo (who insists on the power of the human will to resist love's "perturbation," just as theologians and moralists always insist that man's powers of self-determination can resist and overcome the untoward effects of an unfavorable horoscope). *Turbación,* when allowed to get the upper hand, can, like other passions, upset the reason and produce irrational actions (the *primer movimiento* or "first movement"). Lovers under its influence seldom fail to proclaim their helplessness and speak of their "fate." But in the last analysis they are not excused.[149] In an earlier chapter we quoted from Calderón's *El Mágico prodigioso*:

> Thou hast conquered, woman, thou hast conquered,
> By refusing to give in.[150]

148. Cited by Solé-Leris, *ibid.,* p. 69.
149. On the tyranny of the senses — willingly accepted — and the need of grace to overcome it, see Cervantes, *El trato de Argel,* Jornada II: "Quien con amor amargo se entretiene, / y al duro yugo de su servidumbre / el flaco cuello ya inclinado tiene, / si del cielo no viene nunca lumbre / que aquella ceguedad de los sentidos / con claros rayos de razón alumbre, / todos estos remedios son perdidos" — "He who gives himself over to bitter love and the harsh yoke of love's servitude, if he receives no light from heaven to illumine with the rays of reason his blind senses, will find these remedies useless" (*Obras, ed. cit.,* p. 129a). Strangely enough, the speaker is a Moor.
150. "Venciste, mujer, venciste / con no dejarte vencer."

Cervantes. Miguel de Cervantes published his first book, the pastoral novel *La Galatea*, in 1585. As we have seen,[151] Francisco López Estrada has studied his use, in this work, of the confused concepts Fate-stars-heaven-power of the planets — free will — Providence. His statement will bear repeating: "Cervantes had authority," he writes, "for the use of the terms here enumerated: it is found in the scientific books of the period, in their various aspects. I have sought for it with special care among the texts whose date of publication is closest to that of *La Galatea* . . . and in one of them I have found the following chapter, which brings together in a harmonious and orthodox exposition, as far as doctrine is concerned, the various mixed terms used by Cervantes in his novel."

Let us examine one of Cervantes' dramatic works, *El trato de Argel*, regarded as perhaps his earliest dramatic effort and composed some five years before the publication of *La Galatea*. It brings together a number of the author's experiences as a captive in Algiers. Among the characters are a Moorish witch, Fátima, and the Devil, evoked by her. In Act I the captive Aurelio, in accordance with chivalric practice, appeals for semidivine aid to his absent "lady" Silvia, just as Don Quijote, some twenty-five years later, appeals to his lady Dulcinea:

> Help me, Silvia, my love!
> If you but give me your aid,
> I shall assuredly prevail
> Though the struggle become fiercer.[152]

He is in a difficult situation. Zahara, wife of his owner Yzuf, is adulterously in love with him. He parries her advances:

> Don't you see that I'm a Christian,
> Pursued by ill-luck and misfortune?[153]

Fátima, Zahara's maid, adds her efforts to those of her mistress: the slave will be freed if he loves. Zahara calls herself a "slave of Love, / Who controls and conquers souls" (p. 115b), but the captive cites his religious duties: even if Zahara were baptized, she

---

151. See Chapter VI, note 42 and text, where the following quotation is paraphrased.
152. "¡Valedme, Silvia, bien mío, / que, si vos me dais ayuda, / de guerra más ardua y cruda / llevar la palma confío" (*Obras, ed. cit.*, p. 113b).
153. "con suerte y desdicha mala?" (*ibid.*, 114a).

would still be a wife. He prefers to die. . . . Fátima now shows her Celestinesque ancestry: she will give to her mistress her heart's desire, or die in the attempt (116a).

Aurelio is left alone and prays:

> Father of Heaven, in whose almighty Hand,
> Resides the government of heaven and earth . . .

He prays also to God's Mother — *Virgen Santisima Maria* — and, having prayed, he remembers his love for Silvia. As for Zahara,

> What I owe to God, my debt of love to Silvia,
> Make unendurable those burning eyes.[154]

In the very next line we have the intrusion of the literary, the poetic concepts of blind force, implacable Fate:

> Where are you, Silvia mine? What destiny,
> What sightless force of unrelenting Fate
> Has without cause or reason barred for us
> Our path? What star, oh Fortune, and what sign,
> Has thus our lot determined?[155]

These exterior forces, these accidents of his life, he curses (*maldigo*) while vowing to remain true to his faith, at whatever cost, for his soul's health. The length of his life on earth is of no concern at all.

In the next scene Saavedra (representing Miguel de Cervantes Saavedra) in a monologue accuses Time of having formed a conspiracy with heaven against him. He cries out against his *dura, inicua, inexorable estrella* — his harsh, iniquitous, inexorable star. His companion Leonardo remonstrates that one might better show a bright face to Fortune, whether or not she be bright; his own lot (he is complacent with his mistress) is not so bad. Saavedra will have none of such consolations. If it so be that heaven and his *Ventura* are not in conspiracy against him, and if he ever returns to King Philip's Spain, he will urge the conquest of Algiers (just as Cervantes did.)

Other characters enter and tell their story, or the story of others.

154. "y aquello que a mi Dios y a Silvia debo, / me hace que aun mirarla no me atrevo" (116b).

155. "¿Do estás, Silvia hermosa? ¿Qué destino, / qué fuerza insana de implacable hado / el curso de aquel próspero camino / tan sin causa y razón nos ha cortado? / ¡Oh estrella, oh suerte, oh fortuna, oh sino!" (*ibid.*).

A Valencian priest clothed in the habit of the military Order of Montesa was put to death

> Because these men, deprieved of light,
> Saw on his bosom, gleaming, bright,
> The Cross of his order, and sought to kill
> Christ in the person of one who still
> His emblem wore. . . .[156]

In Act II Yzuf, Aurelio's master, seeks to enlist the latter's help to soften the heart of a lovely Christian captive who is unresponsive to his advances. The maiden is none other than Silvia. Aurelio, left alone, breaks into a soliloquy in which he thanks Heaven for this turn in his fortunes, at the same time that he cries out against his *hado incierto* — his uncertain fate (121b). Then follows a slave-market scene, full "of costumbristic" details suggestive of one of Torres Naharro's *comedias a noticia* (plays of dramatic realism). A character designated only as *Hijo* — Son — asks his father what he shall do, now that a sale — and his *hado insano*, his blind fate — are separating them. "Be a good and faithful Christian," is the reply.

Silvia is presented to her new mistress, Zahara. She too is now a slave because her star so willed it — *que así lo quiso mi estrella*. Heaven — *el Cielo* — gave her a betrothed husband, but has decreed their separation. Zahara enlists Silvia's help in her proposed seduction of Aurelio, but a more dramatic mover of wills appears in the person of the sorceress Fátima, who, like Celestina, summons a devil to her service. Contrary to her expectations, the devil warns her that Christian hearts have little regard for sorceries. Her conjuring has been in vain, he says; yet there are other ways to cause a soul to yield. Two powers of hell can help: Necessity, and *Occasio*. The act ends with the devil's promise to send her those new auxiliaries.

In Act III two Moorish boys taunt two slaves with the refrain *Don Juan no venir* — Don John of Austria (d. 1578) will never come to rescue them. In a highly dramatic dialogue, the two slaves make a desperate plan to escape to Oran (as Cervantes himself tried to do). The scene changes: Aurelio says to Silvia that Fortune has

156. "porque estos ciegos sin luz, / que en él tal señal han visto, / pensando matar a Cristo, / matan al que trae su cruz" (119a).

given him a reprieve: they are together. The two explain their respective plans for deceiving their master and mistress. In the meantime, perhaps inclement Fate (133a) will relent.

In the next scene *Occasio* and Necessity appear as personified abstractions. The former urges Necessity to press hard her conquest of the Christian captive; she, in her turn, will offer him her forelock. The following dialogue between Aurelio and *Necesidad* plays up the Christian's desperate need, and *Occasio* extolls the charms and beauties of Zahara. Who will ever learn of a sin committed in secret? This is the moment! Zahara comes. Aurelio weakens, but recovers his strength. Nothing shall separate him from his God (135a).

Act IV opens as the fleeing captive struggles along the road toward Oran, with bleeding legs, only to be caught and punished. Saavedra and a certain Pedro discuss the problem of collaboration and informing. The Moorish king, a veritable *deus ex machina*, offers Aurelio and Silvia their liberty in exchange for the Christians' promise to send him the money of their ransom. A ship comes bringing two friars with ransom money. Aurelio offers a prayer of thanks to the King of Heaven; others, to the *dulcisima María*, mediatrix between God and men. The author, through Aurelio, offers to the audience this *trasunto* — this series of vignettes — of life in bondage in Algiers.

This drama has been analyzed here not for its dramatic merits or demerits but as an example of the interplay of Christian doctrine and external, decorative concepts inherited from antiquity: Fate and her companions, Necessity, *Occasio*, Destiny, *Ventura*, Heaven, Stars. Against all of these there is much complaint in this play; yet, when it comes to fundamental philosophy, all is Christian doctrine, often wearisomely set forth, as in Saavedra's long expostulation to Pedro, the would-be collaborator (140b). The significance of this interplay is clear: these "pagan" figures symbolize the fact that life here below is often hard and cruel; the sufferer may feel that the blows of misfortune fall at random, that he, like Job, is arbitrarily made to suffer, but though he may make outcry against this arbitrariness — this falling of one Christian soldier, while another is saved — he will always say, as Job said, "Though He slay me, yet will I trust in Him."

We have already seen how Cervantes, on a single page of *Don Quijote*, presents Fortune as both the Divine Will and as a *mujer ciega y borracha* — a blind and drunken woman. Throughout his work he speaks casually of Destiny as a power that, for example, brings one person to engage another in conversation (*Obras, ed. cit.*, p. 500b). Let us now see how Cervantes, when he speaks seriously, deals with the question of Fate. After the freeing of the galley slaves, he causes Don Quijote (on the advice of Sancho) to go into hiding in the mountains of the Sierra Morena, where the two companions make camp. "But Fate, who (according to those who lack the light of our true Faith) guides and controls things as she pleases, brought it about" [157] that Ginés de Pasamonte, one of the men who had received liberty by Don Quijote's foolishly humanitarian action, came to seek refuge in that selfsame place. The result, as readers of the great novel will remember, was the loss to that famous liar and thief of Dapple, Sancho's faithful mount, the apple of his eye.

Don Quijote himself, even in one of his less lucid intervals, makes clear in his reply to the designing Altisidora (the frivolous maid in the Ducal Palace where so many cruel tricks are played on the gentle knight) that the Fates that designated him at his birth as lady Dulcinea's adorer are harmless fates — fates no longer fateful, literary fates that do not exist: "I have often told you, my lady, that I regret that you have centered your amorous thoughts upon me, since I can more readily thank you for them than requite them. I was born to love Dulcinea del Toboso, and the Fates (if there were any fates) devoted me to her service. . . ." [158] Man is not master of his destiny, and that lack of mastery he may, if he wishes, call "fate"; but he is captain of his soul.

The facts thus do not support Aubrey F. G. Bell when he writes: "Cervantes was a fatalist, with that deep Oriental fatalism of the Spanish race which expresses itself in the saying '*Lo que ha de ser no puede faltar*' ('What must be must be')." [159]

157. "Pero la suerte fatal, que, según opinión de los que no tienen lumbre de la verdadera fe, todo lo guía, guisa y compone a su modo, ordenó . . ." (*Obras, ed. cit.*, p. 1118a).

158. "yo nací para ser de Dulcinea del Toboso, y los hados (si los hubiera) me dedicaron para ella" (1512a).

159. *Op. cit.*, p. 46, and note 17, where many references to destiny, etc., are brought together.

Calderón. Calderón is the dramatist of Scholasticism. In his works, different elements of culture are subordinated to Christian doctrine and are utilized to present a philosophical conception based on a cosmic theory.[160] "It is evident," writes T. Carreras y Artau, "that . . . in all Calderón's work we find a juggling and a confusion of terms like heaven, fate, luck, fortune, fatal influence, good or evil star, and their congeners; but if this point is examined with due care, it will be seen that those words are used rather as poetic devices than with true philosophic intent; and it can be easily verified that they all can be reduced to a common denominator, namely the inscrutable designs of Divine providence."[161]

In his plays of human passion, reason corresponds to the universal order, while passion is related to Fate, operating through the influence of each man's horoscope.[162] This highly dramatic theme of passion against reason, of free will against inborn tendency, may be treated comically, as in *The False Astrologer*, or with dramatic profundity, as in *The Daughter of the Air*. Man's nature operates properly when directed by Reason or the Idea of Order; when abandoned to material causality, it moves (or is moved) toward chaos until — the course of events having been changed, or the discordant element eliminated — Order again comes to be the directing force of life.

Calderón, as a writer of dramas, exactly like Cervantes when he composed his plays or his works of fiction, found that the idea of Fate was useful to produce dramatic effects: the hero is victorious or is defeated according as he wins out over, or is cast down by, his natural passions. Perturbation of the will, as we have seen (for example, in our study of the pastoral), makes the struggle difficult; passion, as we know, can debilitate the will; when passion dominates, it propels the individual toward his destruction; it is a voluntary decision that ties the individual to the wheel of Fate (*ibid.*, p. 51). In Calderón's practice, if Fate is to prevail, the characters and the action are given their setting in Antiquity: Narciso fulfills the destiny foretold for him as he drowns in the fountain (*Eco y Nar-*

160. A. Valbuena Briones, "El concepto del hado en el teatro de Calderón," *BHi*, LXIII (1961), 48.

161. "La filosofía de la libertad en *La vida es sueño*," *Estudios eruditos in memoriam de A. Bonilla y San Martín* (Madrid, 1927), I, 158; see also p. 159.

162. Valbuena Briones, *loc. cit.*

ciso), and Faetón fulfills his as the horses of the Sun's chariot run out of control (*El hijo del Sol*). In plays whose setting is Spain, or in others wherein he chooses to portray modern problems, the dramatist affirms that Fatality is the result of a freely made decision of the human will. Weak though a character be, he does not lack a chance to choose:

> Because the most monstrous Fate,
> The most violent inclination,
> The planet most set against us,
> Can the human will incline
> But not force the human will.[163]

This is true because the instincts that have their origin in the natural substance of our bodies can be directed by the will. Fate, in Calderón, is the force that inclines those instincts and tendencies. It is, therefore, the power that leads to the catastrophe if the hero allows himself to be defeated, just as Reason is the dominating force if, through a display of strength, he emerges victorious.

CONCLUSION

All the works studied in the preceding pages constitute a theodicy of greater or less power and scope, but always a theodicy. "To assert the eternal justice," writes E. K. Rand, "it becomes necessary to solve the mysteries of divine unity and goodness, of fate and human freedom," as Boethius did in the *Consolation of Philosophy*.[164] I know of no Spanish author during the five centuries covered by our study (and the Inquisition censored books for less than two hundred of the five hundred years) who questioned that goodness or that freedom; not one who, like Pomponazzi in his *De Incantationibus*, "rises against prayer, declaring it incapable of touching an inflexible divinity, bound like all other beings by the laws of Fate."[165] Whatever the literary or dramatic usefulness of Fate in works of polite literature, when literary considerations

---

163. "Porque el hado más esquivo, / la inclinación más violenta, / el planeta más impío, / sólo el albedrío inclinan, / no fuerzan el albedrío" (*La vida es sueño*, cited by Valbuena Briones, *op. cit.*, p. 53).

164. *Founders of the Middle Ages* (New York, 1957), p. 162.

165. "Pomponazzi dans le *De Incantationibus* s'élève contre la Prière; il la déclare incapable de toucher une divinité inflexible, liée comme tous les êtres par les lois du *Fatum*" (L. Febvre, *op. cit.*, p. 266).

are laid aside and real analysis of causes and effects is undertaken, our authors declare with the fifteenth-century Fernán Pérez de Guzmán:

> There is no Chance, no Ventura,
> Much less is there Fortune or Fate;
> Every one of us is governed
> By Providence inscrutable.[166]

166. "no ay caso nin ventura, / menos fortuna nin fados, / todos somos gouernados / por la prouidencia escura" (*Cancionero castellano* . . . , I, 613).

Bibliography
Index

PERIODICAL ABBREVIATIONS
USED IN FOOTNOTES

Boletín de la Real Academia Española (BRAE)
  Boletín de la Academia Española is the same publication: "Real" was dropped from the title for a short time.
Bulletin Hispanique (BHi)
Bulletin of Hispanic Studies (BHS)
  Bulletin of Spanish Studies (BBS) was the earlier name of this publication.
Comparative Literature (CL)
Hispania (Hisp.)
Hispanic American Historical Review (HAHR)
Hispanic Review (HR)
Journal of the History of Ideas (JHI)
Modern Language Notes (MLN)
Modern Language Quarterly (MLQ)
Modern Language Review (MLR)
Modern Philology (MPh)
Nueva revista de filología hispánica (NRFH)
Publications of the Modern Language Association of America (PMLA)
Revista de archivos, bibliotecas y museos (RABM)
Revista de filología española (RFE)
Revista de filología hispáncia (RFH)
Revista de filosofía (Rev. de filosofía)
Revue de littérature comparée (RLC)
Revue Hispanique (RHi)
Romance Philology (RPh)
Romanic Review (RR)
Romanische Forschungen (RF)
Studies in Philology (SP)
Zeitschrift für romanische Philologie (ZRPh)
  Also abbreviated throughout the notes are Biblioteca de autores españoles (*BAE*) and Nueva biblioteca de autores españoles (*NBAE*), which are series of editions of older Spanish texts.

Bibliography

ARTICLES

Amador del los Ríos, José. "De las artes mágicas y de adivinación en el suelo ibérico: Su influencia en las costumbres," *Revista de España*, XVIII (1871), 1–26, 321–48.

Anibal, C. E. "*Voces del cielo* — A Note on Mira de Amescua," *Romanic Review*, XVI (1925), 57–70.

———. "Another Note on the *Voces del Cielo,*" *Romanic Review*, XVIII (1927), 246–52.

Atkinson, W.C . "Hernán Pérez de Oliva: A Biographical and Critical Study," *Revue Hispanique*, LXXI (1927), 309–484.

Bainton, Roland H. "The Thirst for God in the Renaissance," *Renaissance News*, V (1952), 8–9.

Barrett, L. L. "The Omen in Guillén de Castro's Drama," *Hispania*, XXII (1939), 73–78.

———. "The Supernatural in Juan de la Cueva's Plays," *Studies in Philology*, XXXVI (1939), 147–68.

Bataillon, Marcel. "Du nouveau sur J. L. Vives," *Bulletin Hispanique*, XXXII (1930), 97–113.

Bennett, Joan. "A Note on *Religio Medici* and Some of its Critics," *Studies in the Renaissance*, III (1956), 175–84.

Benzo Mestre, Miguel. "La pura naturaleza humana en la teología de Suárez," *Anthologica annua*, III (1955), 405–520.

Castillo, Carlos. "Cervantes y Pero Mexía," *Modern Philology*, XLIII (1945–46), 94–106.

Christian, William A. "Augustine on the Creation of the World," *Harvard Theological Review*, XLVI (1953), 1–25.

Corts Grau, José. "La doctrina social de Juan Luis Vives," *Estudios de historia social de España*, II (1952), 63–89.

Crawford, J. P. "The Seven Liberal Arts in Lope de Vega's *Arcadia*," *Modern Language Notes*, XXX (1915), 13–14.

———."The Seven Liberal Arts in the *Visión Delectable* of Alfonso de la Torre," *Romanic Review*, IV (1913), 58–75.

———. "The *Visión Delectable* of Alfonso de la Torre and Maimonides' *Guide of the Perplexed,*" *Publications of the Modern Lanuage Association of America*, XXVII (1913), 188–212.

341

Dantín Gallego, J. "La filosofía natural en Huarte de San Juan," *Estudios de historia social de España*, II (1952), 153–208.

Dunn, Peter N. "The Horoscope Motif in *La vida es sueño*," *Atlante*, I (1953), 187–201.

Frame, Donald M. "Did Montaigne Betray Sebond?" *Romanic Review*, XXXVIII (1947), 297–329.

Frutos, Eugenio. "Origen, naturaleza y destino del hombre en los autos sacramentales de Calderón," *Revista de filosofía*, X (1945), 528–58.

Garin, Eugenio. "La *Dignitas Hominis* e la letteratura patristica," *Rinascita*, I (1938), 102–46.

Gembich, E. H. "Boticelli's Mythologies: A Study of the Neoplatonic Symbolism of his Circle," *Journal of the Warburg and Courtauld Institutes*, VII (1945), 13–17.

Gerould, G. H. "The Hermit and the Saint," *Publications of the Modern Language Association of America*, XX (1905), 529–45.

Gilman, Stephen. "Fortuna and Space in the *Celestina*," *Romanische Forschungun*, LXVI (1955), 342–60.

Gilmore, Myron P. "Freedom and Determinism in Renaissance Historians," *Studies in the Renaissance*, III (1956), 49–60.

Green, O. H. "Bartolomé Leonardo de Argensola, secretario del Conde de Lemos," *Bulletin Hispanique*, LII (1951), 382–83.

———. "El *ingenioso* hidalgo," *Hispanic Review*, XXV (1957), 175–93.

———. "*Ni es cielo ni es azul*: A Note on the 'Barroquismo' of Bartolomé Leonardo de Argensola," *Revista de filología española*, XXXIV (1950), 137–50.

———. "Realidad, voluntad y gracia en Cervantes," *Ibérida: Revista de filología*, III (1961), 113–28.

———, and Irving A Leonard. "On the Mexican Book Trade in 1600: A Chapter in Cultural History," *Hispanic Review*, IX (1941), 1–40.

Green, Richard H. "Alan of Lille's *De Planctu Naturae*," *Speculum*, XXXI (1956), 649–74.

Halstead, Frank G. "The Attitude of Lope de Vega toward Astrology and Astronomy," *Hispanic Review*, VII (1939), 205–19.

———. "The Attitude of Tirso de Molina toward Astrology," *Hispanic Review*, IX (1941), 417–39.

Herriott, J. Homer. "The Ten Senses in the Siete Partidas," *Hispanic Review*, XX (1952), 269–81.

Hesse, E. W. "Court References in Calderón's Zarzuelas," *Hispanic Review*, XV, (1947), 365–77.

Keller, Abraham C. "Montaigne on the Dignity of Man," *Publications of the Modern Language Association of America*, LXXII (1957), 43–54.

Krappe, A. H. "Notes on the *Voces del Cielo*," *Romanic Review*, XVII (1926), 65–68.

———. "More on the *Voces del Cielo*," *Romanic Review*, XIX (1928), 154–56.

Ladner, Gerhart B. "Bibliographical Survey: The History of Ideas in the

Christian Middle Ages from the Fathers to Dante in American Publications of the Years 1940–1952," *Traditio*, IX (1952), Section II (Ideas on Nature), 447–53.

Laín Entralgo, Pedro. "La vida del hombre en la poesía de Quevedo," *Cuadernos hispanoamericanos*, núm. 1 (1948), 63–101.

Lapesa, Rafael. "El elemento moral en el *Laberinto* de Mena," *Hispanic Review*, XXVII (1959), 257–66.

López Estrada, Francisco. "Sobre la Fortuna y el Hado en la literatura pastoril," *Boletín de la Real Academia Española*, XXVI (1947), 431–42.

McColley, Grant. "The Seventeenth-Century Doctrine of a Plurality of Worlds," *Annals of Science*, I (1936), 385–430.

May, T. E. "An Interpretation of Gracián's *Agudeza y arte de ingenio*," *Hispanic Review*, XVI (1948), 275–300.

Mele, Eugenio. "Tra vicerè, scienzati e poeti," *Bulletin Hispanique*, XXXI (1929), 256–67.

Millás Vallicrosa, J. M. "El *Libro de astrología* de don Enrique de Villena," *Revista de filología española*, XXVII (1943), 1–29.

Miroczkowski, P. "Medieval Art and Aesthetics in *The Canterbury Tales*," *Speculum*, XXXIII (1958), 204–21.

Morby, E. S. "Levinus Lemnius and Leo Swabius in *La Dorotea*," *Hispanic Review*, XX (1952), 108–22.

Morley, S. G. "The Use of Verse-Forms (Strophes) by Tirso de Molina," *Bulletin Hispanique*, VII (1905), 387–408.

Nicolson, Marjorie. "The 'New Astronomy' and English Literary Imagination," *Studies in Philology*, XXXII (1935), 428–62.

———. "The Telescope and Imagination," *Modern Philology*, XXXII (1934–35), 233–60.

O'Gorman, Edmundo. "Sobre la naturaleza bestial del indio americano," *Filosofía y letras* (1941), núm. 1, pp. 141–48, and núm. 2, pp. 305–15.

Ortúzar, Martín, O. de M. "El Condenado por desconfiado depende teológicamente de Zumel," *Estudios*, IV (1948), 7–14, and V (1949), 321–40.

Paulin [*read* Pollin], Alice M. "The Religious Motives in the Plays of Juan Ruiz de Alarcón," *Hispanic Review*, XXIX (1961), 33–44.

Pierce, Frank. "L'allégorie poétique au XVIᵉ siècle," *Bulletin Hispanique*, LI (1949), 381–406, and LII (1950), 191–228.

Pijoán, J. "Acerca de las fuentes populares de *El Condenado por desconfiado*," *Hispania*, VI (1923), 109–14.

Quirk, Robert E. "Some Notes on a Controversial Controversy: Juan Ginés de Sepúlveda and Natural Servitude," *Hispanic American Historical Review*, XXXIV (1954), 357–64.

Ricard, Robert. "Notes et matériaux pour l'étude du 'socratisme chrétien' chez Sainte Thérèse et les spirituels espangnols," *Bulletin Hispanique*, XLIX (1947), 5–37, and 170–204, and L (1948), 5–26.

Robins, Harry F. "The Crystalline Sphere and the 'Waters Above' in *Paradise*

Lost," *Publications of the Modern Language Association of America*, LXIX (1954), 903–14.

Selke de Sánchez, Angela. "¿Un ateo español en el siglo XVI? Las tentaciones del doctor Juan López de Illescas," *Archivum*, VII (1958), 25–47.

Solé-Leris, A. "The Theory of Love in the Two *Dianas*: A Contrast," *Bulletin of Hispanic Studies*, XXXVI (1959), 65–79.

Spitzer, Leo. "Zur Auffassung der Kunst des Arcipreste de Hita," *Zeitschrift für romanische Philologie*, LIV (1934), 237–70.

————. "Zur *Celestia*," *Zeitschrift fur romanische Philologie*, L (1930), 237–40.

Street, Florence. "The Allegory of Fortune and the Imitation of Dante in the *Laberinto* and the *Coronación* of Juan de Mena," *Hispanic Review*, XXIII (1955), 1–11.

Trinkhaus, Charles. "Renaissance Problems in Calvin's Theology," *Studies in the Renaissance*, I (1954), 59–80.

Valbuena Briones, Angel. "El concepto del hado en el teatro de Calderón," *Bulletin Hispanique*, LXIII (1961), 48–53.

Vosters, S. A. "Lope de Vega y Titelmans: Cómo el Fénix se representaba el universo," *Revista de literatura*, XXI (1962), 5–35.

Williams, Arnold. "Renaissance Commentaries on Genesis and Some Elements of the Theology of *Paradise Lost*," *Publications of the Modern Language Association of America*, LXVI (1941), 151–64.

Wilson, E. M. "The Four Elements in the Imagery of Calderón," *Modern Language Review*, XXXI (1936), 34–47.

Wilson, H. S. "Some Meanings of 'Nature' in Renaissance Literary Theory," *Journal of the History of Ideas*, II (1941), 430–48.

BOOKS

Achútegui, Pedro S. *La universalidad del conocimiento de Dios en los paganos, según los primeros teólogos de la Compañia de Jesús, 1534–1648*. Pamplona, 1951.

Allen, Don Cameron. *Doubt's Boundless Sea: Skepticism and Faith in the Renaissance*. Baltimore, 1964.

————. *The Legend of Noah: Renaissance Rationalism in Art, Science, and Letters*. Urbana, Illinois, 1949.

————. *The Star-Crossed Renaissance*. Durham, North Carolina, 1941.

Alonso, Dámaso. *Vida y obra de Medrano*. 2 vols. Madrid, 1948–58. (A shorter version [*Vida de don Francisco de Medrano*] was read before the Real Academia Española in 1948 and published at Madrid in that year.)

Babb, Lawrence. *The Elizabethan Malady: A Study of Melancholia in English Literature from 1580 to 1642*. East Lansing, Michigan, 1951.

Bainton, Roland H. "Man, God and the Church in the Age of the Renaissance," in *The Renaissance: A Symposium*, The Metropolitan Museum of Art. New York, 1952, pp. 51–62.

Bell, A. F. G. *El renacimiento español.* Zaragoza, 1944.

Benito y Durán, Angel. *La filosofía del Arcipreste de Hita.* Alcoy, 1946.

Bonet, Alberto. *La filosofía de la libertad en las controversias teológicas del siglo XVI y primera mitad del XVII.* Barcelona, 1932.

Carreras y Artau, Tomás. "La filosofía de la libertad en *La vida es sueño* de Calderón," in *Estudios eruditos in memoriam de A. Bonilla y San Martín,* I. Madrid, 1927, 151–79.

Cassirer, Ernest. *The Philosophy of the Enlightenment.* Princeton, 1951.

Castro, Américo. "Incarnation in Don Quixote," in *Cervantes Across the Centuries,* eds. A. Flores and M. J. Benardete. New York, 1947, pp. 136–78.

———. "El problema histórico de *La Celestina,*" in his *Santa Teresa y otros ensayos.* Santander, 1929, pp. 193–215.

Cereceda, F. *Diego Laínez en la Europa religiosa de su tiempo.* 2 vols. Madrid, 1945–46.

Chapman, Emmanuel. *Saint Augustine's Philosophy of Beauty.* New York–London, 1939.

Conger, George P. *Theories of Macrocosmos and Microcosmos in the History of Philosophy.* New York, 1952.

Correa, Gustavo. *El Templo de Diana en la novela de Jorge de Montemayor.* Bogotá, 1961.

Corts Grau, José. "La dignidad humana en Juan Luis Vives," in his *Estudios filosóficos y literarios.* Madrid, 1954, pp. 81–109.

Cotarelo y Mori, Emilio. *Don Juan de Espina: Noticias de este célebre y enigmático personaje.* Madrid, 1908.

Coulton, G. G. *The Medieval Scene.* Cambridge, 1959.

Deyermond, A. D. *The Petrarchan Sources of "La Celestina."* Oxford, 1961.

Eisler, Rudolf. *Wörterbuch der philosophischen Begriffe und Ausdrücke.* Berlin, 1904.

Ferm, Virgilius (ed.). *A History of Philosophical Systems.* New York, 1950.

Fitzmaurice-Kelly, James. *A History of Spanish Literature.* New York, 1900.

Fletcher, J. B. *The Religion of Beauty in Women.* New York, 1911.

Frame, Donald M. *Montaigne's Discovery of Man.* New York, 1955.

Frutos, Eugenio. *La filosofía de Calderón en sus autos sacramentales.* Zaragoza, 1952.

Gallegos Rocalfull, José. *La experiencia de Dios en los místicos españoles.* Mexico City, 1945.

———. *El hombre y el mundo de los teólogos españoles de los siglos de oro.* Mexico City, 1946.

Ganzenmüller, Wilhelm. *Das Naturgefühl im Mittelalter.* Leipzig. 1914.

Gillet, Joseph E. "*So la luna:* Notes on the Life and Death of a Spanish Idiom," in *Estudios Hispanicos: Homenaje a Archer M. Huntington.* Wellesley, Massachusetts, 1952, pp. 193–217.

Gilman, Stephen. *The Art of "La Celestina."* Madison, Wisconsin, 1956.

Gilson, Etienne. *L'esprit de la philosophie médiévale.* Paris, 1944.

González Palencia, A. *Del Lazarillo a Quevedo.* Madrid, 1946.

Green, O. H. *"El Licenciado Vidriera*: It's Relation to the *Viaje del Parnaso* and the *Examen de Ingenios* of Huarte," in *Linguistic and Literary Studies in Honor of Helmut A. Hatzfeld*. Washington, 1964, pp. 213–20.

———. *The Life and Works of Lupercio Leonardo de Argensola*. Philadelphia, 1927.

Guy, Alain. *La pensée de Fray Luis de León*. Limoges, 1943.

Hanke, Lewis. *El prejuicio racial en el Nuevo Mundo*. Santiago, Chile, 1958.

———. *The Spanish Struggle for Justice in the Conquest of America*. Philadelphia, 1949.

Hay, Denys. *The Renaissance in its Historical Background*. Cambridge, 1961.

Heger, Klaus. *Baltasar Gracián: Eine Untersuchung zu Sprache und Moralistik als Ausdrucksweisen der literarischen Haltung des Conceptismo*. Heidelberg, 1952.

Heitman, Klaus. *Fortuna und Virtus: Eine Studie zu Petrarcas Lebensweisheit*. Cologne, 1958.

Iriarte, Mauricio de, S.J. *El doctor Huarte de San Juan y su "Examen de ingenios."* Madrid, 1948.

———. *El hombre Suárez y el hombre en Suárez*. Madrid, 1950.

Jansen, Hellmut. *Die Grundbegriffe des Baltasar Gracián*. Geneva–Paris, 1958.

Kocher, P. H. *Science and Religion in Elizabethan England*. San Marino, California, 1953.

Kristeller, Paul Oskar. "Changing Views of the Intellectual History of the Renaissance since Jacob Burckhart," in *The Renaissance: A Reconsideration of the Theories and Interpretations of the Age*, ed. Tinsley Helton, Madison, Wisconsin, 1961.

———. *The Classics and Renaissance Thought*. Cambridge, Massachusetts, 1955.

Kuhn, Thomas S. *The Copernican Revolution: Planetary Astronomy in the Development of Western Thought*. Cambridge, Massachusetts, 1957.

Laín Entralgo, Pedro. *La espera y la esperanza: Historia y teoria del esperar humano*. Madrid, 1957.

Lapesa, Rafael. *La obra literaria del Marqués de Santillana*. Madrid, 1957.

Lapp, John C. (ed.). *The Universe of Pontus de Tyard*. Ithaca, New York, 1950.

Lea, Henry Charles. *A History of the Inquisition of Spain*. 4 vols. New York, 1906–7.

Lovejoy, Arthur O. *The Great Chain of Being*. Cambridge, Massachusetts, 1948.

Malkiel, María Rosa Lida de. *Juan de Mena*. Mexico City, 1950.

Marías, Julián. *El tema del hombre*. Madrid, 1943.

Menéndez Pidal, Ramón. *Estudios literarios*. Madrid, 1920.

———. "El lenguaje del siglo XVI," in his *Mis páginas preferidas: Estudios lingüísticos e históricos*. Madrid, 1957, pp. 9–45. (Also reprinted in his *España y su Historia*, II [Madrid, 1957], and elsewhere.)

Menéndez y Pelayo, Marcelino. *La ciencia española*. 3 vols. Madrid, 1915–18.

———. *Historia de los heterodoxos españoles*. 8 vols. Madrid, 1947–48.

————. "De los orígines del criticismo y del escepticismo y especialmente de los precursores españoles de Kant," in his *Obras completas*, XLIII, ed. J. Sánchez Reyes. Madrid, 1948.

Michalski, C. *Les sources du criticisme et du scepticisme dans la philosophie de XIVe siécle*. Krakow, 1924.

Moreno Báez, Enrique. *Lección y sentido del Guzmán de Alfarache*. Madrid, 1948.

Morínigo, Marcos A. *América en el teatro de Lope de Vega*. Buenos Aires, 1946.

Morreale, Margherita. *Pedro Simón Abril*. Madrid, 1949.

Nicolson, Marjorie. *The Breaking of the Circle: Studies in the Effect of the "New Science" upon Seventeenth-century Poetry*. New York, 1960.

Paré, Gérard. *Le Roman de la Rose et la scolastique courtoise*. Paris–Ottowa, 1941.

Parent, J. M. *La doctrine de la création dans l'Ecole de Chartres*. Paris–Ottowa, 1938.

Parker, Alexander A. *The Allegorical Drama of Calderón*. Oxford–London, 1943.

Patch, Howard R. *The Goddess Fortuna in Medieval Literature*. Cambridge, Massachusetts, 1927.

Pavia, M. N. *Drama of the Siglo de Oro: A Study of Magic, Witchcraft, and Other Occult Beliefs*. New York, 1959.

Peers, E. Allison. *Spirit of Flame: A Study of St. John of the Cross*. London, 1943.

Picatoste, Felipe. *Apuntes para una biblioteca científica española del siglo XVI*. Madrid, 1891.

————. *Memoria premiada por la Real Academia de Ciencias Exactas, Físicas y Naturales para conmemorar el segundo centenario de D. Pedro Calderón de la Barca*. Madrid, 1881.

Pierce, Frank. *La poesía épica del Siglo de Oro*. Madrid, 1961.

Pring-Mill, Robert. *El microcosmos Lul·lià*. Oxford–Palma, Majorca, n.d.

Puyol y Alonso, Julio. *El Arcipreste de Hita: estudio crítico*. Madrid, 1906.

Randall, J. H., Jr. *The Making of the Modern Mind*. Boston–New York, 1940.

Révah, I. S. *Une source de la spiritualité peninsulaire au XVIième siècle: La "Théologie naturelle" de Raymond Sebond*. Lisbon, 1953.

Reyes, Alfonso. "Un tema de *La vida es sueño*," in *Capítulos de literatura española* (Second Series). Mexico City, 1945.

Rice, Eugene F. *The Renaissance Idea of Wisdom*. Cambridge, Massachusetts, 1958.

Rodríguez Carracido, José. *El padre José de Acosta y su importancia en la literatura científica española*. Madrid, 1899.

Ros, Fidèle de. *Le Frère Bernardin de Laredo*. Paris, 1948.

Salinas, Pedro. *Jorge Manrique, o tradición y originalidad*. Buenos Aires, 1947.

Sánchez-Marín, F. G., and V. Gutiérrez-Durán. *Doctrina de Trento: Imagen del hombre según nuestros teólogos*. Madrid, 1946.

Schmidt, A. M. *La poésie scientifique en France au seizième siècle*. Paris, 1939.

Schütz, L. *Thomas-Lexikon.* Paderborn, 1895.

Scott, Nathan A., Jr. (ed.). *The Tragic Vision and the Christian Faith.* New York, 1957.

Sertillanges, D. *Les grandes thèses de la philosophie thomiste,* Paris, 1928.

Sicroff, Albert A. *Les controverses des statuts de "pureté de sang" en Espagne du XVᵉ au XVIIᵉ siècle.* Paris, 1960.

Silva, Ramón. "The Religious Dramas of Calderón," in *Spanish Golden Age Poetry and Drama,* ed. E. Allison Peers ("Liverpool Studies in Spanish Literature," Second Series). Liverpool, 1946, pp. 119–205.

Simón Díaz, José. *Bibliografía de la literatura hispánica.* 5 vols. Madrid, 1950–58.

Spencer, Theodore. *Shakespeare and the Nature of Man.* New York–Cambridge, Massachusetts, 1947.

Stace, W. T. *Religion and the Modern Mind.* Philadelphia, 1952.

Tillyard, E. M. W. *The Elizabethan World Picture.* London, 1948.

Turnbull, Eleanor L. (ed.). *Ten Centuries of Spanish Poetry.* Baltimore, 1955.

Tuveson, Ernest. *Millennium and Utopia.* Berkeley–Los Angeles, 1949.

Van Horne, John. *El Bernardo of Bernardo de Balbuena: A Study of the Poem with Particular Attention to Its Relations to the Epics of Boiardo and Ariosto and to Its Significance in the Spanish Renaissance.* Urbana, Illinois, 1927.

Vignaux. Paul. *Justification et prédestination au XIVᵉ siècle* (Bibliothèque de l'Ecole des Hautes Etudes: Sciences Religieuses," XLVIII). Paris, 1934.

Watson, Foster. *Luis Vives, el Gran Valenciano (1492–1540).* Oxford, 1922.

Wedel, T. O. *The Mediaeval Attitude Toward Astrology, Particularly in England.* New Haven, Connecticut, 1920.

Wenley, R. M. *Stoicism and Its Influence.* Boston, 1924.

Zavala, Silvio. *Servidumbre natural y libertad cristiana según los tratadistas españoles de los siglos XVI y XVII.* Buenos Aires, 1944.

MEDIEVAL AND RENAISSANCE TEXTS

Acevedo, Alonso de. *La creación del mundo* ("Biblioteca de autores españoles," XXIX). Madrid, 1854.

Alonso de Madrid. *Arte para servir a Dios* ("Nueva biblioteca de autores españoles," XVI). Madrid, 1911.

Autos sacramentales desde su origen hasta fines del siglo XVII, ed. Eduardo González Pedroso (Biblioteca de autores españoles," LVII). Madrid, 1865.

Baena, Juan Alfonso de. *El Cancionero de Juan Alfonso de Baena,* ed. P. J. Pidal. Madrid, 1851.

Calderón de la Barca, Pedro. *Los comedias de D. Pedro Calderón de la Barca,* ed. J. Keil. 4 vols. Leipzig, 1827–30.

———. *No hay más Fortuna que Dios,* ed. A. A. Parker. Manchester, 1949.

———. *La selva confusa*, ed. G. T. Northup, in *Revue Hispanique*, XXI (1909), 168–338.

Castiglione, Baldassare. *El Cortesano*, trans. Juan Boscán, ed. A. M. Fabié. Madrid, 1873.

Collección de autos, farsas y coloquios del siglo XVI, ed. Léo Rouanet. 4 vols. Barcelona–Madrid, 1901.

Córdoba, Fray Martín Alfonso de. *Un tradado del siglo XV sobre la predestinación en castellano*, ed. and with preliminary study by Aníbal Sánchez Fraile. Salamanca, 1956.

Covarrubias, Sebastián de. *Tesoro de la lengua castellana o española*, ed. Martín de Riquer. Barcelona, 1943.

Cruz, San Juan de la. *El cántico espiritual* (Clásicos Castellanos," No. 55). Madrid, 1924.

———. *The Complete Works of St. John of the Cross*, trans. E. Allison Peers. 3 vols. London, 1934–35.

Encina, Juan del. *Cancionero*, facsimile ed. of the Real Academia Española. Madrid, 1928.

Espinel, Vicente. *Diversas rimas*, ed. D. C. Clarke. New York, 1956.

———. *Vida del escudero Marcos de Obregón*, ed. S. Gili Gaya. 2 vols. Madrid, 1922–23.

Estúñiga, Lope de. *Cancionero de Stúñiga*, eds. the Marqués de la Fuensanta del Valle and Sancho Rayón. Madrid, 1872.

Froes de Macedo, André. *Amores divinos*, facsimile ed. of Antonio Pérez Gómez. Valencia, 1959.

Gracián, Baltasar. *El Heroe. El Discreto*. Buenos Aires–Mexico City, 1939.

———. *Oráculo manual y arte de prudencia*, ed. Miguel Romera–Navarro. Madrid, 1954.

Gurrea y Aragón, D. Francisco de (Conde de Luna). *Commentarios de los sucesos de Aragón*, ed. el Duque de Villahermosa. Madrid, 1888.

Hojeda, Diego de. *La Christiada*, ed. Sister Mary Helen Patricia Corcoran. Washington, 1935.

Huarte de San Juan, Juan. *Examen de ingenios para las ciencias*, ed. R. Sanz. 2 vols. Madrid, 1930.

Isidore of Seville, St. *Etimologías*, trans. L. Cortés y Góngora. Madrid, 1951.

Juan Manuel, Prince. *Libro de los estados* ("Biblioteca de autores españoles," LI). Madrid, 1860.

———. *El libro infinido*, ed. J. M. Blecua. Granada, 1952.

Jáuregui, Juan de. *Diálogo entre la Naturaleza y las dos artes Pintura y Escultura, de cuya preeminencia se disputa y juzga* ("Biblioteca de autores españoles," XLII). Madrid, 1923.

León, Fray Luis de. *De los nombres de Cristo* ("Clásicos Castellanos," Nos. 28, 33, 41). 3 vols. Madrid, 1914.

———. *Obras completas castellanas*, ed. P. Félix García. Madrid, 1944.

———. *La perfecta casada*, ed. A. Bonilla y San Martín. Madrid, 1917.

Leonardo de Argensola, Lupercio and Bartolomé. *Rimas de Lupercio y Bartolomé L.* [sic] *de Argensola*, ed. J. M. Blecua. 2 vols. Zaragoza, 1950–51.

López de Ubeda, Juan. *Cancionero y vergel de flores divinas* ("Biblioteca de autores españoles," XXXV). Madrid, 1855.

López Maldonado, Gabriel. *Cancionero*, facsimile ed. Madrid, 1932.

Lull, Raimundo (Raymond Lully). *Blanquerna* ("Colección Crisol"). N.p., n.d.

Mal Lara, Juan de. *Filosofía vulgar*, ed. A. Vilanova. 4 vols. Barcelona, 1958–59.

Martínez de Toledo, Alfonso. *El Arçipreste de Talavera*, ed. L. B. Simpson. Berkeley, 1939.

Mena, Juan de. *El Laberinto de Fortuna o Las trescientas*, ed. J. M. Blecua ("Clásicos Castellanos," No. 119). Madrid, 1943.

Metge, Bernat. *Obras de Bernat de Metge*, ed. Martín de Riquer. Barcelona, 1959.

Mira de Amescua, Antonio. *Adversa Fortuna de Don Alvaro de Luna* ("Nueva biblioteca de autores españoles," IV). Madrid, 1906.

Montaigne, Michel de. *Essais.*, ed. J.-V. LeClerc. 5 vols. Paris, 1826.

Orozco, Alonso de. *Victoria de la muerte*, ed. Biblioteca Renacimiento. Madrid, 1921.

Ortiz, Fray Francisco. *Epístolas familiares* ("Biblioteca de autores españoles," XIII). Madrid, 1850.

Osuna, Francisco de. *Tercera Parte del Abecedario espiritual* ("Nueva biblioteca de autores españoles," XVI). Madrid, 1911.

Pérez de Montalbán, Juan. *Sucesos y prodigios de Amor*, ed. La Sociedad de Bibliófilos Españoles. Madrid, 1949.

Poesías barias y recreación de buenos ingenios, ed. J. M. Hill ("Indiana University Studies," X). Bloomington, Indiana, 1923.

Quevedo Villegas, Francisco de. *Providencia de Dios* ("Biblioteca de autores españoles," XLVIII). Madrid, 1876.

Rojas, Fernando de. *Celestina: A Play in Twenty-one Acts Attributable to Fernando de Rojas*, trans. Mack H. Singleton. Madison, Wisconsin, 1958.

Sabunde, Raimundo (Ramón). *El hombre y sus deberes* ("Joyas de la mística española"). Madrid, n.d.

———. *Theologia Naturalis*, trans. Michel de Montaigne. 2 vols. (Vols. IX and X of *Oeuvres complètes de Michel de Montaigne*, ed. A. Armainguad. Paris, 1924–41.)

Sánchez, Francisco. *Que nada se sabe*. Madrid, n.d.

Sánchez de Badajoz, Diego. *Recopilación en metro*, ed. J. López Prudencio. 2 vols. Badajoz, 1910. Printed also in facsimile ed. of the Real Academia Española, Madrid, 1929.

Sermonario clásico, comp. M. Herrero García. Madrid, 1942.

Terrones del Caño, Francisco. *Instrucción de predicadores*, ed. Félix G. Olmedo. Madrid, 1946.

Thomas of Villanueva, St. *Opera omnia*. Manila, 1881.

Tirso de Molina (pseud.). *El Condenado por desconfiado*, ed. Américo Castro. Madrid, 1919.

Torre, Alfonso de la. *Visión delectable* ("Biblioteca de autores españoles," XXXVI). Madrid, 1871.

Vega, Lope de. *La creación del mundo y primera culpa del hombre*, ed. Real Academia Española. Madrid, 1893.

Vélez de Guevara, Luis. *El diablo cojuelo* ("Clásicos Castellanos," No. 38). Madrid, 1941.

Vicente, Gil. *Don Duardos*, ed. Dámaso Alonso. Madrid, 1942.

Villalón, Cristóbal de. *Ingeniosa comparación entre lo antiguo y lo presente*, ed. M. Serrano y Sanz. Madrid, 1898.

Vives, Juan Luis. *Introducción a la sabiduría*. Madrid, 1944.

———. *Tratado del alma*, trans. J. Ontañón. Madrid, 1859.

Zapata, Luis. *Miscelánea*, ed. Pascual de Gayangos. Madrid, 1859.

Zárate, Hernando de. *Discursos de la paciencia cristiana* ("Biblioteca de autores españoles," XXVII). Madrid, 1926.

Index